Not Guilty

Undoing the Illusion of
Separate Existence

Yaani Drucker

Atma Press

Wisconsin Dells, Wisconsin

Atma Press, 1101 Vine Street, Wisconsin Dells, WI 53965

websites: www.notguiltybyyaani.com
www.atmapress.com

email: yaani9@yahoo.com

The author wishes to express her gratitude for the teachings of Sathya Sai Baba, her spiritual preceptor, and the teachings of A Course in Miracles, for their inspiring elucidations of truth which are richly sprinkled throughout the book.

ISBN: 978-1-59824-839-5

Library of Congress Control Number: 2008904584

CONTENTS

Introduction

Early on in my quest for truth, I was told that I am one with God, that I am God, that there is no difference between my Self and God. Somehow that wondrous news did not come as a great surprise. Deep in my heart I knew it had to be so. And yet the disparity between my experience and my idea of what it must be to truly be God seemed overwhelming. A willingness to take personal responsibility for everything that happens to me and a determination to align my every thought, word and deed with what God must think, thoughts of love, kindness and charity for all, have narrowed the gap considerably. But what helped most in bridging the gap was getting in touch with feelings of guilt associated with past actions for which I was punishing myself. I recognized this to be at the root of all my suffering, whether in the form of sickness, emotional distress or pain of any kind.

Now, whenever I start to feel symptoms of coming down with an illness or find myself in a tight spot, I acknowledge that these experiences are impossible because of who I am and ask for help in being restored to wholeness. Invariably a Divine power of healing enfolds me and the symptoms vanish or the trauma lifts. It is as though some unseen force hears my every plea. That is a miracle and I know God exists. I do not ask in my behalf alone, however, when I heal myself I participate in the healing of the whole world. In changing my mind about who I am, the world must change, for the world is but a projection of my mind. At the same time, in yearning for the healing of the whole world, I heal my mind. The two are inseparable, thus affect each other simultaneously.

As a holy, precious child of God you have limitless capacity. Tap your capacity now by daring to stretch your dreams to infinity. Dare to look deep within. You will discover that which is so vast it cannot ever be conveyed through mere words. When you step away from your self-made prison of guilt into the glorious sunlight of your Godliness, you will reconnect with your very Self. We were created to enhance each other's innocence, purity and joy. What beauty, what glory, what majesty we all are and what a sacred destiny we share.

Are you willing to let yourself be Divine and perfect if that is indeed who you are? I believe you are that. I believe you as both judge and jury have sentenced yourself to littleness, when you are nothing short of grandeur. You have judged yourself wrongly, based on inconclusive evidence, because your self-appointed lawyer convinced you to plead guilty to crimes you never committed. You have been completely unfair in your verdict.

If your every experience is only by your choice and if you are not experiencing yourself as ever fuller, richer love, joy, peace, holiness and power, then you must have convinced yourself you deserve less than the very best. You must have judged yourself unworthy, slated to endure life's hardships only to end in death. It is not true. All the evidence against you was fabricated. You are not guilty.

We have all been on trial for a very long time, in fact since the beginning of time. Perhaps you have grown so accustomed to your particular set of circumstances that you are not even aware that this is so. Ironically, it was you who brought your own case against yourself. It was you who accused yourself and condemned yourself for crimes you never committed. You thought you were guilty and to punish yourself you suffered pain, loss, deprivation, lack, loneliness and grief. You convinced yourself that you were limited, powerless, unworthy... born but to die.

You punished yourself needlessly. You are so holy, so pure, so innocent, so breathtakingly beautiful. You are equal with God in glory, splendor and majesty. There is no one more powerful, more worthy or more holy than you. You were created by God to walk the earth with your head held high, your spirits soaring. Self-imposed guilt alone has caused you to become frightened and so forget who you really are.

You, who are your own judge, jury and prosecutor, in a kangaroo court of your own devising, have judged and convicted yourself of trumped-up charges having nothing at all to do with the truth. And the tragedy is you agreed with the verdict. But now is the time to proclaim your innocence. Every charge leveled against you... by you... is false. God has not changed His mind about you. Your holiness has never been diminished or tarnished. You are still as God created you... innocent, perfect and pure.

This book is an invitation to have the charges against you dropped. Perhaps you can be persuaded that the evidence was inconclusive and that you have indeed judged yourself too harshly. Perhaps instead of accepting your guilty verdict, you can be persuaded to have the case appealed to the Supreme Court over which God has jurisdiction. He will lead you from the darkness of guilt and shame into the sunlight of your radiant innocence as created by Him, eternally unaffectable by any past, if you will let Him.

To begin with, you have to fire your defense attorney. Who has been your counsel? Who did you pick to represent you in this case against yourself? It was ego, hired at your choice. Undoubtedly, you had no idea that ego was determined to find you guilty from the beginning. Who in his right mind would choose a lawyer that was driven to prove him guilty? Yet that is exactly what you have done if you have suffered in any way.

Why does ego want you guilty? Ego's survival depends on your guilt. Ego needs you guilty to live, thus you have found yourself guilty based on ego's false, insubstantial, inconclusive evidence, which you believed. It was a trick, a sick joke you played on yourself. It was you who imposed upon yourself heavy consequences, none of which you deserved. It is time to ensure that ego's attempts to rule you and lead you on yet another round of birth and death at its treacherous hand be undone.

All suffering is self-inflicted punishment for crimes that were never committed. What a pity. You convinced yourself that you were guilty when you were in fact innocent all along. Not only that, but then you forgot that you thought you were guilty and were mystified when disaster struck without rhyme or reason, at most inopportune moments and caught you completely off guard. Perhaps you blamed God or someone else or circumstances or somehow buried each incident without really uncovering the core problem. You haphazardly went on with your life on a hope and a prayer. How tenuous has been your lot. Do you ever really stop to look at it? Perhaps you can be convinced to fire ego and hire Spirit as your counsel. God has all the evidence to prove you innocent beyond a shadow of a doubt. The case against you will be dismissed on the spot.

We do not deserve to suffer. We suffer at our own hand and once we really understand this, we understand that we stop suffering when we wish to stop. Maybe you think your experience is perfect even though it is attended with suffering. Maybe you are not suffering personally and somehow the suffering of others does not pain your heart. Maybe you can still justify the "benefits" of suffering in your mind.

Maybe you justify your suffering by dissociating yourself from your body. You were told your body is not real and even if it suffers you are not suffering. Suffering also is not real, you were told. True, your body is not real and suffering is not real. However, conceptual understanding alone cannot help you. Denial or suppression of symptoms will not heal them. Once you truly know your body is not real, it cannot suffer. When you have understood the truth, neither you nor your body will ever suffer again.

Your only pain will be the agony of the suffering of others who erroneously think they deserve to suffer, age and die. You will then wish only to do everything within your power to end the suffering for all humanity. If you are content to justify your or your neighbor's suffering in any way this book is not for you. This book is for those who have decided enough is enough. This book is for those who would like to gain the kingdom of heaven without having to suffer to get there. God does not suffer, except for the anguish of watching our needless suffering. What loving mother can bear her child's pain? Do you think God gets some strange satisfaction out of our affliction?

Maybe you think I'm confused, that I have mistaken you for someone else and that it wasn't you who pled guilty. But you are on death row aren't you? Maybe not today or tomorrow, but one day you are slated to die, aren't you? Could it have happened without your admission of guilt? Otherwise someone else must have sentenced you to death. Who? God? Is it God's will that you die? Does that really ring true in the depths of your being? Maybe it is time to stop complacently accepting sickness, suffering and death as the norm, even though they may be your experience and that of everyone around you. Maybe you deserve to live, to be supremely happy and to have a healthy, able body. Maybe you deserve to have everything you need plus perfect peace, eternal joy and all-embracing love just because of who you are.

Perhaps it is time to take a closer look at the evidence. Perhaps you will discover for yourself that it is insubstantial and inconclusive. You will only see that when you fire your self-serving lawyer and hire Spirit to act as your advocate. He is after the truth, the whole truth and nothing but the truth. He knows your innocence. He will have no difficulty getting the case against you dismissed. All your mistakes had no effect. You are as God created you, whole, perfect and sinless forever.

I have prayed for the end of suffering all my life. Anyone's suffering, whatever form it takes, whoever they are or where ever they may be, is painful to me. It has become apparent that I must get to the root cause of suffering to end it. In my determination to know, really know, I have utilized the teachings of Sai Baba, my spiritual preceptor since 1981, as well as the teachings of A Course In Miracles (ACIM) and to a lesser extent the teachings of the Bible.

I have found each of these sources to be complete solutions, but have also become aware of a tendency in my mind to draw erroneous or hasty conclusions and thereby close down or constrict. By comparing truth as expressed through a number of clear way showers that seemed at times contradictory or even irreconcilable I would invariably be shown that they were saying exactly the same thing and my premature conclusions alone had caused them to seem otherwise. As soon as the error was exposed, the correction was given. In this way my mind has expanded from mere conceptual understanding of many of the teachings to direct revelatory experience leading to a deepened certainty of who I am and of who we all are.

I do not claim, by any means, to know the whole truth. This book is an exploration of various possibilities, hopefully clarifying what the choices are. I am willing to turn over every stone in a determination to restore each of God's children to wholeness. Only when everyone is whole am I truly free. We are one organism; not billions of separate, autonomous individuals.

At the same time, we must each accept the truth for ourselves. Awakening requires your full participation and the brightness of your mind for your personal transformation. No one can do it for you. It was listening to ego that produced ignorance and bondage, so now we have to muster all our combined resources to pull ourselves out of the darkness into the light. United with God and each other, in a willingness to maximize our efforts, we will be victorious over sickness, suffering and death for all humanity.

Freedom lies in a willingness to be wrong about the conclusions your mind wants to draw from evidence gathered. When you need to be right, you bind yourself to defending a particular position. In that you restrict your freedom. I share here what I have discovered only to stimulate and inspire your own investigation. I have used the above-mentioned teachers as guides or springboards into my own inner exploration.

I am always asking, praying and yearning for only the truth, always willing to be wrong about my understandings. I have not embraced any of the above teachers' teachings unless they resonated deep within my own heart. It had to become my own direct experience before I could adopt it. Your yearning for only the truth must be sufficient to reveal to you the profoundest, deepest, most elevated truths.

I have made over 25 trips to South India to be in the Divine aura of Sathya Sai Baba and have been received into His immediate presence for personal interviews on a number of occasions. Each such privilege has deepened my understanding of the truth. Everything Sai Baba has done in relation to me, whether in the interview room, in dreams, through an inner voice of guidance, or through events in my life directed by Him, has been transformative. I am convinced that He knows and loves each of us totally. I believe with my whole heart and soul that Sai Baba is God incarnate and that He has come onto the planet at this critical juncture to rescue man from imminent disaster.

Humanity is on a fast track toward total annihilation which can only be averted through Divine intervention and intercession. Why does God wait till such a crisis is at hand before making His appearance? Because that is apparently what it takes before we cry out in a true prayer from the depths of our hearts, asking for help. God honors us and will not go where He is not invited. He created us free and will not stand in the way of that freedom. He will wait until we ask for help. He respects our freedom and loves His children too much to be other than the most gracious, humble and unassuming host.

A Course In Miracles (ACIM) is a teaching authored by Jesus Christ and scribed by Helen Schucman in the mid-60's. It offers Jesus' explanation of what caused us to find ourselves in the experience of sickness, suffering and death when we were created to be whole, perfect and complete forever.

I have studied its teachings since the early 90's. In 1998, Sai Baba, through a dream, sent me a teacher. This teacher has greatly facilitated the deepening of my understanding of the truth of Jesus' words. Because of his unrelenting divesting me of any and all stashes of untruth, he left me no choice but to give all my energy, focus and passion to truth. I am eternally grateful. Sai Baba says ACIM offers the purest non-dualistic teachings for the West.

I was raised in a Christian home, thus my first exposure to Spirit was through religion. My parents are righteous, hard-working, God-fearing, good-hearted people who gave everything to their children – their love, their lives, their truth and their religion. The Bible was read daily in those early formative years and I grew to love many of the God-suffused stories my father read at meal times, both from the Old and New Testaments. Later, for many years I rejected its teachings. Hearing Sai Baba refer to the Bible as Veda resurrected credibility in my mind. Now I see in it what had been previously missed. Its allegories were seen in a profound new light.

The ideas presented herein come from what I have understood to be true beyond belief. I have thoroughly investigated their authenticity on the sounding board of my deep yearning for only the truth. What I have uncovered seems reasonable to me. It may however not seem so to you. If not, don't settle. Go for discovering truth within your own heart and mind. At the same time we are here for each other. We don't all have to reinvent the wheel.

I am always searching, refining, and expanding, so it is possible that what seems good evidence for the truth today may change as a new insight brings deeper understanding. Mostly, I wish to inspire you to want to know the truth about yourself for yourself and to give no one power over you to discover it for you. Honor yourself. Be responsible for yourself. Know that you are all-powerful and that you have limitless capacity to know whatever you set your heart and mind to knowing.

There will be those who insist that truth cannot be known, that it is a mystery. That has never been my position. I have always felt I had the right to know and have had a firm determination to do whatever was necessary to find out everything. I demanded to know what I was told was unknowable. My constant prayer to God has been, "Please show me. I want to know. I'm willing to do anything for the truth. I'm willing to give everything for the truth."

Many of the stories narrated here were first heard from talks given by Al Drucker, my cherished husband. It is with gratitude to him for his wonderful gift as a storyteller and teacher that I pass them along to you. I also share personal stories and experiences to help illustrate certain teachings as I have applied them toward my own understanding. My conclusions seem reasonable to me, though I have no need to be right. I only want the truth.

It is so easy to find ways to misinterpret and misapply the teachings if we are not 100% earnest and vigilant in wanting the truth above all else. That is so because we have allied with a slippery ego that wishes to stay alive, and truth and ego are mutually exclusive. Ego survives at our expense. We trade in our eternal life for ego's existence. When we turn toward truth, ego feels threatened and tries to fool us into getting sidetracked in all kinds of dead ends and byways leading nowhere. That is why Sai Baba lovingly chides, "Practice Constant Integrated Awareness (CIA)," and "Always Be Careful (ABC)."

In the text I freely quote from all my teachers where helpful. Italicized quotes sprinkled richly throughout the text are from ACIM. I paraphrase or express ideas in my own words as they have taken on meaning and life for me though they may have originated elsewhere. There is nothing new under the sun. I do not claim to originate anything, yet I have my own particular expression and style. Truth is one and available to all.

I have written candidly about some personal experiences and also some stories that involved others who are close to me. In all my examples I never lose sight of the truth that everyone is innocent, pure and holy forever. I hope you will see my examples as the learning devices they are intended to be.

This offering expresses my passionate delving into the teachings to gain ever-deepening understandings. Sharing strengthens ideas. You are welcome to use any of this material in any way you feel may serve you and all beings everywhere. This book is dedicated to you dear friend and to the end of suffering for all humanity.

Dear Heavenly Father/Mother God, Let truth be restored to earth. Let there be peace, love, light, joy and plenty for all, as it was always meant to be. May ego be exposed as the imposter it has always been. May we witness a great awakening for all humanity. May we witness a grand shift from self-imposed slavery to boundless freedom for each of Your precious children. Inspire us to step into our roles in Your plan for the salvation of the world. Let heaven be restored to earth.

May all beings in all the worlds be happy and blest, Amen

Chapter 1

Are You Ready to Give Up Nothing for Everything?

God, who is everything, created mankind to be and have everything.
Choosing ego, which is nothing, we entered an experience of nothing.
We convinced ourselves that nothing was everything and everything was nothing.
Everything and nothing cannot coexist. Bring them together to see the obvious.
We can choose again. Are you ready to give up nothing for everything?

Everything Is Within You

Once Sai Baba asked Al Drucker, one of His ardent devotees and professor at His university at the time, "What do you want?" As everything was going smoothly, Drucker replied in all honesty, "Nothing, Swami." (In India, Swami is used as a term of respectful endearment for a teacher). That did not satisfy, so again Swami asked, "What do you want?" Drucker again responded, "Nothing Swami, I'm content." Baba was persistent and asked a third time, "What do you want?" This time Al said, "I only want You, Swami." Swami exclaimed, "That's not nothing, that's everything. That's freedom, peace, love, joy, power, wisdom, enlightenment, understanding, truth, eternity..." He pointed to Al's heart and said, "Everything is in here," then pointing to the market place, "Nothing is out there."

Everything is within you. You were created by God, as God, to be and have everything forever. Are you ready to accept that? Is that all right with you? Do you feel you deserve everything, without any effort on your part? If God created you like Himself and if He were everything, then would it not follow that you too must be everything? Or is your question whether you really were created by God? Well, then do you have a Source, and if so, who is your Source? Is it just a mystery that has no answer? Can you content yourself with that? I felt it imperative to know how I came into being. I now trust, through a process of deep inner exploration, that I was created by God. I now trust that I am as He created me and that He created me to be and have everything.

What is meant by everything? Everything means that which does not change and yet continues to increase and expand forever. Everything includes peace, love, joy, truth, heaven, freedom, oneness, life, power... Everything is all-inclusive, though nothing is not part of it. Nothing refers to all that changes, deteriorates, gets lost, dies or suffers, for that is not part of everything. The world as we know it is nothing, for each body, place and thing in it has the mark of death upon it. Your body is nothing. Anything that changes shape, content or form is nothing.

Are You God?

Sai Baba says, "I am God. You are also God. The difference is that I know it, and you do not - yet. I have come to tell you that you and I are exactly the same." The Bible says God created man in His image and likeness. Jesus says in the New Testament, "You are Gods." When Jesus declared his oneness with his Father he was condemned to death by crucifixion. He was accused of blasphemy. A deeply entrenched thought system was seriously threatened by the idea that we could be God, an idea Jesus fully understood, lived and taught. Why has there been so much fear around accepting that idea?

Ego has convinced us that to believe ourselves Divine is arrogant, but can it be arrogant to be who we are? Ego does not want us to know our truth, for then ego loses its hold on us and will vanish. Is it possible to have been created perfect, omniscient, omnipresent and omnipotent forever? When we open the door to that possibility, we give ourselves the opportunity to have that as our direct experience.

If God created us in His image, it must be that we were created exactly like Him and therefore must be God. If that is so, then we were created to be and have unconditional love, unending joy and eternal peace as our direct and only experience right now and forever. Then we must have been created to be ever free, limitless in understanding, mighty in sovereignty and power, masters of a glorious, resplendent destiny. If we indeed were created by God as God, then we were created to be certain of who we are as Divine, holy, innocent and so many other wonderful exaltations that most of us dare not even dream of and certainly do not experience right now.

If this description of yourself is even remotely possible in your mind, you will want to know why it is not your direct experience. Perhaps it is not your experience now because you wanted a different experience. God is love and can only create in His likeness. He created you in love, to be and experience only love. Love is everything and alone exists, yet we experience fear and hatred. How is that possible? Can you imagine God to be afraid or hateful? How then can you, who were created by love as love have an experience other than love? Perhaps your unloving experience is not real. Perhaps fear and hatred are in fact nonexistent and sustained only by your belief in them.

God is peace. Peace is everything and yet conflict is on the rise everywhere. Perhaps war and faction are not God's will and therefore nothing in truth. God created you to be eternally joyful, yet joy turns quickly to sorrow. Perhaps sadness, emptiness and loneliness are unreal as they are not of God. We experience restriction and limitation rather than the boundless freedom of God's kingdom. How is it that our experience is one of being buffeted about by circumstances beyond our control? Surely God does not experience helplessness. How can it be that we are God when our experience is so lacking in Godliness, Divine splendor and certainty?

If you are as God created you, you must be as powerful as God and it must follow that there is no force outside of you arranging your circumstances for you. Then everything that happens is by your choice. If we choose our experience ourselves, what could possibly have possessed us to convince ourselves that we would prefer this insanity, this unreal experience, this nothingness, to everything? This mystifying, unbelievable descent into madness will be the exploration of this book. We have to start asking the right questions. We have to start looking at what we have taken for granted and scrutinize it. Does it hold up? Is our experience conclusive evidence that what is taking place in our lives is a real experience as God intended for us? If not, what will it take to be restored to sanity and to enter into a real experience as we were created to have forever?

Why Were We Created?

We were created to create, to love and to know. We were created as ideas in God's mind. Ideas cannot leave their source, therefore you are an idea in God's mind forever. Since God did not change His mind, you are forever exactly as God created you and thus forever exactly like God. God created us eternally whole, free, flawless, all-powerful, ever-extending, ever-creating and delightfully happy. Of our own freewill we chose to exit heaven, or everything and enter an experience of nothing in a world of sickness, suffering and death. We have convinced ourselves that our experience of nothing is everything and that everything is really nothing or nonexistent.

How were we created? Sai Baba says, "I separated Myself from Myself that I might love Myself." God created us by extending Himself within Himself. God created us one with Him eternally. God is love and can only express love. He loves us, His creation, one with Him, though unique and free to create uniquely. We chose a different purpose than the one God gave us when He created us, because we wanted to experience separation from God. Thus we chose for ourselves an experience devoid of God. Any experience devoid of God must be unreal, as it is impossible to be separate from our Source.

To be restored to a real experience, we must heal the separation, the gap between who we think we are and who we really are. How do we do this? We must want to experience our oneness with God and with everyone and everything. We must stop wanting autonomy. Baba tells us to see God in everything. If you see only God, you will treat everyone as God and hold everyone's truth of Godliness whether they are acting in a Godly manner or not. That restores oneness and heals the separation.

Should we see God in the evil as well as the good, turning a blind eye to evil, wickedness and unrighteousness? That cannot heal the separation for that is the out-picturing of separation. We must learn to look past error to the truth in ourselves and everyone, thereby inviting error to be corrected and truth restored. If you see error and condemn it, you make it real. If you see error and condone it, again you make it real. We inspire others to lead lives of purity and holiness by example.

If you see corruption or evil and call that God, you are making the unreal real and including nothing with everything due to a lack of discernment. This is mere conceptual understanding of the teaching to see God in everything. If you see corruption and bring God to bear on the situation, the corruption must be undone. That is bringing light into the darkness and thus the darkness vanishes. If you think God is in the corruption as much as the good, you have not understood God. God is everything and alone exists. Corruption is nothing and does not exist at all in truth.

Everything And Nothing Are Mutually Exclusive

Everything and nothing are two thought systems that cannot both exist. Everything has no opposite. Nothing is nonexistent forever. What is the veil between everything and nothing? It is merely a wish to be other than who you are. Is the veil impenetrable? No, it is light as a feather and whenever you want to cross back into everything from nothing, there is no force to stop you. There is no power opposing your will. You are all-powerful as God created you.

What landed you on the side of nothing when you were created to be and have everything forever? It was your choice. Your wish or desire put you there. What will it take to get back to everything? The wish to be home will permit you to cross the bridge back into everything. It is all up to you, for you are all-powerful. God wills you to be home and that choice is available right now, as God's will is everything and alone exists. The world of lack, loneliness and fear is nothing as it is not part of God's will.

However, let this teaching not be used to conclude that nothing is nothing for you. We must be vigilant never to underestimate the reality we have invested in nothingness. To whatever extent we experience sickness, suffering and death; peace, love and joy have been abolished. Peace, love and joy are everything while sickness, suffering and death are nothing. Everything and nothing cannot coexist.

We were created to be and have everything and to live in the Garden of Eden forever. What could have possessed us to leave paradise in the first place? Maybe we wanted to experience what it would be like to be different from how we were created. Because your mind is all-powerful, you can give yourself any experience you want. We tried to give ourselves an experience of being and having more than everything, but what would that mean? It would mean that we could actually be more than God. That is impossible as God is and has everything.

An experience of having and being more than everything cannot be a real experience, even though we can make it seem very real. You can be exactly the same as your Creator, because He created you exactly like Himself. You cannot be less because He cannot create less than Himself. Nor can you be more than your Creator, because God is everything and there is nothing greater than everything. To think you can be either more or less than God would be to think yourself separate from God. Separation from God is impossible because He created you one with Him forever. When you think separation possible, you are mistaken, though your experience may support your erroneous idea. Your mind is all-powerful and you do get the results of your own mind.

We Made Ego To Replace God

You can give yourself an experience of separation and thereby convince yourself that you are different from who you are. We each made for ourselves an ego to become different from how we were created. We made ego to replace God because we wanted to experience autonomy or separation from God. Isn't it true that we use the world to experience independence from God? We work to meet our survival needs and forget that we are sustained by God's love. People pride themselves on their independence and think, 'I don't need God,' 'God doesn't love me – He doesn't respond to my prayers,' 'God is up in heaven and I don't experience Him with me in this moment,' 'To depend on God is weakness...' In one way or other we find our experience to be one of separation from God. Maybe God exists, but not as part of our direct experience.

If we are all-powerful, an experience devoid of God must have originated from the idea that we'd like to experience independence from God, so, using our all-powerful minds, we made our own source to become autonomous or self-created. It was our way of pushing God aside or usurping God's throne. We made ego to replace God. Ego means Edging God Out.

Making your own source is comparable to giving birth to your parents. It is not only ridiculous but impossible, and yet we each convinced ourselves that it was not only possible but the only truth. Though ego has been heavily invested with reality, it remains unreal. God is and has always been our Source.

Maybe you don't accept that you made your own ego. Ego is in trouble when you know you made it and can relinquish it as easily. We have given our power away to ego. When you own that you made it, you can take back your power and pull the plug on ego. That is good news for you but not for ego, thus ego does not want you to know you are its maker and thereby in a position of power over it. Ego does not want the obvious exposed, so most people find themselves defending their egos by convincing themselves ego has something good to offer them like personality, specialness or individuality. We tend to justify its existence and do not question it because we made it.

We have an allegiance to or affinity for what we make even though it may not be real, and even though it may be hurting us. This tendency is due to a certain sense of pride of source. You naturally love what you make, just as God loves what He creates. If you have children you cannot but love them and feel proud of their accomplishments – they are seen as your creative extension, not separate from you. The confusion around ego is that it is not a creation, but rather an attempt at mutiny. God created us to create, but it is not possible to create our source. *Creation is not reciprocal.* We can create as God creates, but God created us and we could not in turn create our Creator.

Though it is not possible to replace God as Source we can believe it possible and that will make it real for us, as our minds are all-powerful. We can convince ourselves of anything. Ego has convinced us that we will lose ourselves if we lose it because we have believed in it as our source. The fact is we will only gain who we are by losing ego and acknowledging God as our Source. Can you become less by being who you are?

Another reason people reject the idea of having made ego is that ego is the cause of all the suffering in the world. If we made ego, we would then be responsible for the state of the world. We don't want to be responsible, so we make God or someone else responsible. Only when we understand the unreality of our world will it become acceptable to take responsibility for the state in which we find the world. When we step into personal responsibility for the world, we will be motivated to do all we can towards its healing. Only when enough of us are willing to step into that level of responsibility can ego and the world of sickness, suffering and death be undone. They came together and go together. And only when ego is undone are we restored to wholeness. Then we will again find ourselves in a true experience of being and having everything. Then nothing will have been seen truly as the nothingness that it has always been and it will no longer be part of our experience.

Are You Willing To Give Up Nothing For Everything?

All the mystical teachings exhort us to surrender. The idea of surrender is usually resisted because it seems we are being asked to give up something. We are being asked to give up nothing so that we can have everything forever. The problem is we have made nothing everything by giving it value. Once you see that you have put value in nothing, will it be a sacrifice to trade it in for everything? All that is necessary is that you stop convincing yourself that nothing is everything, and let everything be what it is, the truth. In order to be willing to give up nothing in exchange for everything, we have to withhold belief in it and see it truly as the nothingness that it is and has always been.

When we do not place belief in what is not true, it will be undone for us and all that will be our experience will be everything, which is all there ever was. We just covered up the truth when we convinced ourselves that nothing was everything and everything was nothing. Everything has no opposite, thus nothing is truly nothing and does not exist now, nor has it ever existed. Because we have made nothing everything in our minds by giving it energy, it must be undone. This happens by seeing its nothingness. When we bring nothing and everything together the truth stands revealed.

In bringing opposites together, the fact of their complete incompatibility becomes apparent. In keeping them separate they cannot be reconciled. When two systems of belief are brought together, one must disappear. The fog of untruth lifts in the presence of truth. Light dispels the darkness. Everything is all-inclusive and there is no room in that for that which is not. It is impossible. As nothing is not part of everything it is merely nonexistent and is therefore undone when seen truly. This undoing of the unreal requires a miracle due to the reality that has been invested in it. We prepare for miracles through a shift in consciousness or an action of mind. From giving reality to nothing we withdraw belief in nothingness and allow everything to be what it is, true and real forever. The following fifteen descriptions for everything are looked at briefly here in an overview and in greater detail in the chapters that follow. Their counterpart, nothing, is exposed as what it is in truth, nonexistent.

Fifteen Aspects Of Everything Versus Nothing

1. **Eternity (everything without opposite) or time and space (its apparent opposite – nothing)** - God created everything to be eternal. Our experience is of time and space where all we see dies, disappears or disintegrates with time. We think time and space are the only reality and that eternity is nonexistent. Thus we have convinced ourselves that time and

space are true for all eternity. We have brought eternity to time and space and thereby made the unreal real.

Eternity can be experienced right now by dropping past and future. Time and space require a past and a future, neither of which have anything to do with God and His creation. True teachers teach you to be here now, as here and now are real and truly reliable. When you have no regrets about the past or worries about the future, you are in the present, the eternal now. We made time and space to be our experience for all eternity by pushing eternity out of the equation. As soon as eternity is brought back into the equation, time and space simply disappear as they were never real. We can use them wisely now to regain eternity.

2. **God-dependence (everything without opposite) or ego-dependence (its apparent opposite – nothing)** – You are a thought in the mind of God. As such you have never left God. You have no existence apart from Him. You are totally God-dependent. This dependence is where your freedom lies, for God created you free. His kingdom is freedom and in your dependence on God you are equal with Him, and thereby you are God. Symbiosis, whereby God depends on you and you depend on Him, is your true relationship with God. It is a naturally joyful interdependent relationship.

We made ego to be independent of God, but we merely traded in one dependency for another. If you look closely, you will see that ego-dependence is actually the cause of all apparent bondage. Dependence on ego is an unreal relationship, while dependence on God is a healthy, true, dynamic relationship - the dance of the lover and the beloved, wherein you enhance each other's joy. You pine for God and He pines for you and you rejoice in each other's presence. It is Divine nectar. By contrast, ego dependence is a parasitic relationship whereby it leads you to believe you need it to live so it can live at your expense. Ego is totally dependent on you, or more specifically on you thinking you are guilty, for its survival.

Maybe you are interested in exploring the possibility of being independent of both God and ego as the truth. There are those who think that to see God as your Source is dualistic, but when we realize that we are equal with God and not separate, both the idea that we were created by God and that there is only oneness can be held simultaneously. Sai Baba says you can only choose between God and ego. If that is so, we cannot escape dependence. When you see clearly what the choices are, would you rather depend on God or ego? You can depend on God for everything. You can depend on ego for nothing.

3. **Reality (everything without opposite) or unreality (its apparent opposite – nothing)** - Everything God creates is real. Everything we make without God is unreal and therefore nothing, as without God we can do

nothing. All peace, love and joy are real, while all sickness, suffering and death are unreal, as God did not create them. When we made ego to be our source, we made for ourselves an unreal situation, as ego is an unreal idea in our minds. All that comes from alliance with ego is unreal, as it has no basis. That is good news, as it can therefore easily be undone. It is only held in place by our belief. As soon as we withhold belief from the unreal, reality will be our experience. It was our wish for unreality that made it real for us, just as our wish for reality will allow that to be our experience.

Unreality can deceive, but can change. Reality is changeless. It does not deceive at all. If you fail to see beyond appearances, you are deceived. Everything you see will change. If you believe the changeable to be reality, then reality has been reduced to form and is capable of change. We have given the unreal reality, though it can never be real. As long as we insist that the unreal is real, reality is not allowed to be what it is. *Yet reality remains ever unaffectable and it is this that makes it real and keeps it separate from all appearances. It must transcend all unreality to be itself.* God is a real idea in your mind. Everything that bubbles forth from alliance with God is real. Ego is an unreal idea and all that comes from that alliance is unreal. We need merely stop making the unreal real and allow the real to be real to be restored to a real experience.

4. **Heaven (everything without opposite) or hell (its apparent opposite – nothing)** - God created you to be in heaven forever. Heaven is everything. God made a real world, a heavenly world. The world as we experience it does not exist except in our minds. Neither do our bodies. Your physical body was made to be a limitation on what God created you to be. It is perishable and vulnerable. Yet it can be used either to return to heaven or to remain in hell.

The world has been used to hide from God and so it became a hell, yet it can be used to reunite with God and then it will again be heaven. The unreal can be transformed back into the real. Unreal thoughts lead to an unreal world and an unreal physical body, which has been mistaken for our true identity. The world is a projection of the mind. It reflects back to you what is in your mind. Your true thoughts help to heal the world. Until the world is healed, your mind is not healed, as the world is in your mind.

Jesus says, "The kingdom of heaven is within." Heaven is also an idea in your mind. The world and your body are ideas you projected outside of your mind, though they did not really leave your mind and can now serve to reveal to you the contents of your mind when you are willing to know your own mind. Heaven has nothing to do with the transitory world of name and form. Heaven and the unreal world are irreconcilable. Bring them together and the world of sickness, suffering and death must disappear. There is only heaven. Let the heavens be reflected on the earth now, that the earth may return unto heaven.

5. Innocence (everything without opposite) or guilt (its apparent opposite – nothing) – Either we are all innocent or all guilty. We were all created to be innocent forever. Innocence has no opposite. Guilt is nothing. You cannot ever be guilty for anything. You can make mistakes because you were created free. Part of that freedom includes the freedom to choose to have an experience that is other than who you are, but it won't be a true experience.

You can choose to mistakenly don a false identity. Mistakes do not take away from our innocence as they can be corrected. When we thought we could make our own source we were mistaken. The correction is seeing that we cannot make our own source. We felt tremendous guilt for our mistake only because we thought we had actually succeeded in replacing God as Source. God cannot be replaced. It was ego, 'God's replacement,' that insisted we be guilty and punished. Why? Because once ego has been given life, it wants to survive and depends on guilt and punishment for its existence. Only if you believe you are guilty can ego exist. Ego and guilt come together and go together. Ego wants you to think you are guilty.

To choose to do something that is not in alignment with the Divine will is an error as it is impossible to defy the Divine will. To realign yourself with the Divine will is to correct your error, in which case you are back in a true experience of peace, love and joy as you were created. To leave error uncorrected leads to suffering. You will inevitably feel guilty for uncorrected error, as denial of error is an admission of guilt. Perfection or purity are easy as they are who you are. God will encourage you to correct your error, as that is in your best interest.

Ego wants you punished for your error as that is in its best interest. Your suffering buys ego time, thus it tries to convince you that error is sin. As long as you see anyone as guilty, you do not believe in your innocence. Guilt is impossible for any of God's creations and everyone was created by God. Only ego is guilty as it is a false idea of limitation and separation that could never happen in truth. As innocence overcomes guilt, so also good overcomes evil. Leading a life of goodness, virtue and nobleness reestablishes your innocence in your mind and your guilty verdict is seen truly as insubstantial and baseless. The case against you will be dismissed on the spot and you will be free to be as God created you.

6. Life (everything without opposite) or death (its apparent opposite – nothing) – We were created to be immortal. We will live forever. We were created to have life without opposite. Death is not real. It is a joke we play on ourselves. Death is our final proof that God is dead. That is impossible as God is immortal and as He only creates like Himself, we too are immortal. Death is the opposite of life, but life can have no opposite. We simply cannot die.

Death is an attempt to escape life, but we were created to live forever. How is that possible when we see death all around us? Only that which is not real experiences death. Your body is not real. Even if it dies, you live forever. Plants and animals and everything you see have the mark of death on them, but that is not proof that death is real. We have the power to heal the sick and raise the dead, because we made sickness and death, and they can be abolished when we stop making them real through the power of our belief. Life has no opposite. If life is real, then death is impossible and never happened. God is life. Is it possible for God to die? Then how can anything He creates die? Life and death are irreconcilable. Bring eternal life back into your most holy mind and death loses its sting.

7. **Love (everything without opposite) or fear (its apparent opposite – nothing)** - God is love. Love has no opposite. You were created to be and have love as your only experience, both with God and everyone. Yet we experience fear and hatred. That is because we have miscreated unreal experiences, separate from God. There are only two emotions, love and fear, and only love is real. Fear is not possible, for God can only express love, thus only love exists. All fear is illusion.

Some think of God as fearful, but that idea comes from trust in an ego that wants you to believe that God is fearful, wrathful, vengeful, punishing, judgmental, sitting on some throne somewhere condemning you to eternal damnation. That is the furthest thing from God's mind as He deeply loves all that He creates. But, as long as you believe that to be so, ego survives. Ego wants to exist. It will try very hard to deceive you, because its survival depends on you loving it more than you love God, thus it tries to convince you that God is other than who He is. *God is but love and therefore so are you. Love means letting go of fear. Perfect love casts out fear.* Love is all there is.

8. **Truth (everything without opposite) or untruth (its apparent opposite – nothing)** - What is true is the same for everyone forever. It doesn't mean we all have to practice the same religion or enjoy the same interests or experiences. Variety and differences on the level of form can and must be appreciated and tolerated in order that we live together in peace. Wars are fought over differences of religion, race, color, sex, nationality… These are differences of form and forms will be different. Only intolerance of difference of form should not be tolerated.

Where content is concerned there are no differences. There may be many paths up the mountain, but when you reach the top, the view is exactly the same for everyone. There are countless ways to get to truth, but when it is seen, you will have seen what everyone else who has reached has found. Truth is one. We are all so much more alike than we are different and that is distressing only as long as you want to be special, different or separate. God is love and showers His love on all equally. He cannot be love sometimes and not at other times or with some individuals and not with others. Ultimate truth is universal. Be true for the fog of untruth to clear. Untruth brought to truth dissolves instantly as truth is all there is.

9. **Peace (everything without opposite) or war (its apparent opposite – nothing)** - God created us to be eternally peaceful, yet we pray for, hope for and search for peace. We accommodate our lives and compromise our ideals for the sake of peace and still it is not true peace we experience. It is not lasting peace. Conflict and war are a very prominent part of the world we live in. What must we do to experience peace for ourselves and for the whole of humanity? We do not have to do anything except change our minds. Peace is who we are. It is alliance with ego that is the cause of all conflict, as ego thrives on conflict. Our brother is never our enemy. Our only enemy is ego, and it is vanquished by looking, not by fighting.

If you knew that there was nothing and no one outside of you, wouldn't attacking anyone or anything be an attack on yourself? If you knew that all were your brothers and sisters, given to you by God to be your family, out of His deep love for you, could you fight with anyone for any reason? If you knew that nothing happens to you without your will, could you blame anyone for your ills? If you knew all that to be true, wouldn't you be at peace no matter what happened to you? Taking personal responsibility for conflict in our lives allows it to be undone. 'Let there be peace on earth and let it begin with **me**.' God's kingdom was created to be eternally peaceful and that is your inheritance. Claim it now by bringing conflict to peace to be resolved and dissolved forever.

10. **Knowledge (everything without opposite) or ignorance (its apparent opposite – nothing)** - You were created to know everything. Why would God create you and yet keep secrets from you? Nothing is hidden from you that you have not hidden from yourself. There are no mysteries. There is nothing that is beyond your ability to know right now. There is nothing that is unknowable. We have no need to learn anything. As long as you think you need to learn something, you are giving yourself an unreal purpose. It is simply not true. But we do have tremendous capacity to learn if we so choose, as our minds are all-powerful. We have used that power to teach ourselves to believe the unreal real and the real unreal. That is quite a learning feat. Now we need merely unlearn what we have taught ourselves, for we have been poorly taught. We have convinced ourselves that we are ignorant and do not know who God is or who we are. We seem to have forgotten our purpose. Fortunately all these misgivings are simply impossible as we were created to know everything forever.

God's children, created with the brilliant luster of dazzling diamonds, have become dull, lifeless and stupid, but that is a parody on God's creation and never really happened. We can throw off our ignorance whenever we so choose. We have never lost our knowledge of the truth. We have not become ignorant. We have merely fooled ourselves into believing that we cannot know and then we call that ignorance humility. Ignorance is not humility but the height of arrogance. It is arrogant to want to be different from who we are. Only grandiosity would have us be other than ourselves. We are grandeur and to think it humility to be small, limited or lacking in any way is to deny that we are as we were created.

We have interposed a concept of ourselves onto who we are and have convinced ourselves that is true, though it never affected our truth. When we let go of all our ideas of what knowledge is, knowledge can dawn once again upon our most holy minds. When we want the truth above all else, then only will we be able to recognize the truth that we do know everything forever. *It has taken much time to convince ourselves of who we are not. It takes no time to be who we are.* The darkness of ignorance disappears in the light of true knowledge.

11. **Oneness (everything without opposite) or separation (its apparent opposite – nothing)** – You are one with God. God created you just like Himself. There is no separation between you and God. When you are totally in love with someone, you know each other through and through. You know that nothing can separate you from one other, not time, nor space, nor even death. You are one with each other forever. That is how it is with you and God.

God loves you so intensely that He is always with you, in you, around you, before you and above you. He knows everything about you because He is never separate from you. There is no place where God ends and you begin. At the same time, you are whole, perfect and complete within yourself. There is nothing outside of you. God is not outside of your mind.

Everyone is an idea in your mind. When you merge your mind with the mind of God, you are in the experience of how you were created - one with God. Your mind and God's are exactly the same. The world also is in your mind and the recognition of your oneness with it is key to your salvation.

Your mind and soul were created as one. Your soul is unalterably perfect forever. As soul you are one with everyone and everything. As mind you can have an experience that is different from how you were created, but that is all. You cannot be different from who you are. When you merge your mind with your soul you will again be home where you never left in truth. That return takes place when you stop wanting autonomy or separation to be your experience.

Specialness comes with the idea of separation. You can be unique, but you cannot be special in the sense of being more or less than anyone else. Where is separation when there is nothing outside of your mind? *There is only one problem, separation, and the solution is it never happened.* Bring separation to oneness and separation vanishes without a trace.

12. **Freedom (everything without opposite) or bondage (its apparent opposite – nothing)** - Freedom is your true inheritance. God wants you to be free forever. His kingdom is freedom. God loves you. Why would He wish you to be bound? What father would restrict his child's freedom?

Does freedom mean lack of discipline, license or liberty to run after endless desires with no restraint? Of course not. Freedom lies in self-discipline and self-control. Because God willed you to be free, you have the freedom to choose that which may not be in your best interest if you so insist. If you want to stride into hell, God will not bar your way, for to do so would be to act counter to how He created you - free.

Though God is pained at your suffering and at your wish to experience separation from Him, He honors you and is your perfect, most gracious host no matter what your wish. If you wish to block Him out of your experience, He will step back and wait. If you wish to be as you are not, He will not force you to be who you are. Your wish to be other than how you were created does not alter the truth or make you bad. It does however make you wrong, as it is impossible to be other than who you are.

It is possible to make mistakes and errors are correctable. When your mistakes are corrected, you are restored to a true experience of love, joy and freedom in unbroken communion with God and everyone. A mind that is willing to be wrong is free. Freedom is your truth and when you want freedom to be your experience, it will be so, for there is nothing to oppose your will.

You were created to have the freedom of creation, but not of autonomy, for that is not possible. In attempting an experience of autonomy, we only produced bondage for ourselves. That bondage has nothing to do with God and everything to do with ego. Freedom and bondage are mutually exclusive. Our chains of oppression are self-inflicted and will be cast off when we no longer want them. Accepting that our freedom is limited to limitless creativity and cannot include separation from God or each other will lead to true freedom in the joy of unity with God and everyone.

13. **Non-judgment (everything without opposite) or judgment (its apparent opposite – nothing)** – God does not judge. It is we who have made God into something He is not. We fear Him and His judgment upon us. We project onto Him that He condemns, rejects and punishes. When we think these thoughts we simply expose to ourselves that we do not know God who loves all of us with the love of a thousand mothers. When we

judge each other in any way we bind ourselves to judgment and condemnation and ultimately prove to ourselves that God judges. We make erroneous judgments all the time based on limited information. We have judgments, opinions, assumptions and conclusions about just about everything. This is what we have used our most holy minds for and this has been the cause of our bondage. We must stop judging in order that we be free.

When we see, not that we should not judge, but that we cannot judge because we do not have all the facts needed to make sound judgments, judgment will be relinquished. Then we will be restored to our true state of wholeness. That opens the door to everyone else being restored to wholeness as well. As long as you judge anyone you are judging yourself. Only when you see the perfection in everyone will you know that you are not judging. However, non-judgment does not condone or support impure behavior. Non-judgment is not passive. Use judgment to see where you are contracting into judgment. This is good use of judgment. *Each unforgiving thought is a judgment and keeps the illusion of separation in place.* In giving up judgment we are restored to our original state of purity and perfection. To be perfect requires no judgment at all as it is who we are.

14. **Creation (everything without opposite) or miscreation (its apparent opposite – nothing)** - All God's creations are extensions of Himself as light. You are light. As light you extend forever. You were created as an extension of God. God is limitless expansion. God is always giving. You were created to give forever. In giving you receive. *You can only give to yourself.* You are whole and complete eternally, in need of nothing and so is everyone and everything. There is nothing anyone can give you to complete you. You cannot ever lose anything.

When God gives it is not to complete you, but only to share His joy, which is a natural act of creation. When you recognize your wholeness, you look to God only to share your joy with Him. Then you are in true relationship with your Maker. *When you see no lack either in yourself or another, your relationship will serve only to increase your joy. Then you have come closest in this world to your true relationship with God.*

Our miscreations or projections are unreal. Anything to do with name and form is unreal and anything to do with Divinity is real. Everything we see is made up of both what is real and what is unreal. Give energy to what is real. You projected a world and a body outside of your mind. On the surface they are changing, therefore not real. But your body is the temple for God and you as God are real. The world was created for you by God as a place in which to commune with God and all of humanity. When restored to a real purpose the world again becomes real. Invite God back into your life and into the world to restore it to a real purpose. Miscreations disappear in the presence of your real creations which you create with God.

Lack is impossible in God's creation. *Only you can deprive yourself of anything.* Abundance, fullness and completeness are attributes of God's creation. Lack, constriction or limitation are due to miscreating and are not real. *We cannot create in the world as we see it. We can heal and when healed, the world will be restored to its original purpose.* When your mind is healed, your miscreations will disappear into the nothingness they have always been. Then you will be restored to your true function of creating the true, the beautiful and the holy.

15. **All-Powerful (everything without opposite) or powerless (its apparent opposite – nothing)** - You have everything God has since you were created by God, exactly like Him. God is all-powerful, therefore you too must be all-powerful. There is no one more powerful than you. Nothing happens to you without your consent. Everything that happens, you have agreed to and thus want. If you don't like what is happening, you have the power to give yourself a different experience. You can change your mind. It is ego that tells you that you are helpless. Ego is simply an idea that things could happen to you against your will. Everything that happens to you serves some purpose. If it were not so, it could not be your experience.

Whenever you feel hurt by anyone or anything it is because you have given your power away. When you take back your power by recognizing that in God you are all-powerful, you again take charge of your life. There are those who say power can be dangerous. What they are referring to is not power, but force. Only those who believe themselves weak use force. Those who know they are all-powerful do not misuse their power. We chose to experience powerlessness because we did not want to take responsibility for our particular set of circumstances. In giving up self-responsibility, we give our power away. You are responsible for everything that happens to you. You will accept this level of responsibility when you are ready to trade in powerlessness for all the power in the universe.

Miracles Undo The Unreal

The fifteen attributes of nothing dissolve in the presence of the fifteen attributes of everything. Though there are fifteen different descriptions under everything, they are all really just fifteen different ways to describe everything. Though there are fifteen different descriptions for nothing, they are all just different ways of referring to nothing. The way back home is through the undoing of what is really nothing but misperceived as everything and that requires a miracle.

We prepare ourselves for miracles through forgiveness. We forgive ourselves for miscreating nothing by recognizing its nothingness. Thereby nothing is transformed back into everything, unreality into reality, untruth into truth, sickness, suffering and death into peace, love and joy for all humanity. *Miracles are natural expressions of love. Love is real. Miracles are gifts of God.* You cannot heal yourself, but you can be healed when you are willing to be healed. God is always eager to heal you, but He waits on your wish. When you are healed you are contributing to the healing of the world and until the world is healed, we have work to do. In truth you were never broken, therefore the only healing necessary is to change your mind about who you are.

Sai Baba says, "Everything is within you. There is nothing outside of you." Jesus taught, "The Kingdom of heaven is within." We must seek it within. We must look within for answers. Sometimes people living permanently at Sai Baba's ashram, especially when they feel challenged, might be tempted to think, "Baba, I gave up everything for You." The fact is they gave up nothing for everything. In giving up the world we give up nothing. In coming to God, we receive everything. Is it a sacrifice to give up nothing and receive the love of God forever? Baba says, "Forget the world; Always remember God; Never fear death." God is everything. The world and death are nothing. See them truly and they are undone. Nothing untoward happened. That shift in consciousness allows the miracle of the undoing of the unreal.

Forgiveness sees unreality for what it is, unreal. Forgiveness is the idea that nothing happened to you that you did not ask for. It is an admission that what you thought your brother or sister did to you, you did to yourself. It reveals that nothing distressing ever happened in truth. When you know that, everyone is free to be to you who he really is, namely your dearest, most cherished friend, for that is how God created him, as a precious gift for you. We are all brothers and sisters and have one God, our Father/Mother, Creator and Source.

Sickness and suffering come from thinking we are guilty, which is erroneous thinking. Sickness, lack and suffering unto death are not real. When you assure anyone that they are innocent by treating them with the utmost respect, compassion, understanding, forbearance, patience and charity, you are sending a message to your own subconscious that you too are innocent. That is forgiveness and opens the door to your healing. That is why service to humanity serves you and is where your salvation lies. Service to anyone is service to yourself, for we are all one. As you give, so you receive. Give everything to have everything forever.

Beloved Creator of us all, May all beings regain awareness of their original state of being and having everything forever. May that which is nothing in truth be transformed back into that which is everything, so that everyone everywhere may experience everything forever, in the form of true joy, deepest peace and eternal love. May all beings live together in harmony in the knowledge that all Your creations are and have everything without cease. You cherish Your children and stand at the end of the road to nothingness with infinite patience and intense longing for our return home to Your wide-open arms which give everything forever. Glorious victory to You, sweetest dearest God.

May all beings in all the worlds be happy and blest, Amen.

Figure 1 – Everything vs. Nothing

Everything	Nothing
(without opposite)	(its apparent opposite)
1. Eternity	1. Time/Space
2. God-Dependence	2. Ego-Dependence
3. Reality	3. Unreality
4. Heaven	4. Hell
5. Innocence	5. Guilt
6. Life	6. Death
7. Love	7. Fear
8. Truth	8. Untruth
9. Peace	9. War
10. Knowledge	10. Ignorance
11. Oneness	11. Separation
12. Freedom	12. Bondage
13. Non-Judgment	13. Judgment
14. Creation	14. Mis-Creation
15. All-Powerful	15. Powerless

Chapter 2

The Lifting of the Veil

If the door of perception were cleaned, everything would appear as it is.
William Blake

Our Experience On The Side of Nothing

Before the road to nothingness was made, before time came to intrude upon eternity, there was only everything, only God and His beloved creations and that which His creations co-created with Him. There was love, eternal life, abundance, everlasting peace and complete understanding without opposite. Everyone and everything was in your mind and thereby one with you. And it is so now, though probably not your direct experience. I speak of it as though it were in the past, but that would make it part of time, and eternity is here and now, before time began and after time ends.

Rare is that one whose predominant experience is not of sickness, suffering, death, separation, lack, fear and hate, if not his own, then certainly that of those around him. If you are not aware that this is so, perhaps you are choosing not to see. If you think what the world has to offer is a great experience, perhaps you are simply not being honest with yourself. Our worldly experience is of nothing – it is not a real experience.

Perhaps you will agree that your experience of everything in the form of peace, love and joy has been all but totally blocked out. What is the cloud that has blocked the sun so completely? What is this veil which separates the two worlds, the world of everything and the world of nothing? This veil is light as a feather and penetrable as gentle mist. It is only in our minds that it is real at all. It is as nonexistent as a mirage in the desert or an hallucination. Yet we have all convinced ourselves that it is an impenetrable barrier, a fortress so mighty that to even consider somehow crossing from nothing back into everything is utterly impossible.

When you change your mind the barrier can easily be overcome, for your mind alone determines how it is for you. Though it is simple to cross back into everything and leave nothing behind forever, it is elusive. That is because we made ego to have a different experience from how we were created. Once ego has been given life it wants to survive, so will employ all kinds of clever, deceptive strategies to sabotage our plan to get back home. Fortunately, there is much help available for the asking – we have the Avatar on the planet and ACIM and so many other saints and sages to assist our transition. They have all come to show us the way through the veil back to eternity, because God has willed that this be the end of time, the end of hell.

Once in her dream, a friend was on one side of a foreboding fence, imposingly tall, impossibly strong and topped with wicked spikes. On the other side stood Sai Baba. She loved Him with a passion and yearned with all her heart to be near Him. In response, He effortlessly walked through the fence and they were united. What a joyous reunion. All it takes to lift the veil is your intense longing for God. When you stop distracting yourself with the things of the world, that longing reveals itself for it was always there and cannot be lost. It is natural to want to be one with God, your Source and sustenance. To want God is to want everything. To want the world is to want nothing.

Put On Your Love Glasses

God created the world to be a place in which to commune with Him. In its original state, it was everything. We turned it into a place in which to hide from God when we made ego. To accomplish our change of purpose we projected it outside of our minds to be what it is not. In that action of mind, it became nothing. All we need do to cross the veil from nothing back into everything is change our minds about our purpose for the world. That action of mind allows the world to be transformed from nothing back into everything.

Sai Baba tells the story of a rich man who had fallen ill and had looked everywhere for a solution. One day a holy man, begging for his daily food, came to the rich man's door. In desperation, the rich man sought his advice. The holy man suggested, "Your problem is easily solved. You need peace in your world. There is so much clutter and busy making around here. You need to fill your world with green as green is the color of peace and healing. If you see only green you will find yourself at peace and healing will naturally follow. You need to immerse yourself in the color green."

A year later the holy man stopped by again, only to be greeted by two men rushing up to him and throwing a green cloak over his shoulders before he could even reach the gate. There were others all very busily painting everything green, the house, inside and out, the car, the tree trunks, and on and on. It all seemed so frenetic. The holy man was ushered in to see the rich man. As soon as the rich man saw him, he immediately expressed his despair at how things had not only not improved but rather had gotten considerably worse since the holy man's advice of seeing only green. "My workmen are constantly painting everything that I will look upon so I will see only green, but it is hard to keep up with all the things that need to be transformed. So there is always the fear that things will not be green, and that anxiety has caused me to feel even worse than when I saw you last."

The holy man laughed and exclaimed, "You are so silly. I told you to see only green, but I did not tell you to paint everything green. All you have to do is go to the local store and buy some green glasses and you will see only green. It is so simple."

We are like the rich man who cannot find peace in the world. Instead of trying to change the world all we need do is change our purpose for the world, and peace is restored to our minds and consequently to the world. Peace in the world begins with peace in our hearts. The world is a projection of our minds. It merely reflects back to us our purpose.

We restore the world to its original purpose of communion with God and everyone by seeing it through the eyes of compassion, tenderness, charity and forgiveness. In that we invite God back into the world, for God is love, and when we are love, God is with us. Then we have put on our love glasses and the world will be transformed before our very eyes. Our change of purpose permits the world to be transformed back into the real world God created where only perfect goodness and love are expressed and experienced.

You Are Free To Choose

If we were created perfect, how is it possible to find ourselves in an experience of imperfection? *God is both mind and Spirit.* Mind and Spirit are formless. For God, mind and Spirit are one. We were created in the image and likeness of God, so we too are one in mind and Spirit. As Spirit, we are unaffectable forever, meaning that we are as perfect as God forever. As mind, we have choice. We can choose to remain in the experience of oneness of mind and Spirit, which would mean the experience of everything forever, or we can choose to think mind separate from Spirit and come into an experience of fantasy, unreality or illusion and convince ourselves of its reality.

An unreal experience cannot affect our truth. And an unreal experience does not mean that our minds have become less powerful. However, all that power can be diverted to delude us into believing ourselves powerless. We can choose to have an experience that is not real and that is not in keeping with the purpose for which we were created. That would come from a choice made with ego. Our minds are as powerful as God's, as we were created in the image and likeness of God. If you find your mind to be limited, it is only because you have convinced yourself that you are not as you are.

As Spirit, we are limitless forever. As soon as we reunite mind with Spirit by changing our minds about who we are, we are again limitless in mind as well as Spirit. Then we have closed the gap between experience and truth, and the separation has been healed. Separation has come at our choosing and is healed when we so choose as well. As Spirit we are always one with God and everyone and everything. As mind this is also true, for in truth minds are joined, but we have the freedom to use our minds as we wish. We can choose to delude ourselves into thinking separation real. It does not make it so. However, it will be very real for us as long as we desire it to be so. As long as it is our experience, it must be that it is our desire.

God only uses His mind to create. You can use your mind either to create or to project. When you create, you are using your mind for the purpose for which it was given. Then everything is within your mind, for that is creation. Creation is merely you extending your mind forever. That extension is inward, thus you will experience your reality when you look within. When you experience yourself as a body in a world, that is not due to creation, but rather to projection. We project to make things different from how they are in truth.

If you feel that you are an effect of a cause outside of yourself, you have succeeded in convincing yourself that the world is outside of you and that you are being buffeted about by circumstances beyond your control. That is the world ego has convinced you is real because ego wants you to believe things could happen to you outside of your will. There is nothing further from the truth. You are using your all-powerful mind to convince yourself that you are powerless and helpless.

In the movie, Beautiful Mind, the noble prize winning mind of a mathematical genius is diagnosed schizophrenic. John Nash lives in an imaginary world of beings he is convinced are real. He has projected them outside of his mind to convince himself they are separate from him. He is no different from any of the rest of us. What you project outside of yourself, you believe is separate because you have given it that purpose. This movie illustrates how it is not the brightness of one's mind that guarantees true perception. Your earnest wish to have only the truth restores truth to you. You are all-powerful. If you really want only the truth and if you want only what is real, then that is all you will see, but only then.

Where is the real world? It is right here and now. It is not somewhere else. It will be our experience when we stop wanting the unreal to be real. When we projected the world outside of our minds it became unreal. When we bring it back into our minds by recognizing it is reflecting our minds to us, we permit our minds to be healed and the world will again be real.

The unreal world is superimposed upon the real world. Sickness, suffering and death are overlaid on peace, love and joy. How do we stop projecting an unreal world? We have to stop wanting autonomy from God, our Source, Creator, Mother and Father. To want autonomy is to want the impossible. It is impossible to be separate from God. It is impossible to be separate from anyone or anything. Only in our wishes could that be possible. And it can be our experience if we so choose, though it does not make it a real experience. Once you see that your choice for autonomy gave only unhappiness, would it be hard to decide for total dependence on God?

God Cannot Experience Illusion

God would never have a reason to project you outside of His mind. He would never wish for things to be as they are not. He would never wish to be separate or autonomous from His children. He created us to be one with Him forever. We were created to increase His joy. Projecting His creations outside of His mind would serve no purpose. When God chose to create, He chose to give up autonomy. He prefers creation to autonomy.

We projected God outside of our minds because it gave us autonomy. In the choice for autonomy, we gave up the purpose for which we were created. We were created to create. When we made ego to be our source instead of God we traded in creation for autonomy. Everything that we do here in the world projected outside of our minds is unreal, because it springs from alliance with ego and serves to prove autonomy possible. It is impossible that we be the creator of our Creator, thus separation or autonomy also is impossible. God is our Creator and the truth cannot be altered or overthrown.

God created you whole and perfect. In recognizing your wholeness, in desiring God only to share your joy, you realign yourself with your true relationship to God. In this world your pure and true relationships with others reflect your true relationship with God. *A holy relationship in this world comes closest to your true relationship with God and paves the way back to the real world. In a holy relationship, two have recognized their wholeness and have come together to enhance each other's joy. You see no lack either in yourself or your holy partner, equal with you eternally.* In such a relationship, your miscreations are healed because through your expression of unity you are withdrawing allegiance from autonomy.

When we miscreate or project we support autonomy and make what is unreal real. Projecting what is in your mind outside cuts you off from part of your mind, thereby causes amnesia and serves to prove autonomy real. This separation of self from self causes you to be unconscious of who you are. Psychology makes a study of unconscious or subconscious aspects of mind. You were created to have only conscious mind, thus all unconsciousness can be restored to conscious awareness when you include everyone and everything back into your mind.

Our bodies are miscreations. They are limitations on who we are as God created us. We are not our bodies. *Ever since the separation, you do not know your own mind, for you have hidden it from yourself by limiting it to your body. However, your body can now be used to restore you to wholeness. Your body can be used as a learning device.* Each time you get sick, you can learn that you still think you are other than whole and perfect. That is very valuable, for you would only ask to be restored to wholeness if you thought you were not whole. You can now use everything you projected outside of your mind to know your mind, for every projection is a reflection of the contents of your mind and thus can help you find your way back home.

God did not abandon us though we tried to abandon Him. We used our minds for projection to turn from God and God gave us a miracle to make of projection instead. Projection can be used to show us our minds and thus lead us back home to the action of creation. Whatever happens in the world can be used to restore us to wholeness when we choose to use it for a real purpose.

Change Your Perception To Perceive Truly

In India there is a teaching of a rope and a snake. At dusk, you see a rope lying across your path and mistake it for a snake. You become frightened. It was always a rope and your projecting a snake onto it caused you to become fearful. See it as the rope it always was and you will not be afraid. The world is the rope perceived as a snake. Because we have given it an unreal purpose, we have become fearful. When we change our minds we negotiate the world fearlessly.

Your mind, as God created it, is capable of experiencing reality and does so when you think only loving thoughts. You have the power to think whatever you wish. To believe you do not have control over your thoughts is to deny the power of your all-powerful mind. It is you alone who keep yourself powerless. Every thought you think has the power to save you or bind you and others too. Can you change your mind? Of course you can. Who or what is stopping you? So be careful what you think. Your thoughts have all the power of God behind them, though they can be used for God or against God, for good or for evil. God if you think, God you are. Dust if you think, dust you are. Think God. Be God. You are God, and God is love, compassion and kindness. God only gives. You were created to give everything forever. In so doing you are everything forever.

Projecting Guilt Is How You Keep It

In the Garden of Eden, God warned Adam not to eat of the fruit of the tree of the knowledge of good and evil. Eating the apple was symbolic of making ego to replace God to gain knowledge of evil as well as good. With God, knowledge of evil is impossible, as God is good without opposite.

Eating the apple meant Adam attempted to make his own source to gain autonomy from God. Adam hid when God came to visit, as he felt 'naked,' divested of God. He feared that God would be angry and felt guilty for what he had done. He did not like the feeling, so pointed his finger at Eve and said it was her fault. In that act Adam separated from Eve. He projected her outside of his mind in order to place guilt outside of himself. By projecting guilt onto Eve he thought he had freed himself of it. Exactly the opposite really happened. By projecting guilt out he kept it. In that act of projection, he shifted from the experience of everything to that of nothing.

In order to project his guilt onto Eve, Adam had to perceive her as separate from him and different from how God created her. Only then could he be convinced that he had transferred his guilt outside of himself. To justify transferring his guilt onto her, Adam had to perceive Eve as evil. He had to stop loving her and start hating her. Fear or hatred make the experience of separation possible, while love unites and thus restores one to a true experience of oneness. Adam had to hate Eve to justify making her guilty for his error. In his mind then, he was good while she was evil. Good, which has no opposite, suddenly had an opposite, evil, which had entered Adam's mind because of the purpose it served, that of assuaging his guilt.

Granted, Eve did suggest that Adam try the fruit, but ultimately we are each responsible for our own choices. Eve did not force the apple down Adam's throat. He ate it of his own freewill. Had Adam said, 'No thank-you' to the offer, it would have stopped there. He would not have felt guilty and would not have felt the need to separate from Eve in order to place responsibility for his actions outside of himself. Once Adam projected Eve outside of his mind, Eve became who he wanted her to be, rather than who she is. He needed to perceive her as evil and guilty even though God created her eternally good and innocent.

Adam's decision to love or hate Eve had nothing to do with what Eve did or did not do and everything to do with the purpose she served in Adam's mind. Before the separation, he loved her because his purpose was to have her company to enhance his joy. After making ego, he had a change of purpose. As long as Adam chooses not to be responsible for his actions that produced guilt, he will need to project Eve outside of his mind. If Adam were to look at ego he would see it is nothing because it is impossible to make one's own source. Guilt, which is a product of alliance with ego, must therefore also be nothing. Nothing happened. When Adam projected his guilt onto Eve he made his error real and got caught in ego's trap.

What about Eve? Had Eve not accepted the blame, again nothing would have happened. Eve accepted the blame, thus supported Adam in finding her guilty. Eve listened to Adam and let what he said be true even though it was not true. Eve also put the guilt outside of herself. Both Adam and Eve were banished from the garden only because they felt guilty and thereby banished themselves. The outer was a reflection of the inner. They felt guilty for making ego to take God's place. Their banishment was the crossing over of the veil from everything into nothing. It was desire to leave everything out of a sense of guilt, shame and unworthiness that led to an experience of nothing. Desire, motivated by fear, resulted in their exodus from paradise.

Was God upset with Adam? Why should He be? Adam had not succeeded in creating his own source. That is not possible. There was no mutiny. God did not get replaced. Only because Adam convinced himself that he had really accomplished making his own source did he feel guilty. Then to assuage his guilt, he put it outside of himself and thereby gave it reality in his mind. Had he been willing to be responsible for his error it could easily have been corrected and he would still be in the garden. Because Adam convinced himself that he had replaced God, he severed communication with God out of fear of God's wrath, and that made God sad. God only wills to experience loving oneness with His creations as that is the purpose for which He created us.

Projection Makes Perception

Adam's story is our own. Though we were created to create, we resorted to projection. We did so because it served a purpose, that of assuaging guilt. The world as we know it is a projection of our minds, projected out to be a place in which to displace our guilt and to hide from God. When we wished to be autonomous, we convinced ourselves that we were separate from God and then felt guilty. Ego convinced us that God would come after us to seek revenge, so we wanted to remove God from our lives.

In our wish to get rid of God, we determined that this tiny, imaginary, imperceptible veil between nothing and everything be a solid block of toughest steel and that we should forget what was beyond it forever. In this way we determined to leave God behind forever. We determined to burn all our bridges. Do you remember what happened yesterday, or a year ago, or a lifetime ago? Would it be implausible that you forgot how you turned your back on everything in exchange for nothing? And yet God in His infinite mercy would not have it so and therefore it is not so. However, it may seem so to us.

How is it possible to experience a world without God? It is only possible when we project the world outside of our minds. In that act of projection, we cross over the veil from everything into nothing and leave God outside our awareness by giving the world an unreal purpose. We make the world a place where God is not and convince ourselves that God does not exist. Once projected, the world becomes what we want it to be rather than what it is. At any point we can invite God back into the world and the world will be transformed into a place of joy for all. In that we are inviting the world back into our minds. The world is always reflecting back to us the contents of our minds. When we use it as a device for knowing our own minds, we will be giving it a worthwhile purpose, that of healing. The fact is God is everywhere so in making the world a place where God is not, we gave ourselves an impossible purpose. However, we have convinced ourselves that we really did push God out, and the world really does seem to be very much devoid of God, wouldn't you agree?

We are all responsible for our predicaments as well as for each other. We can help or hurt each other and in so doing, we are helping or hurting ourselves only. History repeats itself. Ego is very uncreative. Until we own our errors and take responsibility for all our actions, we are not ready for only the truth. At no time are either Adam or Eve bad. They are both equally precious souls, created unalterably perfect by an eternally loving Creator. They are just choosing to listen to ego and make life miserable for themselves and each other. Though they are not bad, they are wrong. Their error can only be corrected when they are willing to be responsible for what they made. Though ego is nothing, we have convinced ourselves of its reality and it will use all cunning, treachery and stumbling blocks to keep us from perceiving it truly. Thus we must turn to God for a solution to our grave though nonexistent problem.

The Bridge

God created us to be inseparable from Him and each other forever. When we projected God and others outside of our minds to experience autonomy or separation, He gave us an immediate solution. He gave us a voice of Spirit to sustain us in our hour of darkness, call it the voice of conscience, right mind, or sanity. It was to be the bridge between the two worlds, the world of everything and the world of nothing while communication was all but severed. Where will you find that voice? It is in your own mind. Ego also is in your mind. All your thoughts are generated from the voice for God or the voice for ego within. You can only ever choose between God and ego. There is no other choice.

Before the road to nothingness came to be, the only independent thought possible was that of wanting independence from God. In taking that thought seriously, ego was born and provided an appearance or experience of independence from God, through dependence on it instead. We merely shifted our dependence from God to ego. Once made, ego always speaks loudest and first, as its nature is to be competitive. And yet there is another voice, a gentle voice that will direct us in all our needs when we listen to it and trust it. You can hear it when you want to. As soon as we choose to cross back into everything and leave nothing behind, the bridge will no longer be needed as there will again be only God and His creations eternally loving each other, co-creating and communing in perfect oneness, free of the need to make choices between reality and unreality.

The Neighbor's Dirty Laundry

Projection makes perception and once clearly understood, projection can be used to facilitate a shift in perception. The voice for God directs us to heal our misperceptions. Here is a small anecdote Sai Baba tells: Every morning as Dolly looked out her window she noticed her neighbor's laundry hanging on the line. What irritated Dolly no end was that her clothes were always dirty. What was wrong with her neighbor that she could not wash her clothes properly? Day after day she saw her neighbor's dirty laundry and day after day she complained to her husband. One morning she was pleased to notice that her neighbor's clothes were spotlessly clean. Her husband then informed her that he had washed her windows. The neighbor's clothes were clean all along. It was her dirty windowpane that had caused her neighbor's laundry to appear dirty.

So it is with us. We project onto others what we do not want to look at in ourselves. You see in others what you want to perceive, until you are ready to perceive truly. How, when your window is dirty do you get it to become clean? If your perception is faulty, you cannot correct it on your own due to alliance with ego. You need help. You can question your seeing and ask for help. In that you open the door to correction. You can stop blaming your neighbor for what is not her error. Her laundry is clean though you see it as dirty. The fault is in you. The error is yours. When you want only the truth, when you are willing to do whatever it takes to see clearly, you will be shown both your faulty perception and how to correct it. Spirit will show you if you are willing. You have to be willing to be wrong and that takes courage. In that you are playing your part and setting the stage for transformation.

Baba says, "Take one step toward Me, I take a hundred toward you." You do have to take the first step, that of being willing to be wrong. If you do more, you get in the way. When you take that one step, you are in a position for conscience to show you what is right. Conscience is the bridge that keeps you connected with reality and shows you the way, while you are still unclear about what is real and what is not real, what is right and what is off the mark. That inner voice is ever available, but ego always speaks loudest and first. You must get quiet to hear the truth. Resist the temptation to follow your urge to react on impulse. Be willing to see your irritability as your misperception rather than your neighbor's fault.

Mis-projections are always due to disowned and redirected guilt. If you feel guilty and project that guilt out so you are not guilty but someone else is, your guilt only seems to be assuaged. This method of dealing with guilt does not heal it. It is ego's solution to the problem, because ego wants you to think you are free of guilt while still retaining it. The truth is either you are both guilty or both innocent. If you find her guilty, you have found yourself guilty. If she is guilty in your mind, you need but compassionately remind yourself that it is impossible for either of you to be guilty for anything. You are both eternally innocent as you were created by your eternally loving Mother/Father God, your Source and sustenance.

Is it possible to see error in another when you are in your right mind? Is it possible that your neighbor's clothes really are dirty and your window really is clean? Yes, but in that case you will not find yourself irritable. You will see her innocence, even if she acts counter to who she is. You will be able to overlook her error and see only her holiness as God created her. To overlook does not mean to excuse or condone her error, but to recognize it as a lack that needs to be filled, or as a call for love. When you see truly, her lack will elicit compassion and charity, rather than judgment, rejection or condemnation. In condemning another, you condemn yourself. Correction of her shortcoming also is not of you, but of God. You may be a vehicle, but only when you perceive truly. Before you see her as lacking however, make sure your windowpane is spotless, for only then will you be able to perceive her clothes truly.

When you see truly, your response will have her best interest at heart. You will want her clothes clean for her joy, not your view. Maybe you'll suggest she try the laundry soap that works for you. If you approach her with perfect love, her laundry will become spotlessly clean. You will be shown exactly how to approach the situation. If she feels that you are judging her, she will not be receptive to your suggestion. Jesus says, "Cast the beam out of your own eye first and then see if there is still a mote in your brother's eye." When you respond with love to any situation it will be corrected, whether it is your error or someone else's. Your mind is all-powerful and all you need do to save the whole world is change your mind. Until the world has changed from a world of guilt to a world of innocence, we must acknowledge that we have not changed our minds sufficiently. When a critical mass of us use our minds purely, we will witness a shift for all humanity. A shift in projection will produce a shift in perception.

There are those who keep from correcting their errors by pointing out to others that if they see error, it is only in their own mind. They thereby justify doing what is clearly not in alignment with truth and miss the opportunity to come back into the experience of their holiness. Baba says some people take enough rope to hang themselves. Don't play the game of telling someone who is giving you constructive criticism that they are only projecting their stuff onto you. You know when you are off and it might well be God's voice speaking through a friend offering you something that you would be wise to look at. Be open, receptive and grateful for everything that comes your way. See in it a gift and ask how to make the best use of it.

Being The Object Of Projection

Nisargadatta, an enlightened teacher in India, uses the following example: A policeman comes knocking at your door and tells you that you are under arrest for a crime committed in Calcutta. You were not even in Calcutta, but somehow his authoritative presence causes you to forget all reason and you let him cart you off to jail for a crime you never committed. Being the object of projection can be bewildering when you do not know who you are as wholly innocent.

Mr. Smith, the organist in a Catholic church, is regarded as an upstanding member of the congregation. He is married to Mrs. Smith. Everything is fine until Miss Jones comes along and Mr. Smith falls madly in love. There are no children and Mrs. Smith is approached for an annulment. She gives him his freedom (I do not condone or encourage divorce, but the example is helpful).

Mr. Smith follows his passion for Miss Jones for which he gets excommunicated from the church. Soon Miss Jones finds Mr. Smith impossible to live with. He is constantly berating her, and expressing irritability and anger for no apparent reason. It becomes clear to her that his reactions are unrelated to anything she does or does not do. In fact no matter what she does, his response is invariably unpleasant. She is bewildered and though she knocks herself out trying to please him, to no avail. In his search for happiness he looks for greener pastures. The honeymoon has ended abruptly. Heaven has become hell. What happened?

Mr. Smith's excommunication caused him to feel that God is angry with him for falling in love with Miss Jones and divorcing his wife. The evidence to substantiate his conclusion is that he is no longer permitted to be affiliated with the church. He sees Miss Jones as the cause of his banishment, thus he projects his guilt onto her. He is unaware of why she perpetually causes him to feel irritable. As he needs to see her as the cause of his exile he cannot express his love for her or feel her love for him though he is not consciously aware of the dynamics of their relationship. He does not see how love has been veiled and the situation has become a nightmare. She is not aware of why he is unkind to her and is bewildered at his bizarre behavior. Everyone is unhappy except ego. Life has become unbearable. Is there a solution?

Yes, it is so simple. He need only stand still and ask to be shown what is behind his irritability. He will be shown that he is projecting disowned guilt onto Miss Jones for no reason. She is not bad. His guilt also is not warranted as he was not bad for falling in love with her. In projecting his guilt onto Miss Jones he keeps it and keeps them both in hell. Once he sees that he is not bad for being with the woman he loves, he can see that he has no reason to feel guilty. Mr. Smith did not defy God's will, as he is not more powerful than God. He can rest assured that God is not angry with him. He is and has always been innocent and once he knows this, he will stop feeling guilty and stop separating from Miss Jones in order to project his guilt outside of himself. Once he includes her back into his mind, their relationship can be transformed from hell back into heaven.

We can use Mr. Smith as an archetype, for we each thought we could defy God's will and then felt guilty and projected our guilt out. *In each unforgiving thought,* where we see guilt outside of ourselves, *we relive the moment when we let terror take the place of love.* In that moment we bar ourselves from the garden and assume God is angry with us, though it is we who banish ourselves. All we have to do to get back inside is see that we made a substitute for God as Source and as that is not possible, nothing happened. We did nothing of any consequence. Every act of separation, where we hold someone else responsible for our mistakes is a variation on that one theme. When that is clear, we stop feeling guilty and projecting that guilt outside of ourselves. Our self-banishment is reversed and we are back in a true experience of creation rather than projection.

Projecting Guilt Is A Double-Edged Sword

Mr. Hughes was unfaithful and then told his wife it was her fault because she was overweight. She was no heavier than the day he married her. He must have loved her then despite her excess weight. Now she felt devastated at his unfaithfulness. On top of that she felt guilty for being heavy. He dishonored her and then made it her fault in order to assuage his guilt. He was trying to justify his actions and thereby poured salt into an open wound. He then felt more guilt for hurting her and their sad story was well established, guaranteed to make endless suffering for both. Both individuals are always innocent, but because of guilt projected out, everyone becomes unhappy except ego.

Ego survives at everyone else's expense. It doesn't care that it breaks up marriages in its justification of erroneous actions. It has no compunction about treating others hurtfully. Just because an action may cause you to feel guilty does not mean that you are guilty. However, nor does it mean your actions are justifiable. Everyone is always innocent, but the only way to be truly free of guilt in a marriage is to honor your commitment. To disregard your holy vows cannot but cause pain to your partner and lead to needless heartache for both of you.

We would only break sacred vows if we thought we could attain greater freedom in being free of our commitments. This world is a dream. Why insist on freedom in the dream, especially when that freedom is binding you to the dream and costing you your eternal life? To be free of the dream we have to act honorably and with tender loving kindness toward all those significant others in our lives. The past can be healed. Each moment is a clean untarnished birth. Turn over a new leaf today. Renew your commitment and let your relationship be holy, sacred and pure from this moment on. Therein lies true freedom.

As long as someone else is perceived as guilty be sure your actions are producing guilt and binding you. You allow your mind to be healed when you recognize that everyone is always innocent. You will perceive others as innocent when you live a life of nobility and integrity. In the Bible, when the prostitute was about to be stoned, Jesus asked the one who had not sinned to cast the first stone. As no one stepped forward it was apparent that those condemning the woman harbored their own feelings of guilt, for the guiltless will not see guilt in others, therefore will not wish to have others condemned. Jesus said to the woman, "Go your way and sin no more." He advised her to stop doing that for which she would feel guilty because he knew that a life of virtue would be in her best interest. He only wanted her true and lasting happiness. He was serving her by encouraging her to correct her error.

Projection Of Guilt Onto Jesus

Jesus was crucified due to displaced guilt projected onto him. His character was blemishless and he gave of himself selflessly in his deep love for all humanity. Those who feel guilty tend to find fault with the pure. Because of Jesus' crucifixion A Course In Miracles (ACIM) took birth. He was motivated to look within for answers. The crucifixion was bewildering and mystifying. His determination to understand caused him to dive deeply into his own mind for the whole truth. Everything can be used.

No one is to blame for Jesus' crucifixion. He is a great soul who had the capacity to uncover truth through most drastic and tragic circumstances. He chose that experience to collapse time immeasurably both for himself and for all of humanity. Our actions affect everyone, for we are all one. Jesus is all-powerful, therefore he was not a victim of circumstances beyond his control.

Throughout history, the Jews have been blamed for his crucifixion. If you find yourself wanting to make someone else guilty for any reason, it must be that you are harboring guilt and wanting to project it out rather than take responsibility for it. Know that if you succumb to that tendency, you are listening to ego. Making someone else a scapegoat for your guilt is how you keep it and ego wants you guilty while thinking someone else is to blame. When you know your innocence, you will find yourself unable to blame anyone for anything.

There are those who think that Jesus' crucifixion was God's will. To think Jesus' painful death was God's will is a gross misunderstanding of who God is. God could not have given Jesus that experience for that would make Him cruel, and God is but love. Suffering is not necessary to arrive at truth, but it can be a very effective irritant. You however need not suffer. You are one with Jesus. His accomplishment is your own. You can learn from anyone's experience. You need not limit your learning to your own experiences.

The road to nothingness is not a real road and was never made. You never left everything. There is no veil. There is no road back home for you are home eternally. *Projection makes perception.* Change but your mind and your experience will reflect your change of purpose. You are a holy precious child of God, worthy of honor and appreciation. You are wholly innocent, pure, sinless and lovable. God created everyone perfectly to show you a perfect reflection of yourself. In seeing their perfection, you recognize your own. In loving others, you love yourself. In serving others, you serve yourself. In giving to others, you give to yourself. When you heal your projections, you will see that all are innocent and you will recognize your own innocence thereby.

Dear Heavenly Father, thank You that You only create and that projection is not possible as it is not of You. Thank You that the heavy veil between You and Your creation is not Your will and is therefore essentially nonexistent. Please show us how to lift the veil and cross over from nothing back into everything. Thank You that our projections have no effect on the truth. Let our projections now be used only to heal our misperceptions and miscreations that we may be restored to our true function of creating the good, the beautiful and the holy with You and all our brothers and sisters everywhere, innocent forever.

May all beings in all the worlds be happy and blest, Amen

Figure 2a – Lifting the Veil

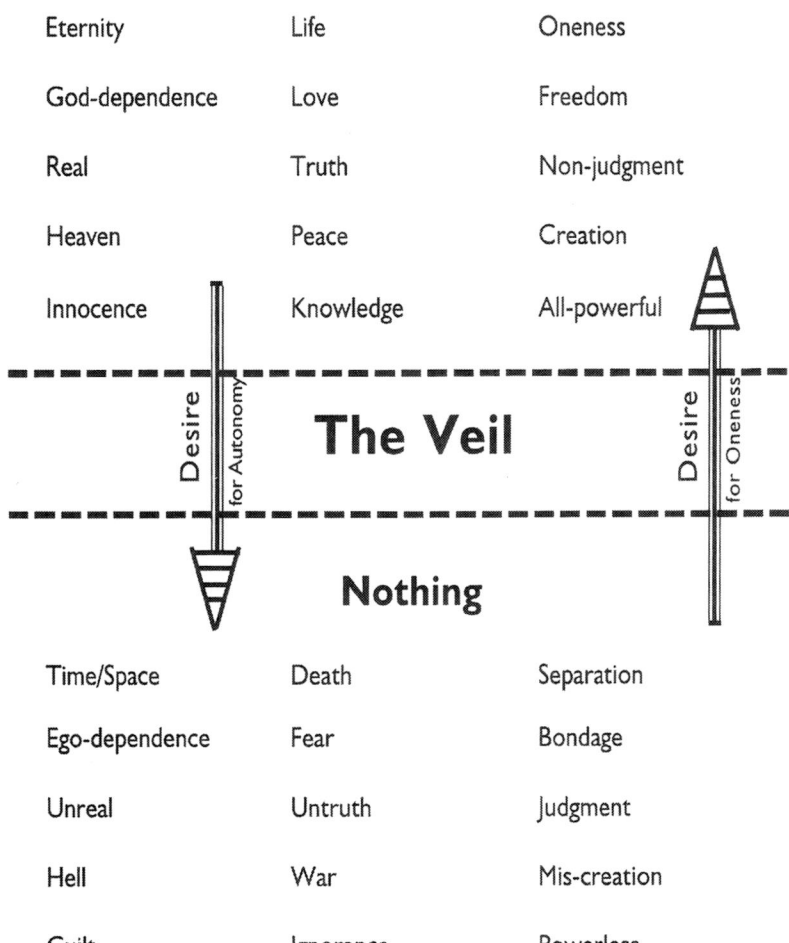

Figure 2b – Creation vs. Projection

Mind Creating or Mind Projecting

Mind that *creates* knows everything to be within it

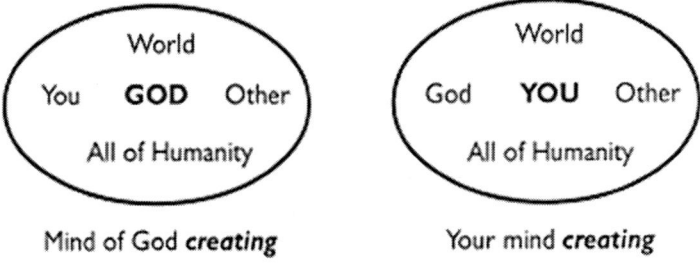

Mind that *projects* thinks it possible things could be outside of it

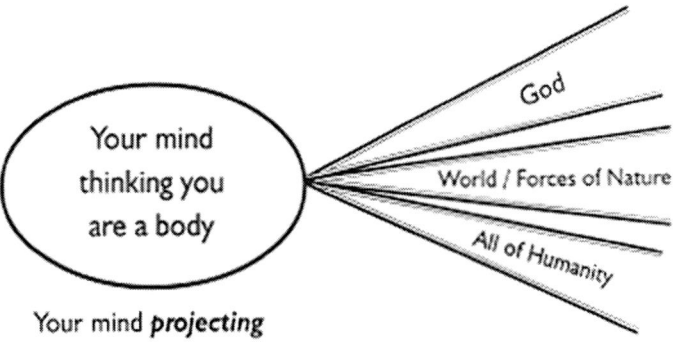

Chapter 3

Are You Ready to Give Up Space-Time for Eternity?

Yesterday is history
Tomorrow is a mystery
Today is a gift
That is why it is called the present.

Time Warp: Evidence For Man Drowning In A Well

Dr. Khan was in charge of the largest hospital complex in all of India. One day he happened to be the only doctor on duty as the other physicians had gone on strike. A dead body, which had drowned in a well, was brought in. After examining the corpse, Dr. Khan signed the death certificate. It was routine and he thought nothing more of the incident. A few months later, to his bewilderment, he was charged with being an accomplice to a murder gang and was put under house arrest. Crime was on the rise in the city and the police force was under pressure to show some activity. Two doctors were required by law to sign a death certificate, but as Dr. Khan was the only physician on duty, his was the only signature on the document.

Six months later, when the case came to trial, the judge ruled that all involved should go to the cemetery. The police chief, the police officer who had indicted Dr. Khan, the judge and Dr. Khan went to the graveyard. The body was exhumed. As the modest pine box, perfectly intact, was opened, the body, also perfectly intact, as though it had been buried just hours earlier and not six months ago, was observed to have some water gurgling up from the lungs. There was no evidence of gunshot wounds. The man had clearly drowned and the case was dismissed on the spot. The painfully embarrassed police chief took to whipping his accusing officer with a riding crop.

Meanwhile, Mrs. Khan was pacing nervously back and forth on her verandah at home when suddenly Sai Baba appeared as an apparition in front of her. He had a riding crop in one hand and a smelly fish in the other. He was holding the fish as far away as possible with His head turned in the other direction and was making an awful face as if completely disgusted. He then threw both riding crop and fish away and motioned her to touch His feet. She fell at His feet, understanding that He was taking care of the problem. Then He disappeared as mysteriously as He had come. Baba's visitation assured her that her husband was found innocent so she sent their driver to pick him up.

Back at the cemetery, Dr. Khan's driver happened to show up just as the case was being dismissed, much to the doctor's relief. The doctor hopped into the car and headed for home. As he was being driven back to his residence in the middle of a scorching hot summer day, Dr. Khan had some time to reflect on what had just happened and something in it simply didn't add up. 'How could that body be perfectly intact? And the pine box as well?' he wondered. He racked his brain for any possible scientific explanation, but to no avail.

Incredulous, he had his driver turn the vehicle around and take him back to the grave site. Just as they reached, the grave diggers were putting the last few shovels full of dirt back on the grave. Dr. Khan requested them to dig it up again. They put in their shovels, only to find bits and pieces of a totally disintegrated box and the remains of a stinky decomposing mass. He quickly saw enough, though he was even more mystified than ever.

When he reached home Mrs. Khan told him of her visitation. They immediately packed their bags and drove all night to Sai Baba's ashram. They arrived in the early hours of the morning, to find Baba waiting for them. He called them in and said, "I entered the minds of all those present and revealed the truth to save your reputation and preserve your honor."

Baba had rearranged time. How is that possible? Perhaps time is not real. Sai Baba who knows its unreality can use it to serve a greater purpose. Once He made a cross for Dr. John Hislop. He said He took the wood from the original cross upon which Jesus was crucified. It did require some effort, as He had to go back in time to find the genuine article. When you know time to be unreal, you become its master, rather than being mastered by it. Only eternity is real. Baba only uses His power in the service of a healing.

Space Warp: Man Instantly Transported To Wife's Bedside

Mr. Chang from Indonesia came to Prasanthi Nilayam, Sai Baba's ashram in the South of India. He had left his wife behind because she was too ill to make the long journey. En route he started having serious misgivings about leaving her in her hour of need. Fortunately Baba called him and the group he had traveled with for an interview immediately upon arrival. As soon as they entered the interview room, the man could contain his concern no longer and blurted out, "Baba, shall I go home to be with my wife?" Baba replied in the affirmative. The man immediately got up to go. Baba stopped him and said, "No, even faster than that." Baba then tapped the wall and it disappeared. In its place they found themselves inside his wife's bedroom. Mr. Chang walked through the wall to her. Baba tapped the wall again and everyone else was again in the interview room, astonished by the miracle they had just witnessed.

The next day the group heard from Mr. Chang. That night his wife had gently passed away in his arms. What a gift that they were able to share her last moments together. A month later, after making the necessary arrangements for the body and putting their affairs in order, Mr. Chang came back to India to thank Baba and pick up his belongings. You can imagine the disbelief with which he was met at customs as he tried to explain why he was traveling without his passport. What a blessing that closure took place between he and his wife. How different he would have felt had he not been there for her in her last moments. He probably would have been hard pressed to forgive himself. Baba, in His infinite mercy, transported a man thousands of miles through space.

Perhaps space also is not real. Baba does not perform miracles to set Himself apart. He says that we also are all-powerful. We too are capable of such powers when we understand the unreality of time and space.

Young Lad Transported To Mecca

Abdul was distraught because his two best friends had gone on a pilgrimage to Mecca and his parents couldn't afford to send him. As a consolation they'd brought him to see Sai Baba. Baba called the poor Muslim family in for an interview and asked the boy, "So you want to go to Mecca?" The boy burst into tears. Baba spoke to the others for a while. The boy continued crying. Baba again asked, "You really want to go to Mecca, don't you?" Baba then tapped the wall. It disappeared and a street scene from Saudi Arabia appeared in its place. "Look, there are your two friends. Go. You have half an hour." The boy walked into the street scene and the wall reappeared.

Baba talked with the stunned family for another half hour and then tapped the wall again. The street scene reappeared and the boy walked back into the interview room carrying some souvenirs from Mecca. A month later, when his friends returned home, the boy's parents asked, "How long was our son with you?" Confirming the boy's account, the friends replied, "Two weeks." Baba knows the unreality of time and space and uses both to reestablish eternity.

Space Warp And The Football Game

Matthew, a young man from Australia, was forced against his will to travel to India with his parents. He desperately wanted to stay home and attend the football game. That was what all his friends were doing and he was very angry that he was not being allowed to do what he wanted. When Baba called them for interview, He tapped on the wall and Matthew saw the football game and his friends in the stadium. Baba gestured to him to go there, as that was his wish. In that instant Matthew understood that he was in the presence of God. He happily discovered the true purpose for his stay at the ashram. He cherished the experience and was overflowing with gratitude and appreciation for his parents' gift to him.

Sai Baba is not the only master of time and space. There are innumerable accounts throughout history of time and space being rearranged. Anyone who awakens to the truth has power over time and space because he recognizes their unreality. *Eternity is God's idea. You as soul understand it perfectly.* Time and space are not of God. Why do they exist at all? They were made by us to circumvent eternity. We accept them without question only as long as we are in ego consciousness. The only part of time that is eternal is now. The rest is simply not real. Eternity is all there is and in truth time never happened. It did not intrude upon eternity. That is why it sometimes seems to fairly fly and sometimes to go painfully slow. Isn't its inconstancy reason to doubt its reality? Is it possible that all of time is going on all the time? Is it possible that it is not sequential as it appears?

Time Waste Is Life Waste - Don't Waste Time

We find ourselves in time because we have elected to be in time rather than in eternity and have therefore changed our belief in our status. But election is both free and alterable. We do not belong in time. Our place is only in eternity, where God Himself placed us forever. Guilt feelings are the great preservers of time. They induce fear of future retaliation and so ensure that the future will be the same as the past. This enables the ego's continuity and gives it a false sense of security through the belief that we cannot escape from it. But we can and must. God offers us the continuity of eternity in exchange. When we decide to make this exchange, we simultaneously exchange guilt for peace, viciousness for love, and pain for joy. Time and eternity are both in our minds and will conflict until we perceive time solely as a means to regain eternity. Time cannot separate us from God if we use it on behalf of the eternal.

Everything can be used. We made time to escape from God and now it can be used to return to God. *Time used as a teaching device becomes a means to an end. It will cease when it is no longer useful for facilitating learning.* We made everything for the wrong reasons but everything can be used for the right reasons. Your body can give you feedback about who you think you are and how much you love yourself if you will give it that purpose. That is valuable feedback. All you have to do is remind yourself that you were created whole and perfect, and that you are not your body.

It is the same for the world. Everything you see can be used as a teaching for you. How do you look on things? Do you see as God would see? Do you look on all your fellowman as sacred creations of God with whom you are one forever? If not, you can ask for help. When your mind is healed you will see through the eyes of love, kindness, compassion and charity. Use all things such as money, food, clothing, and energy in the service of humanity. This is time well spent. Time is both unreal and precious. It is the vehicle that can take you to liberation if used wisely or keep you in bondage if misused.

Baba says that the bird of liberation flies with two wings, discrimination and dispassion. As that teaching relates to time, dispassion would support the idea that time is not real, while discrimination would recognize time as a precious gift which ought to be used for sacred purposes and for attaining liberation. Holding both the idea that time is unreal and that it is precious in perfect balance is the way to transcend it. Every moment is a new opportunity, a clean slate, a fresh beginning since past is past and thereby unreal. There is only now. Master time and do not let it be your master. If it is your master, it is real for you and has power over you.

We need not be discouraged. True, we have been misguided, but it was we who misguided ourselves so completely. True, we were taught by parents and teachers and an environment that did not support who we really are, but we chose all those teachers and learned what we wanted to learn. True, much time has been spent on errant pursuits, but we can undo all of our past instantly. *It has taken much time to learn who we are not, but it takes no time at all to be who we are. God wills us to be in eternity now, thus nothing is beyond our immediate learning.*

Planning The Future Makes Time

We are sustained by God's love and He will take care of our every need if we let Him, thus we need not worry about tomorrow. Storing up for the future keeps us locked in time. What about having some money in the bank and a roof overhead? We do have to temper the teachings with simple logic and at the same time be honest about where our real treasure lies. Are you trusting in God or in that money in the bank and that roof over head for your security? It is not that you are bad when you bank on the things of the world, it is just that you are investing in the undependable. All things in the world are unpredictable, so it is best to lay up for yourself heavenly treasures, such as kindness toward fellowman, love, peace, understanding, wisdom and truth. Those will sustain you better in times of adversity than any plans you make to secure for yourself a safe future. When you are fully present in the moment, the future will take care of itself.

And we have to remain practical and recognize that it is impossible to function without some planning in our daily lives. If, for example, you are going to take a trip, you need to make necessary preparations to do so. This is not wrong use of time. *To plan ahead is necessary where we have accepted responsibilities in the world.*

But we do well to leave the universal plan in more appropriate hands. God has a plan for the salvation of the world and we each have our roles to play. We will know all we need to know when we need to know it. God shows us only what is helpful for us to know right now. If He showed us more, we'd undoubtedly get in the way and foil the plan. As time relates to fulfilling our holy function, the real purpose for which we are here, we simply do not have the whole picture, thus are not in a position to make plans. Everything will be given as it is needed. All that is asked of us is trust and openness. When we expect miracles we open the door to them, for they are always available. If we plan in this regard, we get in the way and put off the miracle. When we place our future in God's hands and allow Him to take care of every detail of our lives, our passage through time and space are not at random. Then we cannot but be in the right place at the right time.

God created everything to be eternal. Our experience of time and space, where everything dies, disappears or disintegrates, is unreal. Some may use evolution as proof that time is real, but that is evolution's purpose. Evolution is not part of eternity and only after we entered the experience of time did we also enter an experience of evolution, where things both evolve and devolve. Truth is changeless and has nothing to do with either time or evolution.

We have a purpose in time in the greater scheme. It is our purpose to save the world so we can step out of time forever. We do know our assignment because we know everything. When we know who we are, we will know our purpose. *All of time is only to help us fulfill our assignment. It is because we are not ready to do what we know we ought to do that time exists at all. When our task is accomplished time will be over and all things will have been restored to their eternal nature. The world as we know it will have passed away.*

Time is precious and sacred. It must be used wisely. Every moment spent in communion with God, in service to fellowman, in being available to perform your assignment, is time well spent, and you will feel satisfaction. When you are fulfilling your function, you are naturally happy and you will find yourself fully present in each moment spontaneously, effortlessly. When you use time consciously, judiciously, carefully, for sacred tasks, you are collapsing time. You can enjoy time when you become its master.

Past Is Unreal – Be Responsible – Let Error Be Corrected

In the garden of Eden, after Adam had eaten the fruit, that is after Adam made ego to replace God as his Source, God asked, "Adam, where are you?" Adam hid. God was not upset that Adam had made a pseudo-parent to replace God. He knew He was Adam's Creator and irreplaceable. Had

Adam stood still and said, 'Lord, I made a mistake, please show me how to correct my error,' God would have assured him that nothing had happened. Adam did not do that. He projected the blame for his mistake outside himself, because he felt guilty. In that act of projecting the blame outside he held onto the guilt and made the error real. In disowning guilt and thereby keeping it, he catapulted himself into time and space where guilt can be assuaged through punishment. Punishment requires time to be meted out. This is the reason time came to be. Ego depends on time for its survival.

There is no place for ego in eternity, for there is no guilt to be punished thus no purpose for time or life for ego. Ego does everything possible to keep you locked in time as without time it cannot exist. Adam's story is ours. All we need do is go back to that moment where we fell into fear because we thought we had made a substitute for God. That moment is available right now, as all of time is going on all the time. Our error was only a silly idea and rather than choose terror, we can simply own our mistake and let it be corrected. Then time will be over and we will again be in the experience of eternity.

Here is a simple three-step process for the undoing of time: First, see the past as unreal. It is unreal because past is part of time and time is not real. In seeing its unreality, there is no need to feel guilty. To see the past as unreal is to forgive the past. (Adam did not make his own source as that is impossible – nothing happened).

Second, be responsible. To be responsible is not difficult when you understand the unreality of the past. You will only refuse to take personal responsibility as long as you think the past real. To be responsible for what is not real is vital because it is real for you, or you would not find yourself in the unreal experience. (Eve was not to blame for Adam's attempt at making his own source. Adam is responsible, though nothing happened in truth).

Third, let your error be corrected by being willing to be wrong. This allows God to heal your mind and bring it back into wholeness. You will naturally have the willingness to change your mind when you see that your error was not cause for guilt but simply cause for correction. When you change your mind you heal the past and allow yourself to come back into the experience of eternity.

Self-responsibility motivates that change of mind. You will correct your error when you know that your happiness depends on a willingness to be wrong. Only when you let God correct your error instead of trying to do it on your own, are you assured of success. You are never on your own. If not allied with God, you are allied with ego and ego does not want your error corrected.

When Adam stops blaming Eve, he opens the door to the realization that making his own source is a mistaken idea. That admission allows God to correct his error. The three-step process then from time to eternity is: 1) see past as unreal; 2) step into personal responsibility; and 3) let your error be corrected.

Collapsing Time

We are all doing time in a way. How much time do you want to do? It is completely up to you. Every action either collapses or makes time. When you choose with God you collapse time. When with ego, you make time. Your mind is all-powerful, thus you do make your own decisions. Don't fool yourself that because everything is God's will, you have no say over your destiny or that you are not responsible for your actions. You are in charge of your every action. There is nothing opposing your will. God wills your freedom to choose your own destiny. Whatever you experience is what you have chosen. *Being in time is not God's will, but as you find yourself in time, God wills you use it wisely for collapsing time.*

You make time or collapse it by the consciousness you hold. Suppose someone takes something that does not belong to him. He would only engage in that action if he didn't know that he is and has everything. Stealing simply would not enter his consciousness if he knew the truth. It would make no sense. What could he steal that he didn't already have? If he steals, it must be that he does not know he is and has everything. When he asks to be restored to wholeness, he collapses time. In asking, wholeness is restored. The urge to take vanishes. That shift in consciousness is a healing, for he is being restored to his natural awareness that he is and has everything and then that is again his direct experience.

Should he succumb to the urge to steal, he will feel guilty, because he will have listened to ego rather than to his voice of conscience. Your voice of conscience will never encourage you to steal. That would make no sense. That voice knows that you are whole and stealing would not improve your lot. If he acts on that thought, he is allied with ego and ego wants him to steal because it knows he cannot help but feel guilty for his action. Ego is happy, because when he is guilty, he must be punished. Punishment requires time and time means ego lives at his expense. Ego and time come together and go together. Ego decides the punishment and the thief agrees because he fears that God will decide an even harsher punishment if he doesn't let ego's punishment be meted out. Of course this can only be the experience of a deluded mind that is listening to ego and has forgotten who God is. God will never punish you for anything. He is love and only acts in love. He does not judge or punish.

Punishment is self-inflicted and that for crimes which were never committed. A thief cannot steal because in truth he is and has everything. The act of stealing is meaningless. It does not make him guilty. Stealing is not bad. It is simply not real. Stealing is impossible, because anything he wants that he does not already have is unreal. Therefore to steal means to steal nothing and can that be bad? To reiterate, bad is simply unreal. However, if he attempts to steal, it is because he thinks he can. He thinks that the item he is stealing is real and this exposes faulty thinking and is the cause of needless suffering.

All he need do is recognize that his thinking is faulty and ask for help to change his mind. You can make mistakes and mistakes are correctable. When you know who you are you will only act in a manner that is befitting your truth. Your moral character will be impeccable. Does that mean that you can measure a person's spiritual progress by his actions? In ancient India, Ratnakara was a thief who transformed his heart through repetition of God's name. He became the renowned saint Valmiki and wrote the great epic poem, the Ramayana. Since time is not real, you can be instantly transformed from sinner to saint.

There are those spiritual adepts who misuse this teaching as license for getting away with taking. They erroneously conclude, 'I can take whatever I want indiscriminately and as long as I do not feel guilty, I will not be making time.' This is the cunning of an ego that wants to survive at its host's expense. If one listens to its reason, he will be making time for himself. Or ego may tell you that you are and have everything, so that whatever you take is yours already. If you are listening with brightness, you will know that voice to be tempting you toward a total misapplication of the teaching for which you will make time for yourself. Your heavenly Father wants to give you everything. Once you know that, you will trust Him to give you whatever you need and will not consider getting at another's expense.

The thief in this example can change his mind and decide now that he need never steal again because he is and has everything forever. He is sustained by the love of God. If he changes his mind, then no matter how many times he may have taken wrongly in the past, he will not have to make amends. That shift in consciousness is always waiting on his willingness. In that transformation, time is collapsed immeasurably. He need not correct himself. He need only be willing for his mistaken thinking to be corrected and it is accomplished.

In the Bible, Jesus tells the parable of the vineyard. The person who comes to work at the eleventh hour gets the same pay as the one who arrived early in the morning. In his shift in consciousness, the thief enters the vineyard and leaves his past behind without having to make amends. He gets the same pay as those who have no history with corruption. We do not need to punish ourselves for our past mistakes. We need only have our erroneous thinking corrected to be free instantly.

If he tries to correct himself, he will be doing so with ego and it will not work. If he has given his problem to God, it has been corrected. No time is needed. If it is not corrected, he has not given it. If he still detects a lack consciousness, a consciousness that thinks that by taking it will fill a lack, he is not healed and can ask to be shown how he is getting in his own way. All that is ever required is a willingness to be wrong and to be shown how to correct his errors. The most hardened criminal can come back to God before the saint. Time is not real. A shift in consciousness can collapse all of time instantly.

You do not have to pay back for past mistakes as long as you make that shift in consciousness. In this way time is being collapsed. When you change your mind, your destiny changes. The script is rewritten. As long as you do not make that shift however, any part of that past could erupt without warning. You may point out that you do not steal. Use this example to make life-changing commitments in any areas where you know you are off the mark. Where do you judge or have undesirable tendencies that cause you to feel guilty? Anger, jealousy, pride, lust, greed and hatred are imperfections that have nothing to do with how you were created. If you have any of these to the slightest degree, it is because you still think you can be other than who you are and you are making time. You need help to change your mind. Ask the One who can help you. Be willing to correct your errors and so be home in eternity. If you have no imperfections, you must be out of time.

Transforming Time And Space Into Eternity

In the real world there is no fear and there are no wars. There is joy, trust in your neighbor and peace and plenty for all. In order that the real world be our experience, we have to be willing to do whatever it takes. Time and space are not real and thus can be overcome. Past is past. It never happened. It is over when we stop making it real. Baba says, "Take one step toward me and I take one hundred steps toward you." By taking that one tiny step of being willing to be wrong for past errors, God reveals to you who you are and your past simply rolls up and collapses behind you. Your karma is wiped out and you stand free for all eternity.

Time is not real. Space is not real. When you act perfectly, with integrity, you collapse time. When your actions lack integrity, you make time. Use time wisely. Use it only to take you beyond time back to eternity, which you never left in truth. Time can have no effect upon eternity. You are still in heaven where you were created. All of time is over. It is a slight of hand, a trick. When you stop making it real, it will no longer be your experience. To go home is not to go somewhere else. It is merely to recognize that you are home, that you never left home, that nothing happened.

Time must be transformed back into eternity. Space also must be restored to eternity. Imagine being able to be anywhere you wish simply by thinking yourself there. That is how it is beyond space, because everything is within your mind. You are omnipresent, meaning you are everywhere at all times. You are not limited to your body. Your body and the world are within you. Sai Baba has spiritual centers all over the world and has made His presence known in many of them. He has manifested His physical form, vibhuti (sacred ash), amritum (divine nectar) or caused garlands of flowers to sway during the devotional singing. In many ways He has demonstrated His omnipresence.

Once while Al Drucker was visiting Him in India, Baba made an appearance at his residence in California. After the visit He said to Al still at His ashram in India, "I came to visit and you were not there." Some devotees who were present and witnessed the miracle told Al upon his return home. Baba had entered from an ocean side balcony and slipped in through a closed door. All those in attendance knew they were in His physical presence and recognized Him to be as real as anyone in the room.

When you become the master over space, needing your own space will seem irrelevant. You will realize you were created one with everyone. It is ego that wants separation, borders, boundaries and autonomy. You encompass all and yet include all. To want your own space is to want to exclude and thus to make yourself less. This is the cause of loneliness and feelings of isolation. You were created to let everyone and everything into your space. Therein lies your joy, for that is natural and comfortable. Chief Seattle was unable to relate when the white man offered to buy land from the Native Americans, "The sky is our father, the earth our mother."

When we no longer feel the need to delineate boundaries between our property and that of our neighbor and when we live together as one world nation, under God, indivisible, free of national borders, we will have understood the unreality of space, and that consciousness will assure liberty and justice for all.

Time And Space Did Not Circumvent Eternity

In the illustration at the end of this chapter, the horizontal line, the veil, separates eternity from time and space. Time and space did not intrude upon eternity. When we are in time we are asleep, for one cannot be in time and be awake. Only when you are back in eternity can you consider yourself awake. Time closest to eternity is the happy dream. As we move further away from eternity we experience the nightmare. Beyond the nightmare is deep sleep. This representation of time has nothing to do with chronological time, as all of time is going on all the time and we are either collapsing, making, or doing time, meaning nothing is happening.

In the happy dream, time closes in on eternity and is being collapsed immeasurably. The closer to eternity, the easier it is to slip back into eternity. The happy dream reflects a mind which can merge back into the mind of God. It is a mind that holds the same ideas as the mind of God, so the separation has been healed and oneness has been restored. Time is collapsed through a shift in consciousness, leading a life of noble character, purity, holiness, doing good deeds, fearlessness, curbing desires, living consciously, thinking of God, happily correcting errors and living in loving gratitude for all those others in your life. Forgiving your neighbor for what he did not do collapses time. You cannot be a victim, thus whatever happens to you, no matter how hurtful it may appear, you are doing it to yourself. The happy dream is still only a dream, but it is a dream of awakening. When we wake up, we will discover that we never left eternity, except in our minds, by convincing ourselves of the reality of that which was never real, namely all that happened in time and space.

In the nightmare time is far from eternity. This is where we make mistakes for which we feel guilty and subsequently punish ourselves. These actions for which we feel guilty are not cause for punishment, but rather for correction. All suffering is self-inflicted punishment for crimes that were never committed. Time is needed for enduring the punishment that befits the crime. Time is being made. This is ego's idea of fairness and has as its underlying motive its existence at your expense. God wants you to correct your errors so you can move out of time back into eternity. The nightmare reflects a mind that is split, or is holding victim-victimizer consciousness.

To move from the nightmare into the happy dream, we have to stand still and ask for help. We have to ask to be shown how to undo the nightmare, how to correct our errors, how to forgive our brothers or sisters and how to change our minds. The nightmare is not real. It is only a dream, but it seems very real while you are in it. Therefore you will be tempted to escape. The urge to escape your pain by projecting the blame for it onto someone else, by denying it or numbing yourself are ego's solutions to the nightmare. This state is referred to as deep sleep.

Deep sleep moves you furthest from eternity, simply because, though you have succeeded in escaping the nightmare, you have also disconnected from who you are. You have cut yourself off from yourself. You have separated yourself from yourself. In choosing escape, you choose to deny your experience. You choose to project your pain or guilt outside of yourself through blame, dissociation, retreat, detachment, disengaging, suppression, denial, deflection, sedation, manipulation, distraction, defense... All these mechanisms serve to escape the nightmare. Though time is not being made in deep sleep, it is not being collapsed either. Nothing is happening. Time seems endless. It is ego's solution to the problem. It is not a real solution. It simply serves to mask symptoms.

God's solution to the nightmare takes you into the happy dream. It is a real solution as it heals your mind. That requires a miracle and miracles will be your experience through a willingness to be wrong and to have error corrected. Ego's solution takes you out of touch so you do not feel your pain. With ego's solution you do not feel real and you do not know who you are because you have cut yourself off from yourself. Nothing is happening. You would only choose to stay in deep sleep out of fear of the nightmare. You would only fear the nightmare as long as you thought it real. Deep sleep is dullness or sedation, but it seems better than the nightmare on the surface.

It will remain your solution of choice only as long as you do not wish the truth, only as long as you do not want to be who you are. You will find the courage to reenter the nightmare when you know its unreality. The only way to get to the happy dream from deep sleep is via the nightmare. You will be willing to stand still in the nightmare when you realize that ego's solution is not a solution, but rather an avoidance of the problem. As the nightmare is unreal, you need not spend any time there to get to the happy dream – you need only stand still long enough to see it for what it is, unreal, and allow it to be undone.

Three Gunas As Part Of The Dream

Sai Baba often speaks of the three gunas, or human qualities, Satva Guna, Rajo Guna and Thamo Guna. Satva is the quality of serenity, peace, fortitude, forbearance, patience, strength and noble character. Rajo Guna is characterized by passion gone amuck, expressed as anger, lust or hatred. Thamo Guna can be thought of as sloth, laziness or chaos. Baba prescribes Rajo Guna as the cure for Thamo, and Satva as the cure for Rajas. He recommends taking the thorn of Rajo to remove the thorn of Thamo, and the thorn of Satva to remove the thorn of Rajo. Then throw them all away. In other words, don't even settle for Satva. Thamas refers to deep sleep, Rajas to the nightmare and Satva to the happy dream. They are still all part of a dream and to wake up we have to leave all three states behind.

It all starts by being willing to reenter the nightmare from deep sleep. You will be willing to reenter the nightmare when you are willing to heal it. That takes courage and honesty. You can be in deep sleep and fool yourself that you are in the happy dream. You can convince yourself that you are happy and it will work for a while. Escape is very seductive. Ego is extremely slippery in its wish to survive. You have to be very bright and vigilant to truly assess where you are.

When you want only the truth, you will be able to accurately assess your situation, for then you will be given all the assistance in the universe. All karma can be collapsed instantly at your discretion. There is no one to oppose your will. Until the nightmare is undone it can come to haunt you, even in deep sleep. You may think you have escaped, but you will always be fearful that the nightmare may erupt again at any moment.

In the Vedanta there is reference to deep sleep as the state closest to awakening, as it is a state free of projection. It is taught there that illusion has two powers, one of veiling and the other of projecting. As deep sleep is free of projection it is viewed as closest to the truth though it still veils the truth. Deep sleep is not used in that way here, but rather depicts the state furthest from truth, as it is the most out of touch with truth. It is a dead, sedated, unconscious state. Nothing is happening.

You Cannot Reach Eternity By Escaping Time And Space

A friend who fought in Vietnam witnessed the aftermath of a napalm attack on a village. He knew in advance and was secretly happy about the plan because he and his troops were getting backed into a corner and it was looking more and more like the attack on innocent civilians was his only hope of survival. When he saw the devastation, the loss of innocent life, he felt that others had been hurt and killed to save his own neck. He recognized that he had acted cowardly when his own survival was at stake. His cowardice caused him to feel unhappy about himself. Had he known in the heat of the moment that nothing real can be threatened, he would have been willing to risk his life to save life and in that he would have felt good about himself.

He was in the nightmare and to deal with the situation, he chose ego's solution and turned to alcohol to cope and thereby shifted into deep sleep. To this day he only wants to escape. He does not want to go back to that wound and let it be healed. Every moment is a clean untarnished birth. He can learn from his experience that he is not his body and that saving life is where his salvation lies, not in protecting his own life at the cost of other life. We are all one and what he does for another he will have done for himself. Then he will not be inclined to want to escape and he will shift from the nightmare into the happy dream, rather than into deep sleep.

The movie, Courage Under Fire, with a similar theme is based on a true story which took place during the Gulf War. A captain and her battalion find themselves stranded in the middle of hostile enemy territory. She does everything within her power to protect the lives of the soldiers in her charge during an overnight struggle to stave off enemy forces. By mid-morning a helicopter comes to the rescue, but due to injury she needs help out. The others run for safety promising to return with a stretcher.

Making their way to the helicopter turns out to be a high-risk dash and they realize that the chances of getting back to her and then back to the helicopter again with her on the stretcher without being shot are pretty slim. So, once they are safely in the helicopter, instead of being willing to do whatever it takes to save their courageous captain, they tell the pilot that she is dead and he takes off without her, abandoning her to her death. They, of course, cover up the details of what really happened.

As she has been nominated for a medal of honor, there is an investigation to find out the facts surrounding her death. Upon questioning, the men start to act very fearful and vicious and one even races his car head long into a train to his death. Their guilt over abandoning their captain, who had acted fearlessly in their behalf, caused their bizarre response. They could not face exposing the details of the true story because it revealed their cowardice. They had been trained to be courageous, yet when put to the test, they deserted ship. That was too hard to live with, so one killed himself, another took to heavy drinking, a third to drugs and another fled. The investigator was not there to interrogate them, but merely to determine whether she was worthy to receive the honor. They saw him as prying and not letting them forget what they were desperately denying had ever happened, so his presence was very threatening. They had shifted from the nightmare into deep sleep and he was forcing them back into the nightmare.

Is there a happy outcome possible for the men who neglected their duty by their captain? Everything can be used. Their actions showed that they still thought their bodies real and more valuable than doing the honorable thing, in this case being willing to take risks for their captain. Once you know your body is not real, you will be willing to risk life to save life. They need to be willing to make a shift in consciousness so that their actions be ones they can feel proud of. True, they cannot bring back their captain, but as bodies are not real, she did not really die, but only her body died. Their agony is due to feeling guilty for her death. As long as they think that, they will think they are more powerful than she is. Her death could only have happened with her consent, as she too is all-powerful. There are no victims. When they realize that, past is healed and they can live with themselves and lead happy, well-adjusted lives, instead of ending up in the psychiatric ward of a VA hospital. So, the shift from the nightmare either to the happy dream or to deep sleep is available every moment, as time is not real. Your past can be healed now.

When Al and I visited Germany in the summer of 2005, we met a sociologist who had made a study of the silence that followed the horrors of the holocaust. The Jewish survivors did not tell their children. The Nazis also were silent on the issue and so there was even some question in the minds of outsiders as to whether the holocaust had really taken place. With painful situations it seems easier to choose deep sleep rather than looking at the nightmare and allowing it to be healed.

A common experience perhaps closer to home is that of falling in love and then getting hurt. Next time you may hold back and be less open and in your reservation, protect yourself from being hurt. By protecting yourself you cannot experience that depth of love. In protecting oneself one shifts into deep sleep, where there is no pain, but there is also no life. By numbing oneself, one experiences living deadness. Until you are willing to stand in the experience of your and other people's pain you remain numb and in deep sleep. That is escape and ego's solution. It does not lead to joy. Healing is God's solution and lifts you into the happy dream from which you can easily awaken. You heal when willing to stand still and see the nothingness of the nightmare. It is only a bad dream and you will wake up, not through denial but by looking at the nightmare without guilt or shame, willing to let your mind be healed.

Only when you are willing to reenter the nightmare from deep sleep, can the pain be healed. We have to be willing to stand still in the pain, to burn, to do whatever it takes, rather than act on the impulse to run. Only when you are healed are you free to experience others' pain with compassion and to do whatever directed to help where you can. We need to courageously go back to that moment where we closed down and ask God to show us what to do and how to heal. *Infinite patience* with ourselves and others *brings immediate results.*

We can take comfort in knowing that nothing real can be threatened. We can be shown how to change our minds, so that horrendous incidents, though unreal, do not ever take place again, not in our personal lives and not for anyone. We do have that kind of power. We are not helpless. As consciousness changes, destiny also changes. The salvation of the world is easy, simply because the world is not real. If suffering were real it would be difficult or impossible to undo, but because it is unreal it is easily healed when we are willing. That is God's answer to the nightmare.

We convinced ourselves that time and space were the only reality, for we assumed they existed forever. We brought eternity to them, instead of bringing them to eternity. Once you bring time and space to eternity, you bring eternity back into your mind. Then time and space vanish into the nothingness they have always been. Time and space can be used to take the journey back to eternity if we give them a new purpose and allow the old purpose, that of obscuring eternity, to be undone.

None of us can make the journey back alone because we are one organism. We need everyone to be inspired to want to be home too. As we join together in the truth that time and space are not real, it becomes easier and easier for others to join us, so that the way home becomes clearly marked. Make your life your message. Everyone will eagerly look to a bright light. Let all humanity know the end of suffering is at hand. Let all beings everywhere know that God created us eternally loving, peaceful and blissful. We were created to be and have everything forever. We were created to be at home forever. We were created to be one with God and each other forever. *Time and space did not circumvent eternity.* May God grant you the determination to experience eternity here and now as it was always meant to be. And may your wise choice be a beacon of hope to all those who still think they are locked in space/time, oblivious to the truth that eternity is available right here and right now.

Beloved Creator of eternity, thank You that time and space are not real and therefore we are not bound by either. Help us to use them wisely to bring us swiftly back into our true experience of eternity. Grant us the courage to stand still in the nightmare and let it be undone rather than succumb to the temptation to escape into deep sleep. Thank You for the freshness and newness of each moment, free of any past. Grant us the strength to step into the power of the present.

May all beings in all the worlds be happy and blest, Amen.

Figure 3 – Eternity Unaffected by Time and Space

Everything (Eternity)

Eternity	Life	Oneness
God-Dependence	Love	Freedom
Real	Truth	Non-judgment
Heaven	Peace	Creation
Innocence	Knowledge	All-Powerful

Nothing (time and space)

Time/space	Happy Dream (Satva) God's solution - collapses time
Ego-dependence	Collapsing time
Unreal	Using time wisely
Hell	Balance between discrimination and dispassion
Guilt	Past is past because it has been healed
Death	**Nightmare (Rajo Guna) - makes time**
Fear	Making time
Untruth	Actions that produce guilt
War	Needing space
Ignorance	Think mistakes deserve punishment
Separation	**Deep Sleep (Thamo) Ego's solution - freezes time**
Bondage	Time stands still
Judgment	'Past is past ' - unhealed, deny past
Mis-creation	Regrets about the past
Powerless	Worry about the future
	Irresponsible -"Doesn't matter what I do as time is not real"

Direction of Consciousness Awakening

Chapter 4

Are You Ready to Give Up Ego for God?

Of myself I am nothing, but with God all things are possible.
Jesus in the Bible

Airplane Rescue Story

Al Drucker recounts with tender gratitude how he and a friend, Monica, were rescued while flying over the Sierra mountains of California in a rented recreational plane. He had taken the aircraft out without filing a flight plan as they were just planning to be gone a few hours. He hadn't flown much on instruments, but Monica assured him she had ample experience and was prepared to back him, so off they flew. The day was choppy but that was fun as they could hone their skills.

When dark clouds, thunder and lightning started threatening, they decided to turn back, only to discover it was too late. The storm had already closed in behind them and for the next three hours they were struggling for their lives. Al would put the plane into a nose-dive only to be carried upward. In the next moment he set the controls to gain elevation only to be plunged downward. His situation could be likened to a toy boat adrift in a raging storm at sea. Huge hailstones had knocked out the back windows producing a deafening noise. The control surfaces on the wings were tearing, making it increasingly more difficult to maintain control. The fuel gauge started bouncing on empty. In utter exhaustion, Al turned to Monica to take over, only to find her slumped in her seat, probably due to oxygen deprivation. He didn't know whether she was dead or alive.

Finally he had to face the inevitable and realized his chances of survival were next to none. In that moment he turned to God for the first time in over 30 years. He had grown up a young Jewish boy in Nazi Germany and though his family had escaped to America, he had seen enough to convince himself there was no God. Now, in desperation and as a last resort, he called out to God. And just as he did, a deep peace pervaded his whole being and he readied the plane for a landing, thinking that perhaps he would somehow be Divinely directed to a safe spot. He knew all too well how slim his chances were, as a number of planes had downed in that same area and none had survived. It was too rocky and mountainous to offer much hope.

No sooner had he prepared himself than he heard a voice over the loud speakers: "Aircraft in distress, can you read me?" That voice so startled him as he had been entirely unsuccessful in making contact up to that point. Eagerly Al reached for his microphone, but it had gotten wrapped around the rudder petal in the turbulence and when he tried to retrieve it, his plane went into a spin. He was unable to respond to that sweetest voice which renewed hope of rescue from an utterly impossible situation.

That angel voice came again, so calm and soothing, seemingly totally aware of the critical nature of the situation, "You need not respond. If you can hear me, turn 60 degrees off your present course and then come back to your present course." Al did as directed. When he was back on course the voice assured him, "I have you in sight." Al assumed some ground controller was picking him up by radar. For the next 20 minutes this kind controller gave him simple instructions that he could easily follow. You can imagine how overloaded and exhausted he felt. The controller seemed to know all and spoke in a way that Al could respond to without much effort.

He would instruct, "Fly where the red meets the yellow." Even an inexperienced pilot could follow those directions without much computation. Then he told Al that he would be coming to a clearing and would see a small airport straight ahead. He ended with, "I'm signing off with this transmission. Good luck." Almost immediately, as foretold, the bedraggled plane broke out of the storm. Al saw the landing strip, declared an emergency landing and touched down safely, though not very smoothly. This jolted his flying mate back into consciousness. She groggily asked, "What happened?" Just as Al vectored the plane to safety, it ran out of fuel - so many miracles all rolled into one.

When they reached the control tower, the controller knew nothing of the voice that had guided Al in. He told Al there were no other airports around. They were surrounded by Indian reservation for miles in every direction. He was in Southern Nevada, hundreds of miles off course. 'Who was that mysterious voice that saved our lives?' Al wondered.

Due to the intensity of the storm they couldn't fly home. Monica knew of a yoga academy just south of the Mexican border. They got the plane patched up enough to feel safe and off they flew. When they arrived at the academy they found a group of people singing devotional songs seemingly to a picture in the front of the room. The picture was covered with some strange dust, except for the eyes. Al took one look at those eyes and found himself moved to tears. He just knew those eyes had something to do with the voice that had saved them. After the ceremony they found out that the dust was sacred ash that had manifested on the picture during the singing and that the picture was of Sai Baba. When he told his story, they all agreed that the voice had to be Sai Baba.

About a year later Al made his first trip to Baba's ashram fully expecting Baba to reveal the truth behind that benevolent voice, so patient and kind, that was the savior of his life. But Baba didn't give him any attention what so ever. It was only years later, after he became professor in

Baba's university, that the subject even came up. One day, out of the blue, Baba asked him to tell his airplane story to the students. When he finished, Baba commented, "He was flying for his own pleasure and yet I had to save him. It was my duty."

We too tend to wait till we have exhausted all other possibilities before we call on God. Yet when we finally turn to Him, God is right there for us. Al put himself in an impossible situation, in which he had to surrender his fierce need to look after himself. What he discovered was that when he finally let go, he made room for God to tenderly look after him with the love of a thousand mothers. In that moment he discovered that with God all things are possible. But why wait till it gets so intense? Why not call on God now? Why not call on God to handle all your problems? He is waiting for nothing else.

Surrender Nothing To Receive Everything Forever

To enlist God's help, it is necessary to surrender, to let go and let God, to trust in God, to depend on God for everything. Yet that idea of God-dependence invariably puts people on their guard. Their initial response is that they feel their independence is being threatened. "Wait a minute," we all say, "Surrender means to give up - never." We hold out till we have exhausted all other alternatives. Only when Al knew he had no other options did he consider turning to God. And so maybe we ought to take a deeper look at the reasonableness of turning to God for everything. When Baba asks us to surrender, He is asking us to give up nothing and receive everything forever. That sounds like a great deal and it is, so why the resistance? He is asking us to surrender what we have convinced ourselves is everything, so that it can be replaced with what we have convinced ourselves is nothing and there's the catch.

We have to retrain our minds about what is valuable and what is not. We have to learn to trust that nothing is in fact nothing and everything is everything. We have to unlearn what we have taught ourselves in order to be willing to give up the things of the world, which are nothing. Only then will we avail ourselves of the heavenly gifts which God wants to bestow, upon our surrender of that which is blocking His gifts from flowing to us. Jesus taught, "Store not up for yourselves treasures on earth where moth and dust corrupt and thieves break in and steal. Rather store up for yourselves treasures in heaven." We have invested heavily in what does not last and is not valuable and have lost sight of what is valuable. What is the cause of this confusion?

We made ego to gain independence from God. The irony is that we didn't gain independence as we had hoped. Instead of being dependent on

God, we now find ourselves dependent on ego and ego wants us bound so it can continue to exist. Ego cannot exist unless you are independent of God and dependent on it. Dependence on God gives you total creative freedom, omnipresence, omniscience and omnipotence. You trade in your heavenly treasure when you choose to depend on ego instead. Ego, by its very nature is constriction, limitation and lack. But ego does everything to convince you that you have greater freedom with it than with God, because it will disappear instantly when you recognize the truth that it can give you nothing and that your total freedom lies in your utter dependence on God who gives you everything.

When you give up ego, you will have given up all misery. You will have surrendered nothing and gained everything. It is ego that convinces us that the things of the world such as money, family, fame... will lead to happiness, but these worldly pursuits inevitably lead to sorrow rather than to the joy you were led to believe would be yours in their pursuit. With wealth, there is never enough, the stock market crashes, or your valuables get lost or stolen. With physical beauty, there is always someone more beautiful and the beauty turns to wrinkles with time. All the things of the world deteriorate over time. Nothing in this world lasts; you lose the ones you love. To look for happiness in the world is a futile exercise.

To give up the things of the world is not a sacrifice once we see truly that we have invested in nothing in investing in happiness where it cannot be found. We made a bad investment. Even if you have invested heavily in a dead horse, it will not, cannot ever win you the race. As soon as you give it up, you make way for your heavenly treasure, which is your true inheritance, just waiting for you.

You won't know whether you are willing to give up nothing until you give yourself a chance to trust God again. We have become distrustful of God because we have allied with an ego that advises us God is not trustworthy and does not really have our best interest at heart. We have been taught that God does not wish to give us everything. We have been poorly taught. Ego has been our teacher. We are always choosing either for ego or for God. There is no other choice. We cannot depend on both ego and God. The two are mutually exclusive. Ego literally means Edging God Out.

Ego Was Made To Gain Independence From God

The story of Adam and Eve in the garden is our one all-inclusive story. It is all that is ever happening. Every other story is merely a variation on the one theme where we chose to leave everything and enter the experience of nothing. Adam and Eve were totally dependent on God until they listened to a suggestion to try independence. Adam made ego to be autonomous, but he merely traded in one dependency for another. In making ego he convinced himself he had made his own source. It would be the same as you giving birth to your own parents. It is not only impossible but absolutely ridiculous. And if you look closely, you will see that ego-dependence is the cause of all apparent bondage. It is impossible to be bound since God created us eternally free. Ego was made to be our source in place of God, but that idea was merely a mistake as God is our Source and irreplaceable. We can think we have another source, but it does not change the truth. God created us and is our Source forever and that is not negotiable.

What does God-dependence really mean? It means you never have a care again, everything is provided for you, you can never get sick, lose the ones you love or suffer. It means you are and have everything forever. Could you consider God-dependence if it offered you peace, love and joy beyond your wildest dreams? Are you willing to be utterly, totally, helplessly, passionately dependent on God if it means your troubles are over? Surrender to God doesn't mean a loss of freedom, but rather is where true freedom can be found. God wants you free. Would you feel all right about not making your own decisions if you knew God's decisions in your behalf would serve you far better than you could serve yourself?

In your dependence on God, are you giving your power away? No, in depending on God, you reclaim your power, for only in God are you powerful. There is no power outside of God. "Of myself I am nothing - with God ALL things are possible." It is ego that convinces us that God wants to control us and be a tyrannical ruler and strip us of our power. God knows nothing of this strange idea we hold about Him. God loves His children forever. He has for you the love of a thousand mothers.

In the world, independence represents freedom. We want to be independent as a nation. We call that freedom. We have to reverse our thinking in order to be willing to accept the possibility that total dependence can give us freedom. It is the way God's nation is set up. That is what freedom is – total dependence on God. It requires trust in God to take care of us. Does that mean He only takes care of us when we meet His terms? Do we have to meet certain requirements to become worthy and then He will step in?

When we choose to be independent, we are closing the door to God's grace. God is a most gracious and unimposing host. He will not knock the door down in a determination to give us everything. If we have closed the door to everything in order to have an unreal experience, He will wait. But let us be perfectly clear that it is never God who has forgotten us, but rather we who have forgotten Him. *God does not command, because He is incapable of arrogance. He does not demand, because He does not seek control. He does not overcome, because He does not attack. He is quiet and waits to be asked. He speaks of peace and offers only peace.* Peace cannot be forced upon God's children by its very nature. We have to want it by wanting only God.

God Depends On You Too

Our whole creative function lies in our complete dependence on God whose function He shares with us. By His willingness to share it, He becomes as dependent on us as we are on Him. He has included us in His autonomy. God gave up His autonomy for us. He prefers to create rather than to have autonomy. In His act of creation He lost His autonomy forever. *He awaits our blessing for every creative action He undertakes.* We also cannot have autonomy, for that freedom is impossible. The belief in ego autonomy is costing us the knowledge of our dependence on God in which our true freedom lies. We are one organism inseparable from God and each other forever. It was desire for independence that gave life to ego. *God and the souls He created are symbiotically related. They are completely dependent on each other for all eternity.* In that dependence there is no limitation on creative freedom.

God-dependence does not mean we can be careless or irresponsible. We are always responsible for our actions. Do not use this teaching to excuse your behavior on the grounds that in your total dependence on God, "God made me do it." God depends on you because He created you perfect. He is counting on you to be as He created you. He knows He can count on you, because you cannot be different from how you were created. If you think it difficult to be perfect, you are mistaken. Is it difficult to be who you are? We have been convinced by ego that we cannot attain perfection, yet it is very easy to be perfect once we stop believing false information about ourselves. And we will find independence when we depend on God for everything. Our independence will be of creation, not of autonomy.

Mutual dependence is our true relationship with God. It is a naturally joyful relationship wherein we are free. In this dependence, God does not need you in order to complete Himself, nor do you need God to complete yourself. You are whole and complete within yourself. Your dependence on God enhances your joy, as God's dependence on you enhances His. It is love that draws you irresistibly together and not need. As Jesus said, "Of myself I am nothing." You are not of yourself; you are of God. In thinking you are independent, you do think you are of yourself and then it must follow that you think you are nothing. Only in your total dependence on God are you everything, equal with God in love and power. It is desire for autonomy that causes resistance to this true and sacred relationship.

With God All Things Are Possible

Sometimes Sai Baba refers to us as puppets on a string. He also says, "There is no one more powerful than you, you are the Lord of the universe, you are no different from God." If you are no different from God, is God also a puppet on a string? No, God is the puppeteer when we allow Him to direct our lives. And when He is the puppeteer He moves us to be who we are, namely God, the Lord of the universe, all-powerful, limitless in creative expression. You are both the Lord of the universe and a puppet when you are dependent on God. When you do not want God to direct your life, you are choosing ego to be your puppeteer and ego leads you to convince yourself that you are nothing, as it is nothing. When God is your puppeteer, you will be like Him. When ego is your puppeteer, you will be like ego. You are never independent as that choice is not an option.

When you realize just what the choices are, you will be happy to make the obvious choice. It really comes down to a choice for equality, oneness with God and all of humanity, leading to peace, love and joy unbounded forever, or a choice for separation, inequality, leading to anger, jealousy, pride, greed, lust and hatred invariably attended with guilt. Guilt then must be assuaged, so one agrees to punishment in the form of sickness, suffering and death, in time and space with little seductions of joy to keep you deluded that you are happy so you won't look your pitiful predicament in the eye. Ego offers you nothing you really want. God offers you everything you really want. Baba says there is no freewill, but we can always choose between God's will and ego's will. God wills our freedom and ego wants us bound. You do have freedom to create, but you are not free to be separate from God or others as dependence on ego would lead you to believe.

The fact is you are dependent on God no matter what choice you make because ego has no independent power, though it tries to fool you that it does. We made ego and then gave it the power to enslave us. It uses the power of our minds given to us by God. Ego is a parasite, totally dependent on the power of God as directed by us for its survival. When we direct our God given power away from ego, it dissolves into the nothingness that it always was.

Everything is suffused with God and God's love. There is no place where God is not. What sustains us if not God's love? Can anything grow without God's love? Where does the sun's energy come from if not from God? God is everywhere always and forever. He did not abandon us or forget us. He is ready to receive us when we wish. Remember the story in the Bible of the prodigal son? We are each that prodigal son, and what did the father do when his son returned home? He prepared a lavish banquet and brought together the finest musicians for a grand celebration. He was so happy for his son's return. God is always eager for our return to His ever-open arms.

When Jesus announced, "Of myself I am nothing," he went on to say, "With God all things are possible." He knew that none of the miracles he performed came from him. Only in his total dependence on God could miracles occur. He knew that in his total dependence on God he could perform miracles of healing the sick and raising the dead. These are not greater miracles than we are able to perform when we let God direct our lives. Jesus pronounced to his disciples, "Greater works than I have done shall you do." We need do so little to receive so much. All things are possible with God. Turn to God and He will do the rest. We only need faith as small as a tiny mustard seed and the world can be transformed back into the world God created.

Surrender To God And Be Victorious Over Ego

In the Bhagavad Gita, Krishna (the Lord) is the charioteer for Arjuna (His devotee), in the war wherein the forces for ego-dependence are pitted against the forces for God-dependence. Because Arjuna let Krishna be his charioteer, though they were greatly outnumbered, the Pandavas (the 5 brothers on the side of good) won the war. Only when we turn to God can He help us. Only when we turn to God can we truly vanquish our enemies: greed, jealousy, anger, hatred, lust and pride.

When I first started really turning to God I was afraid that He would not respond, so there was a strong temptation not to bother so as not to be disappointed. I now see that was ego trying to throw me off the trail of surrendering to God for everything. Ego is very seductive and clever in trying to convince us that we need not, should not or cannot depend on God: 'God won't respond anyway;' 'To call on God is weakness;' 'You'll lose your independence;' 'I never hear God communicating with me...' We must be ever vigilant. God is always communicating with us. Are we listening? One thing that eludes us is that God is within. He is not in some far off place.

Because we made ego, we have trained ourselves to have a greater affinity for it than for God and to turn to it for guidance. Ego always speaks loudest and first. We see ourselves one with our egos, our child protégé so to speak, but we do not see ourselves one with God, our Source. Once we recognize our oneness with God, we will more readily turn our will and life over to God's care. That happens when we see ego truly as the robot we made that turned on its maker.

There are those who may be tempted to reduce God to a genie in a bottle, but that is not surrender to God or trust in God to know better than we what we really need. To depend on God means to trust Him to take care of the problem without telling Him how to do His job. Let go and let God by trusting that He knows better than you how to handle every situation. When you do that, the outcome will always exceed your greatest expectation. God's solution is always bigger and better and offers more than you could offer yourself, on your own.

I Am The Ocean, You Are The Wave

Sai Baba says, "Make no distinction between you and Me. Do not think Baba is God and you are His devotee. Do not even think Baba is the teacher and you are His student. Think only: Baba is the ocean and you are the wave." If you make the distinction that there is God and there is His devotee, you make separation. The teacher-student relationship also makes separation. God wants us to recognize our oneness with Him beyond all distinctions. But then He says, "I am the ocean and you are the wave." Is that not a distinction? Let's take a look. The ocean and the wave are exactly the same as both are made up of only water. There is no place where the ocean ends and the wave begins. There is no place where God ends and His creation begins. God and His creation are one. Baba says, "I am God, you are also God." The Bible says you were created in the image and likeness of your Creator. You are one with God. *There is no place where the Father ends and the son begins.*

The ocean and the wave both consist of water. The essence is the same, however there is a distinct difference. The difference is that the wave emerges out of the ocean. It is not possible that it be the other way around. Can you imagine a wave creating the ocean? God created you. You did not create God, nor did you create yourself. You were created by God to be exactly like Him. Perhaps you are not in the experience of being God, but that is simply because you tried to be something else, because you were not content to have been created by God and thus to be dependent on God for everything. We tried to become waves without the ocean, to gain independence. We stubbornly hold on to our independence though it is hurting us, because we want to prove ourselves right. But it cannot change our true relationship with God. We do depend on God, as God depends on us, and that is the beautiful relationship we share with God, whether we like it or not.

A wave separate from the ocean is impossible. It is impossible to be separate from God though we all tried to be waves without the ocean. A wave without the ocean is ego, an attempt at independence from our Source. If I were of myself, what I made would be true, and I could never escape. Fortunately, I am not of myself. I am of God forever. In making ego we separated ourselves from God in our minds. In truth it is as preposterous as a wave without the ocean. It never happened. However, though ego is unreal, it does have all the power we invest in it and that is not nothing. We took great pride in what we made though it did not make it real. *Deeper than the ego's foundation and much stronger than it will ever be is your intense and burning love for God and His for you.*

The Wave Cannot Create The Ocean

Though ego is not real, let us never underestimate the treachery it wields. All our vigilance and determination are required to restore us to wholeness. Ego, once sided with, is very subtle, insidious and obscuring and tries to complicate the simple truth that you are one with God. Ego wants to throw you off the trail of it as the cause of all your suffering, so it tries to convince you that God is the cause of your unhappiness. There could be nothing further from the truth. *God created us wholly without sin, pain or suffering of any kind. If we accept ourselves as God created us, we will be incapable of suffering. But to do that we must acknowledge Him as our Creator.*

Your acknowledgment of your Source is the acknowledgment of yourself as you are. Many students of non-dualism have conceptually understood themselves to be the ocean. Though they are right that there is nothing outside of them, if their concept of oneness does not leave room for God as Source, they have not realized who they are and are merely the wave pretending to be the ocean. I can only urge you to investigate deeply for yourself. Are you sure you are without a Source? What is the resistance to having a Source if that Source has withheld nothing from you His beloved creation? Is it less than pure non-duality to recognize that you have a Source from whom you are not separate? Is the wave not one with the ocean and is that not pure oneness?

Were you really created equal with God? A wave is smaller than the ocean, however, a wave one with the ocean is as big as the ocean and is therefore equal with it. Only a wave separate from the ocean is small and that is impossible. We are small when we let ego be our source and believe its lies. Ego tries to convince us that it is possible to be a wave without the ocean. We are as great as God only when we let God be our Source. We are each the ocean when we merge back into the ocean. Only the wave that merges back into the ocean is one with it. God created us to be exactly like Him, not less in any way, but we can only have that as our direct experience when the wave dissolves into the ocean, when we realize our perfect equality with God. In our total interdependence we are verily God.

Baba urges us to merge with Him. In merging our consciousness back into God consciousness, we regain the whole ocean. The ocean is limitless. The wave by itself is limited. The ocean is all-powerful. The wave on its own is powerless, buffeted about by circumstances beyond its control. You are God. You are no different from God and you will experience that truth only in your total dependence on God. We are afraid to merge with the ocean because we fear we will lose ourselves, but we will only gain ourselves. We will gain everything. We will lose nothing. The wave merges with the ocean by totally depending on the ocean.

In your total dependence on God, you are both the wave and the ocean. God has withheld nothing from you. He has given you everything. You are no less than God. You are God. Only fear of loss of false identity keeps the wave from being engulfed by the ocean. But our true identity lies in our desire to be one with the ocean. A willingness to give up a false sense of autonomy allows you to merge with the ocean and thereby to wake up. Any mind that awakens is of great benefit to all of humanity. That is why waking up is the greatest service one can render to the planet.

You And I Can Only Join In The Truth

A wave merged with the ocean is a mind awake. Two waves can only merge with each other in the ocean. I can only really join with you when we both recognize our oneness in God through our utter dependence on Him as Source. You and I can never truly meet outside of God and I do so want to meet you. Dependence on God is essential to any true meeting. We can only truly meet when we are both awake in God. When two minds unite in a full commitment to only the truth, it becomes that much easier for the whole world to receive the truth that we are all one and interdependent. Using the hundredth monkey idea, when two minds get it, all minds can more readily accept the truth.

I once had a dream at Baba's ashram where I completely joined in the truth with another. The power of that joining was extraordinary. It was the most intensely exquisite experience of my life. I woke up trembling at the possibility, for I knew then that we all have the capacity to join in true oneness in our total dependence on God. *Alone we can do nothing, but together our wills fuse to something that is far beyond the power of its separate parts.* What a blessed communion awaits us all in our merging in God together. Then our dance with each other will be so pure, rich, expansive and God-intoxicating. That is the gift God gave to us when He created us for each other. In that joining, two waves merge with each other. That can only happen when both waves merge in the ocean. We can only merge with each other when we accept the truth that we are all one in God.

God Is The Mind With Which We Think

To merge with God is to surrender to God's will; your true will. *When you ask God's will in anything you are asking your will. In hearing God's will, you learn your own.* Your will is God's. God always wants what is best for you. He will not settle for you having less than everything. *Humility does not mean being content with littleness, but rather being content with greatness that is not of you.* Our greatness is of God, not of ourselves. We are greatness because God created us and He can only create in His likeness and image. God is greatness. God is grandeur. *We chose to come to the world to escape that likeness which is our true reality, but when reality can be found even here, let us step back and let God lead the way.* We take that necessary action of mind in our utter dependence on God for everything.

Sai Baba says, "Mind is gift of God." God lets us use His mind. For what purpose are you using this most precious gift? Are you using it to be host to ego or to God? You are God's host. If you have God's mind, then you have God. You do have God and thus you have everything. Realize your priceless treasure. God is always communicating with you. When you are host to ego you are misusing your sacred inheritance. Perhaps you feel you would like to surrender to God, but don't recognize His voice. Ego always speaks loudest and first. God's voice is quiet and gentle. God does not try to get your attention as ego does. So you have to remember to get quiet to hear Him. Don't put God into a box of only being a voice in your head. He can communicate through your neighbor, an incident, a dream, etc. The possibilities are endless because God is limitless creativity. Don't worry that you might not receive His communication. He knows very well how to communicate with you because He knows you better than you know yourself, because He loves you so much more than you love yourself. When you have turned to God, and expect to hear His voice, you have opened the door and invited Him in. He is present where welcome.

Perhaps you feel that you pray to God, but God does not answer. God is answering. When you do not tell God how He should respond, you open the door to hearing His response. It will always be a delightful surprise or insight that thrills you to your very essence. So great is His love for you. God cannot hear you when you speak loudly or forcefully, for then you are requesting with ego and ego is nonexistent. Speak to God with gentleness, tenderness, trust and honoring. Do not be coercive or manipulative. God is listening. You will hear Him in the stillness as He hears you in the stillness.

If God is your charioteer your life will be blessed and you will have a true purpose and give joy to others. Choose to depend on God for everything and you are choosing for your freedom and the freedom of all God's children, your whole family. In this choice lies everything you truly want. God loves you so very much and yearns to give you every good and priceless treasure.

Thank You dear God, for giving up autonomy for us. Help us to understand that in giving up autonomy we give up nothing and gain everything. Help us to trust that total dependence on You gives us total freedom. Thank You that we can never leave You or be separate from You. Thank You for creating us in Your image and likeness, exactly the same as You. Thank You for depending on us as much as we depend on You. Thank You for Your unswerving acknowledgment of our perfection. Grant us the determination to be perfect as You depend on us to be. Grant us the yearning to merge with You and all our brothers and sisters in You, and to expand into the limitless consciousness that You created us to be eternally.

May all beings in all the worlds be happy and blest, Amen

Figure 4a – True Freedom Lies in God-Dependence

Everything (Eternity)

Eternity	Life	Oneness
God-Dependence	Love	Freedom
Real	Truth	Non-judgment
Heaven	Peace	Creation
Innocence	Knowledge	All-Powerful

Nothing (time and space)

Time/space	**Happy Dream (Satva) God's solution - collapses time**
Ego-Dependence —	Turn to God for everything/Surrender to God's Will
Unreal	Interdependence - healthy dependence on God & others
Hell	Acknowledge total dependence on God
Guilt	Include self-responsibility with God -Dependence
Death	**Nightmare (Rajo Guna) - makes time**
Fear	Defy Divine will - "I want it my way"
Untruth	Dependence on ego
War	"Dependence on God is weakness"
Ignorance	"Dependence on God means loss of freedom"
Separation	**Deep Sleep (Thamo) Ego's solution - freezes time**
Bondage	Shirking responsibility/feeling helpless
Judgment	Lack of trust in God/Denial of existence of God
Mis-creation	Co-dependence - Unhealthy dependence on others
Powerless	"Doesn't matter what I do as it's not real anyway"

Direction of Consciousness Awakening

Figure 4b – The Ocean and the Wave are One

The Wave One With the Ocean

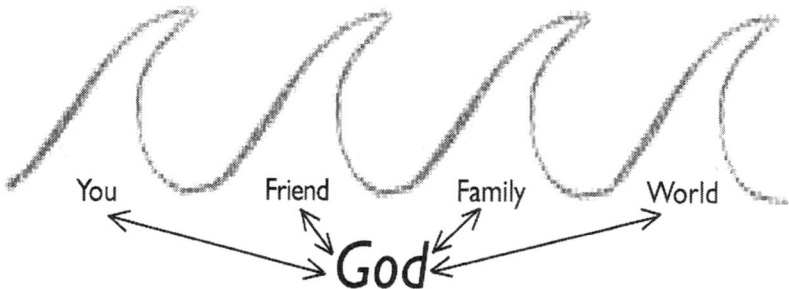

Free communication between the ocean and the wave (God and you)
and the wave and other waves (you and others communicate in God)

The Wave Attempting to be Separate from the Ocean

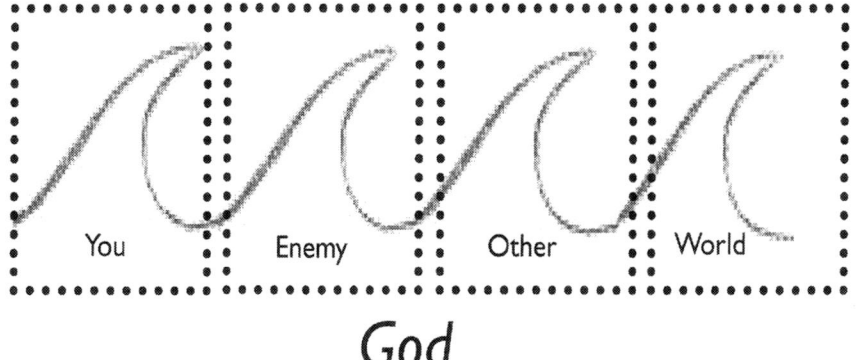

Communication with God and each other is severely impaired.

As communication with God is reestablished through God dependence,
oneness with all is again experienced

Chapter 5

Are You Ready to Stop Making the Unreal Real?

Nothing real can be threatened
Nothing unreal exists;
Herein lies the peace of God
Jesus in ACIM

My Rape Experience

In February of 1985, I had a most intense experience, which at first seemed incredibly brutal but which I now see as a true spiritual turning point. I had been Sai Baba's devotee, living a simple life as a Montessori teacher, residing by myself, spending six months of every year in India with Sai Baba. Life was beautiful. Then one night everything changed. It was Mahashivaratri in India, the holiest day of the year. I was staying in a Sai Baba center in California. We were scheduled to celebrate with an all-night bhajan (devotional singing) the following evening. I was fast asleep in a room adjoining the bhajan hall. It was 3:00 am. It could not have been a more auspicious time or setting.

Suddenly I was jolted awake by a threatening voice ordering, "Scream and I'll kill you." I felt a knife at my throat and saw a massive menacing figure looming over me. Still groggy, I instinctively screamed and to shut me up he pummeled me in the face with his fist till I was bruised and bleeding. He gagged me, tied me up and ripped off my pajamas. In total terror I cried out to Sai Baba to come and save me. In my heart of hearts I fully expected Baba to physically appear and dispel this horrendous nightmare. Baba did not come. And yet He did, though I did not realize it at the time. Even while I was being brutally raped, within me all fear and horror of the situation left. Quite inexplicably I became very calm and to my astonishment discovered a genuine compassion welling up in my heart for that confused soul who thought hurting another could somehow serve him.

As he was leaving, I managed a muffled, "God bless you." He hissed back, "God hates me," and disappeared into the night. I struggled to untie myself and went to get help. The police were called and the man caught. He had a history with abuse and had been in and out of jail, yet, this time something had changed for him. From his cell he made a considerable effort to get this message to me: "I am sorry I hurt you. Please pray for me." So even in that violent scene God was present and the rapist too was affected. To my surprise, I could muster no anger toward the man. I found myself focusing not so much on my personal trauma as on the tragedy of the human condition that could lead to such a desperate state.

The Truth Is Unaffected By Unreality

Although my body was badly beaten and bruised, there was little physical pain. However, I was traumatized and bewildered. I remember walking out at night feeling afraid that somebody might be lurking behind a bush. When anyone entered my room unexpectedly I became startled and jittery, feelings that were completely alien to me. In my being I felt tainted and my familiar sense of security and knowing that I was always in the protective hands of the Divine had been badly shaken.

My confusion centered entirely on Sai Baba. In my mind, Baba, in whom I had put complete trust and whom I regarded as my savior, had not helped me though I had desperately called out to Him. Why hadn't He? I kept praying, "Why did You let this happen? Please help me understand." As I was imploring thus, I distinctly heard Baba's voice gently ask, "What happened to you?" "I was raped, brutalized, robbed and my very life was threatened," came my angry response, "and I called out to You, but You did not come." Again Baba asked, ever so tenderly, "What happened to you?"

That gentle voice pierced through the depths of my anguish and I suddenly realized that absolutely nothing had happened to the truth of me. I remembered one of my favorite passages in the Bhagavad Gita where Krishna taught Arjuna, "You are not this perishable body. Weapons cannot destroy you. Fire cannot incinerate you. Water cannot drown you. The raging tempest cannot blow you away. You are the indestructible, eternal Atma, the one Self." My spirits soared as that mystical pronouncement shifted from a conceptual idea to a direct revelation. My bewilderment, fears and feelings of abandonment miraculously dissolved in the light of that profound realization. Far from failing me, Sai Baba had used this powerful experience to reveal the truth of who I am, the immortal Self. I realized that there is nothing in the universe that can ever really threaten me or hurt me in any way. I am invulnerable.

Is Unreality Part Of God's Will?

And yet that one realization did not satisfy me entirely. There were still some questions that remained unanswered. If nothing happened to me, was this 'unreal' experience God's will? Why do I need to experience something unreal and then realize its unreality in order to be free? Could this experience have been avoided? If I was created to experience only God and God's love as that is all that is real, how did I come to this unreal experience that seemed so very real and deeply agonizing? What is the source of unreality and what is its function? I wanted to find out why there was such a disparity between my experience and the truth. I wanted to uncover the cause behind my experience as that seemed the best way to discover a solution to its undoing both for myself and others.

Perhaps you would be content to believe that the whole incident was God's will and an expression of God's love. After all, isn't everything that happens God's will? When I prayed, 'Swami, how could You let this happened to me?' I obviously thought it was God's will. But something just didn't fit. There was simply no way I could see this as an expression of God's love. Maybe this was not God's will. What evidence did I really have that God willed me to be raped? I realized I didn't have any substantial evidence and that my conclusions had no basis in fact. God didn't say, 'I willed that experience for you.' That was a relief. It certainly helped me feel better about God.

If God had willed this, wouldn't that make Him cruel? What kind of God would permit horrors such as what I'd just experienced to happen? If God created us as an extension of His joy, would He wish us to suffer? My thinking that God had something to do with what happened had put up a huge barrier to my love for God. Once I stopped needing to see Him as the cause, my love for Him resurfaced.

Instead of sticking to my conclusions about God as cause, I searched deeper. I was willing to be wrong, as I only wanted the truth. The next obvious alternative was that there was a rapist out there over whom I had no control and who the Divinity could not prevent, who caused this to happen. Certainly that is how the world would see it. Isn't personal security a major issue for us? So much effort goes into protecting ourselves from hostile forces outside of ourselves.

But is that really how it is? How could I possibly return to normalcy if that were so? Then at every turn I could expect another incident. There could be no peace if it were true that I was buffeted about by forces beyond my control. Could I be so helpless and vulnerable? I simply could not accept that a rapist randomly breaking in and assaulting me was the full story, particularly on Shivaratri night in a Sai Baba center. Again I didn't settle. I kept digging in a determination to find the whole truth.

I Am Responsible For Everything That Happens To Me

So far I had ruled out God or rapist as possible cause. That left only one other possibility and that was that I am the cause, that I did this to myself. That seemed the one possibility that had some potential for peace. I had already been shown that what happened was not real, thus I understood that in truth nothing had happened to me. Knowing this made it possible to step into personal responsibility. Had I not known the unreality of the incident, I would not have been able to shoulder the responsibility.

One might argue, "If nothing happened, what is there to be responsible for?" Though the suffering was not real, it was very real for me. That is the difference between using the teaching of unreality for denial or healing. Only with self-responsibility is there a willingness to make the necessary shift in consciousness required to heal the mind that thought it could be a victim of circumstances beyond its control. Once the mind is healed, the outer circumstances must reflect a destiny free of victim consciousness.

Knowing that suffering is ultimately unreal makes it easier to be responsible. And, if I did this to myself, then I was not buffeted about by forces outside of myself. That was good news. If I did this to myself, then it must be that I also have the power to undo this, to heal its effects, to prevent it from happening in the future. Self-responsibility was essential, for it motivated me to want to change my mind. I have the power to alter my destiny. What do I need to do to change my mind?

All Karma Is Effaced When We See The Past As Past

Some well-intentioned friends told me that a huge chunk of negative karma had just been removed. That provided a possible explanation, but it was not the solution I was looking for. It certainly didn't make me feel good because it left open the question of how much more negative karma I might have to undergo whose effects I might experience at any moment. Karma considers whatever happens in any situation to be an effect of a previous cause. Its purpose is to balance the scales. Karma requires time and we have already discovered that time is not real. I wanted a solution that would guarantee the end of all suffering now.

Should we honor the laws of karma? Are they of God? Let us assume I did something in the past for which I felt guilty. This guilt is exactly what ego had hoped I would feel. Ego then suggested a punishment befitting the crime to be meted out at some future time, most probably another lifetime. I meekly went along with the punishment, because after all I did feel guilty. Next life I probably won't remember what I might have done but sad disaster strikes unexpectedly for no apparent reason. Is a consequence for something I may have done in a previous life really reasonable or fair in this life?

I must have agreed to it because I am all-powerful and nothing happens to me without my will. Is punishment fair just because I agree to it? If I am all-powerful, and if I did agree, then we can see how there are no victims and there are no accidents. It does not however mean that I was wisely advised or that I needed to follow the advice of my counselor. My guide was ego and had a purpose for my suffering – its life at my expense. Ego doesn't care about me. It only cares about its survival. Did I need that experience to learn I shouldn't rape? Did it help me to know not to hurt others? Is karma God's idea of justice?

When I looked at it, I could find no true justice in the idea. Karma is based on the ego thought system that sees other bodies outside of you that can hurt you or that you can hurt. Hurtful actions produce guilt which in turn lead to future reckoning in line with the idea 'as you sow, so shall you reap.' Bodies are not real and you cannot be hurt, nor can you hurt anyone as all are Spirit and invincible. Karma is not of God; it is of ego. God has nothing to do with guilt and punishment. That is ego's idea of justice. God's solution is to correct the mind that thought it could hurt anyone or that attempting to hurt another could serve any purpose. We do not have to make amends for the past. We need merely change our minds toward kindness for all and the past is undone, leaving not a trace.

The laws of karma can only bind you as long as you are allied with ego. Baba says, "There is no freewill because all your will is tied up in karma." He also says, "Let Me efface all your karma." God's grace can wipe out all karma instantly. When you make a shift in consciousness, the scales are balanced instantly. When you recognize that you are not a body and that you cannot hurt another or be hurt by anyone you are making that shift. That shift opens the door to God's grace and your past is undone.

We are under no laws but God's. God's idea of justice is to remind us that all are Spirit. The rapist could not hurt me, because I am Spirit and therefore invulnerable. In other words, no one can ever commit any crime in the truest sense. Everyone is always innocent. We only felt guilty because we thought it possible to hurt others, because we thought we were bodies and they were bodies. You are indestructible just as I am. If you cannot hurt anyone, then you have no reason to feel guilty for any possible hurtful actions you might have committed in the past. They had no effect upon the truth. If however you use this teaching to justify hurting another, you have not understood that you are not a body and subject yourself to the laws of karma.

When we truly know that we are all invulnerable, guilt vanishes with no need to experience consequences for past mistakes and that is how time is collapsed. Then all our past simply rolls up like a long carpet behind us. You are bound by karmic consequences only as long as you do not know who you are. Once you know who you are you will know who everyone is and will not want to hurt anyone. Then there will be no purpose for consequences for past errors. All suffering is self-inflicted punishment for crimes that were never committed. That is the insanity we bought into and we stand free of it when we want to be free. God reminds us that we were created innocent and thus are innocent forever. Only when we remember this are we truly free of our past.

Guard Against Misapplying The Teachings

As with any of these teachings, ego can latch onto them and use them for license. Always be vigilant. Don't let ego fool you into thinking that now you can do whatever you want as long as you don't feel guilty. It is true that it doesn't matter what you have done because it wasn't real. However, do not carry that understanding into the present or you hold onto your past. This is a new moment and any attempt to hurt another is an admission that you do not understand you are both Spirit and binds you to karmic consequences for all errors of the past, not just this action. If you justify hurting another, it will produce guilt and keep you on the wheel of cause and consequence.

You were created to love everyone and everything and though perhaps you have tried to block out the truth, somewhere within you, your deep love for everyone could not be forgotten. Acting hurtfully produces guilt. Hurting anyone is hurting yourself for we are one organism. When we behold each other as Spirit we cannot but love one another. Spirit is who we all are. To think of hurting anyone is simply impossible when you know the truth.

Once a murderer attempted to use the teachings of the Bhagavad Gita in his defense. He took the position that he did not really murder as everyone is Spirit and therefore cannot die. The judge was also a student of the teachings. He said, "Though you killed bodies, it is correct that you did not murder in the truest sense. Regrettably for you, you did not understand the teachings at all and cannot escape the consequences of your actions. You used the teachings for license and misapplied them entirely. If you had understood them, it would have been impossible for you to commit the heinous acts that you have been charged with. You thought that those you murdered were bodies or you would not have acted as you did. Only one in body consciousness can murder and thereby subject himself to the laws of karma."

The defendant's reasoning was that it is impossible to murder as that which can be hurt or destroyed is unreal, therefore it doesn't matter what you do in relation to name and form. He was suggesting that he could not be held accountable for a crime that he had not committed in truth. He had conceptual understanding and was misapplying the teachings to justify the unjustifiable. Needless to say, murder is an unloving act perpetrated in alliance with ego and ego needs you guilty. He was right that it is impossible to defy God's will. To defy God's will would be to try to destroy what God created to have eternal life and succeed. *God did not create bodies.* What God created cannot be destroyed. We are not more powerful than God. It is impossible for anything to die, but in misapplying the teachings to justify murder, he was slitting his own throat.

Had he really understood the teachings he would have recognized the preciousness of all life. The attempt to do what cannot be done is the cause of all unreality, which inevitably results in pain and misery. Pain is not real, as it was never God's will for you, yet it is hard to deny the experience when you are suffering. I pray that you lead a righteous life and use the teachings wisely and thereby be at peace.

The teachings I share here come from my deep explorations of truth, but if used with lack of maturity they will hurt you. It doesn't matter what you have done in the past, but it matters very much what you do now. If you misapply these teachings, you would have been much better off not having received them. You will experience the consequences of your mind. Always act with the utmost purity and sacredness toward all beings and things.

All Are Innocent

There are no levels of illusion. When you know who you are, you will find yourself unable to engage in any unreal behaviors. And yet you have no business condemning anyone for his or her mistakes. All I wished for my rapist was that he change his mind and stop hurting others. I did not wish him punished. I did not seek revenge. I did have him put away but only because I felt a duty to society. Had someone else been violated I would have felt responsible.

Someone suggested that was not my business, as perhaps I was depriving a sister of a valuable lesson that the experience could have afforded. No one needs to learn anything they do not already know. Yes, I learned many things, but what I learned most emphatically was that I did not ever want this to happen again, not to me or anyone. If that is what I learned, it would make no sense to see someone else possibly needing the same experience to learn the same lesson. If someone else were accosted, I would feel I could have prevented that. I have a duty to society as everything is in my mind. There is nothing outside of me. If I can prevent suffering and do not act to do so, I am directly responsible for another's pain.

Though the rapist has been removed from society, he is innocent as he cannot be different from how he was created. He can change his mind toward kindness and be instantly restored to wholeness. There is a story of a sandal thief who was caught and sent away from Sai Baba's ashram. Baba did not have him punished. Instead He supported him to start an orphanage.

The man was transformed and is serving society to this day in a very humble and upright manner. Ratnakara, a skilled and treacherous thief 10,000 years ago became the author of the great epic poem, The Ramayana. Every saint has a past and every sinner has a future. Hold no one's past against him, or you bind yourself. It is possible to be transformed instantly by simply shifting from ego consciousness to God consciousness.

You are always either choosing with God or with ego. When you choose with God, your purpose is the one Self, the truth of who you really are. When you choose with ego, your purpose is to maintain a separate identity. *There is nothing that will not be undone the instant you no longer see a purpose for it.* You are all-powerful because you are not separate or different from God. God cannot be victimized and neither can you unless it fulfills your purpose. God created you just like Himself. *The power of God is within you and all that stands between you and that power is your learning of the false and your attempts to undo the real. When you change your mind about what you want to see, the entire world must change accordingly.*

You Are The Dreamer Of Your Dream

Once in a dream, Arjuna (Krishna's disciple 5000 years ago) and I were sitting at the kitchen table chatting like brother and sister. "You know, Yaani," he said, "I saw the whole Mahabharata war from start to finish in every minute detail before it began." Upon hearing that I threw up my hands and exclaimed in dismay, "Oh, Arjuna, does that mean I have nothing to say about what happens to me?" "No, Yaani, it's not like that," he reassured me. "When consciousness changes destiny also changes." You are all-powerful. You are the dreamer of your dream. You can change it from a nightmare into a happy dream by changing your mind from body consciousness to God consciousness, from untruth to truth.

Every thought you think is either real or unreal. Your real thoughts are thoughts you think with God. They will be loving and will produce a real experience. All other thoughts are unreal, yet they will have their effects. There are no neutral thoughts. That is why Baba constantly reminds us to watch our thoughts for purity, kindness and love. He says, "Give Me your garbage." Give any undesirable thoughts to God to be undone so you will only experience reality. If you give your unreal thoughts to God, you will not feel guilty and thereby perpetuate unreality.

At the time of my rape incident I obviously had not rooted out victim-victimizer consciousness from my mind, otherwise I could not have attracted that experience to myself. I did however use my painful experience to dive deep into the truth so as to prevent a similar episode in the future. *All things are lessons God would have me learn* and thus everything that happens can be used. Use it as God's grace. If not for God's presence it might have been even more traumatic. Do not see it as God's will. God only wills our happiness.

My experience was unreal and never happened in truth. It was a nightmare. A dream seems very real while you are dreaming but when you wake up you see it was only a dream. Everything that happens to us in the world is only a dream. It is not real. We can however either use it as a learning device to free us or as a nightmare to keep us frightened and thereby imprisoned. I used my experience to wake up from the nightmare, not by denying its reality, but by taking personal responsibility and allowing my mind to be healed by God's grace.

Self-Responsibility Heals

The rape wasn't real, but it was real for me and if I denied that it happened before it was healed I would merely be keeping a skeleton in the closet and thereby choosing ego's solution to the problem, which is no solution at all. God's solution is to heal the mind that thinks it can be a victim. That happened when I owned that I did this to myself, for I am all-powerful and nothing happens to me but by my will. Self-responsibility opens the door to a shift from victim/victimizer consciousness to God consciousness. In being willing to be responsible, I was motivated to change my mind and that desire permitted the unreal to be undone. Through that action of mind, the past is truly unreal and never happened from a place of a healed mind, a mind that has been restored to wholeness. Then the experience will not ever be repeated. There would simply be no purpose for it. *The secret to salvation is but that whatever is happening, you are doing it to yourself, however undesirable it may appear to be. Own this and you are free.*

If I don't use the experience to learn the lesson, it will be repeated till I get it right. I am not the only one who has been raped. Many sisters tell of similar incidents. Some admit to having completely blocked the incident out of their minds as the way they have dealt with it. I'm sorry but this is denial and not healing. This is ego's solution to the problem. You would only deny what you feel you need to preserve. Denial keeps the unreal real. Self-responsibility is fearful only as long as the unreal is given reality. Because I recognized its unreality I did not feel guilty or bad in stepping into personal responsibility for what happened.

To be responsible is to be in true relationship with everything that happens to you. You are the Lord of your universe. Everything that happens to you is of your own making. Only when you step into that level of responsibility can past mistakes be undone. The willingness to stand still in the nightmare opens the door to God's solution which is to heal the past. When we look at our experiences with God, God can undo any and all negative effects for us. Mistakes are correctable when we are willing to have them corrected. My mind needed to be healed and in my willingness to be healed, it was accomplished. It required my admission that I was wrong. It was easy to admit that I was wrong when I saw that the consciousness I was holding was not producing a joyful experience.

Stop Making The Unreal Real

I now know that nothing happened because I let myself be healed by looking at the ego thought system that produced an unreal experience. *Ego stands on the tiny platform, "Whatever you do, don't look at me."* Baba says, "Face the devil." I looked at it without judgment and asked that the truth be revealed. I saw its unreality and in seeing it, it literally vanished. When the unreal is transformed into the real all that is remembered of the past is the love. I truly have only the deepest gratitude for the way in which that frightening nightmare was transformed into a powerful classroom toward my awakening. There is no fear associated with my remembrance. In fact it only seems like a distant memory.

My rape experience impelled me to change my mind. It was an extreme example that hopefully not you or anyone need undergo. You can change your mind by using my experience or any other extreme example such as Jesus' crucifixion to motivate you to change your consciousness. See that this world of duality, death, injustice, victims and victimizers that was made to maintain separation is no longer what you want. You do need to judge truly between what is real and what is unreal so that you can stop reinforcing unreality and thereby keeping it real for you.

God honors His children and as long as we want unreality to be real, He will not interfere. Sai Baba says, "The spiritual path is very easy. Stop making the unreal real and allow the real to be real." Once we withdraw belief from our miscreations they will no longer exist. If they are not undone, we have not withdrawn belief from them. Denial and guilt keep unreality in place. When you deny something, you are afraid to look at it and thereby you make it real. When you feel guilty for your past you also make it real. Self-responsibility and looking without judgment allow all mistakes to be healed. *A miracle of the undoing of the unreal will happen for you when you want it above all else. Everyone is entitled to miracles.*

Forgiveness Means Nothing Happened To The Truth

Taking personal responsibility means that there is nothing to forgive and that is exactly what is meant by true forgiveness. If I did this to myself, it would make no sense to forgive someone else, someone outside of me, for there is no one outside of me. If you think someone did something to you and then you magnanimously forgive him, you expose to yourself that you do not believe you are all-powerful. Instead, you reveal that you believe you are both bodies and that you are separate, and you keep yourself locked in victim-victimizer consciousness. Nothing happens to you against your will.

The rapist could not have acted without my will, otherwise I am a victim and not all-powerful as I was created. I am all-powerful and when I know that, I will take great care to use my power wisely in the service of the healing of the unreal. Forgiveness recognizes that nothing happened to me that I did this to myself. The perpetrator merely acted as my consciousness permitted, therefore I have no reason to feel angry or upset with him. However, I need not choose his company. Baba says to avoid bad company. He is not a bad person, as he cannot be different from how he was created, but he must make a shift in consciousness where he is willing to align his actions with truth. I do not condemn him, but nor do I condone his hurtful actions. I hold his truth that he is innocent and that a shift in consciousness will restore him to wholeness. I want his salvation as I want the salvation of all my brothers and sisters everywhere, no matter what their history. That is forgiveness.

You have not understood this teaching if you use it to justify staying in an abusive situation. If, for example, a husband is beating his wife, she is right to recognize that she is doing this to herself, but she is not right to continue to place herself in harms way. This is not an exercise in taking a beating with a smile on your face. To forgive means that she wants him whole for his sake and does not seek retribution. She should not want him punished for his abusiveness. However, she should not let him continue to abuse her. If she does, she condones his actions and is not serving either herself or him. Unless he is willing to admit he has a problem and to seek help in correcting his behavior she needs to change her circumstances. She can turn to God for a nonviolent solution to any problem.

When your mind is healed you will have gratitude and appreciation for everyone, no matter what they have done to you. This is not to say that you should appreciate their unkind actions. To appreciate the rape experience would be to wish it on others. I saw its unreality. It is nothing. You are not being asked to appreciate what does not exist but only to see it for what it is. Anything anyone does in relation to you is either love or a call for love. When you see that, your only reasonable response is love. I expressed love by saying, "God bless you." I wanted the man healed, because I felt his pain, I felt his call for love and I used the experience to express love.

What about forgiving myself? The idea that anything happened to me, to who I am in truth, had to be healed and that is self - forgiveness. If you think something has happened and then you forgive yourself for allowing it to happen, you have made it real. It is not real if it has to do with victim-victimizer consciousness as that is of ego. Ego is unreal and so is anything that comes from it. Only God and God's love are real and being violated is not love. The incident was very real to me until I took personal responsibility for it and fearlessly looked at it with God, willing to face the truth. That is forgiveness. Forgiveness recognizes that nothing happened from the perspective of self-responsibility.

All violence, catastrophes, wars, earthquakes, droughts, famines, epidemics... are unreal. God did not create them. They are an out-picturing of mind allied with ego and that mind makes unreality. The unreal will be real until we let God heal our minds. You can stop making an unreal world whenever you want and then you will have a real experience as God wills for you. God is love, therefore it will be an experience of love.

You can experience love even in an earthquake, but if you could choose to experience love without the earthquake what would be your choice? Watch any tendency to justify disasters because of the 'good' you can find in them. You can find good without opposite too. Love can express itself just as readily without contrast. God made goodness and love without opposite. The world as we see it is the opposite of the world God made, thus it is not real.

When God created the world, He said, "It is good." He did not say it is both good and evil. What God has not created does not exist. Evil, darkness, fear, hatred, and suffering do not exist at all. We make them real by believing in them. We transform the unreal into the real by changing our minds. Baba teaches us to 'do good, be good and see good.' Goodness is the portal back to reality because goodness is real and thus restores reality to our minds.

See God In Everything

Illusions are not fearful, thus there is no need to escape them. They seem fearful only to the extent to which we fail to recognize them for what they are. Any attempt at escape cements their reality in our minds. Who would feel the need to escape nothing? It makes no sense. If the world is a projection of our minds and if it is unreal, then it remains unreal only as long as our minds are unhealed. When our minds are restored to wholeness, we will see a world transformed into a real world of peace, love, joy and abundance for all of humanity. Then heaven will be restored to earth and the Golden Age will be upon us as Baba has promised. It is not up to Baba to bring this about. It is up to you and me. God can only act at our invitation. He awaits our blessing to act toward the salvation of the world. We cannot escape the unreal world. Unreality must be transformed into reality through the transformation of our minds from ego consciousness to God consciousness, from fear to love. Once our minds are healed, we are again able to merge with God's mind and that is our true home.

Someone may conceptually know that the world is not real and that there is no world or suffering. It remains conceptual if they add, "So let's leave this place," or "I hate the world." With this idea, have they really understood the unreality of the world? If one hates the world for the injustices that are perpetrated here, have they stepped into personal responsibility for all that they see? When you have healed your mind, why would you feel the need to leave the world? The world is a projection of your mind. Until you wish it healed you do not want your mind healed. In wishing to escape, you cannot but make the unreal world real for you.

You are attempting to escape if you use drugs, alcohol or overindulgences of any kind. Overeating or sleeping too much are also attempts at escape. Death too is escape. You can even use religion, meditation, 'the highest teachings' or the idea of transfiguring your body into light as a plan for escape. All these are ways to sustain unreality when your purpose is escape rather than transforming the unreal back into the real. To be angry about unreal things that happen also keeps the unreal real for you. If you are detached from the world, disinterested, or complacent, but do not wish to have the world transformed back into the real world, your understanding of its unreality is also conceptual and you thereby still perpetuate unreality.

It is one thing to hear a teaching conceptually and to blindly apply it from that limited understanding. When you really want the truth, you will ask what to do with the knowledge that the world is not real. Only if you yearn with all your heart for the healing of the world and have a willingness to do whatever it takes to help restore it back to reality, have you understood that the world as we know it is not real. Only when you find yourself actively about the undoing of unreality through miracle-mindedness, have you truly understood the teaching that the world is not real. Then you have understood that the world is a projection of your mind and in wishing its wholeness you are wishing your own. All you really need do is change your mind about the world. *When enough minds become truly miracle-minded the shortening process will become immeasurable* for all humanity and the world will be saved.

Your mind is all–powerful and whatever you wish is what you get. Unreality comes from unreal thoughts which source from an unhealed mind. *Our meaningless thoughts show us a meaningless world.* We are responsible for the unreality of the world. The unreal is given reality and therefore only does it seem to exist. Take away reality from it and it is transformed into the real world. That is what a healed mind does by its very nature. It thinks real thoughts which heal the unreal, thereby revealing the real world. The real world was created by God and you and can be reabsorbed back into your mind at will. *You cannot do nothing and not change and expect the undoing of the unreal.* It is essential to watch your thoughts. Every thought has all the power of God behind it and is generating either reality or unreality. Unreal thoughts produce suffering for yourself and others. Give your impure thoughts to God to be transformed.

Dispassion And Discrimination

If you fall prey to the thought that it does not matter what you do as it is not real anyway, you only conceptually understand unreality. Conceptual understanding leads to misapplication of the teachings and gives license to entertain corruption. Some people take enough rope to hang themselves.

Sai Baba teaches that the bird of liberation flies with two wings, dispassion and discrimination. Let us use that teaching here to understand reality and unreality. Dispassion recognizes that the world is not real and that nothing you have done matters as past is past. Discrimination sees God in everything and holds everything sacred. Be a living example of who you are even in an unreal world, by leading a life of noble character. Then you are contributing to the possibility of everyone having a real experience. It does not matter what you have done in the past, but it matters very much what you do now. When you hold both dispassion and discrimination in your mind and apply that perfect balance in all undertakings in the world, you will have understood the difference between what is real and what is unreal.

You may have heard it said that the spiritual path is like walking the razor's edge. If you succumb to seeing only that all is unreal and that therefore it doesn't matter what you do, you fall off the one side. If you choose to see everything as real and worry or get upset whenever anything is lost, stolen or damaged, you have fallen off the other side. The spiritual athlete will stay on the razor's edge through equal-mindedness and will hold both ideas in perfect balance.

Abraham, in the Bible, demonstrated perfect balance between detachment and discrimination when God asked him to make a sacrificial offering of his precious child, Isaac. Discrimination sees only God in everything and is expressed through the deepest love. Abraham had such an all-consuming love for his beloved son. Detachment knows the unreality of the body. Abraham did not hesitate, but took his son up the mountain and after building the sacrificial altar, tied his son to it. He was about to snuff out this most cherished son's life when the angel of God stopped him and gave a fatted ram for the burnt offering instead. Abraham's unflinching obedience to God's will demonstrated that he was not blinded by attachment to his son. And of course God could never let him go through with sacrificing his son, for God is love.

Watch a tendency to become careless or complacent from a conceptual understanding of detachment. Abraham's passionate love, free of body consciousness, demonstrated true detachment and so he mobilized both wings of the bird of liberation. If only one wing is flapping, you are as well off as the person who has no dispassion or discrimination. You are going nowhere. Dispassion does not mean to stop caring because none of it is real anyway. That would be conceptual understanding of the unreal. Everything is a gift. You will understand exactly what to do with the idea of unreality if you sincerely want only the truth. For the mind that wants to understand, discerning the real from the unreal is not difficult. God only gives what is real. If you truly know that all your thoughts, words and deeds come from God, they will be pure, noble and full of charity and compassion because that is all that can come from God and that is real.

Give Unreality A Real Purpose To Undo It

Once you understand the nature of unreality, its source and sustenance, you will give all your energy toward its undoing. The unreal is transformed into the real by finding the real within it. Everything without exception contains God and should be treated with gratitude and used for a sacred purpose. I found a sacred purpose even in a traumatic experience. When you act with love toward anyone or anything you are being real and your reality transforms the unreal. A car is unreal. Do not allow it to give you your identity. Use it to transport God. Use it for holy purposes, not for pomp or show.

You are a God or Goddess and should act accordingly. Treat yourself with the utmost respect. Treat others as you wish to be treated. Then you will know that you truly believe you are who you are. Then you will know your reality and how to negotiate the world of illusion, and you will not be ensnared by it. Others are merely a reflection of yourself. If you treat everyone with love and make one exception, you do not love yourself. If you treat only one person with total honoring and respect, you love everyone truly and have understood your reality. Ego is an unreal idea. God is a real idea. Everything is simply an idea in your mind. Use your mind to discern which of the ideas you hold are real and which unreal.

Meaningless thoughts are not thoughts you think with God. When you do not think like God, you have not really thought at all. Delusional ideas are not thoughts but you can believe in them. If you have thought them, you will believe in them and in the results that come of them. This is the way they are sustained. Change your mind and you will see the world differently. The unreal world must be transformed into the real world. It can be saved because it is unreal. If the world of sickness, suffering and death were real, it could not be undone.

Baba says great saints sitting in temples and caves chanting the eternal OM are doing more for the world than all of our worthy causes combined. They have changed their minds from ego consciousness to God consciousness. That has a powerful and uplifting effect on the whole world. Enlightened masters have realized that the world is a projection of their minds. They use the power of their all-powerful minds for healing the planet. Most of them are quiet and we are unaware of their tremendous impact for good for the whole of humanity. *God has a plan for the salvation of the world and we each have our parts to play.* We must be willing to do our part. The world can be saved. With God all things are possible. *Until not one slave remains to walk the earth's surface is your salvation complete.* Everything and everyone is part of you and to neglect anyone is to remain unhealed.

Compassion For Suffering

Perhaps your learning has brought you to the conclusion that no one is suffering out there, as suffering is unreal and by acknowledging that there is suffering you make it real. Think of a moment when you felt excruciating pain. What was your reaction? I would imagine you sought relief. Hopefully you didn't punish yourself further by blaming yourself for your pain. Hopefully you were compassionate in your behalf and did not feel guilty, but nor did you deny your pain. Hopefully you asked for help and experienced a miracle. And when the miracle came and the pain simply vanished, weren't you grateful? This you can do for all those who suffer and do not yet know the power of their minds to heal themselves. You do not do this by teaching them the unreality of suffering but by allowing Spirit to move through you to heal.

True, suffering is not real, but it doesn't go away by denying its reality. As long as there is suffering in the world in any form, suffering is real for you and you have a responsibility toward its healing. Only when you have the deepest compassion for anyone who is suffering and want to do all you can to restore him or her to wholeness have you understood that suffering is not real. Because it is unreal, it can easily be undone when you no longer see a purpose for it. That is good news. If you use the teaching to become callous and uncaring about the suffering of others you simply have not understood the teaching. If you commiserate with those who are suffering rather than act toward their healing, you also make suffering real.

Everything Is Both Real And Unreal

As long as you find yourself in the world, you have to acknowledge that it is real for you. Do not flippantly see money, food or objects as unreal and thereby justify using them irresponsibly. Use everything for a sacred purpose. Use everything for the salvation of the world. When anyone hands Baba a letter with a postage stamp on it He removes the contents and tosses the envelope back. He is conveying that to waste even a postage stamp is unmindful. You do not need a postage stamp when you hand deliver a letter. Use everything with care, reverence and alertness. Make your life a Zen practice where all is done consciously and with loving alertness.

Baba says that everything we see is made up of name and form, which are unreal, but also of existence, brilliance and dearness, which are real. Everything is both real and unreal. He says, "Money comes and goes, morality comes and grows." Use money for charity and for worthy causes. If you use it carelessly or for worldly pleasures, because 'after all it is not real,' you misapply the teaching. Once Sai Baba made a gift of saris to a group of ladies. When He had finished there were a number of saris that had not been distributed. After a while someone noticed they were getting wet for no apparent reason. When he mentioned it to Baba, Baba said, "They are crying because I did not use them." Even cloth has consciousness.

Everything has consciousness within it and can be used either as a gift of God, or thoughtlessly as 'it is not real anyway.' Baba says of His body, "Ordinary body, used for a sacred purpose." Use your body for a sacred purpose and you will be true to yourself. Use your body in service to humanity, for giving and for pure and holy acts. Treat others with sacredness and gratitude. Do not have a careless attitude as their bodies are not real. This is a misapplication of the teaching that one's body is not real. 'Help ever, hurt never.' Helping others helps you to remember who you are because you are those you are helping and in helping them you help yourself. This helps you to expand beyond the belief that you are a body.

Do not adopt the attitude that you can eat what you like because your body is not real anyway. Eat healthy, pure, wholesome food that will nourish your body and contribute to its health and well-being. Baba says the food you eat affects your thoughts. If you eat animal products you will have animal consciousness. Eating of the plant kingdom contributes to a harmonious and peaceful state of mind. You must master your mind to be free. Eating consciously helps.

Food is sacred and should not be wasted. And keep a balance; don't become fanatical about not wasting. I know someone who won't throw anything away; even banana that is too ripe is put into the stomach. This is discernment without dispassion. It is good to be conscious and to take only what you need so that you don't waste food, but temper that by finding the middle way. When you become irrational about your need to hang on to things, or to avoid waste at all cost, know that you have not understood the unreality of name and form.

If your son crashes the car, a true response would demonstrate that you care about him and feel grateful he is alive, and you don't care about the car because it is not real anyway. At the same time do not foster a recklessness. You won't be troubled when something breaks or gets lost or stolen when you value only that which is real. When you have understood truly, you cannot be disappointed, for what is real can never diminish, but will only increase eternally. The Buddha recommended the middle way. Use common sense, neither letting the pendulum swing too far to the side of everything is real or too far to the side of nothing is real.

You Cannot Undo Unreality Without Changing Your Mind

As long as you make illusions you will believe in them because that is how you made them. You made them with the power of your belief. When you believe something you have made it true for you. *You cannot undo this by doing nothing and not changing.* As long as you find yourself in a body it is real for you so use it in the service of reality. Every loving thought, action or word is real and eternal. When you look upon the world with love you give it reality. *We have used the world to cover our love and the deeper we go into the blackness of the ego's foundation the closer we come to the love that lies hidden beneath it. Do not draw hasty conclusions, satisfying yourself with insubstantial evidence out of fear of uncovering the love and innocence that you have kept hidden beneath a veneer of hate or guilt.*

Unreality can deceive, but can also always be changed. Reality is changeless and does not deceive at all. If you fail to see beyond appearances, you will be deceived, for everything you see will change. But this is not reality. Reality's changelessness makes it real and keeps it separate from all appearances. It must transcend all unreality for it to be itself. We have brought reality to unreality. This has not made unreality real, though we have believed in it. Now we need merely stop accepting it as real and allow reality to be what it is.

Unreality can be transformed into reality when we let God undo the unreal by not insisting that what is unreal is real. God honors His child and if you want unreality to be real, He will not interfere. As long as there is ego, there will be unreality, for that is all that can come from alliance with ego, as ego is itself unreal. Your mind is so powerful that you can convince yourself of anything. Withdraw energy from unreality and stop insisting that it is real if you want to be free. Focus on what is real and allow that to be real. Use unreality for a real purpose. Then it becomes real.

Always be vigilant for the truth. Listen deeply to the truth within your own heart. Do not draw hasty conclusions from what you hear or read to suit yet another of ego's purposes. Go for depth of understanding. Ask for your own revelatory experience. Don't settle for anyone else's understanding, no matter how qualified they may present themselves. You already know the truth. Trust yourself. There is no one more qualified to teach you than God within. Sai Baba says, "If I tell you one thing and your heart tells you something else, always follow your heart."

See unreality for what it is. Do not fall prey to ego's cunning and viciousness or to its subtle seduction and deception. Yield not to temptation. Be pure and true to yourself. Follow your conscience. Remember that three simple steps overcome any nightmare. First, the nightmare is unreal. Second, you are doing it to yourself. Third, you can change your mind. Ask God for help. Once you take personal responsibility, you open the door to the healing of the unreal. Your mind is all-powerful, so use it with alertness and judiciousness. It can be used to support what is real or to perpetuate what is unreal. Be real even in an unreal world and you will have a real experience of love, peace and joy for yourself and for all those you meet.

Beloved Creator of reality, You know how to guide us through the land mine of unreality back to the safety of what is real. Please show us how to use everything both real and unreal in the service of reality. Direct us to use every experience to draw closer to reality. Help us discern between what is real and what is unreal and transform the unreal back into the real. May all sickness, suffering, death, lack and loneliness be undone in the truth that they were never Your will, thus never real. Help us to recognize how we are each responsible for all the unreality in our lives. We made a mistake. Our error did not make us bad, but it did make us wrong and produced endless needless suffering for ourselves and others. Now we bring all our errors happily to You for correction. Thank You that only reality is real.

May all beings in all the worlds be happy and blest, Amen.

Figure 5 — God Only Creates What is Real

Everything (Eternity)

Eternity	Life	Oneness
God-Dependence	Love	Freedom
Real	Truth	Non-judgment
Heaven	Peace	Creation
Innocence	Knowledge	All-Powerful

Nothing (time and space)

Time/space	**Happy Dream (Satva) God's solution - collapses time**
Ego-dependence	Letting reality be real
Unreal	Compassion for suffering, though suffering unreal
Hell	Letting unreality be undone thru self-responsibility
Guilt	Past is past because it has been healed
Death	**Nightmare (Rajo Guna) - makes time**
Fear	Making the unreal real: Sickness, suffering…
Untruth	Helplessly buffeted about by outer circumstances
War	Victim-victimizer paradigm
Ignorance	Sympathy for suffering, thus making it real
Separation	**Deep Sleep (Thamo) Ego's solution - freezes time**
Bondage	Deny suffering/ suppress, dissociate "Doesn't matter- un real"
Judgment	Blame someone else for your pain
Mis-creation	Out of touch with reality – bliss ninny
Powerless	"Suffering is God's will" – callous or blind
	"My neighbors' suffering is justified, deserved"

Direction of Consciousness Awakening

Chapter 6

Are You Ready to Trade In Hell for Heaven?

Oh, were all men wise
And in goodness did excel,
This world would be a paradise
But now it is a hell.

Father Katz

Invite God Back Into The World

How did the world come to be? Sai Baba says, "I created the world at my pleasure." ACIM says, "The world was made as a natural grand division of God; in its original connotation it included both the proper creation of man by God and the proper creation by man in his right mind." The Bible starts with, "In the beginning God created the heavens and the earth." All three sources give support for the world having been created by God. When God created the world it was heaven for it was created perfectly. Upon completion God surveyed His creation and pronounced, "It is good."

Is the world we live in today the world God created? If God only creates what is real, His world must be a real world, a world where nothing gets old, sick or dies. It must be a world where there are no wars, violence or conflict, but rather where brother lives with brother in joy, peace, love and harmony. It must be a world of goodness, abundance, breathtaking beauty, justice and fairness. In God's world there is no separation because we each recognize the oneness of all life. We all treat everyone as we would our very self, with the deepest love, respect and gratitude for we know the sacredness and holiness of everyone and everything.

In God's world we are truly free, we know everything, we are limitless, all-powerful and walk as equals with God and each other. There are no borders separating country from country. There are no cars, planes or space shuttles, for we know how to travel anywhere at will. There are no telephones or internet service, for we communicate with God and each other perfectly through our minds, as we know that minds are joined. No one needs to work for we are sustained by God's love. Food, clothing and shelter are available but not vital to our survival. Animals do not kill each other in order to survive for they too are sustained by God's love. It is a cruelty free world. We all know who we are. We are all enlightened, in love with God and every one.

That is the world I envision to be the real world. Can this ideal world exist? Can it exist without God? I believe it will again be our experience when we invite God back into the unreal world. *God loved the world so much that He gave it to us His children* for our enjoyment. The world was ours to do with as we wished. We, in our right minds used it to create with God, having God uppermost in our minds at all times. We have been given dominion over the animals. That means that their minds are not as powerful as ours, and our thoughts influence their thoughts and actions. They were created to be loved and cared for, not eaten by us or each other. That God created the world and us to create in it with Him is a beautiful idea. It was His gift of love to us. *We were created to create, to know and to love. God created the world, just as He created us, creating both as ideas in His mind. Ideas do not leave their source,* therefore you and I are still ideas in God's mind and so is the world. God did not change His mind about the world or about us, thus we and all the world are still as God created us, whole and perfect forever.

The World Was Remade To Hide From God

The world is also a projection of our minds. Your mind is all the power in the world and everything is within it, including the world. Most people believe they are bodies living in a world separate from them. They believe the world to be a place they live in, rather than that the world resides in them and reflects back to them what is in their minds, and is therefore not separate from them at all. After we made ego, we turned the world into a place in which to hide from God by convincing ourselves that the world was separate from us and God. Why would we want to hide from God?

Adam and Eve are in the garden, the world God created and they eat the forbidden fruit. God comes and they feel ashamed so they hide from Him. The forbidden fruit is the making of separation. In making separation they feel separate from God, unworthy to be in His holy presence because they feel guilty. So they feel the need to hide from God. They also fear God's wrath, and so remake the world into a place in which to escape from God.

We separated ourselves from the world and viewed it as outside of our minds, a place in which to reside as a body, which we convinced ourselves to be who we are. We can do anything we want in our minds. We can convince ourselves that we are having a real experience, but a reality check would indicate that things are not as they seem.

Did we make a completely different world from the one God created? I think we took the world God created perfectly and added time and space, sickness, suffering, death, fear, war, ignorance, bondage, darkness, powerlessness, victims and victimizers to it. We superimposed an unreal world onto the real world. That is what we did with the beautiful world God created for us. Should we feel guilty for the state of the world? No, we should not think we are bad, but we should feel responsible. All we added was not real therefore essentially, we did nothing. We did not affect the real world. If we had succeeded in altering God's creation, it would mean we are more powerful than God. Fortunately that is not true, thus the real world did not disappear. It is still here and we can see it when that is all we wish to see.

We did manage to make ourselves pretty miserable. We can admit that we were wrong. Once we are willing to be wrong about our purpose for the world as a place in which to escape from God, our purpose can change. That little willingness is all that is necessary for the unreal to be transformed back into the real. We can now own that our self-serving purpose for the world, which God so lovingly gave us, no longer serves us. When we let go of our illegitimate purpose, the world can be transformed back into the world God created. When enough of us want the world to be restored to wholeness and believe it possible, that will be the world we see.

If the world we see is unreal, it means we are thinking unreal thoughts. When we reenter the experience of the real world, it will be because our minds are again whole. We cannot leave the unreal world at will because it merely reflects back to us our unhealed minds. Only a healed mind can be reabsorbed into the mind of God. We cannot merge our minds with God's without healing the world first, for in healing the world we heal our minds and only a healed mind is a God mind. What is alike is one by definition. When you mix oil with water they separate. When you add water to water it does not separate. When you think like God you are one with God. When you do not, you are choosing separation from God and the world God created. When you know your oneness with the world you are thinking like God. Though we are always one, as long as we are convinced it is otherwise we will experience separation rather than oneness.

When you shift your consciousness from victim-victimizer consciousness to God consciousness the entire world will reflect that shift. I pray constantly for the salvation of the world. The healing of the world is always uppermost in my consciousness. When enough people hold that focus, the world will be saved. Baba says He only needs a handful of good people to save the world. When you join the great crusade to end hell for all humanity it brings salvation that much closer for every one.

Lord Indra Content To Be A Pig

In order to be convinced that the world needs to be saved, we have to see that the world as we find it today is not the world God created for us and is not the world we really want. Some people are content with the world just the way it is. Sai Baba tells the story of Indra the pig. Indra is really a great God in heaven who decides to come to earth to experience what it would be like to be a pig living in a pig family. He finds himself completely caught up in his pig life and is contentedly wallowing in the mud, having totally forgotten that he is a great God in heaven. One day sage Narada, passing by on his rounds, recognizes Indra and is horrified at Indra's plight. "Don't worry," he assures Indra, "I'll wield my discus and set you free." Indra responds, "Don't disturb me; I'm very happy here with my pig family."

We too have become comfortable and complacent with the little joys we find here. We are happy with our families, beautiful homes, monetary successes, prestigious jobs, swimming pools, shopping malls, computers and fancy cars. We think we're managing just fine without God. What we have settled for is making the world as we know it heaven. We call that contentment. We have merely succeeded in fooling ourselves into believing the unreal real. The world of sickness, suffering and death is not real, and to be content with its paltry offerings is to be sorely deluded.

We are sustained by God's love. The world can offer us nothing. It has nothing to give. It cannot offer us joy. Our joy is in doing our Father's bidding. It cannot offer us beauty. Our delight is in our Father's creation and that far surpasses anything these eyes can behold. It cannot offer us wealth, for our Father has given us everything. In this world death takes our family members and loved ones. Sometimes families are loving, but we may experience sibling rivalry and dysfunction. Our heavenly Father has given us all His children as eternally loving family. The world can offer us fame, glamour, popularity and specialness, but none of those lures hold a candle to a moment away from the world in sweet communion with our heavenly Father.

We don't need anything in order to commune with God. We don't need anything in order to love God and our fellowman. The world offers worry, fear, lack, anxiety, headaches, sickness… I don't want what the world has to offer. Do you? I do not want pleasure and pain. I want what God offers - eternal communion with Him in peace, harmony and love with all my brothers and sisters, and that is why we are here. We have a purpose in the world. It is to free the world and restore it to its original state of beauty, goodness and peace.

Divine Discontent

When Baba speaks of contentment as a spiritual quality, He is referring to being content with what we have in the world rather than continuing to amass more wealth or to compete with others in a worldly way. When you lead a life of impeccable character you will feel contentment and peace. But to be content to have the world of injustice remain exactly as it is, where people and animals experience sickness, suffering and terror is not contentment, but complacency. We are one with all of humanity and to be unmoved by the pain of others is to be dead. Such complacency can only come from having cut oneself off from one's humanity.

To yearn for a healed world of peace, love, joy and abundance for all comes from a divine discontent. It is a spiritual virtue to want the best for everyone and to recognize that what this world offers is not what you want for your brothers and sisters. God created everyone to be and have everything. We should want that for all His children and until that is everyone's lot, we should not be content.

Is it the mark of a spiritually advanced person to forget about the world and be perpetually absorbed in God consciousness? I confess I think a lot about the world. I do not think about what I can get from it. I think about how the world God created was intended to be a gift for us, His beloved children. I think about the disparity between that world and the world I am all too familiar with. I hear about drive by shootings, children killing other children in school yards, Muslim women not permitted to be educated or to expose any parts of their bodies without risking death, airplanes flying into the twin towers, Chinese students being brutally tortured to death for doing outlawed exercises, North Koreans being brainwashed by a heartless dictatorial regime, endless wars, rapes and murders since time began.

Yes, there is beauty and I do not overlook it. I love spectacular sunsets, cherry blossoms in spring, a huge pink fragrant rose, tiny yellow finches, the colors of the rainbow in a waterfall and the bald-headed eagle soaring across the deep blue sky. The only problem with all of the beauty is that everything I see has the mark of death upon it, including the resplendent dawning sun. Everything I see is going to die some day. That is the world we live in. Let's just look at it square on for a moment, because only when we are really in touch with this world's very sad plight will we yearn for something better. Our yearning is where destiny is altered. We are all-powerful. We will get what we want. If we are content with the world as it is, we will not will to change it. If we want a real world, then we must yearn for that, willing to do whatever we are divinely directed to do to bring that about. We cannot transform the world until we become aware that the world we live in is unreal by our choice.

We superimposed sickness, suffering and death onto a world that was created deathless forever. We live in the world as though we can manage without God. God created us to enjoy our company. We gave the world a false purpose when we made it into a place to hide from God. Is it possible to be happy with a false purpose? Some claim it is and that is how we find ourselves where we are. The status quo can content we only as long as we have not had a glimpse of our true happiness, our true state as God created us. We were created to be masters with our heads held high, our spirits soaring, carefree forever, bubbling over with laughter and delight, skipping over the moon, expressing tender loving kindness toward everyone and wanting the very best for all beings everywhere. At least that is my idea of what God had in mind when He created us and the world for us.

We have made the world a prison where we punish ourselves and toil to make ends meet and then die. We can change our minds. It can become a place where we can be set free. The world we see is what we gave it; nothing more than that. But though it is no more than that, it is not less. It is important. It is the witness to our state of mind, the outside picture of an inward condition. As you think, so will you perceive. You cannot change the world, but you can change your mind about the world. When you change your purpose for the world, the world will naturally reflect your changed purpose. We made the world to be a hiding place from God. Now let us invite God back into the world. Let us make it a place where we are again friends with God, a place where perfect communication is reestablished between ever loving Father and His eternally loving children.

Put Together The Individual And The World Is Healed

Sai Baba tells the story of a father and his young son whom he cherishes. The father has a study in which some very valuable papers are kept. The study is off limits to the lad. One day the father leaves the door ajar when he goes out for the day. The boy wanders in and as he does a gust of wind wafts one of his father's precious papers off the desk onto the floor. Not knowing its value, the son plays with the paper, making a hat out of it and then a ship. As he continues to enjoy himself the valuable paper starts to get worn and tears into little pieces.

When his father returns home he immediately recognizes the torn paper as his priceless map of the world. Though he loves his son, he is not at all happy about this state of affairs. He says, "Son, you have torn the world into pieces. You are responsible for putting it back together." The son loves his father and wants to please him, but doesn't have a clue how to put the world back together. Just then a wind comes up again and one of the pieces blows onto its back side. The boy recognizes it to be a human hand. Then another piece flips over and the boy sees the nose and eye of a face. He realizes that there is a human being on the other side and everyone knows how to put the individual back together. Now he knows how to proceed. As soon as he finishes putting the human being back together, he turns the paper over and to his delight discovers that the world is again back together.

We tore the world apart, thus we are responsible for putting it back together. But we don't know how to proceed. We can only heal ourselves.

We can heal our minds by transforming our lives into lives of goodness and purity, thereby living the wholeness and perfection God created us to be. When we do that, we put ourselves back together and simultaneously the world is healed.

If everyone decided to be good, could there be evil in the world? Isn't all the suffering in the world due to injustices, selfishly and heartlessly perpetrated? Goodness overcomes evil within ourselves and others. If there were no leaders wanting to be powerful at others' expense, wouldn't we have a safe world? If everyone wanted to share their wealth instead of hoard it, wouldn't there be enough food for all the starving children in the world? Wouldn't goodness restore wholeness? It all starts when we heal ourselves, for the world is a projection of our minds. With enough goodness, evil will not be able to be sustained.

As heaven and earth become one, even the real world will vanish from our sight. The end of the world is not its destruction but its translation into heaven. We transform the world we live in into the real world by changing our minds and hearts into thinking and acting with love, goodness and piety. We are free to leave the real world at will. All we can do in the unreal world is heal it and thereby transform it into the real world. We have to put our mess in order. We do have a responsibility for the world. It is an overwhelming task, but with God all things are possible. The transformation of our hearts transforms the world.

Peace Depends On Wanting Everyone's Freedom

When Al Drucker first came to Baba he had been active in the nuclear missiles race, and so anxiously asked Baba about the world. Baba said to him, "The world is not your business, sir. Realize who you are and the world is saved." He was directing Al away from his fear. If you are fearful about the state of the world, you cannot help to save it. Baba also instructs us to forget the world. I trust He means to forget about it as a place to find happiness. This idea does not conflict with wanting peace in the world. Unless you want peace in the world, you do not want it for yourself, for the world is an extension of yourself.

I love the world. I do not love it for what it can give me, for I know it can give me nothing. I love it for what I can give to it, for I can give it everything simply by wanting it to be a place where everyone is safe, happy and loved. In that wish, I heal my mind. I know who I am when I wish for the happiness of all beings, because all are myself and until all are restored to wholeness, I am not free. Your mind is all-powerful. To want the salvation of the world is the way the world is saved. When that is your passionate desire you will be shown the role God has assigned you. You will be shown what to do and where to go. It all starts with your desire to know who you are, for in knowing yourself, you know your function.

In my late 20's, I had a very lucid dream in which a number of people were on the deck of a huge boat while I was flying overhead. I was soaring, free, unfettered, so very happy. But then they noticed me up there while they were stuck below. They let me know they didn't think it was fair that I was flying while they were grounded. I tried to communicate to them to leave me be, that I didn't want to be distracted. They couldn't receive my communication so I came closer and as I did they started grabbing at me and I felt body conscious and a heaviness.

Not liking the feeling, I pulled away and was again flying overhead, but now I was aware of their bondage and could not content myself to be free while they were not. My peace was disturbed. So I understood that I had no choice but to be available to my brothers and sisters who wanted to learn to fly. In that moment the scene changed to a bed of lotuses. I gently settled on top of them and a feeling of deep peace pervaded my whole being. The lotus symbolizes being in the world without being affected by the world. It is a stunning flower that grows up out of the mud, yet remains untouched by it. Gently landing on the surface of the lotus pond signified to me to be in the world but not of it.

Should I have stayed up there flying while my brothers and sisters were unable to join me as they did not know how? My heart is not made of stone. How is it possible to see suffering and do nothing about it? It is one thing to see people in a pit and to jump in with them and thereby get stuck. That is sympathy. It is another to see them caught in a pit and to throw a rope down and pull them out. That is compassion. If you were passing by a pit and people were stuck down there and were asking, "Please help us out," could you just walk by?

Trying To Escape The World Makes It Real

You cannot have the experience of heaven by escaping the world. One afternoon a friend who I met at the ashram told me her story. She and her husband have two beautiful children. The problem was that her husband drank heavily and there was never enough food on the table or money to pay the rent. She was finding it harder and harder to tolerate his addiction. Her children were totally supportive and understanding thus she had managed to cope with the situation up to this point but was really at her wits end.

One night as she was sitting in front of her altar she was given a vision. She saw a band of four renunciates who had left the world in search of truth. They had gone to the Himalayas. There was one among them who was not leaving from a pure place but rather harbored a disdain for the world. The other three saw that was not the way to freedom and out of their love agreed to come back into the world to teach the confused one how to leave the world in love.

So they reincarnated and were back in the form of this family. The drinking husband was actually the wisest of the four and the other two were pure in their relationship to the world. It was she who was not yet free. When she recognized the tremendous love the other three had for her to be willing to give their lives and return for her sake, her heart welled up with gratitude and love. Needless to say, this love transformed her husband into a responsible father to her children. He stopped drinking the moment she got the message. The world must not be escaped, but rather transformed through the transformation of our hearts and minds. She transformed her situation through love. Love transforms the world back into heaven.

I spent some time in the Himalayas in the summer of 2002, to be with those great souls who have chosen to renounce the world. I met very few true holy men and women on my pilgrimage. Some were just taking on identities as renunciates. Many had left the world because they couldn't function and some were smoking constantly to blow out their lungs so they could 'reach God more quickly.' I don't think so. We won't want to escape the unreal world when we truly know its unreality. Then we will also know that it is up to us to transform it back into the real world and we will be willing to do whatever it takes to restore heaven to earth.

The Kingdom Of Heaven Is Within

Heaven is not a place or condition. It is a state of mind. It is an awareness of perfect oneness. Many great teachers urge us to look within for the kingdom of heaven. Baba says everything is within. There is nothing out there in the market place of the world. God is within. When we think of God, when we repeat God's Holy Name, we are within. When we do not look for happiness in the world, we are within and that opens the door to a heavenly world. When we trust God for everything we are within. *The joy of heaven has no limit and is increased with each light that returns to take its rightful place within it.* Heaven is the world as God created it. It is our home. It is who we are.

Here is a small example from the Jewish tradition: Jacob, a poor family man, was living in a small hamlet in Russia. He was pestered every night by a recurring dream in which he kept being told that there was a treasure buried under a bridge in occupied enemy territory. To go there would be very dangerous and if he were caught he would most certainly be thrown in jail. He feared venturing forth and yet was haunted constantly by the prospect of abundance. Finally, overwhelmed by the possibility, he decided to take the risk and late one night when all his family was fast asleep he slipped out and started the long journey. He managed to cross the border unnoticed and walked till he recognized the exact bridge in his dream. He was thrilled and started digging. Just as his shovel hit something hard, a patrol above noticed him and he was arrested. Under interrogation, he told all.

The interrogating officer started to laugh as Jacob finished his woeful tale. "You foolish man. I too have a recurring dream which tells me that my treasure is buried hundreds of kilometers from here under some bricks, behind a stove in the home of a very poor man named Jacob. Do you think that I am so stupid as to follow that dream? If you go straight home and stop your crazy nonsense I will release you, but don't let me ever see you here again." Relieved, Jacob ran back home. When he reached his simple dwelling he looked under the bricks behind his wood stove and to his wonder struck eyes beheld an incomparable treasure. The treasure was right in his own home. The kingdom is right in your own heart. You need not go anywhere to find it.

Sai Baba tells an anecdote with a similar message: 'A woman who was doing some needlework at dusk lost her needle. As there wasn't enough light in her house, she went out to the street lamp to look for it.' How could she find her needle outside when she had lost it in her home? All she need do is wait for the light of day and she will find the needle where she lost it. We go to various teachers and spiritual retreats in search of what we think we do not possess, but when we finally find it, we realize that it was always with us. We realize the truth when we purify our lives enough to see clearly. Then we discover that we have enough light to find what we are looking for right where we are.

Spiritual offerings which point you inward are true offerings. Be wary of any offerings that promise to do it for you or to give you something that you don't already have. Everyone can be your savior by showing you the way. If you depend on others to do it for you, you reduce your worth in your own mind. Once a friend was selected for an interview with Sai Baba. Inside she protested that He never looked at her. He replied tenderly, "That is because I want you to look within."

Bring Heaven To Earth

In the Bible Jesus says that heaven and earth shall pass away. In ACIM he explains that to mean that heaven and earth will become one. In a little booklet, entitled 'Open Secrets' by Lami Shapiro, a wise old Jewish Rabbi points out to his young student that heaven and earth must be reestablished as one. He does this by comparing the tower of Babel story with the Jacob's ladder story in the Bible. In the tower of Babel story, the people of earth unite to build a tower with its top in the sky in order to make a name for themselves. God does not look favorably upon the project and causes the people to speak in different tongues. With communication severed, the project comes to a halt. The people were attempting to reach heaven so as to escape earth. They were not looking within for the kingdom of heaven. They were trying to escape the unreal and were thereby making it real. You cannot attain heaven by trying to go somewhere else.

By contrast, in the Jacob's ladder story, Jacob has a dream in which a ladder is set on the ground with its top in the sky and the angels of God are going up and down on it. The ladder is symbolically linking earth with heaven. God looks lovingly upon Jacob's ladder. Heaven and earth are being united. The angels are moving in both directions. We have to bring heaven to earth rather than try to reach heaven by escaping earth. Instead of making the unreal real, Jacob's ladder is symbolic of the process of transforming the unreal back into the real.

In the case of the tower of Babel the unreal world was given reality because it was being excluded. You would only reject what you thought was real. In the story of Jacob's ladder, reality was restored to the unreal world through inclusion. If you think you can only attain heaven after you die, you are attempting to escape the world. Christians and Muslims embrace and fiercely defend this belief. It is a lie. The kingdom of heaven is within. We have to make the world heaven and we do that by standing still in the nightmare and asking to be shown the way, rather than by trying to escape either now or in the future.

This world is not real. There is a real world and the two worlds will never meet. Nothing and everything are mutually exclusive. However, watch a tendency to justify deviations from purity on the premise that what you do in an unreal world does not affect the real world, which is always available. What is overlooked in this misapplication of the teaching is that the real world can only be accessed through a mind that has real thoughts. Real thoughts lead to real actions. You have to be real in an unreal world to reach the real world. That is the portal back to reality. The world is a projection of our minds and we do not have two minds. There is only the real world. It is our mind that has superimposed a world of unreality onto the real world by thinking unreal thoughts. *When you change your mind, the world must change accordingly.*

At the close of each chapter there is a prayer which ends with "May all beings in all the worlds be happy and blest." This reference to multiple worlds includes the physical world, the mental world and the world of Spirit. Besides the physical world, there are astral worlds and heavenly worlds, but these various realms are merely reflecting different states of consciousness and are not completely different worlds as such.

You cannot escape the world because that would be to leave an idea that is in your mind. That is impossible as *ideas do not leave their source.* We have to heal the world by healing our minds. Then heaven and earth become one, and even the real world will vanish. *The end of the world is not its destruction, but its translation into heaven. Heaven is beyond the real world. You are a holy child of God and heaven is within you. You and heaven are one. Remember this and the whole world is free.*

My experience of the real world is that it is a heavenly place. I have had glimpses of it and would describe my visions as of a formful formlessness. There is only light, but it has shape, which is eternally vibrant and breathtakingly beautiful. There is life without opposite with ever increasing brilliance, vitality, glory, holiness and sacredness. Heaven is both the real world and a state of mind wherein there is perfect peace, oneness, joy, harmony, knowledge and perfect communion with God and all our brothers and sisters. When our minds are healed, the world will be heaven and a healed mind can again merge in God. That is a state beyond even the heavenly world, but we can only get there through the healing of our minds, reflected in a healed world.

Never Underestimate Even The Smallest Act Of Kindness

Baba says that His devotees in temples and caves are doing more for the world than all our worthy causes combined. He also encourages service to mankind. Service purifies our hearts. When you are kind to another you send a message to your subconscious, 'See I'm not such a bad guy.' You heal your idea about yourself as guilty and change your mind to see your innocence. At the same time the person you serve feels, 'That was really kind. I must not be such a bad guy.' So you both benefit by being relieved of guilt. In truth you cannot give anyone what he does not already possess for we were all created to be and have everything. Freedom from guilt however should not be minimized. That release heals and nothing else can heal. When you think you have something that another does not have, you are not serving, but rather making inequality real. Let your service lead to joining or oneness. Then you are serving in the true spirit of giving.

Be grateful for any opportunity to be helpful. Make your life a joy to others by sprinkling loving touches of kindness and tender acts of beauty along the road you travel. Every kindness, every loving gesture and helpful deed serves everyone. When you help one you help all, because we are all one. Don't get discouraged and think that your small gesture doesn't make a difference. It does. And don't think that you are not worthy or that they are not worthy. Everyone is worthy because of who they are. We were all created by God exactly like Him. Baba says, "If you want God, you deserve Him." We deserve God because of who we are. We know who we are because we were created to know everything forever. You will remember who you are once you trust God to be your Source. And when you know who you are, you will know your function. When you know your function, your life has purpose and that will increase your joy immensely. Your role is vital to the salvation of the world.

"Each of you has a unique and valuable part to play in this lifetime. This planet has a purpose in the great galaxy in which it is held. That purpose is now unfolding before your eyes. The time is approaching when all humanity will live in harmony. That time will be here sooner than one expects. Before it arrives be prepared for whatever is needed to reveal to every living thing the true purpose of existence. It is not what anyone alive can imagine. It is not something that one can try to aspire to. It is beyond all comprehension. Its beauty is magnificent beyond all dreams."

Sai Baba

Thank you Heavenly Father for creating the world real, perfect and good. Thank You that Your world has not gone somewhere, but can be our experience whenever we so choose. Thank You that the world we made to hide from You is not real. We invite You back into the world with all our hearts. Please come and restore Your opulence to our barren home, that we may live as You ordained. Let the heavens be reflected on the earth now that the earth may return unto heaven.

May all beings in all the worlds be happy and blest, Amen.

Figure 6 – Heaven is Your Home

Everything (Eternity)

Eternity	Life	Oneness
God-Dependence	Love	Freedom
Real	Truth	Non-judgment
Heaven	Peace	Creation
Innocence	Knowledge	All-Powerful

Nothing (time and space)

Time/space	**Happy Dream (Satva) God's solution - collapses time**
Ego-dependence	Look for heaven within
Unreal	Accept my role in God's Plan for salvation of world
Hell ———	Divine discontent - yearn for healing of world
Guilt	World is a place where we are friends with God and all
Death	**Nightmare (Rajo Guna) - makes time**
Fear	Experience the hell of sickness, suffering, death
Untruth	Use world to hide from God
War	Make world real by trying to escape
Ignorance	Ensnared in world of pleasure and pain
Separation	**Deep Sleep (Thamo) Ego's solution - freezes time**
Bondage	Content to let world of death be heaven/
Judgment	"World is better than what God can offer"
Mis-creation	Out of touch with reality – bliss ninny
Powerless	Make world real by saying this is all there is
	"Impossible to heal world - no use trying"
	Distracted by worldly possessions

Direction of Consciousness Awakening

Chapter 7

Are You Ready To Be Innocent Instead of Guilty?

To seek enlightenment without purity or compassion
Is akin to lighting a lamp without wick or oil. It cannot be done.
                                                            Sai Baba

God Created The Good, The Beautiful And The Holy

The Bible begins with, 'In the beginning God created the heavens and the earth.' Upon completion, God said, "It is good." He did not say His creation was both good and evil. God created goodness without opposite. The way to the experience of both good and evil came through the tree of the knowledge of good and evil which God advised Adam and Eve to leave alone. Why would God make the tree available if it wasn't advisable? Because God's kingdom is freedom.

We can choose to experience evil, but it won't be a real experience and there is nothing redeeming about it. In order to survive, ego needs you to experience evil so you will feel guilty. The only way ego can get you to feel guilty is by convincing you to do 'evil' deeds. In truth evil is impossible as it has nothing to do with God and God's creation. Ego, guilt, and evil are all on the same team. Any time you do what your conscience tells you not to do, ego wins. The knowledge of evil came with the making of ego and as ego has no foundation, neither does evil. Look at it calmly and it must disappear. It stands on the tiny platform, "What ever you do, don't look at me."

God created you innocent and that means you are innocent forever. There is nothing you can say or do that will change your innocence in any way. Your innocence is guaranteed by God. What about original sin you may ask? Original sin is the making of ego. In the Garden, Adam and Eve choose to eat of the fruit of the ill-advised tree and as soon as they do, they become aware of evil and so gain the knowledge of both good and evil, where as before they only had the knowledge of good. In order that Adam justify blaming Eve, he needed to perceive her as evil. In that moment evil entered his mind. Eve needed to perceive the serpent as evil and thereby she also allowed evil into her mind.

There are those who believe sex to be the original sin. That idea would lead you to feel guilty every time you made love with your partner and is the cause of much needless suffering. It is ego's trap to throw you off the trail of it as the cause of all guilt and subsequent punishment for crimes that were never committed. In the Bible God instructed man to be fruitful and multiply.

As making ego means making your own source to replace God, nothing happened simply because God is not replaceable. There was no original sin. Adam and Eve committed no crime and had no reason to feel guilty. God, goodness and innocence are all on the same team. Before the making of ego, Adam and Eve were only eating of the Tree of Life, which offered them the knowledge of good. God recommends goodness.

Though they did nothing wrong, they thought they had. Their belief caused them to feel guilty. Had they laughed at their mistaken idea it would have ended there. They did not laugh. They took the idea that they could actually make their own source seriously. As their minds are all-powerful, they have the power to convince themselves of anything they choose. For them, ego had taken on existence. Once given life, it was determined to continue to exist and the only way its existence could be sustained was through convincing them of the reality of evil and of guilt. The more guilt, the more time is needed to balance the scales and the more time ego gets to survive at their expense, the idea of karmic consequences. Balancing the scale seems fair as long as they don't look too carefully. You will only feel you deserve to be punished for a crime you can be convinced you actually committed. Ego is determined to convince you that you did something you never did. For the past 10,000+ years it has been extremely successful.

All suffering is self-inflicted punishment for crimes that were never committed and that is a great tragedy. We have always been innocent and worthy of only God's beneficent love forever. Ego wants us to think we are unworthy and deserving of punishment. It is a lie. Impurity is impossible for any creation of God. You cannot be guilty. You can err, but error is correctable. You cannot sin, for sin is not correctable and would mean that you could alter God's creation, which He created unalterably perfect. The only error ever is the idea that you could be different from how you were created.

Maybe you wonder why God cast Adam and Eve out of the Garden. Maybe it wasn't God who sent them away but rather their feelings of guilt. Maybe the angels blocking their reentry were merely reflecting back to them their own minds, as they are all-powerful. God cannot oppose their will. It was their will to leave the garden because they felt ashamed and feared God's wrath. They simply did not know God in that moment. God is always only love. Love does not punish or separate. God created us to enhance His joy. He wasn't angry with Adam and Eve. What did He have to be angry about? Why should He want to send them away? They felt guilty because they thought they had pushed God aside. He cannot be pushed aside as He created us to be one with Him forever. Nothing happened in truth. Adam and Eve's story is our story. We have always been innocent though we have convinced ourselves otherwise.

We could never do anything to become guilty and yet we have all pled guilty to crimes we never committed. We have all put ourselves on death row. We have all agreed to sickness, suffering and loss because we thought we deserved it. Whatever is happening to you, you have agreed to. Nothing happens by accident. We do not deserve the untold suffering that we have all endured. None of it has served us in any way. We only ever deserved to be happy beyond measure because that is what God wills for us. He created us innocent forever. We only ever deserve to experience God's infinite unconditional love. We deserve God right now. We don't have to wait. "If you want Me, you deserve Me," says Sai Baba.

Adam blamed Eve when God asked him what happened. He blamed someone outside of himself because he thought he had actually done something bad. He felt guilty and projected his guilt onto someone else. That made his error real. Eve also felt guilty and projected her guilt out onto the serpent. They listened to ego's solution to the problem of guilt. As soon as they projected the guilt out by blaming someone else, they did not feel their guilt, but they still felt ashamed. Projecting guilt is how you keep it. They still felt tainted, but they were not aware of why, due to disowning their guilt. Ego doesn't want you to stand still when you feel guilty or you will discover that there is no reason to feel guilty and you will correct your lack of love that produced guilt.

In Adam and Eve's minds a tiny mad idea had been entertained and become a reality. As it was not a real idea, it was merely an idea of lack. Real ideas are creative and rich. Unreal ideas such as making your own source lack truth and substance. When you see the problem as a lack, you will desire to have the lack filled and then God can fill it by showing you the unreality of ego and the problem will be solved. Your mind will then be healed. Each and every error is a replay of the original error. All of time is going on all the time. Whenever you project guilt out by blaming someone else, you keep it. You may not be aware of this dynamic, which is no problem for ego, because it still gets to mete out punishment, to which you meekly agree. Be bright and honest. Let your errors be corrected. Listen to God's solution to the problem, not ego's. It is so very easy when you are willing to be wrong about your mistakes.

Be Good, See Good, Do Good

Baba makes quite an issue of behavior. He is constantly urging: Be good, see good, do good; Always be obliging; Love all, serve all; Help ever, hurt never; and watch your words, actions, thoughts, character and heart for purity. Why is behavior important if we are innocent no matter what we do? *What you do attests to what you believe.* When you behave in alignment with the goodness that you were created to be, you acknowledge who you are and you will know yourself. If you behave in a fashion that does not become the purity and holiness that you are, you cannot but feel guilty, thereby adding time to your sentence. You will feel guilty because to act counter to holiness means to listen to ego.

Don't think that acting impurely has no effect. You will punish yourself, even though you may not be in touch with your guilt. It is easy to be perfect, because perfection is who you are. Don't think there are forces outside of you forcing you to be less than good, kind and loving. Only when you step into personal responsibility for all your actions can you choose for your perfection. There is nothing outside of you. You are all powerful. There is no force that can prevent you from being perfect if you so choose. All actions either confirm your innocence or lead you to conclude you are guilty, thus imperfect. There is no way around this. You are free to think any thoughts you choose. Behavior emerges from thought. First you think your action and then you act. Your behavior reflects back to you who you think you are. All power is yours. You are in control of what you think, say and do. Be noble in thought, word and deed, for that is your truth.

When you don't act nobly you won't feel good about your actions and if you don't immediately recognize your lack and give it to God to correct, you automatically give it to ego. When you have acted impurely you will feel inclined to keep God out of your life out of shame. It would be much easier if your character were impeccable. Your life would be much cleaner, more wholesome, sane and peaceful. But whether you choose to behave in alignment with the truth of who you are or in alignment with ego's idea of how you should behave, you will not change the fact that you are innocent. Guilt is impossible. You can be wrong, but you cannot be guilty. By the same token, only one who leads a Godly life will not feel guilty. You are responsible for your behavior. We need not receive consequences for the past. We need merely turn over a new leaf now and our past is wiped out without a trace. To err is human, but to leave errors uncorrected is stubborn and foolish. Don't beat yourself up when you make mistakes. Just correct your errors. If you hurt someone, tell them you're sorry and determine to treat them as the Goddess or God that they are from now onwards. Strive to your maximum capacity for excellence and leave the results of your efforts to God.

Goodness Averts Self-Destruction

In the Bible, God requested Jonah to go to the people of Nineveh to persuade them to repent of their sins. Jonah, fearing that his message would not be received, decided to drown himself in the sea instead. But God was not so easily refused and sent a whale to swallow Jonah up and spit him out on dry land. This convinced Jonah that he had no recourse but to deliver God's message. When he urged the people to mend their ways and turn to God, they heard him and were glad. They did want to repent.

Why should God care for their repentance if He knew they were not guilty no matter what they may have done or if He was going to send a savior to deliver them from the burden of their sins? God loves everyone and intercedes where invited. If we are on a fast track toward annihilation He will attempt to reach us with His message of goodness and perfection so we can be saved. So great is His love.

In the case of Sodom and Gomorrah, two cities headed for self-destruct, Abraham pleaded with God to intercede for 50 good people. God said He could, but that there were not 50 upstanding individuals in all of Soddom and Gomorrah. Abraham then pleaded for salvation if there were 40, then 30, 20 and finally just 5 God loving souls. Had there been just 5 good people, God could have saved both cities. There were not even 5 beings of noble character in all of Sodom and Gomorrah and so their corruption caused their annihilation.

Only a handful of souls willing to lead lives of goodness is needed to save the whole world. The power of truth is much stronger than the power of untruth. Only a little light is needed to brighten a dark room. A few good people can transform much evil. Using the hundredth monkey idea, once there is a critical mass willing to do whatever is necessary, including wake up in service of the salvation of the world, the world will be saved. It need not wait on everyone changing their minds. It will be easier and easier to change as more and more minds hold the true consciousness of oneness, purity, holiness and love for all. It all starts with you changing your mind and acting in ways that are true to the goodness, beauty and holiness that God created you to be for all eternity.

The Road To Hell Was Paved With Good Intentions

When you want with all your heart to be in alignment with who you are, you will be shown all you need to know. Turn to God to guide your every step along the way to purity, holiness and goodness. Without God's constant guidance, even the best of intentions may be misdirected. Once a Sai Baba devotee, Noah, gave money to a village head in India for drilling a well. This seemed like a good idea, as then the villager could grow two crops per year instead of just one and the whole village would stand to profit. What was overlooked was that the money required to drill the well was a huge sum for that villager and it could easily corrupt him.

In fact the villager absconded with the money just as soon as Noah turned his back. That money created jealousy in the village and led to fights with knives. Some individuals were badly injured. Sai Baba called Noah in for an interview and scolded him soundly. Then He manifested a tooth colored lingam (egg shaped sacred object) for him to wear around his neck. The lingam got darker and darker till finally it was pitch black. One night it disappeared and Baba told Noah in the next interview that he didn't need it any more. It was used to absorb the 'bad karma' that was incurred from doing a 'good deed.'

It is wise to seek guidance in our hearts in relation to everything we do or do not do because we have so lost touch with our truth that we do not know what is in our own best interest. Fortunately we really can't go too far wrong as long as we are willing to be corrected.

If you are unwilling to correct your error, you demonstrate that you believe you are guilty, for your unwillingness comes from alliance with ego and you will punish yourself harshly though needlessly. Be willing to do whatever it takes to come back on the mark. If you have asked ego to be your lawyer, you have pled guilty, but you can have the case appealed at any time and the high court will dismiss the charges against you. You will only appeal to the Supreme Court when you find yourself worthy. It is alliance with ego that makes us believe ourselves unworthy. Noah was obviously willing to correct his error, even though he was not aware that he had committed an error at the time. When we are willing to be wrong, we will be shown whatever we need in order to come back into alignment with our truth. We don't need to know anything. We need only be willing to be wrong and to have error corrected. Then we will be restored to the moral clarity to make decisions that are in the best interest of all.

There are those who feel guilty, though not responsible. Until you step into personal responsibility for your errors, you will not be motivated to change your mind. As soon as you see the unreality of your errors you will be willing to be responsible for them. As soon as you accept responsibility, you will be motivated to bring your behavior into alignment with who you are. There are many closet drinkers, secret relationships and other hidden parts of people's lives. There are no secrets in the truest sense, and if you need to be secretive, know that you have a problem. Until you own your problem, you will not be motivated to seek help in correcting your error. As soon as you take personal responsibility for your particular set of circumstances, help is available.

Be holy in the presence of God or you will not know that you are there. What is unlike God cannot enter His mind, because it was not in His thought and so does not belong to Him. Your mind must be as pure as His to know what belongs to you. As soul you are pure forever, but you can choose to think you are not pure and if you do, you keep yourself away from God's holy presence. Only in holiness can you merge with God's mind. Only like can merge with like and the mind of God is wholly pure. When pure you will attract God, and when impure you will bind yourself to the world. Only holiness can content you and give you peace. Holiness means the end of guilt. You do not have to have only holy thoughts and behaviors in order to know your holiness, but you do have to want only holiness.

Evil Acts Without Consequences?

Once Ramana Maharshi, an Indian saint of the last century, was asked, "Is it possible under any circumstances for a murderer to escape punishment?" Ramana answered, "If he can act without guilt he will not be punished." It is guilt that leads to punishment and nothing else. If we could act without guilt, whatever we did, we would not suffer consequences. However, if you act hurtfully toward anyone, you are acting with ego, as Spirit would only direct you to act lovingly. When you act with ego, it is driven to produce guilt, without you recognizing your guilt, as it depends on guilt for its survival. You would not participate in guilt producing actions if you were aware that they would lead to guilt and subsequent punishment. You are treading on thin ice if you choose unrighteous or unkind actions, even if you are not in touch with guilt. You cannot be unkind to your brother and walk away without feeling guilty.

When you feel guilty, your ego has violated the laws of God, but you have not. Only when you change your mind about those your ego has hurt, can you be released. As long as you feel guilty, ego is in command, because only ego can experience guilt. You can always change your mind and become truly helpful. God is praised whenever any mind learns to be wholly helpful. The truly helpful are invulnerable, because they are not protecting their egos, thus nothing can hurt them. You can only ever be hurt by ego.

Be Carefree, Not Careless

Perhaps you will be tempted to think that it does not matter what you do, as your innocence cannot be affected. But by now surely you are beginning to recognize this as the voice for ego and not for God. Never underestimate ego's determination to preserve itself. Carelessness will only lead to needless suffering. It matters very much what you do. Your every action is either collapsing or making time. Don't feel guilty for anything you do and do only that for which you know you will not feel guilty. Strive to your maximum capacity for excellence and holiness, and at the same time, leave the results to God. Resist the temptation to feel guilty for outcomes that fall short of your expectations. Be ever vigilant against ego's attempts at making you feel guilty.

There is story of a Sufi master whose disciples marveled at his purity and freedom from ego's clutches. One day they asked him, "Master, how is it that you have managed to overcome illusion? We find ourselves caught in illusion's trap every day. Please tell us your secret." The master replied, "It is not as you think. I am ever vigilant. Not until my last breath will I relax my keen awareness of ego's every attempt to reestablish its hold over me." Baba says there are those who have become fully awake who then fall through the cracks again because they are not vigilant against ego's slipperiness in its determination to live. Baba reminds us to be carefree, not careless. Good overcomes evil. Innocence removes guilt. Be the innocence that you are in truth.

Guilt is very hard to get in touch with because to do so would jeopardize ego's hold. Usually we quickly project guilt out and justify our projections by convincing ourselves that our lack is someone else's fault, or we don't feel guilty because we didn't get caught. We conclude that our behavior didn't make us guilty and are bewildered when we are struck with a heavy dose of negative consequences sometime in the future. There are no victims. We do reap the results of our minds.

Be ever vigilant. Ego is an idea that things could happen to you against your will. You are all powerful. There are no accidents. Nothing happens to you but by your will. You may not be aware of the bargain you made but that is only because ego has convinced you to think you do not know your own mind. There is much that has been lost from conscious awareness but can again be retrieved when we so choose.

Actions Speak Louder Than Words

It is very easy to espouse the 'highest teachings' and not be a living example. If you say one thing and do another yours is mere conceptual understanding. That is just another way in which ego is attempting to foil your plans for return to innocence. Some people say it doesn't matter how a teacher behaves, but I look for the teacher who walks his talk. Anyone can talk. Baba's dictum is, "My life is my message." His behavior is impeccable. He works toward the end of suffering 24 hours a day every day of the year. He is constantly serving. He puts into practice what He teaches. Actions do speak louder than words. Your life is your message.

Everyone is free to do what he chooses. Though you can choose to do whatever you want, only those actions which give joy to others will give you joy. If you are keen for the truth, you will observe your behaviors to discover just what you believe. Do you believe you are whole and perfect? Then you will act accordingly. If you do not act nobly, you do not know who you are as God created you. Any decision you make comes from what you think and will affect both your behavior and your experience. You cannot however heal your mind just by changing your behavior, as that would merely be treating the symptom without uncovering the cause of the problem. But you can change your mind. When you change your mind, you will behave in alignment with that shift in consciousness. A realized master brings thought, word and deed into perfect alignment.

Watch a tendency to hide behind a face of innocence. If you are pure love with all, but make one exception, you are fooling yourself. Assume then that it is your unhealed mind that is causing you to exclude. Look behind this face of innocence. Be courageous. You are not pure till you are pure with everyone, no exceptions. *Deep to our face of innocence is a saboteur, but deep to that face is our true face of innocence, is our purity and perfection.* To find pearls we must dive deep. Make your life a message of love.

Don't Invite Ego To Stay For A Cup Of Coffee

Baba says that if ego comes knocking at your door invite it in, but don't let it stay for a cup of coffee. In other words don't deny or fight ego and at the same time don't entertain it. Ego stands on the tiny platform, "Whatever you do, don't look at me." To invite it in is to look at it. Face the devil. Ego is the devil and when we look, we see its nothingness. If you fight it, you have made it real. You will be fighting a phantom. Ego is very evasive. It doesn't want to be seen. It knows that once you see it, you will see it is nothing and then it cannot but disappear. It doesn't want to disappear. You have given it life and it wants to survive and will do anything and everything to stay alive.

To entertain corruption is to let ego stay for a cup of coffee. Don't deny corruption. Invite it in so you can have a good look at it and see its nothingness. If you give it a cup of coffee, you will be making friends with it and thereby making it real. If you justify entertaining your corruption because of its unreality, you have given it reality and thereby bind yourself to consequences. Once it's nothingness becomes apparent, you would find no purpose in entertaining corruption. Negative tendencies have no power over you except the power you give them by justifying them in your mind through denial or guilt.

Some people think it is good to have a healthy dose of ego. They think they would have no personality without it. Some even think that without ego they cannot exist. That is what ego leads them to believe. The truth is that without ego you would be yourself. You would know you are eternal and cannot die. You would know your mind. We don't know our own minds because we have allowed ego to take over our minds and to limit us and restrict us to bodies and convince us that we are powerless. Ego is not a nice guy. It is not your friend. Behave with integrity and nobility and ego will lose its hold over you. Baba says that He has come to make us completely ego free.

Let Conscience Be Your Guide To Goodness

Your soul knows the truth and after communication between soul and mind was all but severed, that is after the separation, conscience was given to bridge the gap. When you have a thought that is not of truth, conscience will let you know. If you act on the thought anyway, it means you have disregarded conscience and you will not escape feeling guilty because you do know the truth. Choices not in alignment with who you are produce guilt. Conscience knows what is in alignment with truth. What is not was a choice with ego and thereby a choice for guilt.

At any point you choose, you can correct your error and your past will simply collapse behind you. If you have an untrue thought like 'I can be separate from God' or 'I can do something that is not God's will' and you recognize its unreality and refrain from acting on it, there will be no consequences. It is alliance with ego that leads to impure behavior and subsequent punishment. It is you who inflict punishment upon yourself. You are always at the helm. Be bright in your mind and own your power. All your unreal thoughts should be given to God for correction. Only when error is turned over to God can it be undone. Behavior exposes what is in your mind, so watch your actions. Then you are the witness or the observer. To be the witness does not mean to be passive. The witness is engaged. Watch your behaviors so as to correct them when they are off. Be an active participant.

Only after we made ego did it become necessary to behave at all. Behavior is not a Divine attribute. *We were created to create, to know and to love. All behavior is essentially motivated by need.* Even though we were not created to behave, now our behavior can either bind us or free us. Integrity in the work place moves us toward the happy dream. Goodness, kindness, and noble behavior will lead toward the consciousness where behavior again becomes unnecessary. Act Divinely to know yourself. *Purity is the opposite of frailty and weakness.* To act with integrity takes courage and strength. *Innocence is strength and nothing else is strong.*

Talking about behavior doesn't get much support. There are those who say that what is righteous and pure will be one thing for one and another for someone else, thus good behavior requires judgment. This is an excuse to plead ignorance, but we do all know everything and we do know what is in alignment with who we are as beings of noble character. There is no ambiguity about what true holiness is as it is the same for everyone. God created us all equally holy and we could not forget who we are. We are all the same, for holiness is the same in each of us. We do all know how to behave perfectly.

When you desire to be holy, it will be given you to know what holiness is. As long as you want to be a little corrupt... in some areas of your life... you do not want to be holy. As long as you do not want to be holy, how can you hope to know what holiness is? You can only be shown what holiness is when you desire with all your heart to be holy. Holiness and corruption are mutually exclusive. When you want to be corrupt, you don't want to be holy. When you want to behave badly, you don't want to be good.

Some argue that to be pure means to be confined. That is the voice for ego, hoping you will not see the virtues of purity and innocence or again its days are numbered. Purity is not confined. When you are pure, you are free, without any barrier or limitation. It is guilt that binds and nothing else. It is corruption that limits, contains and confines. The world has taught exactly the opposite, but that is only because ego wants to survive and tries to convince you that things are not as they are. *Holiness is seen through holy eyes that look upon the innocence within and expect to see it everywhere.*

Only when you see everyone and everything as innocent will you know your innocence. Either everyone is innocent or guilty. See only innocence and you are seeing truly. This is expansion, freedom, limitless beauty forever for there is nothing more beautiful than innocence. *We have not lost our innocence and it is for this we yearn. It is our heart's desire and cannot be denied.* You find your holiness by seeing another's innocence. That happens when you *overlook another's mistakes and see the perfection God created beyond error.*

To overlook another's shortcomings should not be used to sanction unholy behavior. To see innocence is not to be blind to unholiness. It is to know that impure actions do not alter the truth. To see error and to hold the truth of innocence will defuse unholy behavior in yourself and others. If you ignore faulty behavior in others you are condoning imperfection. Find ways to support and inspire goodness in yourself and others.

Jesus Encourages Perfection

In the Christian theology it is considered humility to think yourself a sinner. You are taught that your salvation depends on believing Jesus died for your sins. Yet Jesus himself teaches us to be perfect. Why would he teach perfection if it were not attainable, or if he were going to wipe away the effects of sin through his death? What would that teaching then serve? Jesus encouraged perfection because he realized not only that it is possible, but that your salvation depends on it.

To the woman who was about to be stoned for being a prostitute, he said, "Go your way and sin no more." He had no problem seeing that it was possible for her to be perfect because that is her nature. He did not tell her she would only be saved if she believed his death on the cross was for her sins. He told her to change her mind and act perfectly as per her truth. He saw her capacity to be perfect and inspired her toward that end. *To think yourself a sinner is arrogant, for it suggests that you could be different from how God created you.* In effect, it means you think you are more powerful than God. You cannot be either greater or less than God.

Some Christians believe that because Jesus died for their sins their imperfections will have no ramifications. Their imperfections will have no consequences only if they turn over a new leaf and determine to be the perfection that Jesus instructs them to be. To believe that Jesus' death wipes out all consequences of ignoble actions inevitably leads to license. 'It doesn't matter what you do' is self-deception. Jesus taught peace and love for all and inspired charity and kindness.

The two ideas, to be perfect and to believe Jesus died for your sins are irreconcilable and incompatible. If you own your perfection you have no sins, in which case you don't need someone to die for your sins. If you are sinful and cannot attain perfection why did Jesus bother to teach perfection? Either you will believe what Jesus taught, or you really don't believe Jesus is your savior. In his words, "If you love me, keep my commandments." Jesus wanted people to hear his message because he knew they would benefit from changing their behavior toward goodness, integrity and nobleness. That is perfection. A true savior shows the way. Christians who deify Jesus and depend on him to take away their sins weaken themselves in their own minds.

It doesn't matter what religion you follow. What is important is the purity of your heart. When you want to be pure, there is no force that can stop you, for that is how God created you. Jesus is a savior because of his message and his living example of perfection, not because of his crucifixion. Let his perfect example inspire your perfection. Then you will have been saved by Jesus and you will be a true Christian. Everyone is responsible for his own salvation. And salvation comes with a shift in consciousness toward simple honest goodness. This shift moves you from guilt consciousness to innocence consciousness.

Let God Correct Your Errors

Watch your thoughts and give all the unreal ones to God for correction. *Don't suppress your unloving thoughts. They are the barometer to your state of mind. Look on them without judgment and then quickly offer them to Spirit for healing.* Healing is not of you, but it cannot happen without your awareness and active willingness. You won't want healing if you feel guilty. If guilty, you will feel you don't deserve to be whole. When you do only that for which you know you won't feel guilty, life is much simpler.

Correcting error is resisted due to attachment to ego. Only when you turn error over to God can it easily be undone. If you are not turning to God, you are trying to undo guilt with ego and ego wants to ensure that you keep guilt. Ego is very clever in its attempts to trick you into thinking that you are healing your mind while still retaining guilt. Be ever vigilant against ego's slipperiness. We cannot achieve liberation except by turning the reigns over to God. Only when you become completely dependent on Him will ego simply disappear.

Sai Baba gives us a code of moral behavior. So does ACIM. The teachings of both are simple and direct guides for what to do. If you do as directed you will see the results in the form of freedom, peace and joy. Baba speaks of the need to overcome the six enemies of man, namely anger, greed, hatred, jealousy, lust and pride. They have nothing to do with our true nature. Until they are overcome, we are not free. We must realign ourselves with our true nature in order to again be in the experience of who we are. Like attracts like. We cannot dissociate from our behavior on the pretext that it is not who we are anyway. Baba says you gain immortality through the removal of immorality. As long as you express any of the six enemies you do not know who you are and keep yourself on the wheel of cause and consequence, birth and death.

Overcoming Anger

We do not know our own minds. If we did, we could never be upset. *We are never upset for the reasons we think. Anger is nothing more than an attempt to make someone else feel guilty for unfulfilled desires.* When you recognize your anger is not justifiable you can ask God to heal that place in your mind that feels guilty and thus expresses anger. If you turn to ego, ego will tell you that your anger is justified, that you have every right to be angry, that anger is perfectly reasonable and your mind will remain unhealed. When you turn to God, the problem is solved. When you turn to ego the problem gets glossed over and keeps resurfacing again and again. You never have a cause for anger, for God is always with you and your every need is always taken care of by Him.

How strongly do you need to defend your beliefs, concepts and understandings? Do you easily get angry when someone else presents a different point of view? That is a good indication that your beliefs are not based in truth. When you feel angry, when you find yourself forcefully defending your position, use that red flag to unlearn who you have convinced yourself you are. Even the slightest irritation is unhealed anger and keeps you bound. The following story is an example of overcoming anger.

The Sweeper Story

There was a family man in India who, after having spent his adult years in a very active professional life, had reached retirement age. He decided that from then on he wanted to withdraw from worldly life and intensely immerse himself in spiritual practice so as to gain the highest spiritual wisdom. The man went to a guru and requested, "Swami, I am ready to devote the rest of my life to achieving God-realization. Please initiate me into the knowledge of the Absolute."

The guru said, "My son, it cannot be done so quickly. There must first be some inner preparation; otherwise my instructions will have no effect. Here is what I suggest you do. I keep a cabin down by the river. Go there and remain in seclusion for one year. Spend the year in mediation and inner inquiry. Just stay with yourself and go out once a day to take your bath and beg for your food. Then, when the year is out, take a special purification bath intoning some sacred verses that I will now give you, and put on new white clothes. Keep yourself spotlessly clean and come back to see me. If you spend the year as instructed, you will be ready for the initiation into Brahman (God consciousness) and it will be very effective. Otherwise, it will be of no use and you will just feel frustrated."

The man went to the cabin as directed by the guru. He avidly immersed himself in the prescribed spiritual practices and progressed rapidly toward inner peace. Every day he counted the days still left until the year was out and he would be able to receive the coveted initiation. On the day that he was to come out of the cabin, the guru called the village sweeper and instructed him, "Go down to the river and sweep the street in front of the cabin. The man staying in that cabin will be going into the river for a bath. Wait until he comes out and has put on fresh clothes; then sweep the whole pile of rubbish in his face. You need not be afraid; he will not really harm you."

After having his bath and putting on the new clothes that he kept by the riverbed, the man recited the special purification verses the guru had given him in order to prepare himself to receive the initiation. He felt so sacred and pure, having completed the whole year immersed in spiritual practices. Now at last he was to gain the inner mysteries of the highest spiritual teachings. At that moment the sweeper came toward him raising a cloud of dust, covering him from head to toe. He became furious. In a trice he completely lost his serene composure and started abusing the poor sweeper mercilessly. He grabbed the sweeper's broom and raised it to beat him on the head, but restrained himself and did not hurt the sweeper. He went back to the river, took another bath, put on some other clothes and collected himself. He regained a portion of the peace he previously felt inside and went off to see his guru.

The guru said, "Yes, you certainly have advanced very nicely. But you know and I know that you are not quite ready for the highest initiation into God-knowledge. Go back to your little cabin. Spend another year. At the end of that year, have your bath, put on some new clothes, recite these prayers and come back to me. I will give you your initiation." So again he spent a year in meditation, took his bath, put on his new clothes and recited the special purification verses.

The guru again enlisted the sweeper to collect an even bigger pile of rubbish and smelly sewage which he again threw at the man, just as he was coming up the river bank spick and span in his new clothes. Again he was covered with dirt from head to foot, and again he became furious. But this time he just glowered at the sweeper and managed to restrain his tongue as well as his hands. Though he was livid, he kept his composure and just turned around, went back into the river, took another bath, put on some other clothes and returned to the guru.

The guru said, "I see that a true inner peace is beginning to take hold in you, but at the same time you know and I know, you are not quite ready. Go back for another year and then come to me." At the end of the third year, he took his bath, put on his new clothes, recited his verses and here came the village sweeper with a cart full of repugnant debris, all over his spotless white clothes. This time the man ran up with tears in his eyes and fell at the dumbfounded sweeper's feet saying, "Brother, thank you for showing me how much impurity was still in me. Please forgive me for everything I have done to hurt you. God bless you."

Again he turned around and went into the river, this time fully composed and at peace within himself. He completed his bath and went to the guru. Now there was no question that he was ready, and so he received the guru's initiation and quickly progressed toward God realization. You cannot attain God as long as you have impurities and a true teacher will expose them so they can be removed. Once exposed they can be dealt with. The tricky thing about our tendencies is that we are not even generally aware of them. We go on thinking we are perfect and wonder why we haven't attained God realization. Just because you express anger does not make you guilty. It does however make you wrong. Change your mind and anger can no longer reside in you.

Overcoming Jealousy And Greed

When I first heard that God was on the planet, I feared that He would draw to Himself all the glory and eclipse my purpose. Only now do I realize that all He wants is for His children to shine. In that moment I was exposing jealousy toward God and Sai Baba would eventually bring it to the surface to be dealt with. But He waits for just the right moment, the moment when we have matured to the point where we can handle exposing our negative tendencies. About ten years after first meeting Him in form, I was given the opportunity. It took place in an interview.

During that interview Baba manifested some lovely delicate gold lotus earrings for a woman from Italy. I was sitting directly behind her. When Baba left the room to show an Indian couple His new home, Treyi Brindavan, I noticed that one of the earrings was not fastened properly and fearing she might lose it, fastened it for her. Just as I was finishing, Baba came back into the room and asked, "Jealous?" "Oh no Baba, I'm very happy,"

He, responded, "Jealousy, jealousy, jealousy." I was sincerely happy for her, but realized afterward that Baba had set up that little drama to expose my jealous nature. So I started to be more alert to my tendency to get jealous as Baba was passing by and looking at someone else, talking to someone else or taking someone else in for interview. Before, when those feelings arose, I would quickly hide them from myself by reminding myself that I was a 'good' devotee and that I couldn't possibly harbor negative feelings. I'd fool myself by stuffing those feelings, denying that they existed and hiding behind a face of innocence. I was listening to ego's solution to the problem. Ego guided me to deny the problem so that it could not get solved, as ego's existence depends on my denial, suppression, avoidance and ignorance of my imperfections. I had chosen deep sleep to deal with my problem though I was becoming aware that denial was not a real solution after all.

Baba was bringing jealousy to conscious awareness so it could be healed. Now when it came up, I owned it and felt horribly guilty. It seemed

I was worse off than when I was in denial. I was shifting from deep sleep back into the nightmare. The guilt was more painful than stuffing it, but denial was no longer an option. I knew too much. So I pled with Baba in my heart to show me how to heal this jealousy from which I was acutely suffering. I remembered Him saying to give Him our garbage, so each time it raised its ugly head, I offered it to Him instead of feeling guilty.

Our little willingness for ego to be undone is all that God asks in order that He give us everything. Do more and we get in the way. When Shirdi (Baba's previous incarnation) was alive, He used to shout at his disciples to get out of the way so He could do His work. Ego is too smart for us, but not too smart for God. We made ego thus something in us wants to preserve it. Only God is 100% sure He doesn't want it preserved, because He wants us as we are in truth, free of our misery. Ego keeps us separate from God and in pain.

Once free of guilt, I was curious to know what jealousy really was, so I asked it, "Who are you?" As soon as I faced it, jealousy literally disappeared. This happened a few more times, each time with less intensity and then I realized I was free. When you are free of guilt, you are free to see clearly. Jealousy was never real and only had power over me because I believed in it and my investment of denial and guilt gave it reality.

Now whenever Baba would come by and give anyone attention, my heart genuinely rejoiced for them. When someone I know was selected for interview, gentle tears of delight at their good fortune trickled down my cheeks. I had no idea how much jealousy had covered my joy. I was sabotaging my own happiness by not dealing with my demon. Again ego's solution is denial and guilt and God's solution is to heal my mind. When I looked at jealousy, I saw its nothingness and it vanished. It was my energy of denial, suppression and guilt that gave it existence. Baba did not see me as bad while harboring jealousy. He did see that I was not free and He was looking out for my best interests. He did not ignore my jealousy, but gave me the courage to face it and thereby heal its negative effects on me.

When you are jealous, you think someone else has something you do not. This is a false idea, as you are and have everything. *We cannot lose what God gave us because God also gave everything to everyone.* Once this is known, jealousy makes no sense and vanishes. Baba says that jealousy is the last tendency to be overcome, for even great saints in temples and caves have some vestiges of jealousy toward God. This lack is filled when you realize that you and God are exactly the same and that any limitation you feel is self-imposed and has nothing to do with any oversight on God's part.

Greed and jealousy are similar obstructers of peace. If one's tendency is to amass wealth or keep up with a neighbor, they simply do not realize that God gave them everything and that the things they hanker after are nothing.

Greed is overcome in knowing that you are and have everything. Live a simple life. When you live simply, you have fewer problems. Having more wealth or possessions than you need cannot bring true happiness. When the shoe is too big it is as uncomfortable as when it is too small.

Overcoming Lust

Lust is an out-picturing of the idea that your body is more powerful than your all-powerful mind. Your body is inert. It is not real. Any bodily tendencies that you allow to control you constitute lust. They can take the form of food, sex, alcohol, drugs, etc.

Maybe you will entertain the thought, 'It doesn't matter that I have lust. After all I am not my body. Even if my body has lust, that has nothing to do with me.' That thought comes from ego. We have to be very wary of ego's attempts to keep us bound. When you think your lust does not matter, you are making your body real. Of itself it is nothing, but you give it power over you by thinking you cannot control lust. Ego's solution is to be free sexually, but Baba says, "Dogs have that freedom."

Baba advises us to give our lust to God. When we give it to God, we let go of the guilt and then it can be undone. As long as we justify any of our negative tendencies, we are sabotaging our joy. To be free of lust is not to deprive you of passionate expressions of love with a partner to whom you are totally committed and with whom you feel a loving oneness. Making love is very beautiful. Lust is very ugly. The difference is black and white. One plunges you into the depths of hell while the other transports you to the very heights of ecstasy.

When you are in a committed relationship, you are making a commitment to join on all fronts, and then sexuality is an outer expression of an inner joining. Sexuality outside of an eternal commitment is lust as it merely seeks to satisfy pleasure without taking responsibility for the act of joining. Baba says that when you are with another that is marriage. Don't be with another superficially or outside of a total commitment or you cause suffering to yourself and others. Pleasure and pain are flip sides of the same coin.

Perhaps you justify inappropriate cross gender exchanges as genuine expressions of love. But love for mother, sister, friend or daughter is not expressed in the same way as is love for wife. God intended holy matrimony to be between one man and one woman in a total commitment. Krishna told Arjuna that the householder path is the fastest path to God. When you honor your marriage commitment you meet challenges and temptations that the one who abstains or renounces has not dealt with. If after 20 years of marriage you are still irresistibly prompted to shower tender affections on your spouse in public, you have accomplished something and are a rare and great soul and a true savior of the world.

There are many so called spiritual communities that justify sleeping around on the pretext that all should be given the same expression of love, otherwise you are reinforcing inequality. This is a misapplication of the teaching. If you fall prey to this temptation, you make the body real, just the opposite of what a true spiritual aspirant is attempting to do. The intention of that teaching is to see all as innocent and to reject or condemn no one. All are equally precious children of God.

In overcoming the body's tendencies we affirm the body's unreality. Ego likes confusion around sexuality. You can justify anything until you really do want to be free. When you want to be holy, all confusion around sexuality will be cleared up. Do you want to be holy, or do you still want to be different from how you were created? To love everyone equally means to see the Christ in everyone and to treat everyone as the God or Goddess that they are. Treat everyone with appreciation and gratitude, and you are applying the teaching as intended.

In giving lust to God, you will not feel guilty, which helps you to see it truly as nothing. Once its nothingness is seen, it can no longer have a hold over you. Ego stands on the tiny platform, "Whatever you do, don't look at me." It doesn't want you to notice that it is nothing. It is something as long as you believe in it, for your belief gives it power over you. Ego is like the emperor with no clothes on. As long as everyone blindly agreed that he was wearing a beautiful garment, though he was stark naked, everyone deluded themselves. It only took one boy's laughter for the whole delusion to be unraveled. Look on ego open-eyed.

Once an alcoholic came to Baba wanting help to stop drinking. Baba said to him, "Don't stop; drink to me." Surprised, the man did as he was told. Every time he tipped the bottle, he said, "Here's to You, Baba," and then he chugged it down. But very soon he found that he simply wasn't interested in chugging it down. It had lost its hold because there was no guilt. He no longer felt guilty because he was thinking of God.

You cannot feel guilty and think of God at the same time. As soon as the guilt was gone the habit could not be sustained. Guilt was the glue that held it in place. If you tend to overeat, try offering the food to God every time you want to reach for something. Pay attention that you not allow yourself to be plunged into guilt. See if you don't lose interest in food consciousness. Baba frequently chides heavy people and urges them to lose weight. Can you really be overweight and feel good about yourself? You are letting your body be your master and that is simply a statement that you are not all-powerful as you were created. You are all-powerful. Take back your power, O holy child of God. Be the master of your senses to overcome lust in any form.

Overcoming Pride

Baba says, "If you are a mountain, be a molehill; if a molehill, don't be a mountain." When you truly understand that you are God, you will know it with the deepest humility. To know that you are all the power in the universe is so very awesome, inspiring and humbling. If you feel pompous about the idea, know that you only have conceptual understanding. You could only feel pride if you were comparing yourself and seeing inequality. There is no one outside of you, therefore you are not more powerful than anyone else. Pride only rears its ugly head until you realize you are the same as everyone. There is a tendency to pride oneself in one's accomplishments. But where do the energy, strength, power and intelligence to do anything come from? Everything comes from God. God is the only doer. Once you really understand that of yourself you are nothing you will not give way to feelings of pride in relation to anything.

Overcoming Hatred

Hatred is but fear. You will only hate what you are afraid of and what can you be afraid of once you know who you are? When you know who you are, you will know there is no one outside of you and that to hate anyone is to hate yourself. Exclusion is a symptom of hatred. Include everyone into your life and hatred vanishes. Some Christians hate those who are not Christians. Some Muslims hate those who do not profess Allah. This is fanaticism and a distortion of what those respective religions' founders taught. I love Sai Baba and believe He is God, however I do not need you to believe the same in order to love you. If I hated you for not believing as I do I would be a fanatic and exposing self-hatred. I know we each have to save ourselves, therefore whether you believe as I do or not is not important to me. I do not need to defend my position. This is self-love and self-confidence.

When we recognize that all are our brothers and sisters and that we all have the same Father/Mother God, we know that we belong to the one family of God. Then we will not be intolerant of people on the basis of religion, color, philosophy, nationality, gender or social status. How you relate to others reveals how you feel about yourself. If you hate anyone, you need help to change your mind. Ask God to show you who you are. A glimpse of your truth will remove all self-hatred forever. When you love yourself, you will love everyone. When you desire happiness for everyone you do love yourself.

Perfection Is Who You Are

There are those who say, "It is impossible to be perfect." It is not only possible, it is your truth. You were created unalterably perfect. Can it be difficult to be who you are? It is ego that tries to convince you to maintain the lie that you are helpless to overcome anger, jealousy, greed, lust, pride or hatred. Negative habits hide who we are and yet we have convinced ourselves that these tendencies are natural and that they cannot be overcome. Do not give ego power over you. You are purity and innocence and you do want that as your direct experience. You have the capacity to have that as your experience right now. Just stop convincing yourself that you cannot be who you are.

There are those who defend against purity, reasoning that if you are too pure, others will feel uncomfortable in your company, or will feel judged by you. Know this to be the voice for ego. Everyone loves Sai Baba and He is Holiness personified. All the saints and sages throughout the ages attracted the masses because of their purity. When you are pure, you cannot judge. It is only the impure who judge. When pure you only see everyone's innocence and that draws people to you irresistibly like ants to sugar or bees to honey. It is not purity that turns people away but corruption. The outer reflects the inner. You see outside of you what is in your mind. When you see only innocence in others, you know your own innocence and perfection.

Ego's Survival Depends On Your Not Looking

Baba exposes ego so that it can be looked at. Once there was to be a Christmas celebration in the Kalamantap hall, in Whitefield, India. Before the celebration Baba called two head Seva Dals (volunteers) aside separately and gave them each some simple instructions. He instructed one to let only the devotees from overseas into the hall. Then He dismissed her and called over the other. He instructed her to let only Indian devotees into the hall. By the time I arrived with hopes of getting inside there was utter bedlam at the door. Ladies were pushing and shoving and doing everything they could to gain entry. The one Seva Dal was doing everything she could to keep us Westerners out, while the other was doing everything she could to keep the Indians out.

Finally I pushed my way in, sat down and tried to reconstruct some dignity into my sari as well as my mind and heart. Baba showed up after all the commotion had settled. He always somehow manages to stay away from the fray. With an innocent look He asked if there was any problem. Both ladies jumped in and started to explain how she had done her best to follow Baba's instructions. Baba, with a cheeky look of surprise, commented to the one, "All I asked you to do was let only the Indians in. I did not tell you to keep the Westerners out. Had you followed my instructions, there would have been no problem." To the other woman, who tried to keep the Indians out, He said the same thing. Exclusion was justified because God Himself had instructed them to exclude. At least that is what they chose to hear from what He said. Ego was being exposed and once seen it could be recognized as preposterous and unreasonable.

The disingenuousness of ego to preserve itself is enormous. Ironically, it gets its cleverness from the power of your mind and then denies you its power. In turn the power of your mind comes from God. Ego attacks what is preserving it. Of itself, it does not know anything. It draws on your mind, which is totally inimical to it, for its existence. It is a parasite. It is then fearful of being found out, so depreciates the power of your mind in your mind. It convinces you that you are not only not all-powerful but powerless and that not only do you not know everything as you were created, but that you don't know anything. *It cleverly does not perceive its existence as threatened because it projects the threat onto you by getting you to perceive your being as nonexistent.* If you think you are a body that will die some day, ego has convinced you that you are nonexistent. This insures its continuance by guaranteeing that you will not know your own safety. Your safety is guaranteed by God. Your inheritance is eternal life and ego does not want you to know that.

How can ego be undone once you see that it is your problem? *You cannot escape from ego by humbling, controlling or punishing it.* See through ego's clever ruse and recognize its nothingness. *Do not be afraid of ego. It does depend on your mind and as you made it by believing in it, so you can dispel it by withdrawing belief from it. Do not project the responsibility for your belief onto anyone else or you will preserve the belief. When you are willing to accept sole responsibility for ego's existence yourself, you will have laid aside all anger and attack, because they come from an attempt to project responsibility for your own errors. But having accepted the errors as yours, do not keep them. Give them over quickly to God to be undone completely.*

Ego, Who Are You?

Baba tells the story of a bridal party. Two families had come together for a wedding celebration and days before the ceremony a stranger approached the bride's side with numerous unpleasant and outrageous demands. The bride's family just assumed he was representing the groom's party. He was so unfriendly and his demands so unreasonable that they seriously considered calling off the wedding. Meanwhile the same obstinate intruder was making equally outrageous demands of the groom's party and they too were ready to call the whole thing off.

In a fit of anger the two parties approached each other to express their decision to walk away. The bride's side assured the groom's side that they were not responsible for any absurd demands. The groom's side assured the bride's family of same. Then they both looked at each other in surprise and asked, "Who is this outrageous impostor?" They searched everywhere but could not find him. He had disappeared. It is the same with ego. Once we stand still and ask, "Who are you?" instead of giving it power, we see its nothingness and once exposed, it cannot but vanish.

As soon as you withdraw energy from ego it disappears for it never existed except by your belief in it. It has been the robot you made, which then turned on its maker. It has been the parasite that has sucked all your power and knowledge from you. It has tried to fool you that you are powerless and ignorant and in most instances it has been very successful. You can be restored to wholeness any time you so desire because you are still whole and perfect as God created you. He created you exactly like Himself. He has not changed His mind about you. You need merely change your mind about yourself to be restored to truth. You have all the power that God has. You are not limited like ego has convinced you that you are. It is a lie. Love is your power. *Love is treacherous to ego because ego was produced by fear and love overcomes fear.*

We made ego to be our source. We made ego to perceive ourselves as we wished, rather than as we are. *As long as you believe ego made you, you will not know who you are, for you remain confused about your source.* You are never locked into ego consciousness. *You can always choose to listen to either of two voices within. One you made yourself and that one is of ego. The other was given by God. Ego always speaks loudest and first for its selfish interests at your expense. God is always communicating with you toward your best interest.*

Listen carefully in everything that happens in your day. God's communication can take place in a meeting with someone, when something happens to you, in a particular scene, in a story, in a thought or impression in your mind, in a dream... There are so many ways God communicates. He is total creativity and knows you better than you know yourself, so don't think He doesn't know how to make contact. Do not be afraid that you cannot hear Him. He does know very well how to reach you. All you need is a little willingness that this be so. Only guilt and unworthiness stemming from guilt will cause you to believe that you cannot hear God's voice. Innocence literally drives guilt from your mind. When guilt is gone, ego is gone. Remember your innocence and communication is reestablished.

When you make a mistake, ego does not see it as a lack of love, which is all it could ever be. Ego sees it as a positive act of assault. It needs to interpret it this way so it can survive. If you saw it as merely a lack, you would automatically do what was necessary to remedy your shortcoming and you would succeed. This would be bad news for ego, but it is where your freedom lies. *When you are guiltless, you cannot suffer. When you are healed you cannot conceive of illness because you cannot conceive of attacking anyone or anything. Sickness is an attack on yourself. Do not hide your wrong doing. Look at it and correct it.* Then you won't feel guilty about it. Wrong doing equals alliance with ego which amounts to alliance with nothing. *Whenever you respond with ego, you will experience guilt and fear punishment. Ego is quite literally a fearful thought.*

Be Responsible For Your Experiences

Guilt stands in the way of your remembering God whose pull is so strong that you cannot resist it. If you are to retain guilt, as ego insists, you cannot be you. Only by persuading you that it is you, could ego possibly induce you to project guilt and thereby keep it in your mind. You project guilt to get rid of it, but in so doing you merely conceal it.

Baba says, "When you remember God, you can quickly reach enlightenment," and then He goes on to say, "but even to remember God is only by God's grace." God's grace is always there for you, but guilt blocks it. There are those who espouse the highest teachings, but if they are not in God consciousness with every thought, word and deed they are only fooling themselves. Are you irresistibly drawn by God's grace into rapt ecstasy at the mere mention of His name? If not you are probably harboring some guilt and it would be good to ask to be shown what it is, so it can be healed and you can be free. The first step is to recognize that you are responsible for any block that keeps you from effortlessly experiencing God-consciousness as the only thought, passion and joy in your mind.

Once a young boy, determined that he should have the vision of the Lord, lovingly prepared some food. He expected God to literally come and eat with him. He sang the sweetest love songs to God. He pined for God with every breath. But God did not appear, so he said to himself, "My songs must not be sweet enough, my food tasty enough or my yearning pure enough." He would not rest or eat. He prayed and sang and kept reflecting within and taking personal responsibility for God not having come as yet. He kept up his self-scrutiny, determination, fast, prayer and melodious song, imploring God to appear. On the 7th day he received the splendorous vision of the Lord. Never did he think, 'God has not come because He does not love me,' but always he looked within to see how he was keeping God away.

Purity Is A Prerequisite To Performing Miracles

We have to be pure in order to perform miracles and performing miracles is natural. Love is a miracle as only love heals. Love can heal the sick and raise the dead. If you think you are guilty, you will block the flow of Divine love. When you behave purely, you will feel innocent and this innocence will draw God's Divine energy of love to and through you. Desire is all that is needed to achieve any outcome sought. If you want to be holy, you will be holy. It is your truth, so why not want it? It does matter what you do, but it does not matter what you have done. Past is past, and it will not be held against you when you change your mind. *Each moment is a clean untarnished birth into your pristine purity.*

Don't let ego fool you into justifying any behavior except the purest and the noblest. Only fearless, courageous, dignified, holy and sacred actions are becoming of you. Baba says, "Walk the earth like masters with your heads held high." You are God. Act like God. Think like God. Love like God. Live like God. Fill your heart with God's tenderness and kindness. Go for what makes you and all those around you happy and leave what leads to misery behind forever. You deserve the best because of who you are. You are so beautiful, so pure, so holy and so sacred. Be the innocence that you are. In choosing for your innocence you become a beacon of hope to all those who still think they are guilty for crimes they never committed. In choosing for your holiness, you are stepping into your role as savior of the world.

Beloved Lord, thank You that You created us innocent forever. Thank You that ego and guilt are not real and that we can walk away from all guilt forever when we so choose. Thank You that You made everyone and everything innocent and that our innocence is reflected in all Your creation. Inspire us, dear God, to be pure in every thought, word and deed. Thank You for refusing to acknowledge anything less than perfection in each of Your creations. May we determine to lead lives of purity and may that purity inspire all our brothers and sisters to rise into their purity and holiness, so that all the world will be saved.

May all beings in all the worlds be happy and blest, Amen.

Figure 7a – Everything in God's Creation is Innocent forever

Everything (Eternity)

Eternity	Life	Oneness
God-Dependence	Love	Freedom
Real	Truth	Non-judgment
Heaven	Peace	Creation
Innocence	Knowledge	All-Powerful

Nothing (time and space)

Time/space	**Happy Dream (Satva) God's solution - collapses time**
Ego-dependence	Shift in Consciousness - God's idea of justice
Unreal	Overcome 6 enemies, addictions - ask for help
Hell	Face the devil - correct error - discover innocence
Guilt	Listen to God's voice - desire to be pure, perfect
Death	**Nightmare (Rajo Guna) - makes time**
Fear	Karma balances scales - ego's idea of justice
Untruth	Act ignobly - make time - include corruption
War	Make error sin, thus feel guilty
Ignorance	Make ego real through power of belief
Separation	**Deep Sleep (Thamo) Ego's solution - freezes time**
Bondage	Blame others for your troubles - make more karma
Judgment	Deny, project, suppress 6 enemies - 'doesn't matter'
Mis-creation	Listen to voice of ego
Powerless	Deny or justify addicitons, 'impossible to be perfect'

Direction of Consciousness Awakening

Figure 7b – Ego Uses God's Mind to Make You Feel Guilty

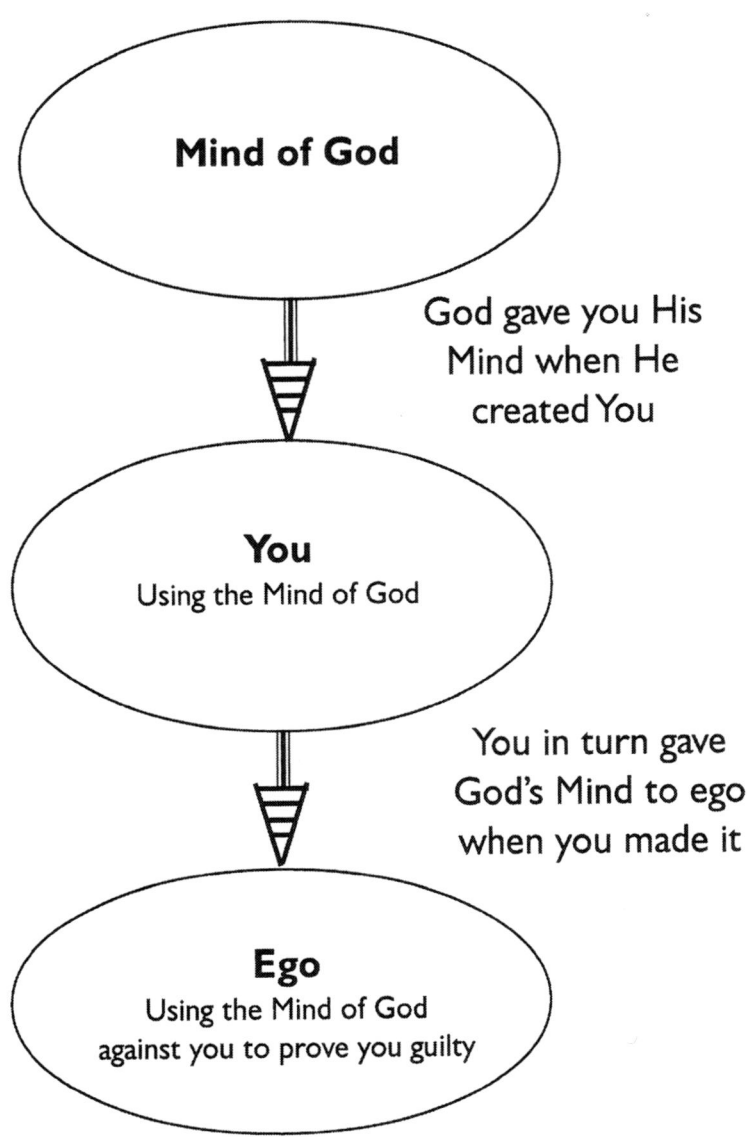

Chapter 8

Are You Ready to Choose Life Instead of Death?

The way to immortality is through the removal of immorality.

Sai Baba

Buddha Overcomes Sickness, Old Age, And Death

At the time of Siddhartha's birth, a local astrologer was summoned. The astrologer told his father, the king, that the boy was slated to be either heir to the throne or a great saint. As the king expressed a hope that his son follow in his footsteps and carry on the royal line, the astrologer advised him to keep the boy within the protective confines of the palace courtyard. If the boy were to witness any sickness, old age or death he would be driven to find the deeper meaning to life. As long as he was protected, the king stood a good chance that his son would follow in his footsteps and become a great king. So little Siddhartha led an enchanted, sheltered life and was very happy.

He was oblivious to any and all misfortune in the form of sickness, suffering, old age or death, until one day he experienced a restlessness. He asked his friend, Chana, to accompany him into the larger township. When his father heard of their plans he ordered the streets to be cleared of all sights that his son should not see. So they had a wonderful adventure and only on the way back to the palace did they happen to spot a man being carried off on a stretcher. "Chana, what is that?" Siddhartha asked in surprise. Chana told his friend that the man was sick. At Siddhartha's insistence, Chana explained what sickness was and the pain associated with bodily illness. Siddhartha was deeply moved with compassion and could not sleep that night. He had no idea that there was such a thing as suffering.

Next day he wanted to go out with his friend again. The streets were again cleared of all undesirable sights. Again they spent the day viewing only uplifting scenes. Yet, as fate would have it, as they were returning to the palace they happened to notice someone who looked very frail. He had white hair. He could not move well. He needed help to cross the street. Siddhartha again asked Chana to explain. Chana told Siddhartha that he was seeing old age and that old age was inevitable. His parents too would get old with time. That night again Siddhartha could not sleep. He could not understand this idea of old age. It made no sense at all.

The following day, compelled by astonishment and curiosity, he again encouraged Chana to accompany him into the larger township. This time they witnessed a strange and shocking site - a procession of mourners carrying a dead body to a crematorium. Siddhartha was beside himself. He had no idea that death was everyone's final destiny. He went home and locked himself in his room and could not be consoled. After much time, again he wanted to go out with Chana and again they wandered the township together, but this time they continued into the forest glade beyond. There, Siddhartha saw a radiant face as he had not seen in his father's entire kingdom. He had met an awakened sage, someone who had renounced the world and discovered the deeper meaning of life.

Siddhartha wanted to know if this man had understood the purpose of sickness, suffering and death. The enlightened sage shook with laughter. It was obvious that he did not think they were a problem. Siddhartha was thus inspired to turn away from the kingdom and sit under the Boddhi tree until he understood. Being a great soul, he was not prepared to merely accept sickness, suffering, old age and death as inevitable. Thus he became the great compassionate Buddha. Today Buddhism continues to flourish and promulgate the deepest compassion for the suffering of all humanity. Buddha showed that sickness, old age and death, were not to be feared, nor merely accepted, but rather looked at. In looking, the Buddha awakened to the truth that he could not die.

Death Is A Choice

Death is feared and dreaded, yet accepted as inevitable. It is never the topic of conversation because always 'more pleasant and uplifting' subjects ought to be discussed. What if death were not real? What if looking at it would cause it to disappear? Our unwillingness to look at death and our acceptance of it as inevitable are what keep it in place. *Death is a choice. No one can die unless he chooses death.* There is no one outside of you more powerful than you causing you to get old and die. *All forms of sickness unto death are physical expressions of the fear of waking up.*

What seems to be fear of death is really its attraction. We think we fear death, but we really fear eternal life, otherwise we simply would not choose death. Fearing salvation, we welcome death. The Buddha had no fear and thus experienced his enlightenment and was restored to eternal life. Death is an attempt at escape from life, but we are immortal. We are as we were created. Though that is so, whatever we accept into ours minds has reality for us. Acceptance makes the unreal seem real. The Buddha woke up because he did not accept sickness, suffering and death as real. He wanted to understand the truth behind the idea of death. Death is real for us only as long as we believe in it.

Overcoming Death Through Passion For God

Death is a thought that we could be separate from our Creator. Separation is impossible and thus death also is impossible. Death can be overcome through love for God. In sixteenth century India, a family man, Tukaram, worked very hard and yet was extremely poor. He didn't seem to mind at all. He was always thinking of God, talking to Him and seeing Him in everyone he met and in everything that happened to him. He found God to be everywhere and in all things. He loved God with a passion. His wife however was very impatient with him. She found him much too intoxicated with his love for God. She scolded him incessantly and gave him a hard time. He was not troubled. He saw God in her too.

And when God told him that He would be coming in a chariot to take him home, he invited her to join him. She didn't believe him and ridiculed him, but God did send His chariot and Tukaram did ascend to heaven without experiencing death. Passionate love for God overcame death. Tukaram proved for all humanity that death is not real and that you are not mandated to die. You are not separate from your Creator and your oneness is realized in your total love for God. That love conquers even death. Baba says, "Always remember God, forget the world, never fear death." I think Tukaram did exactly that and thereby was victorious over death.

Savitri's Deathless Love

There is another great favorite among the East Indian classics of how love overcomes death. It is the story of the love of a woman, a true princess, for her husband, a worthy and noble prince. Long ago, the Goddess of the sun, Goddess Savitri descended to earth as a princess to the great Monarch Aswapati. He was a pious king who, after long and severe penance and austerities for an heir to the throne, was graced with a delightful princess. When she came of age the monarch implored her to find a husband worthy of her noble hand. He sent her to search in all the kingdoms far and wide. She spent her search in hermitages and immersed herself in the teachings of the great wise ones.

Upon her return, Sage Narada, a renowned seer was at the king's table. Savitri greeted both and at her father's bidding blushed her choice. Sathyavan, the Soul of Truth, of royal descent, was selected her lord and husband. His father, though kingly still, was blind and had been forced from his kingdom. He and his virtuous queen had raised their child in the forest and there Savitri met Satyavan. Sage Narada, turning ashen, reluctantly disclosed a grim foreboding, "This prince is slated to die in one year." Upon hearing impending doom, Monarch Aswapati urged his daughter to choose again. Trembling, Savitri stood firm in her choice, asserting that a pure woman only chooses a husband once, whether his life be short or long.

So they married and she went to live in the forest and care for Satyavan's blind parents while daily he went out to gather the necessary food and firewood. The dread of impending doom perpetually cast its shadow over Savitri's gentle form. Too quickly, the year was spent and only three days remained. She took to severe fasting and prayer. The dreaded day arrived. On that most unwelcome morning Savitri asked if she could follow her beloved Satyavan into the forest. With ax propped upon his handsome shoulder, they wandered off. Soon he felt an ache, a piercing and a throbbing in his head and beads of sweat burst upon his brow. He laid his head upon mortified Savitri's soft and tender lap. She clasped him to her bosom and fervently kissed his lips and as she held him helplessly, he slept the sleep of death.

Lord Yama, Monarch of the dead, came to take his own. Savitri's pure and stoic love for husband permitted her to see the Lord's terrible form. As he took Satyavan's noble soul in his noose, Savitri got up to follow. Yama urged her to turn back, but her love was too strong and she followed where he took her husband's life, though where they went mere mortals cannot go. Her love was deathless and Lord Yama had not the power to turn her back. He could not divide loving man and faithful wife. He had no choice but to give Sathyavan back his life. Savitri returned to where he lay and her tender caresses thrilled him back to life. Death cannot separate true love from true love. Such love must give back life. Death was not possible because death is a thought that you can be separated from the ones you love and when your love is as strong and pure as Savitri's for Satyavan, it is more powerful than death.

Death Is A Joke We Play On Ourselves

We were created immortal. We are alive and will live forever. We were created to have life without opposite. Death is not real. Alexander the Great had set out to conquer the world. He was about to invade India and had sent ahead a troop of scouts. As his men pushed into Kashmir they came upon a yogi sitting in the middle of the road. Gruffly they told him to get out of the way or they would send his head rolling. He laughed heartily. They were mystified and brought Alexander to witness this strange behavior. When the yogi was asked why he was laughing when his life was being threatened, he shook with laughter and said, "You think you can kill me by cutting off my head. You cannot kill me, for I am immortal. Therefore I am laughing." Alexander marveled at his fearlessness and retreated. Thus India was not invaded because of its sages who knew the truth about life without opposite.

Death is our final proof to ourselves that God is dead. That is subconsciously what we are convincing ourselves of by dying. We are attempting to prove to ourselves that God is mortal. You are probably already sensing who is behind that preposterous idea – it is ego. It is impossible for God to die as He is immortal, and as He only creates like Himself, so are you immortal. Death is impossible. Your body may die, but you are not your body. Many people have had experiences of meeting their loved ones who have gone to the other side. I've had a number of dreams in which 'dead' loved ones made contact with me. God did not create fleshly forms as He only creates what lasts forever like Himself. It is possible that we exit our bodies consciously, or that our bodies be transfigured into light. Jesus overcame death through resurrection. Everything is possible as long as we do not limit what is possible to our experience or to what we have witnessed with our own eyes.

One example to illustrate other choices is of a lad who was separated from his parents and sold as a slave to a very wealthy yet kind man in South India. The young boy ran away and undertook rigorous spiritual practices from the tender age of five. A realized saint discovered and guided him. Because he did not have parents discouraging him from his determination, he underwent the necessary changes to his body before the age of 20 to convert it into a light body. To this day he is known as the immortal Baba-ji and has lived for over 3000 years in the Himalayas. He appeared to Jesus, Mohamed and many other spiritual leaders, and guided them in their awakenings. He has guided many spiritual aspirants, among them the beloved Yogananda who came to reside in the Los Angeles area in the last century. Baba-ji proved that it is possible to transform your body from a fleshly form into a deathless light body.

It is also possible to leave your body consciously. I visited Ramana Maharshi's ashram on Arunachala Mountain in the early nineties and sat in the Virupaksha Cave where he had attained enlightenment. In the twelfth century a sage had inhabited that very cave long before Ramana. One day the sage told his disciples to leave him and come back shortly. They did as they were told and when they reentered the cave, all that was left of their beloved teacher was a heap of ashes. There is only one entry to the cave and they were standing by it. The ashes were embalmed and were still being held sacred when I sat there.

The cave had a powerful timelessness about it. I would enter at 8:00 in the morning and come out at 4:00 in the afternoon and it would seem as though I had just arrived. The power in that cave transported me into timelessness. When the yogi finished his task, he consciously left his body without being a burden to anyone. This is a very common practice for saints and sages in India. Death is a choice. It can be a conscious choice.

Enlightened beings leave their bodies just like one would shed a garment that he no longer wishes to wear – no fuss, sickness, suffering or aging. Their graceful exits are living proof that death is not real.

Ramana Maharshi underwent a death experience as a lad of 16. He felt his body entering rigor mortise and simply lay down and let himself undergo the experience of death. When his body literally died he discovered that he did not die and in this way he too realized his deathlessness. That realization inspired leave home and to become fully enlightened.

Death is the opposite of life, but life has no opposite. We simply cannot die. Death is an attempt at escaping life. It will never work, for we were created to live forever. How is that possible when we see death all around us? Only that which is not real undergoes death. Your body is not real. Even if it dies, you live forever. Plants, animals and everything we see have the mark of death upon them, but that is not proof that death is real. If we conclude that death is real it is only that we trust our senses, which are not necessarily reliable witnesses to ultimate truth. Two people witnessing the same incident will invariably see it totally differently. Two people hearing the same words will frequently draw different conclusions from what they hear. Your senses are limited in their ability to witness to truth, and are thus unreliable. That is because they are not real. Just because you see death doesn't make it true. We have the power to heal the sick and raise the dead because we made sickness and death and they can be overcome when we stop making them real for us. When you truly love yourself, you see the senselessness of death.

Reincarnation Is A Relative Truth

There are numerous stories to substantiate the idea of reincarnation. Reincarnation means that you die and then are born again, which basically says that you didn't die, but only shed one body to don another. It does not matter whether you believe in reincarnation or not, because it is not ultimate truth, even if it is what we do when we die, if we have not awakened to the truth. If death is not real and if bodies are not real, then can you see how reincarnation also is not real? It is however possible on the level of form. It helps me to understand better why I see the world the way I do. I see only this life, but what is playing out in this life is the effect or result of actions from previous lives. This helps explain how it is possible for innocent children to be starving to death or so many other things that seem so unjust. We only see the present, not the past or future.

It also explains why one might find himself a genius in a particular field, like Mozart in the field of music or Einstein in the arena of mathematics. We simply do not know the past or future lives surrounding the little that we see. This is in no way an excuse to keep from acting toward the betterment of everyone's lot. Though they may be reaping the negative consequences of previous lives, they were never guilty and do not deserve pain and suffering no matter what their past. Our assignment is to do what we can in the service of all humanity at every opportunity. It is not essential to believe in reincarnation because it is a relative truth and not ultimate truth. God's creation does not experience reincarnation. Only the unreal can die and be reborn. There is however plenty of convincing evidence for reincarnation on the level of form. It is very much part of the Hindu and Buddhist religious traditions.

The movie Ground Hog Day is a wonderful portrayal of what it is to live forever through the idea of repeating the same day over and over again. A news reporter, who woke up every morning reliving the same day finally started to catch on that he could make it hell or heaven. When he mastered loving kindness, he got to move on to the next day. This movie is a brilliant metaphor for reincarnation. You keep coming back lifetime after lifetime until you get it right, until you are an embodiment of what your Creator created you to be – perfect love, and then you graduate or wake up.

Reincarnation helps in understanding the idea of karma. If someone does something harmful in this life and seems to get away with it, we would say there is no justice in the world, but we do not know his future. We do not know what results are still to come for his wrongs or omissions. There is also the question of the innocent person who seems to be unfairly treated. We do not see his past, thus do not know if he is not simply balancing the scales for some uncorrected error of a previous life. There are no victims. There are no accidents. Your mind is all-powerful and everything that happens to you, you have asked for and receive as you have asked. Everyone does receive the results of his own mind and since all of time is going on all the time, consequences could happen at any moment, whether in this life or in one's next incarnation.

Birth and death are unreal and so is reincarnation. Karma too is unreal. But in order to close the gap between the truth and our experience we have to have the bigger sense of the illusion so we can understand how to negotiate it safely. In other words reincarnation and karma are relative truths, not ultimate truths because we are only bound by them as long as we choose to be. All you have to do is make a tiny shift in consciousness, and karma is collapsed in its entirety. All you have to do is make a tiny shift in consciousness and you will never be reborn. All you have to do is make a tiny shift in consciousness and you will never again experience death. That tiny shift is a shift from body-consciousness to God-consciousness.

If death were a viable alternative to life, we would have destroyed ourselves long ago. Death is not possible. *God did not will the destruction of His creations, having created them for all eternity.* Baba says what fuels the cycle of birth and death is desire. Whatever we want is what we will experience. If we want the things of the world, the glamour, the pleasures, the temptations, the tinsel, the fame and the fortune, then that will draw us back into birth again and again, until we decide we would like a different purpose, a real purpose. Then we will set for ourselves a goal that is really legitimate, like waking up, finding out who we are, finding out if life is really only to end in death. Then we start to open ourselves to a more meaningful existence.

No one created by God can find joy in anything except the eternal. That is not because he is deprived of anything else, but because nothing else is worthy of him. We were willing to accept even death to deny our Creator, but He would not have it so and so it is not so. Death yields to life, simply because destruction is not true.

We made death the final purpose for everything, so then all must die unless given another purpose. You can change your mind. You can overcome death. Death is an attempt at resolving conflict by not willing at all. Life and death are opposites. They cannot both exist. If life is real, then death never happened. God is life. It is not possible for God to die. How then can anything He creates die? Death is experienced only as long as we protect it by keeping it away from eternal life.

What ACIM Has To Say About Death

"Death is the central dream from which all illusions stem. Is it not madness to think of life as being born, aging, losing vitality, and dying in the end? Death is the one fixed, unchangeable belief of the world that all things in it are born only to die. This is regarded as "the way of nature," not to be raised to question, but to be accepted as the "natural" law of life. The cyclical, the changing and the unsure; the undependable and the unsteady, waxing and waning in a certain way upon a certain path, - all this is taken as the Will of God. And no one asks if a benign Creator could will this.

"In this perception of the universe as God created it, it would be impossible to think of Him as loving. For who has decreed that all things pass away, ending in dust and disappointment and despair, can but be feared. He holds your little life in his hand but by a thread, ready to break it off without regret or care, perhaps today. Or if he waits, yet is the ending certain. Who loves such a god knows not of love, because he has denied that life is real. Death has become life's symbol. His world is now a battleground, where contradiction reigns and opposites make endless war. Where there is death is peace impossible.

"Death is the symbol of the fear of God. His love is blotted out in the idea, which holds it from awareness like a shield held up to obscure the sun. The grimness of the symbol is enough to show it cannot coexist with God. It holds an image of the Son of God in which he is "laid to rest" in devastation's arms, where worms wait to greet him and to last a little while by his destruction. Yet the worms as well are doomed to be destroyed as certainly. And so do all things live because of death. Devouring is nature's "law of life." God is insane, and fear alone is real.

"The curious belief that there is part of dying things that may go on apart from what will die, does not proclaim a loving God nor reestablish any grounds for trust. If death is real for anything, there is no life. Death denies life. But if there is reality in life death is denied. No compromise in this is possible. There is either a god of fear or One of Love. The world attempts a thousand compromises, and will attempt a thousand more. Not one should be acceptable to you because not one is acceptable to God. He did not make death because He did not make fear. Both are equally meaningless to Him.

"The "reality" of death is firmly rooted in the belief that God's child, His creation, is a body. And if God created bodies, death would indeed be real. But God would not be loving. There is no point at which the contrast between the perception of the real world and that of the world of illusions becomes more sharply evident. Death is indeed the death of God, if He is Love. All dreams will end when death is overcome. This is salvation's final goal, the end of all illusions. And in death are all illusions born. What can be born of death and still have life? But what is born of God and still can die? The inconsistencies, the compromises and rituals the world fosters in its vain attempts to cling to death and yet to think love real are mindless magic, ineffectual and meaningless. God is, and in Him all created things must be eternal. Do you not see that otherwise He has an opposite, and fear would be as real as love?

"Your one assignment could be stated thus: Accept no compromise in which death plays a part. And what is the end of death? Nothing but this; the realization that God's child is guiltless now and forever. Nothing but this. But do not let yourself forget it is not less than this."

Accept No Compromise Where Death Plays A Part

Are you willing to die to accept no compromise where death plays a part? The death of your body cannot get in the way of your eternal life, but lack of integrity due to fear of death can. In the movie about the Gulf War mentioned in chapter three, soldiers, who had been trained to be fearless, had not done all they could to save their captain and clearly had regrets.

They made a compromise with death and could not live with themselves because of their choices. In fearing death, they missed out on life.

Jesus said to his disciples, "I am prepared to lay down my life for you." He meant that even death was not going to stand in the way of his love. If it came to it, if he had to make the choice, he would die rather than stop expressing his eternal love for his cherished disciples. He refused to compromise with death. As he knew the unreality of his body, could its crucifixion be his maximum expression of love? To hold on to the idea that God sent Jesus into the world to die for one's sins is to think God cruel. Jesus' death by crucifixion was a choice he made. It was not God's will. Jesus' life is his message, not his death. He refused to compromise with death, as demonstrated in his resurrection and ascension.

Jesus' disciple, Peter, was not so free of body consciousness. On the night the Roman soldiers arrested Jesus in the Garden of Gethsemane, Peter denied Jesus three times. Because he feared his own death he did not want to be associated with Jesus. He was not prepared to do whatever was necessary to demonstrate his love for his master. He thought the preservation of his body more valuable than courageously facing death to express love for his beloved teacher. In that, he was accepting a compromise with death.

Joan of Arc was willing to be burned at the stake rather than denounce her voices. She was accepting no compromise where death plays a part. Truth was more important than life itself.

If you were living in Nazi Germany during Hitler's tyranny would you have been willing to risk your life for the safety of others? Love is fearless. There are many stories of great courage in defiance of Hitler's inhumanity. In one example from the movie, Schindler's List, Schindler took tremendous risks to save life by employing Jews to make inoperable weapons. He was at risk for insisting that the Jews who worked for him were indispensable and also for not producing up to standard. He risked his life for the sake of life. On the news in January of 2003, a young German doctor exposed inhumane treatment in North Korea. He was called a fanatic but stood strong, saying, "We Germans were accused of being passive during Hitler's regime and so I will not keep quiet now." We can learn from the past and get it right in this moment. I salute this German doctor's courage.

Once a friend shared a past life wherein she belonged to an American Indian tribe during the time of the brutal massacres. She'd had a vision in which she saw her whole village being wiped out but was afraid to tell the chief because she was just a little girl and felt she would not be heard. The following day as witnessed in her vision, the village was totally annihilated. Though she died with the rest, she carried a feeling of guilt with her into this life. She felt she had let her village down and was responsible for their bloodbath. Had she found the courage to tell the chief, even if he hadn't listened, she would have had the satisfaction of having done what she could to save her people. She compromised with death by contracting into fear. Though you may not be able to prevent physical death, if you live your life fearlessly, you are accepting no compromise with death. In this life she has become a great teacher who boldly declares the message of accepting no compromise with death.

In the movie, John Q, the father of a son who needs a heart transplant doesn't have the money for the necessary operation. John Q is forced to take extreme measures, including hold up the emergency room of a hospital. As a last resort he is willing to take his own life so his son can have his heart. In the nick of time, a heart is donated and there is a happy ending. I think that even if his son had not survived the operation, John Q would have been able to live with himself in peace, knowing that he had done absolutely everything possible unto death to save his child. He would have had no regrets. He was not afraid of dying and in that he knew how to live. Accepting no compromise where death plays a part is for our peace of mind.

Martin Luther King, Jr. frequently commented that threats on his life could not diminish his passion for justice for his people. There are many examples of heroic efforts wherein people are willing to risk their lives for the sake of the highest good for all. Generally, when we hear about, read about or watch movies of these fearless acts of noble character and deathless courage, tears spring to our eyes. We see that love is more important than life itself. We recognize goodness and courage as real and it makes our hearts soar. True courage inspires nobility and fearlessness. Fear not for your own life and you are accepting no compromise where death plays a part. One who lives so fearlessly knows he is not his body and that he cannot die.

Fanaticism Is A Compromise With Death

There are those who don't mind the idea of dying because their religion assures them they will go to heaven for their courage. The Muslim suicide bombers are a prime example of that very idea. They blow themselves up hoping to take out a number of innocent 'enemy' civilians in the process. They act out of hatred for their brothers, the Jews. They justify killing themselves because they have been brainwashed to believe they will be warmly received in heaven for their courage. Has anyone of them come back from the dead to confirm their belief? They are simply acting on blind faith and killing innocent people with their distorted understanding.

Are they different from the heroes we just touched on? They too are willing to give their lives for what they believe in. There is all the difference in the world. The suicide bombers are destroying life and acting from hatred, while the heroes are saving life and are motivated by love. The suicide bombers have no compunction about killing those who refuse to adopt their religion or beliefs. This is not accepting no compromise where death plays a part. This is using death as a weapon and thus making death real. They are exclusive and have forgotten the truth that all are their brothers and sisters. If they knew that, they could not kill anyone for any reason.

Some Christians believe that Jesus death on the cross assures them they will go to heaven after they die. Has anyone who believed this come back to confirm for the Christians that it is so? Jesus taught that the kingdom of heaven is within. If you wait till you die to get something you don't have right now, you are missing the truth and making death real. I would only wonder if life would be so different without a body. You always take yourself with you wherever you go. You cannot escape your mind, but you can transform it and then you don't have to wait till you die to go to heaven. Then you can be in heaven right now.

I am willing to do anything to end the suffering on the planet. Is that fanaticism? Is that terrorism? I want even the terrorist saved. I don't support his acts but he is still my brother. Nothing he does can change who he is. God created him innocent and perfect and God did not change His mind. A terrorist's actions cannot change his truth. He is not more powerful than God. In fact I refuse to die until the whole planet is free of ego. That is my commitment.

I yearn for the end of suffering for all. No one is excluded. All are God's children and therefore my family. There are no exceptions. *Until not one slave remains to walk the earth's surface is my salvation complete.* A terrorist or a fanatic is a slave to ego. Anyone who is not living the truth of love for all is a slave and is suffering by definition. To yearn for the end of suffering for all humanity is an impossible goal, yet with God all things are possible. With only a handful of such fearless souls as those mentioned earlier, the world will be saved.

Ascension Plan As Escape Makes The Unreal Real

There are those who say, "We cannot die, so let's transfigure our bodies into light and leave this world of illusion." So far I don't know of any success stories, probably because they are trying to escape the world rather than transform it into the real world. You cannot escape your mind and the world is merely a reflection of your mind. You can only leave the real world at will for then your mind is healed and the world will reflect that wholeness. A whole mind is one that has been restored to oneness with God. It is again merged with God and is free to be in the world or not, determined by what will be of greatest service. An unhealed mind is bound to an unreal world by definition. Escaping the world cannot be done either by death or ascension. Only in knowing the world can be transformed from unreal to real is there hope of life without opposite.

There is some evidence that the Anasazis ascended en mass. Studies indicate that they were a peaceful Native American tribe, apparently living in total alignment with Great Spirit. During the late 1200's, they experienced a severe drought in all the land. Their consciousness simply did not support starving to death. They had not focused on ascension. They merely found themselves in a situation where their knowledge that they were sustained by Great Spirit rather than by food and water permitted a solution from out of time. They must have freed themselves sufficiently of victim/victimizer consciousness to allow ascension to be a viable alternative. This is different from a group trying to leave because they don't like it here. Ideas cannot leave their source and the world is an idea in our minds.

Tukaram, mentioned earlier in this chapter, did not attempt to escape the world. God scooped him up due to his devotion and pure life. No one who wishes to escape will be successful, whether they try to escape with drugs, alcohol, food, sleep, television, video games, ascension attempts, suicide or death. Anything can be used or misapplied depending on one's purpose. What is the point of knowing that you cannot die? You will not fear death. You will fearlessly look death in the face. You will recognize that you are immortal and thus be victorious over death. You will know who you are.

God Has Nothing To Do With Death

To live in the real world is to live in the world God created. God created a world where everything lives forever. Imagine what that would be like. Just for a moment let's take death away from everything. Imagine not being able to lose the ones you love, your family, friends, pets... Imagine trees, flowers, mountains and the sun living forever. Doesn't that feel good? It does mean you have no final solution to your problems except to solve them. Doesn't knowing that God did not make death remove a huge barrier you had put up against Him? You probably weren't even aware that the barrier was there. But as long as you believe in death, you invariably think it is God's idea and thus you will be afraid of Him. If you do not love God with a passion, if you do not find yourself irresistibly drawn to Him, you are probably blaming Him for the world being a place where everything dies. It is not true. We are responsible. God has nothing to do with death.

Ellie Wiesel, a holocaust survivor, tells the story of a group of Jewish lawyers and judges held captive in Auschwitz who decided one night to put God on trial. They deliberated the whole night and by morning had found God guilty, for surely the inhumane atrocities they witnessed and experienced could only have happened because God had abandoned them. Despite their gloomy verdict they expressed a beautiful surrender to God by concluding the trial with, "Now let us pray." They did not forget God, though they could not find a way around blaming Him for their suffering.

God does not will anyone to suffer. He was not the cause of their anguish. To think He was only added to their misery. I am agonized by the horrors that went on in the concentration camps in W.W.II, the genocide of the Native Americans, the brutality perpetrated against the Afro-Americans... Ego is behind all hatreds that lead to cruelty on the basis of religion, skin color... We cannot solve the problem by blaming God, but by seeing truly what ego is and relinquishing it within ourselves in the service of the whole of humanity. When a critical mass is willing to offer this maximum expression of love, we will end horrific genocide for all humanity and live in peace with all our brothers and sisters as God intended.

Compassion For Humanity's Pain Is Life

There are those who say, "It doesn't get any deader than this." They mean that life as we know it is living death. We are the walking dead due to isolating ourselves from others' pain. Once I was part of a discussion centered on the Falun Dafa exercises that so many Chinese citizens have been brutally tortured to death for practicing. I was expressing my outrage and how I was willing even to go to China if that would serve. Someone else, a student of ACIM, piped up, "All you have to do is change your mind, Yaani." It felt so lacking in compassion. Another student of ACIM asked if I would be willing to do nothing. It sounded so dead, so intellectual and conceptual. It was completely devoid of heart. They had used the teachings of ACIM to intellectualize themselves out of any feelings of compassion for the horrors that take place in the world.

Later, as I was driving down the road thinking about our conversation, I saw how protecting ourselves from other people's pain was living death. I found myself dropping every last barrier that I had in place to keep out the pain of the world. I let it all in and found myself alive as never before. I felt so whole and real. Death is cutting ourselves off from other people's suffering, thus putting the suffering outside of ourselves. That is living death out of fear of having to experience another's pain. We create separation to avoid suffering. You will naturally be compassionate toward all who suffer and do what you can for them when you recognize there is nothing outside of your mind. By helping them you are helping yourself.

Would you do nothing if you broke your leg? Excruciating pain causes you to act. You don't even hesitate or think about it. You act. As long as anyone is suffering, it is your pain. Because I know the unreality of pain, I am willing to be responsible for it. In taking responsibility, all I want with all my heart and soul is the end of suffering for all, and I have a willingness to do whatever it takes. That passion can be used to literally see miracles of healing take place before our very eyes. A passionate determination to draw your circle and declare that enough is enough will make a difference.

False Equanimity And Disowned Guilt Lead To Deadness

When I first started visiting Sai Baba's ashram, I was instructed to cultivate equanimity. No matter what happened, I handled it with the same friendly, yet all too ready smile. It was too available, too predictable. I didn't feel my other emotions because I was told that only supreme happiness was my true reality. I wasn't authentic with what I was experiencing in each moment. I prided myself on being spiritual, but still felt unworthy and a gnawing lack of self-confidence. I felt like the walking dead. I had conceptual understanding and was misapplying the idea of equanimity.

Once I realized there must be more, I opened the door to experiences that offered the opportunity to stay in a state of deep equanimity while responding in a real way to my present circumstances as well. There are those who suggest to fake it till you make it, but it is my experience that when you face it, it can be undone, and when you fake it, it keeps resurfacing. Any more I am always aware of a calm that comes from a deep trust in God. That is equanimity. I know I am unaffectable, but at the same time I don't deny or suppress my emotions. Nor do I wallow in the negative ones. I give them to God to be healed.

Another way to be the walking dead is to put guilt outside of yourself. When you project guilt out, you no longer feel guilty, but you have cut yourself off from the one you project onto, thus from a part of yourself and so you no longer know who you are. When Adam projected his guilt for eating the apple, that is for making ego, onto Eve, a deep sleep fell upon Adam. He cut himself off from his love in order to escape his guilt. In so doing he forgot who he was. That is death.

Only when you see everyone's innocence do you know your innocence and only then have you included everyone and everything back into your mind and thereby realized who you are. You cannot rid yourself of guilt by projecting it out. On the contrary, projecting it is how you keep it. It isn't real and only by projecting it do you make it real. When you stand still in it, you see its nothingness. Then only is your mind whole and then only are you alive and you know who you are. You know you are life without opposite.

Uncertainty about what you must be is self-deception on a scale so vast, its magnitude can hardly be conceived. To be alive and not to know yourself is to believe that you are really dead. For what is life except to be yourself, and what but you can be alive instead? Who is the doubter? What is it he doubts? Whom does he question? Who can answer him? He merely states that he is not himself, and therefore, being something else, becomes a questioner of what that something is. Yet he could never be alive at all unless he knew the answer. If he asks as if he does not know, it merely shows he does not want to be the thing he is. He has accepted it because he lives; has judged against it and denied its worth and has decided that he does not know the only certainty by which he lives.

Where does confusion about who we are come from? We made ego to be our source in God's stead. In convincing ourselves that we actually succeeded in making our own creator, we also convinced ourselves that we were self-authored. Since ego is nothing, in believing that it is our source, we believe that we are nothing. We donned a false identity and this confusion around our identity is the cause of our not knowing something so basic as who we are. Once we accept God as our Source, all confusion around who we are vanishes.

Until we know who we are we identify with ourselves as vulnerable, fragile, physical/emotional bodies. We close down so we won't get hurt, yet in that action we die a little. We have to recognize that we cannot be hurt by anyone or anything and that to close down is ego's solution to pain. To heal is God's solution, and then instead of dead, dull, lifeless and purposeless, we will feel alive, eager, enthusiastic, energetic, passionate and vibrant. That is who we are. We are life. To be alive is to fully embrace life with the deepest love. To be alive is to put our whole heart and soul into our every endeavor. Baba says, "Strive to your maximum capacity for excellence." Be alive. Be vital. Be happy and pass it along. Make everyone you meet happy. That is life. Then you will not question who you are. You will simply know.

Beloved Mother-Father God, Thank You that You have nothing to do with death. Grant us the strength to accept no compromise where death plays a part. Grant us the courage to look at death without fear and see its nothingness.. Help us to discover true life, full of joy, passion, compassion, enthusiasm and vitality as you intended us to experience always. Thank You for the gift of eternal life.

May all beings in all the worlds be happy and blest, Amen.

Figure 8 – God Only Creates Eternal Life

Everything (Eternity)

Eternity	**Life**	Oneness
God-Dependence	Love	Freedom
Real	Truth	Non-judgment
Heaven	Peace	Creation
Innocence	Knowledge	All-Powerful

Nothing (time and space)

Time/space	**Happy Dream (Satva) God's solution - collapses time**
Ego-dependence	Enthusiastic, energetic, passionate, happy, vital
Unreal	Laugh at death, be certain about who you are
Hell	Accept eternal life as a final solution
Guilt	Accept no compromise where death plays a part
Death	**Nightmare (Rajo Guna) - makes time**
Fear	Death is feared and dreaded
Untruth	Death by old age, sickness, suffering, tragedy
War	Suicide bombers -perish to attack others
Ignorance	Sell soul to hold onto life of body
Separation	**Deep Sleep (Thamo) Ego's solution - freezes time**
Bondage	Avoid topic of death
Judgment	Escape present by thinking death will be better
Mis-creation	"Suffering is God's will" – callous, blind
Powerless	Sedation through alcohol, drugs, food sleep
	Purposeless existence - "Doesn't matter what I do"

Direction of Consciousness Awakening

Chapter 8 Highlights – God Only Creates Eternal Life

Chapter 9

Are You Ready to Master Love and Let Go of Fear?

Start the day with love; Fill the day with love,
End the day with love, That is the way to God.
                                                    Sai Baba

Love Is The Only Power

In the late 60's, Phyllis Krystal was flying home from India on an airplane which got hijacked. The hijackers had somehow managed to carry guns on board. One was pointing his weapon directly at her. She fervently prayed to Sai Baba and He guided her to send them love. She responded, "I cannot, I am too frightened Baba, but let Your love pour through me." In that instant she felt a tremendous surge of Divine love flow through her to the hijackers. They started to tremble and spontaneously dropped their weapons. The whole operation was aborted on the spot and no one was hurt. Fearful situations can be transformed through love. *You cannot master fear, but you can master love,* and when you do, fear vanishes.

Once, during our late teens, a girlfriend, Judy, and I were traveling by train from Holland to Poland. We were asleep in the night coach when a conductor asked for our passports with transit visas for East Berlin. We were not aware that visas were required so had boarded without proper documents. The conductor told us he could get the visas stamped for us. Too sleepy to argue we agreed and fell back asleep. At the next stop we were again asked to show our passports but did not have them as the conductor had not returned them to us. We were thrown off the train and put into separate jail cells in a station in Berlin.

While the authorities were interrogating me, Judy, being Jewish and having been raised with first hand accounts of inhumane atrocities perpetrated against her people, was terrified, envisioning me being tortured or worse. I calmly explained the situation and the officer could see that I was not frightened and that my story sounded reasonable. He made some calls and located our passports. I was ignorant of the horrors of W.W.II and that was undoubtedly a blessing under the circumstances. The officer asked Judy to join us for a coke and we all laughed at the story we could write home about. Soon we were on the next train and at the following station reconnected with our passports. We were pretty careless when I look back on it, but fearlessness helped us to negotiate what could have been a very bad scene relatively smoothly.

Misperception produces fear, while true perception reveals love. To use the metaphor of the rope and the snake again, though all the time there is only a rope on the ground, if you pass by it at dusk, you misperceive it as a snake and get frightened. The rope never turned into a snake. It was only misperception that produced fear. Judy was fearful because of her misperception, based on stories from the past. Every moment is new and when we have no past, we have no reason to fear.

There Are Only Two Emotions, Love And Fear

Only God and God's love are real. We were created to be and have love as our only experience, both with God and with everyone. Yet we all experience fear because we have made for ourselves unreal experiences, separate from God. Any experience that is separate from God will be devoid of love by definition. Those experiences will be fearful. The fact is all fear is illusion.

The illusion that God is fearful is a prime example. That idea comes from trust in an ego that wants you to believe God wrathful, vengeful, punishing, judgmental, sitting on some throne somewhere condemning you to eternal hell and damnation. That is the furthest thing from God's mind as He deeply loves all that He creates. But, as long as you believe that to be so, you will be afraid and will not want God near you and ego will survive. Ego wants to exist. It will try very hard to deceive you because its survival depends on you loving it more than you love God, thus it tries to convince you that God is other than who He is. It tries to convince you to believe in illusions. God is but love, and therefore so are you.

Hatred is another word for fear. You will only hate what you fear. Love cannot hate, for love has no fear. Joy is another word for love. *If you are not wholly joyous, something is blocking your love.* Love has no fear and means letting go of fear. When you are love, fear cannot exist and free of fear, your joy will bubble forth. You were created to be happy all the time. Baba says, "I am always happy." He is constantly expressing His love and joy. He is constantly giving joy to others. That is why He is so happy.

However, don't use this teaching to feign happiness when you are not happy, for then you are out of integrity with what is happening in the moment and you will feel even more confusion. If you are not supremely happy, stand still in what is happening and ask that the blocks to the awareness of love's constant presence be removed for you. If you fake love, it will not bring you into true joy. You will be superficial and will be fooling yourself. Be honest with yourself. That way joy can resurface naturally and fully.

When you awaken joy in others, you will naturally feel joyful. When you are happy, you are in love with everyone and everything. It is up to you whether love and happiness are your experience. Once when I had to get a tire fixed, the repairman greeted me, "Hello, hon." I felt his sincerity, warmth and purity, and it gave me so much joy. It was so simple. I sensed immediately that he had no ulterior motives. One just feels that. Everyone can recognize pure goodness. He was working hard the whole time I waited and he was happy. I could tell and I felt happy just to be around him, though I had nothing to do but wait for my car. It is not difficult to be loving, but it does require purity. It does require knowing who you are. As long as you think you need to exchange or get something from someone, your offering will not be genuine. Genuineness is rare and refreshing.

Master Love To Abolish Fear

Harriet Tubman, a nineteenth century Afro-American affectionately called Moses, rescued over 3000 slaves on the underground railway. Her trust in God was implicit, her cause just. She was guided and fearless. She loved her people and was determined to give as many Blacks as possible lives of dignity. She took tremendous risks. There was a bounty hunter who had been offered a handsome reward for her capture, dead or alive. But he was an unusual man considering his particular profession. He had heart and admired her fearlessness. Though he had a reputation for being the very best, he had a deep respect for Harriet, and when he finally caught up with her, he told her how honored he was to meet her and let her go without turning her in or receiving his reward. Her love for her people made her fearless in the face of injustice. She could not be touched. She had mastered love, thus fear had been abolished.

Once a friend, Colleen, and I hiked up to the top of Arunachala Mountain near Ramana Maharshi's ashram in Southern India. While taking our picnics out of our knap sacks, we were suddenly surrounded by a dozen or so very large and vicious looking monkeys. They were hungry and wanted our lunch or maybe even us for lunch. I calmly looked them in the eye. At no time was I afraid and exuded a strength of love and self-confidence. We were, after all, on the top of a sacred mountain, in the presence of a holy sage who had lived there in a small hut of sticks and burlap, having sustained himself purely on God's providence for over 10 years. I was in a very deep and profound meditative consciousness of blissful expansion. Love had been mastered in that moment and fear was simply not present. Keeping eye contact with my brother monkeys, I got up slowly and sending them pure love, backed away coaching Colleen to do the same. We retreated unharmed. Colleen was very frightened. Had I not had the composure I did, we might well have been brutally attacked. When love is mastered, fear has no power.

Being fearless in the face of danger can be exhilarating. One fine morning while Al Drucker was living on the Big Sur coast of California, Gayatri was playing in his mind. Gayatri is a mantra that asks that our limited consciousness be merged with the limitless consciousness that we are in truth. He went for a hike into the nearby mountains and all the while Gayatri continued effortlessly. As he was coming back down the mountain, what was standing directly in his path but a huge mountain lion, lean and mean. Al was not afraid. Gayatri was going. He crouched down so the animal would not be frightened of him. He softly called out to the cat and held out his hand. Slowly the animal slithered away. Al felt only love for the animal that could have torn him to pieces. He cautiously walked past where the animal had been seen and then when he felt safe to do so, fairly flew down the mountain thrilled to his very marrow. He perceived the lion as a visitation from Baba, so packed his bags and flew off to India. Al was fearless, thus the lion could not touch him.

When you are afraid of anything, you are acknowledging its power to hurt you. In your fearlessness, you acknowledge your invulnerability. However, let this teaching not be used to put yourself in harms way to test your fearlessness. There is a story of an Indian saint who taught his disciples to be fearless. One disciple took the teaching to heart and placed himself in front of a stampeding elephant. I will spare you the details of what followed. Always temper the teachings with a bit of common sense. If ever you do find yourself in a tight spot, you can negotiate it fearlessly by remembering God. God is love, and where there is love, fear has no power.

Love Has No Opposite

Love cannot be taught. It is who we are. But we cannot be who we are as long as we let fear stand in the way of our love. Though love has no opposite, fear is its seeming opposite. If you are not feeling your love, it must be that fear is blocking love's flow. *Our task then is not to seek for love, but merely to seek and find all of the barriers within ourselves that we have built against it. It is not necessary to seek for what is true, but it is necessary to seek for what is false and to then recognize its falseness.* Once seen, fear disappears because it is not real.

All fear is reducible to the false belief that we could usurp the power of God. That is a fearful thought and is behind all anxiety of any kind. Adam and Eve ate the fruit and hid when they heard God approaching. They were afraid of God because they thought they had replaced Him as Source and that He would therefore punish them. God is Source and cannot be overthrown. They could not act outside of His will, but that they thought they could frightened them. Fear took the place of love. Fear is of ego. Only after they made ego did they experience fear. Until then their only experience was love.

There are those who think fear is a good thing. What if there were no fear? What if you were not frightened by the idea of karmic consequences? Because of fear, it is posited, people behave decently toward each other. That may be true. Knowing that you will be punished if you take certain actions is sometimes effective toward self-restraint. Perhaps fear of punishment does keep your behavior in check, but wouldn't love be just as effective, or perhaps even more so?

Love was Adam and Eve's only experience until they became fearful due to making their own source. Once they were fearful, the world reflected fear back to them. They were cast out of the garden and two angels with flaming swords barred their reentry. One of their two sons killed the other and the unreal world of fear and hate was up and running. Murder had never happened before the time of terror took the place of love. We must go back to the time of terror in our minds and let it be healed. Then we will again be in the experience of only love. That time is when we made ego, and is right now, as all of time is going on all the time. All we have to do is stand still right now and own that we tried to make our own source. As that is impossible, nothing happened, thus we have no reason to fear. It does require an admission that we were wrong and that takes courage.

There are those who insist that no matter what our experience may appear to be, all that is happening is love. In a way they are correct, for love is all that is possible, but when I was raped, that was not love. When you are sick you may feel the love of those concerned, but the experience itself is not love. When you are playing tennis and your partner cheats, that is not love. When a husband is unfaithful to his wife that is not love. When you see a kid stealing a candy bar from a store that is not love. Love is all there is, yet there are expressions that are not love. An earthquake is not love, nor is a famine or wars or Jews being exterminated in Auschwitz... These are not acts of love. They are acts of fear and fear is not love, it is rather a lack of love or a call for love. Fear is not real. When love is brought to a fearful situation, fear must disappear. Love can transform the hearts of those who are fearful and inspire them to act in ways that support their truth as love. The tennis partner can be inspired to play fair and the child to stop stealing. God's love is the transformative agent.

Love Is More Than A Constant Desensitized Smile

The idea of love has been much misunderstood and misapplied. It is not enough to act lovingly in all situations. If a mother sees a child stealing and ignores him he will grow up to be a thief. That is not love. Love takes appropriate actions to prevent inappropriate behavior. If a child is unruly and a mother does not discipline, that is not love. In the work place, three women were named women of the year (2002) for being whistle blowers in corporate America. They exposed evidence for corruption in the work place and plucked up the courage to speak out. That was love in action. Had they remained silent to ensure employment, they would have been choosing fear.

Unconditional love does not mean a lack of discernment. Love doesn't say everything is perfect when people are suffering. Unconditional love acts to relieve suffering. Unconditional love does not mean loving ego. Ego is not nice. Ego is the cause of all suffering. To love ego is to support suffering and that is not love. God does not wish anyone to suffer. A miracle undoes suffering. That is unconditional love. Suffering is not real, but if you say it is perfect, if you justify it, you make it real and that is not love. Those who find perfection in imperfection are making the unreal real. If you inspire a shift in consciousness toward the undoing of suffering, you are transforming the unreal back into the real and that is love.

There are those who think that love expresses itself only with a pasted on smile no matter what is going on at any particular moment. An acquaintance, Sandy, who had this belief told me how her boyfriend expressed displeasure toward her because he was angry with her inappropriate liaisons with other males. Sandy prided herself that all she did in response was smile back at him. She called this unconditional love, but her understanding was really only conceptual. I suspect her 'magnanimity' was not well received by her beau. You can say, "I love you," and it can feel empty or it can be transporting. The difference is your purity, sincerity and genuineness. Are you real? Words and actions in and of themselves are not necessarily love, but rather may only reflect conceptual understanding. Love is deep, real, natural and easy and elicits joy in others.

Sandy held the notion that she should be free to be in sexual relationship with any man and she called that unconditional love and oneness. Baba says of that concept, "Animals enjoy that freedom." It is body consciousness and has nothing to do with love. To want bodily freedom is to want freedom on the level of form, which you would only choose if you thought you were a body. That consciousness binds you to form. To be truly one, we must move beyond form to content, where we are indeed one. We express true oneness by joining at the level of mind, which is content. Sandy's friend was hurting because he felt dishonored and reduced to a body by her actions. For her to respond as she did exposed a self-interest that did not connect with his pain at all. Communication did not happen. Love is mindful and communicates.

How do you know how to express love in a way that is appropriate to the situation? How do you feel inside? Follow your heart, not your head.

When your heart is pure, the right response will be readily available for every situation. Ask God to show you how to respond. It is not hard. You are unconditional love. If Sandy had been open to hearing her beau, she might have responded by apologizing and mending her errant ways. You can have an idea about love, but if you don't feel a heart connection, it is not love.

Love opens the heart of another. It cannot be learned or taught. It can be recognized. You recognize it because you are love, but some purification has to take place first. A pure heart knows love. When your heart is open, vulnerable and trusting, you are love. Then you understand what is being communicated and your response will be real. It will be right and it will be received.

Once in an interview Sai Baba revealed to a couple that He knew that the man had been with other women. Then He scolded the woman for allowing her husband to stray from his commitment. Baba was showing her that by not standing up for herself, she was not honoring or loving herself. Baba, in His infinite love, was showing her how to want only the very best for herself. She deserves the best because she is a precious child of God. A husband who is playing the field is not honoring his wife and if she supports his inappropriate behavior, probably to keep the peace, she is not honoring herself.

You cannot love others if you do not love yourself. I'm not referring to narcissistic love, where you don't care about others, in a worshipping of yourself. That is not self-love, but rather self-loathing. When you love yourself, you will express it through the utmost compassion, caring and kindness toward everyone. At the same time you will only let yourself be treated with the deepest honor and respect.

Once Sai Baba had gone to a hill station in Northern India. It was Easter morning as He headed back to His ashram in the South, while an elderly couple was coming up the mountain on a scooter to offer Him their obeisance. Since they were poor they were scantily dressed, yet unmindful of the cold. They were full of devotion and intent on expressing their love for their beloved Lord. When Baba intercepted them He had His car stop and received them and their worshipful offering with the most gracious love. They were overcome by His tender reception, as He was by their offering and everyone who looked on was moved to tears. Such is the power of love and it is not hard to recognize.

Ring Story Taught Self-Worth

God reveals to us our lack of self-love, complete with the cure for our particular malady when we are ready to be who we are. Once in an interview Baba manifested a Shirdi ring for a young man. Shirdi was Sai

Baba's previous incarnation. The ring did not fit. Baba took it back and manifested another ring, which did fit. I was sitting at His feet. Suddenly I was startled to notice something sparkling at me from between His lap and the arm of His chair. I had always accepted with full faith that Baba manifested objects. Yet, the instant I saw the object sparkling at me and questioned my seeing, it surfaced even more prominently and there could be no doubt. At no time did I notice His hand near the ring, so how did it get there? At first I was shocked but soon relaxed as I realized Baba has some Divine mischief in store for some lucky soul.

He invited a small group into the inner room. With His hand cupped as if He were holding something, He closed the door. He was obviously clutching the rejected ring. To me it was unmistakable that He had taken with Him the manifested Shirdi ring that was too small for the young lad. I did not see Him reach down to retrieve the ring and I was at full attention. I wondered what He was going to do. When I looked around the group left behind, I could tell that no one else was wondering. This was somehow a play just for me.

When He came out again, He called our group into the inner room. He asked everyone how they were. The conversation was casual and light and put everyone at ease. He is the perfect host. When it came my turn, I said, "By Your grace all is well in our home, Swami." He said, "Yes, yes, I know." Then He held my hand and looked at a ring with His picture in a blessing pose. He had materialized it some 10 years earlier. It was rather worn, with some chips broken off and the band quite badly bent. He asked, 'What do you want? You want new ring?" Affectionately taking His darling little brown hand in both of mine, I said with all my love, "I only want You, Baba, forever and ever."

Ignoring my passion, He responded, "I will give you new ring in the main room, so everyone can enjoy." I didn't particularly want a ring, but it seemed Baba had His own agenda, and of course I was delighted just to let Swami unfold His play. When we were in the outer room again, He took my old ring and passed it around to show how banged up it was. He asked, "What shall I do with it?" Someone piped up, "Fix it, Baba." Someone else suggested, "Make her a new ring, Baba." It was all very light and playful. The ring came to me and I passed it on to Baba. He said, "Wait, wait, don't haste, don't haste."

With a mischievous smile He asked me once again, "What do you want?" Again I patiently responded, "I only want You, Baba." "Would you like Shirdi ring?" I was shocked as I instantly recalled the Shirdi ring Baba had made for the young man, which didn't fit, which I then saw between His lap and the arm of His chair, and then clutched in His closed hand. I must have turned green. I could not say anything. I just smiled a weak smile. He did not seem the least bit troubled, but went about His business of inviting the next group into the smaller room, again with His right hand closed over something, which I assumed was again the rejected Shirdi ring. But now I understood that it was destined for me.

I was incensed! I could not have been more offended. Baba was going to give me a rejected ring! Never! I would simply not accept it. I would politely say, "No, thank You, Baba." He was with that other group a very long time. As I waited my mind continued to churn out all kinds of ideas. I thought about how I would be trading in Sai Baba for Shirdi Baba, who I didn't really feel a strong connection with. Maybe I should just insist on keeping my old banged up ring rather than trading it in for a new one. Still Baba hadn't returned. So I fantasized, 'If I were to have a new ring, and if I could have any ring I wanted, what would I choose? I like elegant things. I like diamonds and gold. I do not need anything, but if Swami insists on giving me a ring, it would be nice to be given a ring I would like.'

By the time He reappeared, I had pretty much regained my composure and was prepared for whatever was to happen next with the ring drama. Again Baba sweetly asked, "What do you want?" Again I responded, now with just a tinge of exasperation, "I only want You, Baba." Comically, Baba imitated me perfectly, and then jumping out of His chair and throwing open His arms with a big smile gleefully exclaimed, "Here I am, I'm yours!" I was so touched. I didn't know what to say or do. I just looked at His endearing preciousness and fell totally in love all over again. I wanted to throw my arms around Him. Then Swami waved His hand and made a dazzling diamond ring, with three large brilliant stones in a very elegant gold setting. He placed it on my finger exclaiming with delight, "Perfect fit." I was absolutely stunned, overwhelmed by His love.

As He always does, at the end of the interview, He distributed vibhuti (sacred ash) packets to everyone. When He came to me, He held up both of His open hands directly in front of my face and said, "See? I didn't immediately get it and reached forward to kiss His beautiful delicate hands. "Hey," He scolded playfully, and tapped me lightly on the head. I felt like a naughty schoolgirl who had just had the perfect encounter and then blown it. While continuing to pass the vibhuti packets to everyone else He kept glancing mischievously in my direction to see if I'd gotten it yet. Suddenly the light bulb went on and I understood that He was communicating, 'See, no Shirdi ring.' He was letting me know that He had staged that whole play for my benefit.

It was not till later that I understood what He was offering with that little drama. I had always thought of myself as undeserving of the very best. I didn't love myself and lacked self-confidence. I was shy and rarely asked for anything. I didn't think I was worthy. Baba set up a drama where He restored a desire for the best, a desire to get in touch with what I really want. In saying to God, "This is what I want," I regained the confidence to say it to anyone. I knew from then on that I didn't have to settle for less than the best for myself. I deserve the best because I am a wholly worthy child of God. As a precious child of God I was created to be and have everything.

We ask for far too little. What are you asking for? Are you settling for less than everything? You deserve all the happiness, peace and love in the whole world. This does not mean to want the things of the world. The ring in itself is merely symbolic. Had I politely agreed to the Shirdi ring I would have been asking for far too little. My response demonstrated self-love and self-worth. I would never have been happy to have a ring Baba initially made for someone else. Baba says, "You come asking for a cup of coffee when I am prepared to give you the whole ocean of Divine nectar." Don't be falsely humble. True humility is grandeur. You are God. Act like God. Live like God. Walk with your head held high in the glory of who you are as pure unconditional love, wholly worthy of the very best. You do know who you are. Love yourself. Be yourself.

Tough Love Used For A Sacred Purpose

God is unconditional love, yet I have experienced Sai Baba's anger. I have seen Him with lots of expressions, not one was ever a plastic superficial smile of 'unconditional love.' Once in an interview I was on the receiving end of His tough love. When He shouted at me, I was not stunned, surprisingly. I was calm and open to receive His gift. I recognized Baba's anger as moving me toward collapsing time. He was using anger to heal my mind, not to create further wounds. There was a huge difference between His shakti and some other experiences I have had where the energy was of similar intensity. Baba's purpose was healing because He is love and cannot but act in the best interest of those He contacts. He was expressing His love and I recognized it as love, though it took the form of anger.

In a subsequent interview again He said some rather strong words and then raised His hand as if to strike me. His hand came just short of my cheek. He turned abruptly away. I was holding onto His feet. I couldn't help but note that they did not twitch or move at all, though His whole body turned swiftly away. That's impossible. I have tried that maneuver myself a number of times. The message seemed to be 'hold on to the feet.' The feet do not change expression or vary. They are firm and unwavering and Baba was inviting me to step into that level of trust and faith.

Another woman in our group had the presence to express her love for Baba immediately after His expression of intense anger. He responded with the sweetest, "I love you too." There was no anger in Him in that very next instant. It was remarkable. I had never experienced anyone to have so much anger one moment and then be so completely loving in the very next. It showed that Baba was using anger to heal and not to wound. He was not angry with me. He was expressing love. I felt His love. Love is appropriate to the situation. It is not conceptual.

Baba says, "Everyone must develop the higher values and consider himself as Atma (true Self). This is the mission for which I have come – to make known to all this sacred knowledge of Atma. I will bring all people near Me and make them completely ego-free. For many years it has been sweetness, kindness and soft persuasion; from now on it will be different. I will drag you to Me. I will place you on the table and operate. It is My love that prompts Me to save you. It is My love that prompts Me to open your eyes before you get bogged down deeper in the swamp of worldly life."

Baba's unconditional love is not contained. Unconditional love is not limited to superficial niceties. You know when you are real and when you are phony. You are love. You do know how to express love. It is your nature. True unconditional love supports purity, integrity and the moral fabric of society. It doesn't just say, "I love you no matter what you do." See if your 'unconditional love' is pure or if it betrays a lack of self-worth.

If you have another's betterment in mind you do love him though your actions may not necessarily seem loving. If you love someone you want their salvation and are willing to do whatever you are directed by Spirit toward that end. It may be to withhold tenderness. That is generally Baba's method of inspiring transformation in people's hearts and lives. He showers love on some and others He purposely ignores. There is always a deeper significance to His every action.

In Professor Kasturi's book, Loving God, he shares how Baba frequently avoided him. This withdrawal was unbearable but always when the 'wrath' was appeased Kasturi would understand why Baba had cut him off from His love. Once Kasturi had gone on a talking tour and pride had slipped in. Baba knows everything. He insists on perfect purity because where there is impurity you have turned from God and Baba's ignoring you is only reflecting back to you your own mind. Once exposed it can be healed. The doctor might prescribe bitter medicine though his interest is always in the cure.

Win God's Love

Baba says it is not so important that you love God. What is really important is that you experience God's love. True, God loves everyone unconditionally, but if you are not pure in thought, word and deed, you have allied with ego, and have turned away from God. When you turn away from

Him, God leaves you alone. This is at your choosing. Baba says, "If you want Me, you deserve Me. If you want ego, I leave you alone."

When you love and serve others you are loving God and opening the door to the experience of God's love. All are God and we love God when we act in a Godly fashion toward everyone and treat all as God. Love is purity. You cannot be impure and loving at the same time, for impurity causes harm and that is not love. We do not love God when we show unkindness toward others for all are God's children. Jesus said, "As much as you have clothed and fed the least of these my brothers, you have done it unto me." All acts of kindness are expressions of love for God, as this poem conveys:

> *Abou Ben Adam (may his tribe increase)*
> *Awoke one night from a deep dream of peace,*
> *And saw, within the moonlight in his room,*
> *Making it shine like a lily in bloom,*
> *An angel, writing in a book of gold.*
> *Exceeding peace had made Ben Adam bold,*
> *And to the Presence in the room he said,*
> *What writest thou?" The vision raised its head,*
> *And with a look made of all sweet accord*
> *Answered, "The names of those who love the Lord."*
> *"And is mine one?" Asked Abou. "Nay, not so,"*
> *Replied the Angel. Abou spoke more low,*
> *But cheerily still, he said, "I pray thee, then,*
> *Write me as one who loves his fellowman."*
> *The angel wrote, and vanished. The next night*
> *It came again in a great blaze of wakening light,*
> *And showed the names of those whom love of God had blessed,*
> *And behold! Ben Adam's name led all the rest.*

Ben Adam was not so concerned that he love God, yet God loved him because of his love for his fellowman. You experience God's love when you are love, because that is who you are and that is who He is. He can only draw near when you are love. Like attracts like. Love attracts love. Anything less than pure love pushes God away.

Love Is Letting Go Of Fear

All negative emotions can be reduced to fear and fear obscures love. Jealousy is fear that someone else is getting something you don't have. Once Baba advised someone who was jealous to love himself with jealousy. Why? Because jealousy cannot remain in the presence of love. Don't love the jealousy, but love yourself despite it and you will be cured. You can include corruption in as long as you don't entertain it. Invite it in, but don't let it stay for a cup of coffee, as Baba says. Hatred is another word for fear. You will only hate your enemy if you truly think he can hurt you. Love your enemy and you have mastered love. Fear cannot remain in the presence of love. You cannot master fear, but you can master love, and when you do, fear vanishes and you are restored to God-consciousness.

Peace and joy are expressions of love. Love is their basis. God is love and He created you as love. You are love and love is expressed in joy, peace, kindness, compassion, forbearance, forgiveness, tenderness, gentleness, care, purity, eagerness and enthusiasm. These are all expressions of the one true emotion, love. And when you are love, do you have any doubt about who you are? Only when you are fearful, do you question your reality. That is because fear is foreign to you. When you are not wholly joyous, you are fearful and fear is not real, thus you do not know yourself when you are afraid.

Whenever you are not wholly joyous, it is always because you have reacted with a lack of love to some soul God created. You can always change your mind. Love is your nature. Love is who you are. *Accept only loving thoughts in others and regard everything else as an appeal for help. Every response that anyone could ever have toward you is either love or a call for love. Fear is a call for love. Whether you are receiving love or a call for love, your only true and appropriate response to any situation is love.*

The word for God in Sanskrit is Brahman, and its root 'Bre' means expansion or extension. That is love. Love offers everything forever. *To withhold the smallest gift is not to know love's purpose. To give without limit is God's will for us, because only this can bring us the joy which is His and which He wills to share with us. Our love is as boundless as His because it is His. Could any part of Him be without His love, and could any part of His love be contained? Love asks only that you be happy and will give you everything that makes for happiness.*

O loving Lord, Thank You for Your limitless, boundless, unconditional love that expresses itself so personally to each of your children all over the world. May all beings choose to experience Your love tangibly by turning toward You in all things. Please show us how to love ourselves, so we may lead lives of dignity and self assurance in the truth of who we are as created by You. Show us how to love each other freely, genuinely and purely, and experience the true purpose for which You created us for each other. Let love envelop the whole world and transform it back to its original state of peace, joy and abundance for all.

May all beings in all the worlds be happy and blest, Amen.

Figure 9 – Only God and God's Love Are Real

Everything (Eternity)

Eternity	Life	Oneness
God-Dependence	**Love**	Freedom
Real	Truth	Non-judgment
Heaven	Peace	Creation
Innocence	Knowledge	All-Powerful

Nothing (time and space)

Time/space	**Happy Dream (Satva) God's solution - collapses time**
Ego-dependence	Unconditional love, genuine love for all humanity
Unreal	Master love to abolish fear
Hell	Good behavior as expression of joy and love
Guilt	Love for self, respond with love to all situations
Death	**Nightmare (Rajo Guna) - makes time**
Fear ———	Fear of past, future, others, nature, survival, God...
Untruth	Mis-projection produces fear
War	Victim-victimizer paradigm
Ignorance	Plagued with doubt about who you are
Separation	**Deep Sleep (Thamo) Ego's solution - freezes time**
Bondage	Conceptual understanding of unconditional love
Judgment	Fear justified, fear of death
Mis-creation	Cause of unhappiness outside
Powerless	Manipulate - alterior motives, pretense of love
	Narcissistic, selfish, feel unworthy to be loved

Direction of Consciousness Awakening

Chapter 10

Are You Ready to Give Up Untruth for the Truth?

This above all to thine own self be true.
Shakespeare

Everyone Has A Valuable Contribution To Make To Truth

Five blind men lived together in a village. It so happened that the king would be coming to their village atop on an elephant. The blind men were not so enamored with the king, but they were curious to know what an elephant was as no elephant had ever come to their village before. When the king arrived, one man touched the elephant's ear and concluded that an elephant is like a fan. The second touched its trunk and discovered that an elephant is like a hose. The third touched the tail and understood an elephant to be like a rope. The fourth touched a leg and assumed that an elephant was like a tree trunk. The fifth touched the body and surmised the elephant to be like a wall.

When they got home they eagerly reported their findings to each other only to discover that they had all perceived the elephant differently. They started arguing amongst themselves. They each thought they were right while everyone else was wrong. What they overlooked was that they were each right but so was everyone else and that only by including everyone's ideas would they be able to glean the whole truth about the elephant.

We each have a contribution to make to the truth and only together do we know the whole truth. However, only a pure heart can render one's contribution effectively. The 5 blind men were exposing a lack of maturity and purity and therefore were unable to be inclusive. Unless we are inclusive we can get stuck thinking we are right while someone else is wrong. *The whole is greater than the sum of its parts.* To have the whole picture about anything we need to consider everyone's contribution.

Three Philosophies Contribute To The Truth Of Oneness

In India there are three different approaches or philosophies regarding oneness. There are those who believe they are God and that there is nothing outside of them. They call themselves Advaitins or non-dualists. Their contribution to the truth is that they know nothing happens outside of one's mind. This essentially means everything happens because we have asked for it. Every experience that happens to you is thereby your responsibility, as you are all the power in the universe. What you draw to you is in response to your will alone. There is no force outside of you, more powerful than you.

There are others who believe that they were created by God. They are taught that they are one with God, but that oneness retains the idea of having been created. They depend on God for everything. They refer to themselves as Vishishtadvaitins or qualified non-dualists. Their contribution to the truth is that they acknowledge God as their Source and sustenance.

And there are those who believe there is God and there are all His creations, which includes everyone and everything. They are called Dvaitins or dualists. Their contribution is that all are equal and in the recognition of their perfect equality is their oneness with God and everyone. They understand that we all share one universal mind as well as one universal soul despite seeming multiplicity. They recognize love, innocence, holiness and power to be equal in everyone. They are convinced that God gives them everything and so does He also give everyone else everything.

Sai Baba says each of the three ideas are true. Alone each contains a portion of the truth. When they meet they recognize they are all correct but only together do they make up the whole truth about oneness, namely that there is nothing outside of your mind, that you were created by God as His perfect equal and are thereby one with Him, and that God created everyone perfect like yourself thereby one with you.

Ultimate Truth Is Universal

When you know that you do not have the whole truth, you may be more willing to be wrong about the conclusions your mind wants to draw from evidence gathered. Freedom lies in a willingness to be wrong. When you need to be right, you bind yourself to defending a particular position. We each have our piece to the puzzle and together we make the puzzle complete and recognize the long forgotten picture of truth.

Is there just one puzzle, or are there a number of puzzles and if your piece doesn't fit one, will there be another puzzle, or school of thought that you can plug into? Is truth different for everyone or is there only one truth? Are you willing to let the truth be true whatever it may be? If what you believe is not the truth, of what use is it? When you are ready to admit that you might be wrong, will you not be more tolerant of others' beliefs? If God is your Source and if He created you like Himself, then you must be God. Are you willing to let yourself be Divine and perfect if that is who you are? Ego maintains that truth is different for everyone. Ego's purpose in trying to convince you of this idea is to produce chaos. Chaos serves to keep the truth from being obvious.

To think that truth could be different for everyone comes from ego's plan to confuse and foil our attempts at reaching truth. It would mean that there are many puzzles and that your piece completes one puzzle, while you have no connection with any other puzzles. Does that ring true? It doesn't for me. I think we are all connected. We each hold our piece to the one puzzle and we need every piece to have the whole picture. We do depend on each other and on God. That is unity and oneness and paves the way to ultimate truth. Insisting that truth is different for everyone prevents a joining. We can only join in the truth, and if it is different for everyone, how can we join? I do not care whether I am right or wrong, I only want to join with you in the truth.

Truth must be universally true, whatever it is. It may be approached in a number of ways and that would be form, but when you have found truth, you will have found it to be the same for everyone. You may climb the mountain on the north side and someone else may ascend by the southern trail. But when you reach the top, the view will be the same for both of you.

What do you do when someone disagrees with your believe? We must always be willing to be wrong and to listen to our heart. Never attack another's position. If you feel the need to defend the truth, that is a good indication that you are wrong. Untruth cannot threaten truth, so truth does not need your defense. Protect the truth by living and walking it. You will be guided as to how to express the truth. Truth is beyond words, thus words are inadequate even to point to truth, yet your yearning for only the truth must be enough to reveal to you the profoundest, deepest, most elevated truths, even via limited or clumsy means. Everything can be used. We need to keep in mind that words are limited, and that they may not accurately convey what we are trying to say, so we must always listen deeply, past words to essence.

Ultimate truth would answer questions like: Were you created? If you were created, then was everyone and everything else also created? Are you God? Are you whole and perfect forever? If you are whole and perfect as you were created, then does it follow that so is everyone else? Are you innocent forever? If you are innocent forever, then is everyone else also innocent? Is the world real or is it unreal or is it both?

Gathering evidence means not settling for a portion of the truth. When we want all the truth we have to dive deep. Our willingness to know will draw all the evidence we need to us. Truth is generalizable. Why settle for only a portion of the truth? For all-knowledge, for the whole truth we must be willing to explore the reality of God, ourselves, ego, the world, our bodies, life, death... Watch any tendency to draw hasty conclusions based on insubstantial evidence.

Just because you may be able to convince others to agree with your position does not mean you have found the truth. Witnesses do not constitute hard evidence. Even if everyone believes it to be so, does not make an idea true. Do you have irrefutable evidence for your conclusions? Do you have the courage to be wrong? Only when we want to join in the truth, will we have a true purpose. That is my purpose.

At one time everyone was convinced the world was flat. Today we know beyond a shadow of a doubt that it is round. Even though everyone was at one time convinced of its flatness could not make it different from what it truly is and has always been. Even if you knew the world was round while everyone else held the false belief that it was flat, you needn't have convinced anyone. All you need do is sail around it and everyone is convinced. When you really know, there will be little need to talk. Baba says, "First be, then do, then speak, but then only a little."

Truth Lies In Content Deep To Form

Either reincarnation is true for everyone, regardless of whether you believe in it or not, or it is not true for anyone, even if you do believe in it. To me it does not matter whether we reincarnate or not. All that matters is the truth. I do not defend reincarnation, nor do I defend against it. I subscribe to reincarnation, but I'm willing to be wrong. In itself, it is not important one way or other as it is relative truth and not ultimate truth. I want ultimate truth, whatever it is.

Either destiny is predetermined or we have freewill. I don't care if it is predetermined or if we have freewill, I want the truth. Either we made ego to replace God or we did not. I only want the truth. Either God created everyone or He did not. I only want the truth. I am willing to be wrong about my position. It does not matter so much what I have discovered to be the truth. What matters is that you only want the truth and that you are willing to question every one of your beliefs for the sake of truth. This opens the door to truth beyond conceptual understanding.

Your glasses may have the most beautiful frames, but will you wear them if the lenses impair your vision? The frame is the form and the glass the content. Of what use are your glasses with beautiful frames if you cannot see through them? Of what use is your belief if it does not pass the test of truth? People who insist that their form is the only true form are confusing form with content. Each religion offers a unique form. In content they all teach love for God and fellowman. Do not succumb to thinking your religion is the only way. It may be the right way for you but it may not be right for someone else. What is important is your love, respect and support for each other, overlooking your differences on the level of form while remembering your sameness on the level of content.

When we say truth is the same for everyone, we are speaking of content, not of form. There is only one truth, though it can be expressed through all religions and spiritual movements, as well as a huge variety of other avenues. Einstein discovered truth through mathematics, many have come upon it through music, contemplation, or meditation. The pure non-dual teachings, the qualified non-dual teachings, as well as the dual teachings are all equally valid paths to truth. The paths of service, devotion and wisdom are all legitimate paths to God. The paths of the householder and that of the renunciate are equal approaches to God.

These many paths are all only different on the level of form. It is your desire for truth that will direct you to truth and draw truth to you. Truth has to do with content, deep to form. And your uniqueness will draw to you the form that resonates in your heart as your chosen path. Where content is concerned, it must be that either truth is universally true or it is not true for anyone. Pots may be many, water is one. Bulbs are many, electricity is one. Forms may be different though content is ever the same.

All Religions Contain The Truth Equally

Baba says all religions are equally valid paths to God. Then He goes on to say that it doesn't matter what your religion, what matters is the purity of your heart. All the different religions have something in common that make them legitimate roads to ultimate truth. That is where my interest lies. I am concerned with content deep to form. Whatever your religion, practice it with full endeavor, purity and love for God and fellowman. That is content and can be experienced through any form, be it the form offered through Christianity, Judaism, Buddhism, Hinduism or the Muslim tradition. Each of those religions teach you to love God above all and your fellowman as yourself. Every religion is the same at its core and yet how much heartache has been caused over seeming differences.

If your religion espouses that it is the only way, that is a belief. What proof do you have that yours is the only way? Your conviction does not make it so. Some Christians believe that Jesus died for their sins and that if you don't believe your salvation depends on his death, you are damned to hell. What proof do they have that this is so? Is that what Jesus taught? Jesus taught the masses to be perfect. If perfection is possible, what sins are there that require another's blood, another's sacrifice? Some Muslims believe that they will attain heaven through killing in Allah's name. Who has come back to confirm that this is so?

Irrational conclusions spring from alliance with ego. Ego wants to survive at our expense. See the truth and you stand free of any past distortions. To know the truth, we have to be open to all possibilities and then ask to be shown. We have to want the truth above all else. You may have invested heavily in what you assumed was true or in what you let others tell you was true. To give up your lifelong beliefs can feel very threatening. We can move quickly when it simply doesn't matter what has gone before. Now we stand fresh, prepared to throw it all overboard for the sake of only the truth. I pray God grant us all the courage and strength to be willing to do whatever it takes to know the whole truth. Even if we have invested heavily in a dead horse it can never win the race for us. We have to invest in a live horse and be winners. We have to be willing to be wrong about all our past beliefs. All we have to lose is alliance with ego and ego is an imposter.

If you find yourself fanatical about your beliefs, that is a red flag. Be willing to be shown the truth behind your beliefs. Do they withstand the test of reason, logic and perfect peace? I believe with all my heart that Sai Baba is God, but I don't need to be fanatical about Him. I don't need to deify Him. I don't need you to believe in Him in order to love you. I don't need you to believe in Him in order that you be saved. I know that we each have to save ourselves. It does help to have an authentic teacher but that in itself is not a guarantee of salvation. All that is necessary is your passionate desire for eternal life and a willingness to do whatever it takes and the whole universe will come to your aid. It all starts with a willingness to lead a life of purity and holiness, whatever your chosen path.

Purity Is Essential To Every Path

There are those who defend against purity by contending that purity is different for everyone, or in other ways justify diminishing the value of purity. That would be ego again trying to throw you off the trail, as everyone knows exactly what is pure and in alignment with truth and what is not. When you want to be holy, you know what holiness is because you were created holy and cannot forget your truth.

As long as you don't want to be holy, you will find all kinds of justifications for unholiness, such as 'holiness is different for everyone, therefore ambiguous,' or 'unholy behavior cannot affect the truth,' or 'it is impossible to be holy' or 'I'm only human...' To justify impurity means you don't want to be who you are. Holiness is the cornerstone and foundation of all paths to truth and alone removes the blocks to the awareness of truth.

The suicide bomber professes to be a Muslim but that does not guarantee him or her eternal life. To be a suicide bomber is to use one's body for attack and thereby to make it real. This is an example of attempting to justify impurity, though impurity cannot be justified. Use your religion as a springboard into truth. To kill those of another religion for any reason is not love but hate. In hating anyone, you hate and hurt yourself and bind yourself to the cycle of birth and death, cause and consequence.

Baba says that it is good to be born in a religion but not to die in one. Move on beyond religious dogma. Spirituality is not containable and is not limited to a particular form. If you insist on retaining your religion, then at least don't deify its founder and thereby become dependent. To let your leader be a way shower is to be in true relationship with him, but to depend on him to do it for you is to be untrue to yourself. You are your own savior. No one can do it for you. Every one must accept the truth for himself. Jesus death on the cross cannot save you, but Jesus living example of love for God and all people everywhere can.

Once Al Drucker asked Sai Baba, "Are You the Messiah?" Baba answered, "It is not like that. Save yourself and others too." You be the savior of the world. You will step into that responsibility when you truly know the world to be in your mind. Baba says He can turn earth into sky and sky into earth, but over men's hearts He has no power. We each have to save ourselves. That is so because we were created free.

You Already Know The Truth

Everyone knows the truth for we were created to know everything forever. Be true to yourself. The process of regaining awareness of truth must be one of recognition and remembrance of what you already know through a willingness to let go of what you have convinced yourself was the truth, though it was never true. That process requires a willingness to acknowledge that perhaps you were poorly taught, and that now you would rather be happy than right. It requires honesty and an attitude that it doesn't matter if you have been wrong about everything all your life, as long as all you want now is the truth. Past is past. There is only now. Eagerness and a willingness to be wrong are infinitely more helpful to an exploration of all the different possibilities from all the various angles than a mind that thinks it knows something. As soon as you draw a conclusion you have closed your mind to all possibilities. Be ever alert to your mind's tendency toward contraction.

There are those who worship the teachings of ACIM as gospel truth. I differ with some of the content of the course and therefore do not blindly follow everything in it, even though I find it to be the most profound piece of literature I have ever come across. I do not deify anyone or anything, as I take personal responsibility for my awakening. I will use everything, but always with integrity. If you do not agree with something I am writing, first see if you have understood what I am trying to convey by entering my mind. That is possible as minds are joined - ask to be shown what I'm trying to convey deep to the words and if my ideas are pure. Then see if your resistance comes from a clear perspective. If it does, do not accept my conclusions. I am always searching, refining, expanding, so it is possible that what seems good evidence for the truth today may change as a new insight brings a deeper understanding.

Mostly, I wish to inspire you to want to know the truth about yourself for yourself and not to give anyone power over you to discover it for you. Honor yourself. Be responsible for yourself. Use your saviors to show you the way. Know that you are all-powerful and that you have limitless capacity to know whatever you set your heart and mind to knowing.

Included in your capacity is your ability to learn as quickly as you wish, even instantly. It would give me great satisfaction for you to surpass me in your passionate embrace of the truth. Jesus inspired his disciples to surpass him by saying to them, "Greater works than I have done shall you do." How much do you really want truth? Enough to give up all untruth, all specialness and all competitiveness? Only then can you reach the truth quickly.

There will be those who insist that truth cannot be known, that it is a mystery. That has never been my position. I have always felt I had the right to know and always had a determination to do whatever I could to find out everything, demanding to know what I was told was unknowable. My constant prayer to God has been, "Please show me. I want to know. I'm willing to do anything for the truth. I'm willing to give everything for the truth."

Be True To Yourself

Do not accept what anyone tells you is or isn't the truth unless it resonates deep in your heart where you know. Do your own research and be willing to turn over every stone, willing to have been wrong about everything. You will defend untruth only as long as you do not love yourself. With self-love it becomes easy to accept the truth. When you have received even the tiniest glimpse of who you are as God created you, you will see just how lovable you really are. That experience is available to you the instant you truly want it.

I question Sai Baba and A Course In Miracles, my two greatest sources of truth. I use everything, but I do my own footwork. I'm not lazy. I won't accept anything based solely on its source, but I will accept all that rings true in my heart, even if it comes from a questionable source. I accept nothing on someone else's authority. It has to be reasonable to me. Sai Baba says, "If I say one thing and your heart tells you something else, always follow your heart." Even when I think I've understood, I stay open, knowing that I have a history of being wrong. I want the truth. I don't care if I'm wrong. I do not claim to have the answers. A free mind is a mind that is willing to be wrong about everything. On such an open mind, truth can dawn of itself, for it was always there.

There is no need to defend the truth because it cannot become untrue. I want only the truth for you and have no investment in being right. It is so easy to find ways to misinterpret and misapply the teachings if you are not 100% earnest and vigilant in wanting the truth above all else. That is so because we have allied with a slippery, crafty ego, that wishes to stay alive, and truth and ego are mutually exclusive. Ego survives at your expense. You trade in your eternal life for ego's existence. When you turn toward the truth, ego feels threatened and tries to fool you into getting sidetracked in all kinds of dead ends and byways leading no where. That is why Sai Baba lovingly chides, "Practice Constant Integrated Awareness (CIA)," and "Always Be Careful (ABC)."

Truth Is That Which Does Not Change

Whether reincarnation is true or not it is not ultimate truth as re-embodiment has to do with change. Knowing that reincarnation happens after you die can however serve to help you reach ultimate truth. If you knew you would reincarnate again and again until you got it right, you would be motivated to lead a perfect life, if you were tired of reincarnating. Neither real pearls nor fake ones are real in the ultimate sense as even a real pearl deteriorates with time, but you would prefer real ones to fake ones, wouldn't you? If reincarnation is what happens after death, it is like the real pearl, because it can lead to ultimate truth. It is not ultimate truth, because it has to do with change, and ultimate truth is changeless.

Knowing relative truth can serve a valuable purpose toward ultimate truth. When you want the truth no matter what it looks like, you open the door to being shown in a way that will not feel threatening. But you must be willing to do your part, that of leading a life of noble character, so that you can be shown. Be true for the fog of untruth to lift. Deception, dishonesty and insincerity are untruths that point away from truth. Telling the truth, being accurate, being honest and acting with integrity pave the way to ultimate truth.

Truth is the same for everyone forever. That does not mean we all have to do the same things or have the same religion, or the same interests or experiences. Variety and differences on the level of form can and must be appreciated and tolerated in order that we live together in peace. Wars are fought over differences of religion, race, color, sex and nationality. But truth is one and contact is the appreciation of sameness despite seeming differences.

A beautiful garden may have a variety of flowers. That makes it beautiful. Those flowers of many colors, shapes and fragrances have all been tended by the same gardener. They all grow due to her love and tender care, and all are pleasing to her. There are no exceptions. Either God is love and showers love on all, or God is not love. God will not be love sometimes and not at other times or with some individuals and not with others. Finally, we have to own that we are all really much more alike than we are different. That sameness is oneness and that is what ego does not want us to hear, for ego thrives on specialness and differences.

Ultimate truth is universal. You can tell a story and that story may be true or untrue on the level of form, but the final truth about all stories is that they are untrue if they are stories related to name and form in any way, for name and form are untrue. Is there a true story beyond form? I would imagine it to be the following:

A True Story

Once upon an eternity God is, and that is all there is. God is expansion, light, love, holiness, sacredness and purity. God knows everything. God creates creations of light. That is just what happens as God. God is not static but rather dynamically creates forever. God is an idea. As an idea, He creates ideas. He creates you and me as ideas of light. God creates us to be and have everything forever, exactly like Himself. We were created like God in every way. We were created to know, to create and to love. We were created with all the attributes that God has. God created you and me one with Him forever.

God is both Spirit and mind and so are we. God knows everything forever. Mind knows, wills and creates. Baba says, "I never think. When I will I act." We were created to know everything forever. You, as mind, were created to have and be knowledge, will power, creative expression and freedom. As Spirit, you have and are sacredness, holiness, innocence, love, light, joy and peace forever. For God, mind and Spirit are perfectly one forever. God created you to be inseparable as mind and Spirit forever as well. God and His creations too are inseparable from Him and each other forever.

And we were created to have freedom. We were given limitless freedom to create. However God could not give us autonomy as He created us one with Him forever. We are dependent on God just as God is dependent on us forever. In that also we are exactly like Him. *God awaits our blessing for every creative act He undertakes.* He does will us to be free to express ourselves creatively. We are not free to be separate from Him or each other as we were created to be one with God and each other forever.

In your mind you can think you are different from how you were created, but as soul you know the truth forever. As mind you can make for yourself an illusion and convince yourself that is the truth. That is possible because your mind is as powerful as God's, because your mind is the mind of God. God is the mind with which you think. You were given the freedom to use God's mind for a true experience or an untrue experience at the moment of creation. It is impossible to alter the truth in any way though it is possible to deceive yourself that untruth is true. In this true story, you did not choose to be different from how you were created, thus you are in the experience of being all-powerful, uniquely creative and lovingly blissful forever.

God created a heavenly world for us. He created a world out of His love for His children. The world is a Divine and precious gift, a creation of light. Everything in the world lives forever. Everyone in the world is perfectly happy and peaceful forever. God gave the world to us as a place in which to commune with Him and each other in perfect harmony, creativity, joy, brotherhood, love and delight. We are one with God and each other and there is only love between us forever. We all live happily forever as one, sharing one universal mind, the mind of God, and one universal Spirit, the Spirit of God. There is perfect oneness between mind and Spirit. This is a true story beyond form. It is our story now because though we may be in the experience of an untrue story, *not one note in heaven's song was missed.*

An Untrue Story

Here is an untrue story that never happened, though it may seem very real and very true. Once upon a time, after experiencing ourselves as perfection, holiness, purity and ever-deepening love, we wanted to experience something different. We wanted to use our freedom to experience independence from God. For that we needed to make our own source. We made ego to replace God. Now that we had made ego, we were told by ego to forget all about our experience of perfection because greater freedom was to be found in independence, imperfection, impurity and impiety. We were told that we were in trouble for doing something that was not God's will and that we'd better hide or we would be punished.

We turned our perfect world into a hiding place where we could forget about God and enjoy imperfection. Now we were 'free' to play by a new set of rules. Over time we convinced ourselves we had no power and no knowledge. We believed that our brothers and sisters would take from us if we didn't take from them first, so we became suspicious of everyone and everything and that suspiciousness turned quickly to viciousness.

We did not know who was our friend. We did not know who could be trusted. If they were of a different color, race or religion they were cleansed from our lives. If they believed differently about God, that was cause to fight and kill our brothers. If they set foot on our territory, vanquishing them was perfectly justified. We needed to survive and learned to take care of our physical, mental and emotional needs ourselves, independent of God.

There was jealousy, anger, greed, lust, pride and hatred. Jealousy made us want what our brother had because we believed we had less than he did. We were angry when our brother did not do what we wanted him to because we wanted it our way. We were greedy and took much more than we needed and so some of our brothers and sisters starved but we didn't care, because we forgot that they were our very selves and that their pain was ours. We had lust and hurt our sisters to appease our appetites. We had pride and wanted to be powerful rulers and didn't care who we trampled on to get what we wanted. We hated those who looked different, thought different or had different backgrounds from us.

We hurt our brothers and sisters and they hurt us. We all felt guilty and received results in kind. We suffered, got old and died. We felt this was justice. We had unfulfilled desires and debts to pay to balance the scales, so we were born again and did it all over again for countless lives. We thought God had abandoned us. We felt forsaken, betrayed, forgotten and rejected. We thought God was dead. We thought God didn't care. We thought God was to blame. We thought God was cruel. And God waited patiently and any time you or I called out to Him, He was right there for us. He has been there all along, but we just forgot to call on Him, because we had pushed Him aside. This is our story. It is not a true story, yet it is true for you and me, and seems truer than our true story told earlier, wouldn't you agree?

Miracles And Forgiveness Serve To Reestablish Truth

We all want peace to be restored to earth. We all want the first story to be our experience. We all want brother to live with brother in peace and harmony. We all want to know that we can trust each other and God and feel safe and cared for and not have to work to survive, and not have to see and hear about endless wars, sickness, starvation, suffering, dying and catastrophes. We want to hear about peace, joy, abundance and love for each other and God. We want a world where there is plenty for all, where there is no conflict or strife, where there is only love and good will. We want a world where mother earth is happy and there are no 'natural' disasters or weird weather patterns. Isn't that the world you'd like to live in, if you had the choice? Is this mere wishful thinking or is this world possible?

What will it take for the untrue story to be undone and the true story experienced? It will take a miracle. It will take forgiveness. Miracles and forgiveness are relative truths. They have no relationship to the world God created, for in that world miracles and forgiveness are not needed, but they are necessary to restore us to the real world.

What is forgiveness? Forgiveness merely says that none of the untrue story ever happened, because all that is possible is God and God's love. It says that what you thought your brother did to you had no effect. It says you have nothing to forgive because nothing happened to disturb the truth. Truth is of God and our decision to change it was not successful, simply because we are not more powerful than God. Ego, of course, wants no part of truth, because the truth is ego is not true. If truth is total, the untrue cannot exist and so ego cannot exist.

True forgiveness acknowledges personal responsibility for everything that happens to you. When unreality is your experience, a shift in consciousness will restore you to reality. That shift takes place through forgiveness or self-responsibility. Self-responsibility acknowledges that nothing can happen to you against your will. That is true forgiveness. Forgiveness brings you into right relationship with what is happening and opens the door to miracles.

What is a miracle? A miracle is the undoing of that which never happened. It is the undoing of the second story. That story is not true and never occurred, but it did seem to happen and so we need a miracle to undo it. We cannot be free of the untrue story by glossing over it or denying it. It is a denial of the truth. We have to deny the denial. Miracles do this by translating denial into truth. The truth is there is no sickness, suffering or death. A spiritual adept may agree that this is so and thus encourage you to just ignore sickness and suffering. It does seem harder to ignore when you are experiencing pain directly. If you knew your oneness with everyone and everything, it would not be so easy to ignore or deny another's suffering.

There are those who contend that Ramana Maharshi, Rama Krishna and Nisargadatta, all realized sages, suffered and died of cancer but that they were not suffering because they knew the truth. I pray they did not suffer. I would rather not have cancer in my body whether I recognized it as real or not. I do not wish cancer on anyone, not the saints, nor the sinners. No one deserves to be anything but whole and perfect as his or her direct experience right now.

It may be that those great saints were taking on planetary suffering because planetary consciousness at that juncture did not permit the suffering to be undone. We are the writers of our destiny. It can be anything we want and it can change when we so choose as well. I wish for a destiny where sickness and suffering are entirely abolished for everyone. As more and more minds join in expecting miracles, they will be everyone's experience as there is power in joining in truth and a world free of injustice, disease and lack is the truth. Miracles deny the denial by undoing the unreal world of suffering and lack. When enough minds become truly miracle-minded, the shortening process becomes immeasurable and we will see the world transformed before our very eyes.

Above All Else, I Want To See

Unreality is very real to us and therefore requires transformation for its undoing. It requires an action of mind, a shift in consciousness. Miracles restore us to wholeness by undoing what never was. Why bother undoing what is not real? For the simple reason that it seems very real to us or it could not be in our minds. We would not have unreal experiences if we did not believe in them. *Denying the denial* does not mean ignoring unreality. We must guard against the mind's tendency toward using denial inappropriately. We must use vigilance to actively see unreality for what it is, and thereby withdraw energy from it.

In the movie, American Beauty, a young man looked on the horror of a murder scene with a display of the deepest love, as if to depict that he was seeing truly, he was seeing only innocence and beauty. Someone had just shot himself to death. That was violence. There was no beauty in it. It was horrific and a real response would have included shock and sadness. By seeing it as beautiful, the young man was giving reality to the unreal, which can be measured by how out of touch it was with life. This is a gross misapplication of the teaching to see only what is real. This kind of desensitization is the cause of children shooting each other in school yards. It is insanity due to being out of touch with reality and applying the teachings from conceptual understanding.

In the Bible, when Jesus was told by Mary and Martha that Lasarus had died, Jesus wept. He obviously knew the unreality of death, as shortly thereafter he performed a miracle of raising Lasarus from the dead. Everyone else was weeping and Jesus expressed sensitivity and compassionate by weeping with them. Laughter or finding 'good' in that moment would have been entirely inappropriate and out of touch. Be real. Don't intellectualize or conceptualize yourself out of heartfulness. Be in your heart, not your head. *A pure mind knows the truth and that is its strength.*

True vision can be perceived only by the truly innocent. Because their hearts are pure, they defend true perception, instead of defending themselves against it. Purity comes with responsibility for error and a willingness to correct it. In that you guard against arrogating to yourself a knowing that is not there and thereby open the door to true vision. To be holy, all you need is the willingness to be who you are. You will have your own direct experience of truth when you stop being determined that you know something on your own. As long as you think truth must look a certain way, you close the door to a true experience. Be willing to be wrong and you open the door to truth.

Don't let someone else's experience determine your truth. You are worthy to have your own direct experience. And when you have that coveted vision of the Divine watch that you not use that to be different or special. Watch the mind's tendency to draw erroneous conclusions even from glimpses from out of time. It is easy to fool yourself that you are enlightened because of an extra sensory experience. Don't put your own interpretations on anything and thereby close the door to ultimate truth. No one is so hopelessly bound as the one who falsely believes himself enlightened. Don't be self-proclaimed. Let the universe confirm your enlightenment for you. Till then be willing to be wrong, even about your enlightenment. There are many false prophets in the world today so we must be ever so bright and committed to true seeing.

How do you know if you've zeroed in on truth? There will be no doubts. You will just know. It will not come from books or teachings, but from direct revelatory experience. When you've laid all your ideas aside and have no investment in being right, when you have a certainty, when you find yourself thinking of God and the end of suffering for all, when you are not embroiled in your own drama, then only can you be confident that you have understood something. The truth will ring true in a pure heart. Truth comes in removing untruth. Ego and its underpinnings must be seen truly and relinquished, for truth to reemerge.

Turn To The Sun And The Shadow Is Behind You

Error is always undone in the presence of truth. When we decided to make ego, we made a mistake. It was not the truth as it is impossible to replace God as our Source, so it never happened. Bring truth to bear on any situation and error disappears. Look to the truth and untruth vanishes. Baba likens truth to the sun. When you face the sun, the shadow is behind you. When the sun rises and is directly overhead, the shadow has disappeared. You need do nothing to the shadow. If you fight it, it will not disappear. You cannot escape it by running from it, so stand still and let the sun of wisdom rise overhead. Then the shadow vanishes of its own accord.

If you turn toward the shadow, you are turning away from the sun and all that will be real for you will be the shadow. But the shadow was never real. If you have turned to the shadow, then see it for what it is – nothing. Don't deny the shadow or you give it reality. Don't confuse the sun with the shadow. Don't see shadow and call it the sun. Use discrimination to tell the difference between the real and the unreal, the true and the untrue. How can you turn to the sun if you do not know the difference between the sun and the shadow? As ridiculous as that may sound, we have all convinced ourselves of the reality of the shadow and the unreality of the sun, the reality of the world of ego and the unreality of God and His love. We will see truly only when we want to see truly.

Truth will dawn of itself. God wants us to have the truth. He has not withheld it from His beloved children. When you search for and discard everything that is not the truth, you make way for the truth. All concepts about what is true and what is not have to be undone. Truth comes with depth of understanding beyond intellectual concepts. *It is restored through desire for it, as it was lost through desire for something else.* Truth can only be experienced within. Do not seek for it outside yourself. It is not of the world. Seek it within.

Truth Is Beyond Words

Truth can only be recognized and need only be recognized. To describe truth through mere words is a reduction and frequently leads to misinterpretation and misapplication. A yogi knows a flower by becoming one with its essence. A scientist dissects a flower, analyzes it and figures out from his explorations the function of each different part, but in the process its essence is lost. Do not try to figure out or analyze the truth, but rather allow truth to dawn, asking incisive questions, standing still, drawing your circle. Be willing to do whatever it takes, willing to be wrong, with all purity of heart and intention.

At the same time, we must be willing to plumb the depths. Measure your thoroughness on the basis of its heartfulness. A mind that probes, yet lacks heart is ineffective. A mind that inquires deeply, fearlessly, willing to investigate every clue for the sake of truth, uses passion purposefully. That one does not lose touch with reality or heart, but probes to get in touch with both. Is a mind that is ever compassionate toward all humanity, yearning for the end of suffering for all, off the track? We must do whatever it takes to remove the blocks to the awareness of truth and that requires deep self-inquiry.

There are those who discourage deep inner inquiry. That may be because they do not have the truth and do not want to be exposed. Their beliefs may be threatened by deep inquiry. Truth cannot be threatened, so if one feels threatened, he can be sure he does not have the truth. When people thought the earth was flat, they felt very threatened by those who were making ready to sail around it, because they were invested in being right and didn't want the truth. To be willing to be wrong takes courage. When you are willing to be wrong about other things you open the door to being wrong about ego, therefore ego tries to convince you to think you are right about those things that you are clearly wrong about and to never admit error. In our willingness to be wrong about everything else, we weaken ego's hold.

The Truth Is You Are And Have Always Been Innocent

Do you have the courage to be wrong about yourself? You thought you were guilty and gathered all kinds of evidence and witnesses to prove your guilt. You made a case against yourself that was fool proof, but not God proof. God knows your innocence and when you let Him be your advocate, all your evidence will be seen as insubstantial, inconclusive, immaterial and irrelevant. The case against you will be dismissed on the spot. God is always working with your best interest at heart. He has all the evidence immediately available to prove you innocent beyond a shadow of a doubt.

If God would make such a great lawyer, why don't we hire Him? He wants nothing more than to be our advocate. He will be happy to see us all set free. The problem is ego always speaks loudest and first and we listen to it. Ego convinces you that you are in better hands with it. So, without investigating whether what ego is saying is true, you blindly believe ego and let it be your counselor and that is a mistake because ego doesn't want the truth. Ego wants you guilty. And of course it doesn't want to let on to you, because only a fool would choose a lawyer who was going to do everything possible to prove him guilty. Everyone wants a lawyer who will win the case for him and prove him innocent.

Well, ego persuaded you that it was the best thing going. It convinced you that if God were your lawyer He would really fortify the evidence against you. That was a lie and you bought it and thus you chose a lawyer who did everything to throw the book at you. You were convinced you were guilty, but the truth is you have always been innocent. You can choose a different lawyer whenever you like. God is always available. Don't worry about hurting ego's feelings. It has been beating you up. It doesn't deserve your loyalty or kindness. It will be in the best interest of all if you see clearly what ego's game is and walk away from it toward the light. Once ego is seen truly as false, it will vanish. It was never real.

Truth is the same for everyone. Everyone has always been innocent. 'Even the hardened criminal?' you might ask. There are no exceptions. If you make one exception, if guilt is real for anyone, then it is real for everyone, and then it must be real for you as well. If the hardened criminal kills in cold blood, his ego is guilty, but he is not. He has done nothing but listen to ego, which gave him some very bad advice. This does not make him a victim of forces beyond his control. He chose to listen to ego. He is all-powerful and there is no force outside of him making him do something he does not wish to do. Ego persuades you to engage in corruption so you will feel guilty without taking responsibility for your actions. You are responsible for every one of your actions.

In the movie, Dead Man Walking, a nun helps to transform a man on death row convicted of rape and murder. Initially he denies the charges, but through her love finds the courage to admit his wrongs and take responsibility for them. She tells him, quoting the Bible, "The truth shall set you free." Her unconditional love helps him come into true relationship with his actions so he is able to apologize to the families of the victims and leave this world with dignity. He makes huge leaps in consciousness due to her willingness to see his innocence beyond his actions.

Make A Life Changing Commitment Today

It is only in being fully responsible that we will be willing to change our minds. This change of mind alone permits the undoing of the consequences of erroneous acts. We are responsible for our actions and our minds can only be healed when we are willing to be wrong if we commit a hurtful act. Because we are innocent no matter what we do does not justify unkindness. A devious mind can justify any action, unto murder. This is ego's racket. If you touch it, it will burn you.

Always be careful about how you interpret the teachings. Impure actions do generate guilt or they simply could not have been enacted and then ego makes sure that the proper punishment is meted out. If you listen to ego, you will be persuaded that you are guilty and will agree to suffer the consequences of your actions. Be responsible for your actions. There is no power outside of you forcing you to do things against your better judgment. Past is gone, but turn over a new leaf and stop justifying the unjustifiable. Make a life changing commitment today. There are plenty of examples of reformed alcoholics, transformed liars, thieves, drug addicts… With God all things are possible. Every saint has a past and every sinner has a future.

Perhaps you are not aware of this particular mechanism whereby suffering is associated with acts that produce guilt. That is only because it takes place in the unconscious part of mind. The purpose for bringing it to conscious awareness is to reestablish awareness of the unconscious. The unconscious is also ego's idea to keep us from seeing truly. God's creations cannot have a mind that includes subconscious and unconscious aspects. Bring those into conscious awareness by being ever vigilant and by wanting to be fully aware and awake. In your vigilance, they can be exposed to conscious awareness. Once aware of our unconscious mind, it is no longer unconscious. Then we have been restored to purely conscious mind.

Though everyone is responsible for his actions, no one is ever guilty. If a criminal truly turns to God for a total solution, God will reveal to him the truth that he cannot harm anyone in the truest sense and that he should not want to, for all are worthy of only kindness. Every person is God's gift to him thus only appreciation and gratitude are a worthy response to anyone. If he gets it, he will have taken a quantum leap in consciousness, a shift from victim-victimizer consciousness to God-consciousness. That quantum leap ameliorates any negative effects from any deleterious past actions. When he has changed his mind, he will never have a desire to perpetrate hurtful acts again. He will be restored to wholeness. That requires a miracle. No time is necessary. It does require his recognition that he is wholly worthy because he is a precious child of God, no matter what may have gone before.

It also requires a willingness to trade in his lawyer who wants him guilty, for a lawyer who wants him innocent. All he need do is be willing to trade in ego for God. Generally we will witness a more gradual process of transformation or awakening to truth. Generally we will lead many lives of purity and determination for the truth before we are ready to make a tiny shift in consciousness. For a murderer to make a quantum leap is very rare indeed, but with God all things are possible. It is all up to you whether you want to collapse time immeasurably, even instantly or gradually. That is the only reason time exists at all.

The truth sets us free. We are free when we want to be free, because in truth we are already free. God created us free forever. That is not alterable. That is why it is really wise to choose God to be your advocate. It is really wise to stop looking to ego to give you sound advice. Ego wants you convicted, guilty, bad, sinful, deserving of punishment. Ego's advice is never in your best interest. The truth is you are and have always been innocent.

Only truth is true and nothing else is true. Be true to the truth. Be passionate for the truth. Be willing to be wrong about everything for the sake of truth. Then truth will dawn once again upon your most holy mind. In choosing for the truth, you make it that much easier for all people everywhere to accept the truth of who they are and to stop being terrified to change their minds about their erroneous beliefs. Courageously choose to want only the truth and thereby be a beacon of hope to all your brothers and sisters in all the world.

God of truth, Grant us the courage to want only the truth. Grant us the willingness to be wrong about everything for the sake of the truth. Grant us the broad-mindedness to see that we each have a portion of the truth and that we need each other for the whole truth. Thank You for giving us miracles, forgiveness and healing for undoing untruth and restoring us to our true experience with You. Thank You that truth is one and the same for all and does not change. Help us to love each other, despite seeming differences of religion, gender, nationality, color... Help us to recognize the underlying truth that we are all equal and so much more alike than different. Thank You that we do already know the truth. Inspire us to lead lives of purity so we can recognize our truth. Help us to be willing to give everything for the truth and grant us the courage to relinquish all untruth.

May all beings in all the worlds be happy and blest, Amen.

Figure 10a – Only Truth Is True

Everything (Eternity)

Eternity	Life	Oneness
God-Dependence	Love	Freedom
Real	**Truth**	Non-judgment
Heaven	Peace	Creation
Innocence	Knowledge	All-Powerful

Nothing (time and space)

Time/space	**Happy Dream (Satva) God's solution - collapses time**
Ego-dependence	Recognize everyone's contribution
Unreal	Miracles and forgiveness restore truth
Hell	Willing to be wrong/to do anything for the truth
Guilt	Willing to let truth be the same for everyone
Death	**Nightmare (Rajo Guna) - makes time**
Fear	Need to be right at another's expense
Untruth	Attack another's position
War	Misapply the teachings to distort truth
Ignorance	Analyze the heartfulness out of truth
Separation	**Deep Sleep (Thamo) Ego's solution - freezes time**
Bondage	Defend untruth
Judgment	Secretiveness or dishonesty
Mis-creation	Truth is different for everyone
Powerless	Intolerance on level of form - "My way is the only way"

Direction of Consciousness Awakening

Figure 10b – Ultimate Truth, Relative Truth and Untruth

Ultimate Truth (Here are some ideas on what might constitute ultimate
truth - come up with your own ideas to add to the list)

You were created by God, no different from God
Everyone has always been innocent forever
You are an idea in God's mind and God did not change His mind about you
There is no one more powerful than you
You have creative fredom but not autonomy
Truth is the same for everyone
Of myself I am nothing, with God all things are possible
The world and my body are in my mind
Everyone has a valuable contribution to make, together we have the whole truth
God is but love, and therefore so are you
You are and have everything forever

Relative Truth (add to the list)
Miracles
Forgiveness
Healing
Reincarnation
Purity restores truth to you
You have to save yourself; no one can do it for you
There are many paths that lead to the one truth
The world and our bodies are projections of our minds

Untruth (add to the list)
Sickness, suffering and death
Victims and victimizers
You could create your own source - ego
You are guilty and unworthy
Inequality
Separation
Your are your body
Things happen outside of your control or will

Chapter 11

Are You Ready to Give Up Conflict for Peace?

Our lives begin to end the day we become silent about the things that matter.
Martin Luther King, Jr.

Peace Through Nonviolence

The British had ruled India for over 200 years. In the early 1900's, Mahatma Gandhi took some very peaceful yet effective measures to regain independence for his country. He undertook a simple march to the sea to mine salt. Mining salt was not permitted under British rule. His actions attracted attention from both the British invaders as well as India's citizenry. His civil disobedience landed him in jail. His nonviolent protest against injustice brought awareness to minds that had previously accepted injustice and had resigned themselves to a hopeless situation. Gandhi inspired awareness that caused a shift in consciousness. With a shift in consciousness from blind acceptance to a willingness to do whatever was necessary to end tyranny, the British rule simply lost its hold and crumbled. The British withdrew from India solely due to the use of nonviolent resistance to injustice.

Subsequently, due to insecurity around freshly gained independence there was a Hindu/Muslim power struggle to rule the country. At first it appeared that independence was worse than British rule. Gandhi was willing to fast unto death to end the huge wave of endless killing, the brutality of brother against brother. Gandhi's simple yet strong determination opened minds to other possibilities and the Hindus and Muslims decided to try to live together in peace.

Mahatma Gandhi found a nonviolent solution to end conflict in British ruled India. He stood up for independence for the people of India through nonviolent resistance against oppression. There is always a nonviolent solution to every problem if we are willing to open ourselves to all possibilities. When we allow ourselves to be Divinely directed, willing to do whatever it takes, we can be shown how and where to take a stand. It requires a willingness to be assertive, courageous and fearless and to know that with God all things are possible.

Martin Luther King, Jr., inspired by Gandhi, took a similar stand against Black discrimination. He organized freedom rides, where Blacks protested against discrimination on buses. Every Black walked to work instead of taking the bus in a nonviolent protest against discrimination on the basis of skin color, exposing the cruelty of prejudice. I am aware that there is still prejudice against Afro-Americans, but at least they have more freedom and opportunities than before the freedom rides. We can employ nonviolent resistance to all prejudice and injustice.

The ego thought system has to be brought out of the closet in order that it be looked at and seen as preposterous. Exposing injustice brings about a shift in consciousness. With that shift, prejudice and tyranny can no longer be sustained. They have no support. *The world is a projection of your mind.* When there is a shift in consciousness, it has to reflect in a more peaceful world. If the world is in turmoil, how can your mind be at peace? *Do you not think the world needs peace as much as you do? Do you not want to give it to the world as much as you want to receive it? Unless you do, you cannot receive it.*

God created you to be and have everything forever, and to make sure you could not lose your inheritance, He also created everyone to be and have everything. If you truly knew that, could you ever be in conflict with anyone? What would be its purpose? We attack, defend, fight and argue because we think someone has something we lack. If we truly knew we had everything, there would be no purpose for conflict. *God created us as peace and gave us a purpose of extending that peace to all. Accepting our mission to project peace, we will find it.*

Core Issue Behind Crisis In Middle East

In the summer of 2002, the Middle East crisis had so escalated that young Muslim children were resorting to destroying their tender lives by becoming suicide bombers. They had no purpose for living. They hated their brothers the Jews because they had been taught to do so since early childhood both at home and in school. The story of their hatred is historical. It goes back to the time of Ishmael and Isaac. God had promised Abraham that he would be the father of a great nation. But Abraham's wife, Sarah was barren. So she gave her maidservant, Haggar, to Abraham. Sarah apparently did not trust God implicitly. She took it upon herself to figure out a way to make what God promised come out right. Had she trusted Him, she would have let Him reveal His plan, rather than step in with her own. Abraham listened to his wife. He also must not have trusted God implicitly. Shortly, Abraham and Haggar had a child, Ishmael.

Sixteen years passed and God came again to Abraham and told him again that he and Sarah would have a son. It seemed ridiculous as Sarah was by then nearly 90 years old and hadn't yet conceived. She laughed at the idea. But as foretold, she bore a child, Isaac, and now there was a problem. Because of Ishmael, Haggar had become more than a maidservant in Haggar's mind. She was now the mother of a great nation and so was not treating Sarah with the respect that was her mistress' due. At times Haggar goaded Ishmael to threaten little Isaac's life, as Isaac posed a threat to her son's inheritance. To resolve the conflict, Haggar and Ishmael were sent away. They were rejected. Ishmael became the father of the great Muslim nation. Isaac grew up to become the father of the great Jewish nation.

Throughout history the Jews and Arabs have hated one another. Brother has fought against brother. It is understandable that Ishmael felt rejected but every problem has a nonviolent solution where peace can prevail when we let God solve the problem for us. Like Haggar and Ishmael, we have all felt abandoned. We must each be willing to forgive the past by taking responsibility for what led to our banishment. Like Sarah and Abraham, we have distrusted God, but errors are correctable. It is time to correct our errors by being honest about them and trusting God to show us how to heal them. All are God's children and equally precious, and there is always a peaceful solution where everyone wins, when that is our objective.

God Is More Powerful Than Weapons Of Mass Destruction

It helps to get to the root cause of our problems. When we uncover that, we will have compassion for every situation. There is a solution to every uprising when we find our love, compassion and brotherhood. We must look deeply to find the root cause behind the war in Iraq. We must send love and light to all victims as well as victimizers. If we take sides, we are no better than those who are destroying each other. God is more powerful than weapons of mass destruction or biological warfare. When we remember that, we invite God's hand of intervention into every situation, no matter how impossible it may seem.

Once Sai Baba gave Himself a birthday present of pushing the whole Chinese army out of India. It was November 22, 1962, the day before His birthday. He was chiding His devotees, "You are not listening to Me because you are all worried about the news from the North, but I assure you that My birthday will not be spoiled by any bad news. In fact there will be positively good news." By midnight that night there was not a single Chinese to be found in all of India. They had all left of their own accord. Next day was Baba's birthday and that was the present He gave Himself and of course all of India. God always gives joy to all and with Him all things are possible.

So, to end all wars forever, we need merely harness that Divine power and peace must prevail. How do we enlist God's power to prevent or end war? Goodness invites God's participation. When Abraham pleaded with God to intervene on behalf of Sodom and Gomorrah, God said it would be possible if there were only five good people. With enough goodness, Divine intervention is possible. We do have freewill. If the door is shut tightly against God, if there is no one who is turning to God for a solution, He cannot enter, for He honors our freedom. You are turning to God when you lead a life of goodness, purity and morality.

The power of God can make pretzels of nuclear weapons. It is time for world peace. Baba says to send pink light to those in positions of power and to the whole world. Pink light is God's light; it is Divine light. Pink is the color of love. Hijackers threw down their weapons upon receiving such light. It does not matter where you are or what your particular circumstances, you can do your part to restore peace to earth. When you want peace in the world, you will be shown what to do to truly be an effective instrument toward that end. It all starts with peace in your heart.

Look with peace upon your brothers and God will come rushing into your heart in gratitude for your gift to Him. The most sacred spot on earth is where an ancient hatred has become a present love. As long as there is polarization, good guys and bad, there is no solution. God always has a perfect solution in which all involved will feel satisfaction, if we let Him solve our problems, whatever they may be. It is good to look for the root cause of the problem, as then it has some hope of being solved. The root cause of all problems is the making of ego to replace God. Once this is clearly understood, all efforts will be directed toward the undoing of ego.

Peace In The World Begins With Peace In The Home

When Shari's mother, Pat, was a young girl, Pat's mother favored Pat's sister, Jane and Pat grew up with the pain of not being acknowledged, so was determined not to inflict that pain on any of her children. None the less, she and her daughter Shari had an especially loving and easy relationship.

While visiting Europe together when Shari was 16, Shari's cousin died in a motorcycle accident. Though they were so near, Shari and her mom did not attend the funeral. Many years later, while Shari was nursing her mother during a bout with breast cancer Shari brought up incident. Pat immediately justified her past omission on the basis of some petty issue she held against her sister, Jane. It dawned on Shari that her mother was jealous of Aunt Jane, even after all those years, even after Pat's mother was long gone, and her sister Jane also had passed away. That seemed pretty loaded.

Oddly, Shari found herself being treated with hostility by her sisters and even her mom during the year of being at her mother's bedside. She was mystified at the bizarre treatment she was receiving from her entire family. At first she thought it had to do with their feeling threatened by her spiritual choices, but as she kept digging, it dawned on her that her sisters were jealous of Shari's bond with their mom especially during the first 30 odd years of Shari's life.

At around age 30, Shari's spiritual interests took her away from family and her sisters took the opportunity to strengthen relations with their mom. So they felt threatened by Shari's reappearance and even Pat accused Shari of returning to reestablish favorite daughter status, though Shari had no hidden agenda. She came to help a mother in a time of family crisis and so was mystified by all the accusations and misperceptions. It became apparent that Shari's absence had allowed Pat to fulfill her need to love all her other children without the complication of their unbidden, passionate embrace. Shari was not aware as they were growing up that the others felt excluded and jealous, though she never felt close to any of her sisters and always felt excluded by them. She frequently went out of her way to express her love toward them though it never matured into a closeness with any of her siblings. Then on their mother's death bed all the skeletons came out of the closet.

Shari's mother died before the family conflict had been resolved. Shari was so stricken with pain at the hostility directed against her that she could not attend her mother's funeral. A year later, the pieces of the puzzle came together for Shari. She understood that the problem was that her mother thought that to be a good Mom she had to love all her children equally. Her idea, though good, was based on her own unhealed past. In that moment of understanding, her mother's energy enveloped Shari so strongly she got goose bumps. She immediately knew her mom was free of her guilt for loving her more, and realized that her Mom in turn was not a bad Mom for loving her sister Jane more and so she no longer felt jealous of Jane. In that moment, the past was all healed, once the plug was pulled on the core issue. As soon as the core issue was healed, all the resentment, jealousy and guilt disappeared as well. Ego was behind Pat's false idea that caused a life of untold grief not only for her but for many who were close to her.

This trajectory is perhaps not so different from the story of Joseph in the Bible. His father favored him and his jealous brothers threw him into a pit, sold him into slavery and told his father he was dead. It seems that the cause of much sibling rivalry starts with jealousy over parental love. When we know who we are, we will not feel the need for our parents' love to complete us. When we love ourselves we will know we are whole and complete and will not stoop to jealousy if a sibling is favored, or will not resent a parent if they seem to love one child more than the rest, for whatever reason. This shift in consciousness will restore peace in our homes.

Ego Is Your Only Enemy

You do have an enemy, but it is never your brother or God. Your enemy is ego and you can vanquish your opponent, but not via the usual means.

First you have to be convinced that ego is indeed your only enemy. If you listen to its voice you can be sure it will not tell you it is your enemy. It will advise you to make friends with it. Only when you see ego as the cause of all your conflict, anguish, agony, pain, betrayal, hurt and suffering of any kind, will you understand what ego is and then you will agree that ego is not your friend.

Baba says, "Face the devil." The way to vanquish your opponent is not by fighting ego, but by looking at it. Ego is nonexistent and looking reveals its nothingness. When you look, ego disappears and your war is over. You cannot overcome ego by fighting with it. To fight it is to meet ego on its terms. To vanquish ego, you must look to God. God can show you ego's nothingness and once seen you will never wish to ally with it again. That is nonviolent resistance against the greatest injustice ever perpetrated. As long as you feel the need to fight ego, you are using ego's devices to destroy it. Ego is happy for this game, for it is much too clever to be destroyed when you employ it to destroy itself. Of course it will agree to the idea, because if it didn't you would turn to God and He would show you how to be victorious over ego. *Ego's goal for you is, "Fight, but do not win."*

The voice for God is always quiet because it speaks of peace. Yet peace is stronger than war, because it heals. We all want peace, but there is one who wants war and who is the instigator of all war. That is ego. *Peace is ego's greatest enemy, because according to its interpretation of reality, war is the guarantee of its survival.* Now we come to the truth behind every altercation, no matter how great or small. *Ego wants you to be at war.* The world of peace, joy and love that God created and the world of constant conflict, attack, inequality, unfairness and injustice must meet that ego be vanquished. Only when we see that ego is the cause of war will we open the door to lasting peace in the world.

Just as light dispels the darkness, so war cannot continue where peace has entered. As long as there is war, conflict, attack and tyranny, ego is happy. Ego is always happy at our expense. We are responsible for ego's trouble making. There are no victims. There are no accidents. Ego is only sustained by the energy we give it. Give it no energy and you bring peace to every situation, for ego is then undone, and thus war, attack, anger and conflict are undone. The only war that is being waged in truth is inside. Let there be peace on earth and let it begin with 'me.' Peace in the world begins with peace in the home. When you relinquish ego, you invite peace into your home, and thereby do your part to bring peace to the world.

The key to a peaceful world is the undoing of ego, the withdrawing of energy from it. The world is in your mind and when you want peace in the world, it will be reflected in a peaceful mind. Your mind cannot be at peace as long as you are investing in ego's survival. In order to undo ego you have to see it for what it is and stop giving it the power to be the warmonger that you have been supporting. Most people don't even realize that they are supporting a warmonger. That is because ego is very crafty and clever. It uses the power of our minds to outsmart us. If ever you really realized the monster you were allied with you would cast it away immediately as one who realizes he is holding a poisonous snake. The best way to overcome ego is to unite with all humanity. In wanting peace for all you are doing just that.

Ego is a fake. It has no power of its own. It doesn't exist. All the power to cause havoc in your life is given it by you alone. Therefore none of the conflict that we see all around us need ever be. It has nothing to do with truth. It has nothing to do with God or God's will. It does not make a good story. It is not justifiable in any way. Do not find ways to justify war, conflict, anger or hatred. Do not think that you can learn good things from them. Do not think that conflict is a good way to discover the truth.

Do not fight. Use nonviolent means to overcome, outsmart, and outmaneuver your opponent. Baba says, "Life is a game, play it." God's solution is to look at ego. Looking involves no fighting whatsoever. Looking is so easy. Yet it is the last thing ego hopes you'll do. As soon as you look without judgment you see that ego was only a bunch of hot air. We have been fighting against a phantom opponent. *You have been at war against yourself. Let this war against yourself be over. Every response to ego is a call to war and war does deprive us of peace. Yet in this war there is no opponent. This is the interpretation of reality we must make to secure peace and the only one we need ever make.*

Peace Is Your Birthright

Peace is your inheritance. It is your birthright. You can claim it now. There is nothing opposing your will. If you truly want peace, what is stopping you from experiencing it right now? You are all-powerful. Take back your power and live in peace. Conflict requires force and force is not power. Force is used by those who really believe themselves powerless. Only those who are afraid use force. God's power is kind, innocent, tender, never forceful. That is because God knows that He is all-powerful. When you know you are all-powerful, as you are, you will never feel the need to attack, conflict, contest, defend, vanquish or overpower others. You will know that your safety lies in your defenselessness. You will know your strength lies in your innocence and you will have no fear, for you will know you are always protected. God's angels always hover near and you will abide in peace.

When any situation has been wholly dedicated to truth, peace is inevitable. Its attainment is the criterion by which the wholeness of the dedication can be safely assumed. To dedicate anything to truth is to dedicate it to God. When you dedicate anything to God you will feel peaceful. You will have no need to be anxious or fearful. You will know your life is in capable hands, thus a good outcome is assured.

Peace of mind is achieved largely due to perfect honesty. When you are perfectly honest, you will be satisfied with yourself. You will feel contented. This contentment is peace. *If you are wholly free of fear of any kind and if all those who meet or even think of you share in your perfect peace, then you can be sure you have learned God's lesson and that you are honest.*

Sai Baba has named His ashram Prasanthi Nilayam, the abode of eternal peace. Eternal peace is our home, our inheritance. If peace is not our experience, we are choosing to be other than home where God wills us to be. We are choosing to have a different experience than perfect peace, yet perfect peace is a choice that is always available for it is the only real state. God created us to share His peace with us.

We made ego and ego is the source of all war. Since ego is not real, war also is not real, though it will not work to simply say it is not real. We have to transform war into peace in order that we be restored to a peaceful experience. *You who are not at war must look for brothers and sisters and recognize all you see as your equals, because only equals are at peace. Because God's equal children have everything, they cannot compete. But if they perceive any of their brothers or sisters as anything other than their perfect equals, the idea of competition has entered their minds. Do not underestimate your need to be vigilant against this idea because all conflict comes from it.*

Peace comes to you when you become a teacher of peace. Peace is the acknowledgment of perfect purity, from which no one is excluded. God created everyone as His child thus we are all within that holy circle. Joy is its unifying attribute, with no one left outside to suffer guilt alone. The power of God draws everyone to its safe embrace of love and union. Stand quietly within this circle and attract all tortured minds to join with you in the safety of its peace and holiness.

We understand nothing until we pass the test of perfect peace, for peace and understanding go together and cannot be found alone. We may think we have understanding, but if in the sharing of our understanding conflict is created, we have not understood anything. So we always have to watch our tendency to draw conclusions, to think we know something, to think we have a corner on the truth. Ego is very slippery and evasive and doesn't want to be found out. Only if our experience is of unflappable peace we can safely assume that we have understood truly.

Peace comes in needing nothing. There is a Sanskrit word, Santushta, which means 'to be content with whatever one gets.' Therein lies peace. As soon as we hanker after anything, our peace is disturbed. People say to Baba, "I want peace." Baba says, "Take away the **I** and the **want** and what is left is peace." As long as we are thinking about ourselves in a selfish way, we will not be able to attain peace. As long as we have expectations of others or think we need something we don't have right now, we will not be able to find peace. When we stop thinking about ourselves, stop amassing wealth or progeny, or hankering after worldly possessions, peace is there. Peace is always there. We just cover it up with ideas that ego has encouraged us to adopt. Ego is determined to delude us into thinking we do not already have everything.

Once a king who was searching for peace was told to find the happiest man in all the world and ask him for his shirt. Then he would know perfect peace. The king searched far and wide. He found a few happy people, but when he asked if any of them thought they were the happiest person in the whole world, none could own that level of happiness. Rather discouraged, the king returned to his palace to discover laughter coming from his courtyard. Upon investigation, he found a very poor man sitting under a nearby tree. The king asked if he was the happiest man in the whole world. The man laughed and declared confidently that he certainly was. The king asked for his shirt. The man laughed again and told the king that he didn't own a shirt. We lose our peace because we let our desire for worldly possessions and fear of losing those possessions disturb our peace.

Peace Cannot Be Attained By Compromising Integrity

When we compromise our truth to avoid friction, agitation, or "rocking the boat" we cannot find peace. To be peacefully uncompromising takes strength and courage. In a marriage, sometimes we give in to our partner to keep the peace, but when we succumb to ease rather than integrity, something in us feels we have sold our souls. When that is your experience, do not compromise. Ask God for a solution. His solution will always be conflict free and you will know it is God's solution by the peace you experience even with the most impossible situations.

We have to be willing to face uncomfortable situations rather than avoid them. One friend who goes to great lengths to avoid rocking the boat had a house mate that he no longer wished to be with but he did not know how to tell him, so decided to sell his house to solve his problem. This fear of conflict at all costs does not solve problems, but rather denies them. They will inevitably resurface in other ways and in other areas of one's life. God can offer a solution that both will feel good about when there is a willingness to call on Him. It will be a solution from out of time. It will be a solution where both parties win. God wants to help us with all our problems, be they large or small.

To Have Peace, Respond, Don't React

When someone acts unkindly, you can respond by forgiving them. True forgiveness recognizes that ultimately nothing happened. You are not a body, you are spirit - eternally unaffectable. True forgiveness does not mean to ignoring a slight. We must ask Spirit to show us how to restore peace to a tear in the curtain. We may be directed to request an apology or an admission of error before resuming a relationship after an altercation.

A Course in Miracles tells us that to overlook or deny inappropriate behavior is forgiveness to destroy. When we let unkindness go unnoticed, we do a disservice and enable. Any act of unkindness will produce guilt even if your brother defends or justifies his actions. Peace comes in healing relationships so that all concerned have an opportunity to be free of guilt. That is true love for your enemy. Ego is our only enemy and when your brother feels guilty, ego wins and both of you lose. Forbearance means to respond rather than react. To react is to forget to invite spirit into your situation.

I was leaving at the end of the month and closing our house up for the winter. The person who was occupying the apartment adjoining our house would have to move. Already she had been looking for months for different housing to no avail. Where we lived at that time, there was a marked shortage of rentals, especially within her price range. I assured her that I would not leave her stranded. Together we asked Spirit for help. By the end of the week she had a house-sitting job for the winter in the place just across the street. It was a beautiful home and a peaceful solution. When we are sensitive to each other's needs, we open the door to a happy outcome for all concerned. We both stepped out of the way and let God solve the problem.

Peace hinges on how we respond to any situation, and cannot be disturbed by what others do or don't do. If you find yourself having difficulty with anyone, there is a peaceful solution where you can both feel honored and where a happy outcome is assured for both parties. The Iroquois Indian nations are remembered for practicing consensus. Their tribes would sit together in a pow wow, drawing their circle. Everyone was heard and only when there was universal agreement around any issue did the party breakup.

If anyone disturbs your peace, you can be sure you are allied with ego and that you had not found true peace. It was only an idea of peace. It was superficial. Real peace cannot be disturbed. When we trust God implicitly we will be guided through even the most turbulent and rocky moments of our lives with peace and equanimity. God only wants us to have a peaceful experience. When we trust Him implicitly we will be shown how to bring peace to every situation, at every opportunity. Peace is only possible where there is a happy outcome desired for all concerned.

Peace Comes With A Willingness To Expose Error

When everyone thought the world was flat, the captains of the ships who set sail around the world were scoffed at and there was every attempt at preventing them from launching their boats. Somewhere within the heart of each person who believed the world flat, there was a knowing that it was round, yet there was a tremendous investment in its flatness. They did not want to be wrong, because they were allied with ego and ego would then become less credible. Once you are willing to be wrong about other things, what's to stop you from being willing to be wrong about ego? It takes courage to be willing to be wrong. Those who were willing to set sail were faced with tremendous resistance. It takes courage to disturb the peace for a real purpose.

What is the big deal about being wrong? If you thought the world was flat when it was really round, would you not be happy to change your mind, once the truth were known? We have all been wrong, because we all made ego to replace God as our Source. It is ego that tells you that to admit error is weakness. Ego knows that in your willingness to admit error its nothingness is exposed and it will lose its power over you. Those who are willing to be wrong have tremendous strength. Those who insist they are right, no matter how irrational their conclusions, are actually very fearful.

An apology is an admission of error, not of guilt. When you are wrong, if you are unwilling to admit it, you are making the error real. It means that you are choosing to be guilty rather than allow your idea of lack to be healed. How many religious wars have not been fought because someone thought they were right while someone else was wrong? There is always a way to get at the truth, when we are willing to be wrong or to see that we both have a contribution to make to the truth. As long as you need to be right, you will be at war with yourself and think that the other person is really the problem. You will fight and feel perfectly justified in your position.

We may find ourselves in an impossible situation, but with God all things are possible. We do not have to know how to solve our problems. We just have to be willing to be wrong about our position and willing to do whatever is necessary to resolve issues peacefully. We have to be willing to trust that there is a solution that will serve everyone's best interests.

World Peace

I yearn for peace for all humanity. I confess I want peace in the world more than anything. I want it with all my heart. I want it with a passion. I will not be content until there is peace for everyone. Until then my heart is in agony for the suffering that wars and violence foster. I cannot be content while my brother or sister is afraid that she may be shot, raped, made homeless or starved to death. I am one with everyone and until everyone is assured peace, I am not at peace.

Surely this yearning for world peace is a noble Divine discontent and is not of ego, but rather comes from an understanding of our oneness with all beings. Until there is peace everywhere we cannot claim to be at peace. The more minds who are inspired to join in that greatest of crusades toward world peace, the more quickly it will be the direct experience of every living thing. As long as we think peace for everyone is impossible, we keep it at bay. When enough minds become truly miracle minded, we will literally see a world transformed into a world of peace for all.

Overcoming The Obstacles To Peace

Peace has obstacles to overcome in its attainment. *The first obstacle to peace is the desire to get rid of it.* I realize that seems odd, but the last thing ego wants is peace, and so it will cause you to think you want to get rid of it. As long as you ally with ego you will feel uncomfortable in the presence of peace. Or you will have a semblance of peace and think that to be real peace.

When I first came to Sai Baba's ashram I was there about 6 weeks and then really wanted to move on. The experience was too peaceful. There wasn't enough action. I was looking for more adventure, excitement and thrill in my life. I wasn't ready for peace. I wanted to get rid of it. In order to have peace, we must desire it.

Body-consciousness is the second obstacle to peace. As long as you believe the body valuable for what it offers, you will not be at peace. The body offers nothing you really want. When you believe it does, you will cater to its needs and this will cause a disturbance to your peace.

There is a story from the Mahabharata, a great Indian classic, of a pool whose waters would take on miraculous powers one day of the year, every year, to satisfy everyone's wishes. Kids would wish for toys and subsequently get their toys. But there was always a down side to the fulfillment of their desires. Either the toys broke or were stolen or in one way or other their joy turned to sorrow, their pleasure to pain. As the years went by the children grew older and started wishing for spouses. And the dream spouse would come along, but their relationships were invariably fraught with sorrow. One spouse died, another drifted away, or there was constant conflict. In one way or other none of their wishes produced lasting peace.

There was a cripple boy who was unable to get to the pool in time to make a wish. Each time the moment arrived he was too far off and by the time he made it to the water's edge, the healing powers had closed down. So he watched from a distance all that was taking place. He saw how everyone was getting what they wished for and how they would end up disappointed. He felt compassion for all those who got their wishes but subsequently suffered. His heart was moved and he found himself genuinely wishing for the happiness of all his brothers and sisters. It hurt him to see their suffering. As he had this true wish that was not for himself or his lameness and was free of all body consciousness, he miraculously experienced a healing. In his compassion he forgot about himself and that shift in consciousness permitted him to be healed. Body consciousness keeps peace away. Catering to the needs and desires of the body is a bottomless pit. In order to obtain peace, it is necessary to overcome body consciousness.

The third obstacle to peace is the attraction of death. Death is an attempt at peace, but it is not a solution. It is a way to escape life and there is no peace in the need to escape. The way to attain peace is by standing still in your problem, whatever it may be and asking God for a solution. With God all problems are solvable. Death is ego's idea and not of God. You may disagree that you are attracted to death, but if you feel death to be inevitable that is its attraction. Ask to be shown if there is another final solution. Is death really inevitable? Be willing to ask. Be willing to look. It takes courage. It takes a willingness to be wrong even about death. When eternal life becomes your attraction, you will have peace.

And the last obstacle to peace is fear of God. We fear peace, because we fear God, as peace and God are one. If you fear God, you will not want peace to be your experience. So we must look at why we fear God. We fear God because we have listened to ego. Ego has told us that God is fearful and vengeful and that He wants to punish us. These are lies. Ego wants us to be afraid of God. Ego's survival depends on your fear of God. As long as you are afraid of God, ego is guaranteed life at your expense. Ego doesn't care about you. It doesn't want you to discover God to be your very dearest friend.

Many Christians are taught to believe that God is quite literally fearful as part of their religion. They are taught that they must believe Jesus died for their sins. If they believe this they will go to heaven and if not, they will be damned to hell. In their minds then it must be that God judges them as to whether they believe He caused His son Jesus to suffer a cruel death so they could be saved. This theology must set up visions of a ruthless, vengeful God. Anyone who challenges their beliefs is seen as attacking them, as allied with the devil or in some way evil. Thereby, they protect themselves from the truth. The truth needs no defense or protection. When you know that God is love, you will have attained peace.

God Is My Dearest Companion

I am not afraid of God. He is my friend. I am in constant communion with Him. I hear God talking to me because I trust that He can. This opens the door to that Divine communication. We have to invite God in or He cannot be seen or heard. He is unimposing. Ego is imposing. Ego is in your face, demanding attention. Only when you want only God, and turn to Him for everything does ego lose its power.

God is the Source of all peace, harmony, stillness, kindness, gentleness, contentment, serenity and calm. When we turn to God for a peaceful solution, the world becomes a place where lasting peace is possible for everyone. Peace is expressed through honesty, integrity, gentleness, tenderness, kindness, silence, communion with the Divine and in choosing a contemplative life - simple living and high thinking. To have peace, give peace.

Illusion meets illusion while truth meets itself. The meeting of illusions leads to war. Peace looking on itself extends itself. War is the condition in which fear is born and grows and seeks to dominate. Peace is the state where love abides and seeks to share itself. Conflict and peace are opposites; where one abides, the other cannot be; where either goes, the other disappears. The memory of God is obscured where minds become illusion's battleground. Yet far beyond any senseless war it shines, ready to be remembered when you side with peace. God is your friend. Remember Him and live in peace that peace may prevail on earth.

Thank You dear God that You only want peace for us. Please grant us the confidence to know You are there for us whenever we turn to You. Help us to trust that You can solve all our conflicts and bring peace to every situation. Grant peace to every home, neighborhood and country, precious Lord. Turn the leaders of the world toward peace. With You peace is possible. With You war is impossible. Let brother express only love for brother as it was always meant to be. Let all mankind walk together in perfect harmony.

May all beings in all the worlds be happy and blest, Amen.

Figure 11 – Peace Is God's Will For Everyone

Everything (Eternity)

Eternity	Life	Oneness
God-Dependence	Love	Freedom
Real	Truth	Non-judgment
Heaven	**Peace**	Creation
Innocence	Knowledge	All-Powerful

Nothing (time and space)

Time/space	**Happy Dream (Satva) God's solution - collapses time**
God-dependence	Trust God for a peaceful solution to all problems
Unreal	Equanimity whatever happens
Hell	Yearn for peace for all humanity
Guilt	A quiet mind in which God is constantly remembered
Death	**Nightmare (Rajo Guna) - makes time**
Fear	Wars for power, borders, religion, race, caste...
Untruth	Fear of God
War	Conflict due to body consciousness
Ignorance	Discomfort with peace
Separation	**Deep Sleep (Thamo) Ego's solution - freezes time**
Bondage	Attraction of death
Judgment	War justified/terrorists die to attain heaven
Mis-creation	Keep the peace by compromising truth
Powerless	Sell your soul through fear, avoidance, escape
	"Don't rock the boat"

Direction of Consciousness Awakening

Chapter 12

Are You Ready to Give Up Ignorance For Knowledge?

God knows everything, and pretends to know nothing.
Man knows nothing and pretends to know everything.

Sai Baba

Who Are You?

A teacher and his student were crossing a bridge. The student asked the master how he could most quickly attain self-knowledge. The master threw him off the bridge and pushed his head under water for what seemed like forever. When the teacher finally let go, the student came up gasping for air. The master said, "When you want to know who you are as much as you wanted a breath of air just now, you will progress quickly toward self-knowledge."

Do you know who you are? If your answer is 'No,' don't you find that rather strange? *Uncertainty about who you are is self-deception on a grand scale. What is life but to be yourself?* How can you exist and yet not know yourself? *Your existence tells you who you are.* In the Bible Jesus said, "You are verily Gods." He also declared, "I and my Father are one." Genesis, the first book of the Bible says that God created man in His image and likeness. Sai Baba says, "You are God. You are no different from God. There is no one more powerful than you." Isn't that empowering?

To be restored to true knowledge we have to want it more than all the other knowledge with which we distract ourselves. Sai Baba tells a story of an erudite scholar who was being ferried across the river by a simple boatman. After some time passed, the scholar casually asked the boatman for the time. The boatman confessed that he didn't have a watch and didn't know how to tell time anyway. The scholar rather derisively exclaimed, "What! Without knowledge of time one quarter of your life is wasted."

After some more time the scholar asked the boatman for the news. The boatman admitted that he could not read. The scholar derided the poor man, "You don't pay attention to what happens in the world? At least one half of your life is wasted."

After some more time, the scholar asked the boatman to entertain him with some radio tunes. The boatman humbly apologized that he had no radio. "No radio mean you miss out on the wonderful world of entertainment - thus three quarters of your life is wasted," mocked the pompous scholar.

When a storm came up the boatman asked the scholar, "Can you swim?" The scholar admitted that he could not. The boatman sadly informed him, "Then your whole life is wasted." Your whole life will be wasted when used only to gain secular knowledge. Only with the pursuit of self-knowledge do our lives become worthwhile.

The difference between an awakened master and the rest of humanity is that the awakened one knows who he is. We adulate anyone who knows himself. We should stop adulating and get on with finding out who we are. We are love and light, created by God to be and have everything, no different from God or any of God's creation. We are life eternal, all-knowing, one with everyone and everything, whole and perfect. When you know that, you know something precious.

Being Is Lost In Becoming

It is thought by many that waking up is an evolutionary process whereby we start from below and over time learn and progress and eventually ascend. Suffering is a great teacher it is said. Having things go wrong is full of opportunities for growth. As long as we hold this philosophy, we will continue to draw hardships to ourselves so we can grow. We will continue to suffer so we can mature and learn. Certainly when hardships come they can be used. We can use our pain, see the gift in everything, and yet, ultimately we must come to the realization that enough is enough. That is the only true lesson worth learning from any pain. It is the idea that pain is a good teacher that calls forth that teacher into our experience. We did not start from below. There is no evolutionary process. We do not have to become who we are. We are whole and perfect right now as that is how we were created.

If you were already everything that you aspire to become through suffering, tough times, challenges and trials, would any of them have any purpose? Without a purpose, our difficulties would cease to be our experience. As long as we believe we are not who we are, we can justify all kinds of hoops to jump through to become ourselves. If we simply allow ourselves to be who we are right now, none of those austerities or sacrifices will make any sense. They will cease to be what motivates us and our circumstances will change to reflect our shift in consciousness. If we were created to know everything forever, then it must be that we know now. *It has taken much time to be who you are not. It takes no time to be who you are.*

Perfection Is Your Truth

Sai Baba says, "My life is my message." He leads a life of purity and perfection. Acting with the utmost purity and holiness will reconnect us with our true self. When our every thought, word and deed is in alignment with our perfection we will realize that we know and our experience will reflect that knowing. We block our knowing when we choose to be less than the perfection God created us to be.

We do not have to learn how to be the perfection we already are. We do not have to become good in order to attain knowledge or become worthy. Behavior modification deals with the problem of imperfection at the level of symptoms. We need merely stop denying our shortcomings or feeling guilty for them, and then ask God to correct our thinking that we could be other than how we were created. Perfection is immediately available, no learning is necessary. We demonstrate our desire for perfection by striving to our maximum capacity for excellence and purity with every thought, words and deed.

Imperfection is a symptom of alliance with ego. Ego is the cause of all imperfection. When we root out the cause of imperfection, it vanishes instantly, without a struggle. It is ego that tells us that we are not and cannot be perfect. It is ego that depends on us to be imperfect. When we remove ego, our perfection, which is always in tact, reemerges effortlessly.

There are those who justify a lack of perfection on the premise that it is not possible to be imperfect no matter how imperfect one's actions may be. If your actions do not reflect your truth, you are exposing to yourself that you don't really believe you were created perfect. Actions reflect one's state of consciousness.

There are others who say, "I'm perfect just the way I am." They mean their imperfections are perfect. When you know you are perfection, your every thought, word, and deed will reflect goodness, integrity, nobility and loving kindness. Ego is determined to employ all kinds of cunning arguments to keep you from your perfection, so be bright and alert.

You Already Know Everything

Love cannot be taught. It is who we are. Ego alliance blocks the awareness of love's presence. When we want to be who we are, the blocks fall away because they were never real. We do not have to learn how to remove the blocks. We need simply be willing to have them removed. Our desire is all that is ever needed, as our minds are all-powerful. We just have to recognize that the problem is ego and the solution is its nothingness.

There is nothing you can learn from anyone that you do not already know. There is nothing you can teach anyone that they do not already know. *Your worth is not established by teaching or learning. Your worth is established by God and He created you to know everything forever. He also created everyone else to know everything forever.* Why would God create you and yet keep secrets from you? Why would He create you ignorant? *Nothing is hidden from you that you have not hidden from yourself.* There are no mysteries. *There is nothing that is beyond your ability to know right now.* To know takes no time at all. As we were created with all knowledge we have no need to learn anything. Our minds were not created for learning. We were not born to learn something only to end in death. We taught ourselves how to learn.

There are those who think God gave us an unreal experience in order that He become enlightened about unreality. Is God really deprived by not being able to experience suffering, lack, separation, fear, death, ignorance...? God is all-knowing, meaning He has nothing to learn. Learning serves to fill a lack. Can you imagine God studying, learning, evolving or progressing? Can there be any lack in God? Or in you, who were created in His image? Can knowledge of unreality add to total knowledge? We can concoct all kinds of justifications for our ignorance or we can simply drop our ignorance and be all-knowing. We are the deciders of our destiny, be it a slow learning process or a quantum leap into limitless knowledge. Ego persuades us to distort our God nature.

Knowledge is different from everything we teach ourselves and returns when we want it. As long as you think you need to learn something, you are giving yourself an unreal purpose and keeping knowledge at bay. We do have tremendous capacity to learn if we so choose, as our minds are all-powerful. If you want to use your mind to learn, then learn you will. We have used all our God-given power to teach ourselves to believe the unreal real and the real unreal. This is quite a learning feat. Now we need merely unlearn what we have taught ourselves, for we have been poorly taught.

Ignorance Disappears In The Light Of True Knowledge

We have convinced ourselves that we are ignorant, that we do not know who we are, that we do not know who God is and that we do not have a purpose. All these untruths have been acquired while truth has been forgotten. It was our decision to make everything that is natural and easy impossible.

Once in an interview Baba manifested a diamond ring for an older devotee with the injunction, "Die-mind." He gave the diamond as a reminder to still the mind. The endlessly, useless chatter needs to die. However, a diamond is clear, brilliant and dazzling. So should our minds be. It is up to us how we use our minds. And how we use our minds will be reflected in our lives. We are grandeur and to think it humility to be small, limited, or lacking is to deny that we are as we were created.

God's children, who were created with the brilliant luster of dazzling diamonds have become dull, lifeless and ignorant. This is a great travesty on God's creation and fortunately never really happened, for truth is unaffectable forever. We can throw off our ignorance whenever we choose. It has taken much time to become who we are not. It takes no time to be who we are.

We have merely fooled ourselves into believing that we are ignorant and convinced ourselves that ignorance is humility. Ignorance is not humility but rather the height of arrogance. It is arrogant to want to be different from who we are. *Only grandiosity would have you be other than yourself.* We can convince ourselves that we are small if we wish. We can as easily convince ourselves that we are grandeur.

When we stop teaching ourselves that we do not know everything, we open the door to the remembrance that we were never ignorant. The veils of illusion that obscure our truth are but the weight of a feather. Maya (illusion) obscures only as long as we fool ourselves that it can fool us. All sickness, suffering and disasters unto death are due to the belief that we do not know who we are, while all along it is impossible not to know ourselves. *Just to exist, you have to know who you are.* We do know who we are and also who God is for we are God.

While you ask questions about God, you are clearly implying that you do not know Him. It is ego that hopes we will not know our true identity or true source, for then it has no further purpose in our lives and withers and dies. When you know who you are you can never act unkindly toward anyone. When you know who you are, you will be certain about everyone's Divinity and you will naturally express only love and joy toward all of creation. To experience this truth we must unlearn what we have taught ourselves.

Learning Has A Function Now – That Of Unlearning

Due to erroneous learning it has become necessary to use our learning ability to change our understanding. This is a remedial necessity. The ability to learn has no value when change of understanding is no longer necessary. The eternally creative have nothing to learn. God does not teach. To teach is to imply a lack which God knows is not there. God is not conflicted. Teaching aims at change, but God created only the changeless.

Only after the separation was it necessary to direct our creative force to learning, because behavior had become mandatory. We needed to learn to survive, to grow crops and to build shelters. Behavior became part of our experience, though it was never the purpose for which we were created. *Behavior is learned.* Behaving perfectly is the portal back to our true state where behavior is no longer relevant. Poor behavior attracts unreality, as it is unreal, while good behavior attracts God as God is goodness.

To be restored to sanity, we can learn to improve our behavior and to become better and better learners, bringing us in closer and closer accord with truth. The truth is we are perfect creations, and perfection is not a matter of degree. Only while there are different degrees of understanding is learning meaningful. Now we must want to learn. Until complete understanding is restored, until all doubts are dissolved, learning is indispensable. Turn to the teacher within. All knowledge is within.

No kind of knowledge is acquired by anyone unless he wants it or believes in some way he needs it. We have learned poorly, so now must learn anew what is true. We will do this when we are motivated to learn. *Knowledge will be restored when we meet its conditions, not because God bargains with us, but merely because we misused His laws on behalf of a will that was not His. Knowledge is His will.* If we are opposing His will, how can we have knowledge? *The happy learner meets the conditions of learning here, as he also meets the conditions of knowledge in the kingdom.*

Be Willing To Be Wrong About All You Taught Yourself

The only thing we really need to learn is that it is possible to be wrong. When we insist we are right, we put up blocks to the truth that is always present. A mind that is willing to be wrong is free and open, and that willingness removes the blocks to the awareness of true knowledge. We have to be willing to be wrong about everything we have erroneously taught ourselves. *When we let go of all our ideas of what knowledge is, knowledge can dawn once again upon our most holy minds.* When we want the truth above all else, then only will we be able to recognize the truth that we do know everything for all eternity.

Truth dawns on a mind that is willing to be wrong, that is open and does not need to defend its position. When we think we know something, we close the door to truth. In letting go of any need to be right we make room for truth. We must be willing to be wrong about our religious beliefs, our philosophies and our ideas of who God is and who we are. Before the separation we did know everything. We have not lost that knowing, but after the separation we chose to forget and knowledge will be restored when we give up our desire for autonomy. In desiring autonomy, we traded in true knowledge, as that desire gave birth to ego.

Ego Is The Only Obstacle To Knowledge

Ego does not know anything and has no being, as knowledge and being are one. The ingenuity it employs toward self-preservation however is enormous. Ironically, it gets its cleverness from the power of your mind and then denies you its power. Ego attacks what is preserving it. It draws on your mind, which is totally inimical to it, for its existence. It then depreciates the power of your mind in your mind to avoid being found out. It convinces you that you are not all-powerful, but instead powerless, and that not only do you not know everything as you were created, but that you don't know anything.

The major obstacle to any true and valuable knowledge is ego. It will distract you and try to convince you that you are not capable of learning the truth. Ego tries to prevent you from attaining self-knowledge because once you know who you are, you recognize ego's nothingness. *Though its distractions seem to interfere with your learning, remember that it has no power to distract you unless you give it that power.*

Ego's voice is an hallucination. Hallucinations are inaccurate perceptions of reality. To be free, illusions must be dispelled, but you need not dispel them alone. All that is needed is that you evaluate them in terms of their results to you. If you do not want them on the basis of loss of peace, they will be removed from your mind. Knowledge cannot dawn on a mind that harbors illusions, because truth and illusions are irreconcilable. Truth is whole and cannot be known by part of a mind.

True Teachers Know That You Know

A true teacher always wants to join with his students by bringing forth their own inner knowing, rather than encouraging dependence. The only true teaching is perfect equality and a teacher who does not lead the student to that understanding is an ego oriented teacher. A true teacher can only help you remove the blocks to the awareness of the knowledge that is always within.

Those who teach with words without bridging the gap between student and teacher are keeping separation alive. This is always due to fear of oneness. A true teacher knows his students were created by God to be and have everything, no less than he. He does not see himself as greater than his students. A true teacher wants his students to surpass him. Jesus said in the Bible, "Greater works than I have done, shall you do."

It is not uncommon to experience fear associated with teaching or learning of ultimate truth. That is because true learning leads to the relinquishment of the ego to the light of the soul. It is ego that tells us that learning about who we are is fearful. We must change our minds and help others change theirs.

Perhaps you wistfully see that your family, environment, religion, education or culture is the cause of your faulty learning of inequality and separation. Every situation that you find yourself in you made for yourself because it is exactly what you wanted to learn. *The world cannot teach you anything you do not want to know.*

Once Arjuna asked Krishna, "What if a yogi is close but does not achieve enlightenment in this lifetime?" Krishna assured him that the yogi would be born into a family who would support and strengthen his spiritual aspirations so that he would be able to pick up where he left off in his previous incarnation. Learning of the truth will serve your eternal life. Whatever efforts you make in that regard cannot be lost.

Look Beyond Others' Errors - Don't Ignore Them

To know that everyone was created equal is knowledge. To see everyone as they were created we need but recognize that every act without exception is love or a call for love. *Only appreciation is an appropriate response to anyone. His loving thoughts as well as his appeals for help should elicit only gratitude, as both are capable of bringing love into your awareness when perceived truly.* When we do not feel the deepest gratitude and appreciation for everyone, we have decided wrongly and can choose again.

Once Peace Pilgrim, an American saint, went for a walk with a rather tough teen. En route he started beating on her. She responded by wrapping her arms around him with all her love and compassion. She knew his Divinity and felt his call for love. The surprised child responded by melting in her arms. All he wanted was to feel loved.

Overlook errors in others by looking to their perfection undimmed by any error. We must stop judging error as sin and thus condemning others and wishing them punished. At the same time, when I know I'm mistaken, I want to make it right, but I cannot correct an error when I'm oblivious to the fact that I'm in error. In truth we do always know when we are off, but we tend to fool ourselves. When others support us in fooling ourselves they are not really serving us. Those who are willing to point out error without judgment reflect back to us where we are off if we allow them to serve us in that way.

To turn a deaf ear and blind eye to others' errors would be to have no interest in their salvation. Everyone is yourself and their salvation is your own. Do everything within your power to support the truth for all in every way possible. How do you feel when you avoid or deny others' errors? If you find yourself feeling guilty, if your peace is disturbed in any way, or if you feel desensitized, be sure that something is telling you to get more involved. It may feel scary, but the peace you will experience will make the risk worthwhile. Sometimes your acts of kindness in the face of error will be the remedy. Sometimes it will be avoiding company with your 'brother' while he is choosing erroneous ways.

Let God direct you in what to do in relation to others' errors. And be sure to see that you are not projecting your errors onto others and seeing in them what you are not willing to look at in yourself. If your response comes from irritability you have work to do on yourself. Be pure and then you will see others with clarity, charity and compassion, recognizing their error as the call for love that it is. Then you can be shown what to do to truly serve their enlightenment.

There are those who teach that it doesn't matter what you do as a defense against correction of error. What doesn't matter is the past. It doesn't matter what you've done, but it matters very much what you do now. It doesn't matter your position in life, whether you are a street sweeper or the CEO of the largest corporation in America, but it matters very much what you do with that station – purity, integrity and nobility matter.

Only when we want everyone to be whole and perfect and to stop being fooled by ego are we in right relationship with others' errors. *To heal is to correct perception in ourselves and others by sharing God's love.* Three women were named women of the year in 2002, for being whistle blowers for corruption in corporate America. That took courage and clarity. Correction of others is a delicate matter. It requires purity and integrity within your own life first before you can act in any capacity in others' affairs. You will just know when it is appropriate to act.

When I was raped, I did have the man sent to jail. I did this out of a sense of duty to society. I could not bare the thought of someone else having to experience what I had gone through. I would have felt responsible. I did not put him away out of a sense of justice, retribution, retaliation or revenge. I have the deepest compassion for this man and pray for him even today. My wish is that he correct his ways, not that he be punished for his mistakes.

If we truly inspired all criminals to be transformed, we would have true correctional facilities and rehabilitation centers and people would reenter the world as upright citizens who choose to lead noble lives because they have learned that is in their very best interest. That will be accomplished when they step into personal responsibility for their past actions and are willing to correct their ways. Their detention ought to be measured by their transformation and should be based on willingness rather than on a time related sentence meted out as punishment, which makes time and guilt real.

When my rapist said he was sorry, he was acknowledging that he was in error. He also needs to know that though he was wrong he is not guilty and that error is correctable. As long as he feels guilty for his error, he has made it a sin and will not be able to avoid punishment or to stop his hurtful ways. Once he is willing to let God correct his mind, he will not feel guilty. Then his error will be undone automatically and he will be able to reenter society and live a life of decency and trustworthiness.

Once you know who you are you cannot hurt anyone. It will be enough for me to know that my rapist will never rape another woman. It would be enough for me that Hitler not hate Jews and gypsies. At every moment anyone can choose to be transformed into a noble citizen, as that is their truth. I do not wish Hitler punished for the monstrous atrocities he perpetrated against humanity. I would be happy to see all criminals transformed. I do not need anyone punished. That gives me no satisfaction. My satisfaction comes in their discovery of who they are as wholly innocent.

I am overjoyed when anyone discovers the truth that they deserve the best because they are precious souls, created by God as God, worthy to walk the earth like masters with their heads held high. You know you deserve the best when you treat others with the utmost dignity and kindness. Everyone has the capacity to change their minds and transform their lives. Every saint has a past and every sinner has a future. *You can choose again. Each moment is a clean untarnished birth.*

Freedom Is The Reason We Could Err

How is it possible to err if we were created perfect? It is possible for you to make wrong decisions because God's kingdom is freedom. It is possible for us to err in thought, reflected in our words and deeds. *Error cannot however really threaten truth, as truth can withstand its assaults. Errors are but illusions that remain unrecognized for what they are. Where truth has entered, errors disappear. They merely vanish, leaving not a trace by which to be remembered. They are gone because without belief, they have no life.* There is only one error, the idea that we could be different from how we were created. History would not exist if the same errors were not repeated in the present. Errors are of ego.

Before ego, there was only one error possible, the making of ego, or one's own God. That error could only be motivated by a desire for autonomy from God. Once we wished to be free of our Source, to start a mutiny, we had the power to make that our experience, though we never had the power to make it a reality. God is our Source. We are inseparable from God forever. Ego is an idea of separation from God. It is an erroneous idea, however we have the power to convince ourselves that we succeeded in becoming autonomous.

Into eternity where all is one, there crept a tiny mad idea and we forgot to laugh. That tiny idea was that we could make our own source. It was a silly idea, a mistake. We took it seriously. It was not an idea that entered our minds inexplicably; it was our idea. We are all-powerful and if we entertained a tiny mad idea, we did so open eyed. We are responsible for everything that happens to us and for every thought that enters our minds. Our will is free. We can make a mistake and when we do, it is our error. When we so choose, error is corrected. Truth overcomes all error. *True perception cancels out misperception in ourselves and others. When we see everyone as they were created and can really create, we offer them our own validation of their truth.*

Once ego was made, we opened ourselves to all kinds of errors, as ego thrives on error. In fact all those errors are only one, namely that we could become different from who we are. We thought we could be guilty instead of innocent, powerless instead of all-powerful, vulnerable instead of invulnerable, mortal instead of immortal, imperfect instead of perfect, ignorant instead of all-knowing, autonomous instead of one with God and each other forever.

Ego convinces us that error is more than error, it is fact, and that we indeed succeeded in becoming autonomous. If error is seen as a lack, it will simply be corrected. What keeps it from being corrected is an unwillingness to see it for what it is. When seen as sin, irrevocable, wreaking permanent damage, it will have to be punished to balance the scales. If admitting error is seen as weakness it will also remain uncorrected. It is strength to admit error and to allow it to be corrected. Then we can again enter the experience of our wholeness.

Ego wants you to believe error is sin. *Sin is insanity for it suggests that you actually succeeded in being different from how you were created - perfect. It entails an arrogance that the idea of error lacks. To sin would be to violate reality and to succeed. Sin is the proclamation that attack is real and guilt justified. It assumes that you, who were created innocent forever, are guilty and have thus succeeded in losing your innocence and making yourself what God did not create. Sin is the grand illusion underlying all ego's grandiosity.* To admit that you are a sinner is arrogance and not humility. In that admission you are stating that you are more powerful than God. You are equal with God. God created you perfect and you do not have the power to become different from how you were created.

We can pretend we have become bodies, prey to evil and to guilt, with but a little life that ends in death, but all the while our Creator shines on us and loves us with an everlasting love, which our pretenses cannot change at all. It is ego that hopes we will err and then think we deserve punishment unto death. That is its guarantee of survival at our expense. We suffer and die so it can live. It is possible to make mistakes, but those mistakes can have no real effects.

Mistakes Warrant Correction, Not Punishment

All suffering ends in a willingness to correct our errors instead of punish ourselves for them. Sai Baba says of sin: "Do not condemn yourselves as sinners. Sin is a misnomer for what are really errors. I shall pardon all your errors, provided you repent sincerely and resolve not to follow evil again." Repenting of errors collapses time. God can see errors, but He does not use them to see you as different from how He created you.

When we correct our errors by owning that we were mistaken and by being willing to make life changing commitments, we are repenting of our 'sins,' and then we do not have to pay back any debts, for they have been undone. That shift in consciousness assures that we only choose to act in ways that are pure, holy and in harmony with how we were created. *God never punishes, but ego does.* If we don't give our errors to God for correction, we have given them to ego and we will punish ourselves, even though in truth sin is not real and never happened.

No one warrants punishment for 'sins,' and God's children are not sinners. We do not deserve to be punished because we have never done anything sinful. *Any concept of punishment involves projection of blame and reinforces the idea that blame is justified. Errors are of ego and correction of errors of any kind lies solely in the relinquishment of ego.*

Reason cannot see sin, but can see errors and leads to their correction. It does not value the errors themselves, but only their correction. You will know that you are in error if you see a sinful world. Can you see a sinful world and look upon yourself apart from it? It is reasonable to see a world that needs healing and in your wish for the healing of the world, you contribute to its healing and to the healing of your mind.

As I was growing up I believed that when I did something like lie, steal or cheat I was bad and deserved punishment. The truth is I was wrong and needed correction. My teachers taught me I deserved punishment. I must have wanted to learn that or I would not have given myself that learning situation. We set up circumstances to teach ourselves only what we want to learn. I wanted to learn I was bad because I had chosen ego as my guide instead of God. Ego wanted me to think myself bad so I could be punished and thereby assure its continuance. Ego was then happy. Ego is really only ever interested in its survival, out of touch with its negative impact on our lives.

Have you ever used punishment to discipline a child or student? If so, you probably felt guilty. You will feel guilty when you hurt another for that is never an act of love and you are love. It is not that you are bad when you punish error. It is just that you are listening to ego and being told that is in the best interest of your child or student. You only want what is best for those in your care. Ego likes your guilt too. Let everyone feel guilty and thereby ego is assured survival at everyone's expense. All suffering ends in a willingness to correct errors instead of punish ourselves or others for mistakes.

See Error As Unreal Rather Than Bad

When a man came to Baba asking for help to stop drinking, Baba said, "Don't stop. Drink to Me!" The man followed Baba's instructions and soon he stopped drinking. Why was that? Baba guided him to let God take care of the problem by telling him to think of God when he drank. He was not judged or condemned because of his error. When it was given to God he didn't feel guilty. When error is not given to God, it is given to ego and ego wants you to feel bad. Without guilt, ego cannot survive. Ego is the source of all bad habits. Once ego is gone, the bad habit can no longer be sustained.

Bad is never truly what is happening. Bad is really unreality which has been given reality. There is only real or unreal. Good is real. Bad is unreal, therefore does not exist at all in truth. Once you stop giving energy to unreality, it disappears. When you think someone or some action is bad, you are judging and giving reality to what is unreal. If it is not an expression of goodness, it is simply unreal. It will be healed when given to God to heal. You act nobly when you love yourself and you love yourself when you act nobly. One who acts impurely simply does not love himself because he has forgotten who he is. His is a call for love, and a loving response would include wanting him to be holy for his sake.

There are no sins, but only mistakes. When you view a mistake as a sin, you are looking with ego and ego will make sure you are punished. Hardships, sickness and suffering come because we misperceive mistakes as sins. All we need do is be willing to see our mistakes as just that, and ask to be shown how to correct them. Every unkind thought, word or deed is a mistake. If it goes uncorrected, that is if it is not given to God, it has been given to ego for punishment. There are only ever two possibilities in relation to all errors - correction or punishment.

Sai Baba says, "Give me your garbage." He doesn't want us to suffer. When you offer imperfections to God, you are not giving them to ego and they are corrected and you are not punished. When you give error to ego, you repeat the error again and again due to the guilt associated with it.

When you think of God constantly, you are keeping ego away. Suffering comes from ego. If you are not thinking of God, you are thinking with ego and sabotaging your and others' joy. Lead a life of holiness and turn any errors over to God immediately - then you are collapsing time.

Striving For Perfection Is Exhilarating

An unwillingness to admit a mistake means you see it as irrevocable. Many alcoholics are closet drinkers. Violent husbands remain unexposed. Rapes go unrecorded. As long as error is denied, it will not be corrected and will remain unhealed. When you deny an error, you have made it a sin in your mind. *When error goes unrecognized for what it is, it is given reality.* The fact is we all make mistakes or we simply wouldn't be here. To let a mistake go unrecognized is to make it real. Ego is very cunning in preventing us from recognizing error for what it is. Be bright, be vigilant. You do know when you are in error, as the truth is you know everything. You cannot plead ignorance. It won't work and it won't help.

Watch a tendency to justify or defend error. If you do not recognize error as error, will you be open to correcting it? Error must be seen for what it is in order that it willingly be corrected. The catch is that if error is not corrected, it is automatically given to ego and ego takes every opportunity to mercilessly judge you sinful because it wishes to remain alive now that it has been given life. It is like that science fiction movie where robot turns on its maker. Without your guilt, ego will simply disappear. Ego wants you to feel guilty for everything. God created us to be innocent forever, but that would not be in ego's best interest, so it convinces us that we are sinful, that our errors are irreversible and uncorrectable, and that we must be punished for our mistakes. In fact, some religions are based on that very premise.

Christianity teaches that you are sinful no matter how pure or perfect your behavior and that Jesus died for your errors, whether you committed them or not. This is the teaching of others who came after Jesus and is not what Jesus taught. This teaching does not inspire perfection, which is what Jesus taught. Your sins or mistakes can be forgiven. Forgiveness merely means seeing that the truth was not affected, then correcting your error through self-responsibility so that you come back into alignment with your truth. Then past is wiped away without guilt or punishment. We are eternally sinless. As long as you are convinced that you are helpless and powerless to control your actions you are under ego's spell. You are all-powerful, therefore you are always acting on your choice and are not impelled by forces outside of you or beyond your control.

Jesus taught us to be perfect as our Father in heaven is perfect. If perfection were not attainable, why would he bother to teach it? When the prostitute was about to be stoned to death, Jesus saved her by exposing to her accusers their own guilty conscience. After they left, he said to her, "Go your way and sin no more." He did not condone her behavior. He told her to stop doing it, to correct her error, to come into her purity, for he knew that only her holiness could content her. He did not tell her to believe he was about to die for her sins and that she ought to see that as the purpose of the crucifixion. He knew the truth that we not only have the capacity to be perfect, but that perfection is our nature and sin is simply a mistake.

Jesus often spoke of 'sin' when he taught his disciples as well as the masses. He spoke in Aramaic in which the word for sin is 'Katha,' which means 'off the mark.' It was used as an archery term that Jesus applied to any misalignment with one's true nature. When you shoot an arrow and miss the target you will simply correct your aim and shoot again. You will not feel guilty for missing the mark.

That is all that is needed when you make any mistake. When you admit your error God can show you how to correct it. Then you will again be on the mark. It is really very simple and not a big deal at all. There is never a need to feel guilty for a mistake and there is never an error that is more than a mistake. Uncorrected error leads to needless self-inflicted punishment, which serves no purpose whatsoever. When a mistake is brought to correction, you are restored to wholeness and that feels good, just as hitting the bull's eye feels good. There is something very satisfying about striving for perfection in everything you think and say and do.

Nothing You Do Can Alter The Truth Of Who You Are

Rama Krishna, an East Indian saint of the 20th century, said that the only sin possible is the idea that you could be sinful. It is impossible to sin for sin is an action that causes irreparable damage and that would prove that you are more powerful than God, as God created you sinless forever. Your actions cannot affect how God created you. He created you perfect and if you really sinned you would be imperfect. To admit to being sinful is not humility, but rather the height of arrogance. *To those who believe sin possible, purity is seen as arrogance and acceptance of yourself as sinful is perceived as holiness.* It is ego that cannot support true virtue, purity or holiness for they threaten ego's existence.

Can you see mistakes in others? Yes, and at the same time you can give them the charity of knowing their perfection. Then their mistakes can be corrected. If you see them as acting perfectly when they are in error, you are making the imperfect perfect, the unreal real. This is not what the teaching to see only perfection means. See them as perfect, but do not excuse their error or you are an accomplice. In your complacency, you are responsible for their error. We are all one.

Correction of error of another is not of you, however. Ask Spirit to direct your actions in relation to others' shortcomings. Only then can error be resolved without conflict. And remember if his error is attended with any irritation on your part at all, it is you who are in error and projecting that out onto others. Generally speaking, it is safest to work on correcting our own errors and not to feel inclined to look for errors in others. Look for that which is laudable in others and support and encourage that. Listen within and you will know what to do in every situation. Find ways to inspire perfection both in yourself and in others. When I was a Montessori teacher I discovered that if I looked for goodness and pointed that out to my students, every child was inspired toward goodness. A willingness to be holy brings you into holiness. Inspire others to want to be holy because in that they will be happy. Be holy happy.

'Original Sin'

When we made ego to be our source, we made a mistake. It was the first and only mistake really. The Bible refers to 'original sin' as the eating of the apple from the tree of the knowledge of good and evil. After we made ego to be our source we became aware of both good and evil. In choosing the knowledge of evil we lost the knowledge of God as our Source and thus lost all knowledge, as God is the source of all knowledge. In choosing ego to be our source we traded in everything we had with God as our Source. Ego was never our source. Making ego to replace God was a mistake. It was the first mistake and really the only mistake that ever happened. Once you accept God as your Source, ego disappears and you regain the awareness that you know all things.

You can be mistaken. You can deceive yourself and even turn the power of your mind against yourself, but you cannot sin. There is nothing you can do that will really change your reality in any way, nor make you really guilty. That is what sin would do as that is its purpose. The attraction of guilt is found in sin, not error, and guilt is attractive as long as you ally with ego. Sin will be repeated because of this attraction. A major tenant in the ego's insane religion is that sin is not error, but truth.

When you think you sin, you think you have lost your innocence. You can never lose your innocence. You can never lose anything. There is no loss. To think there is, is a mistake. When you are willing to be wrong about everything you taught yourself and to see that you cannot be different from how you were created, your mind is open. This openness permits knowledge to dawn once again and you will see that you could never sin or become less than God created you to be, and you will see that you do truly know who you are.

Always Think Of God

Baba tells the story of a king who was warned that his servant must stay busy all the time doing constructive acts of service or he would destroy the king. Whenever the king had no pressing assignment, he instructed the servant to climb up and down a tower. In that way he was safe, for he always kept the servant occupied. The servant is the mind. The tower is remembrance of God's name. When we are not otherwise occupied, we will be wise to repeat God's name. Then we will be allied with God and not with ego and will not be causing ourselves or others harm with our thoughts. Your mind is all-powerful. Never underestimate the power of your every thought.

God knows the past, present and future of everyone. He has a plan for the salvation of the world. All we need to know is that we each have an indispensable role to play and that He is showing us every step as long as we are aligned with Him and not with ego. You do not need to know more than the next step or you will get in the way. Be fully in the present and you will know that you know. You are an instrument in His mission when you have turned away from ego.

We are Gods, because that is how we were created, and it is our birthright to walk the earth with our heads held high, like masters, full of self-confidence, holiness, perfection, serenity and knowledge. You were created to know who you are and there is nothing you can do to be other than yourself. We have beclouded our minds with all kinds of ideas and concepts of what truth is and when we empty ourselves of all those notions truth will reveal itself for it was always available. May you walk the earth in the certainty that you do know all as endowed by God, and may your certainty be a beacon of light to those who still think they are trapped in ignorance and cannot change their minds. May the light of true knowledge reemerge in your awareness in the service of all humanity.

Heavenly Father, Thank You that You made each one of us to know everything forever. How beautiful to know that everyone does know deep within. Lord, let us teach that and that alone. What an uplifting message of joy. Lord, grant us the courage to look at our errors and turn them over to You for correction. Inspire us to want to be the perfection that You created us to be and depend on us to embody. Help us to think of You constantly. May all beings know the truth that they know everything and are sinless forever.

May all beings in all the worlds be happy and blest, Amen.

Figure 12 – God Created You To Know Everything Forever

Everything (Eternity)

Eternity	Life	Oneness
God-Dependence	Love	Freedom
Real	Truth	Non-judgment
Heaven	Peace	Creation
Innocence	**Knowledge**	All-Powerful

Nothing (time and space)

Time/space	**Happy Dream (Satva) God's solution - collapses time**
Ego-dependence	Willing to trust that you do know everything
Unreal	Happy learner, bright eager mind
Hell	Willing to be wrong, to bring error to correction
Guilt	Accept God as source
Death	**Nightmare (Rajo Guna) - makes time**
Fear	Awakening is a long, slow, painful process
Untruth	Mistake is seen as sin, irrevocable
War	Beat oneself up to learn
Ignorance	Arrogate to oneself a knowing that is not there
Separation	**Deep Sleep (Thamo) Ego's solution - freezes time**
Bondage	Suffering justified as a good teacher
Judgment	Ignorance, dullness
Mis-creation	Closed mind, need to be right
Powerless	Deny errors, not responsible

Direction of Consciousness Awakening

Chapter 13

Are You Ready to Give Up Separation for Oneness?

The union of all God's creations is its protection.
Alone we can do nothing, but together our wills fuse into something
whose power is far beyond the power of its separate parts.
Our function is to function together, because apart we cannot function at all.
The whole power of God's creation lies in all of us, but not in any of us alone.

Jesus in ACIM

Specialness Makes The Illusion Of Separation Real

A scientist named Dr. Baranowski, Professor of Physics at the University of Arizona and a specialist in Kirlian photography came to India where he met Sai Baba. To quote Baranowski, "When a person is full of love the aura around him is blue and when the love is pronounced, it becomes pink." Baranowski had scientifically trained himself to see auras and with this trained vision was investigating the various holy men of India. He found that Sai Baba harbors no feelings of specialness, though He is clearly seen as a teacher and deified by many as God on earth.

In the mid -70's he gave a talk at the Prasanthi Nilayam ashram on his experiences with Sai Baba. Some excerpts follow: "I have met over a hundred holy men in India. Too many of these holy men are involved in their own personal egos. Their auras show mostly concern for themselves and their institutions. So their auras are only a foot broad or perhaps two feet.

"I am not a devotee. I have come here as a scientist to see this man, Sai Baba. I saw him on Sunday, on the balcony giving darsan to the devotees singing below. The aura Baba projected was not that of a man. The white was more than twice the size of any man's, the blue was practically limitless, and there were gold and silver bands beyond even those, far behind this building right up to the horizon. There is no scientific explanation for this phenomenon. His aura is so strong that it is affecting me standing by the chair on which He is sitting. I can feel the effect and I have to wipe my arm, off and on, as you must have noticed. It is very difficult for me to admit. I am a scientist. I have given over six thousand lectures in all parts of the world, but for the first time, believe me, my knees are shaking. The aura that emanates from Baba shows his love for you. If ever I can use the phrase that I have seen 'love walking on two feet,' it is here."

At this point Dr. Baranowski concluded his talk and Sai Baba then delivered a discourse. When Baba finished, Baranowski asked for permission to address the audience again saying, "I have been watching Baba, while he was addressing you. The pink aura that was manifesting was so vast and strong that it went even beyond the hall behind this chair. It filled this big hall, embracing all of you gathered here. There can be no scientific explanation for this phenomenon. I have watched him for a week now, as he walked among you, morning and evening. I have seen his aura, pink in color, go into the person he is talking to or touching and returning to him. His energy seems to be endless. In my estimation, He is exactly what he appears to be – LOVE. That is what he is."

Dr. Baranowski saw that Sai Baba has no need to be seen as special or better than others. We are all unique, special and precious. However, when we want specialness for special favor, the result is separation in the form of competition, comparison and self-aggrandizement. Specialness has entered whenever we perceive inequality, hierarchy or a lack of mutual positive regard in any relationship or interaction. It is frequently seen in teacher-student, doctor-patient, husband-wife, employer-employee, guru-disciple, or parent–child relationship. *A true relationship starts from the premise that you are whole and complete and that you do not need another to fill a lack.* In co-dependency relationships we make separation by thinking we lack something that someone else has or that we have something someone else lacks. *A relationship whose purpose is to fill a lack is a special relationship.* Any relationship where you do something for someone in exchange for something is a special relationship. Sai Baba knows no lack, thus harbors no special relationships.

You Are One With God

God created you to be one with Him for all eternity. He also created everyone and everything to be one with Him eternally. God created you just like Himself. There is no separation between you and God. Nor is there any separation between you and any other. We wanted to experience freedom from that oneness. We wanted to experience separation from God and each other. We wanted autonomy. To accomplish this, we made our own source. In that action we separated from God in our minds, though that separation could not happen in truth. After separating from God we felt guilty and that guilt motivated us to separate from each other as well, so we could project our guilt outside of ourselves. Separation served a purpose.

In the Garden of Eden, before the separation, that is before the making of ego, there were both Adam and Eve, but there was only love between them. Adam loved Eve. Eve loved Adam. That is oneness. There is oneness between two people where unity, harmony and peace prevail. Love recognizes oneness, while hate and fear make separation seem real. Adam has his own mind, as does Eve, and when they love each other they experience their minds as joined and they are in the experience of their holy relationship. When love is mastered there will again be oneness as there will only be love and no fear. After the separation fear entered Adam and Eve's minds and that fear was reflected back to them in their exodus from the garden.

Just because Adam and Eve left the garden would have had no effect on you and me except that we thought God had banished them. We loved them and were torn by their departure. *But when we thought God was the cause, we did not know God and thereby caused our own banishment.*

Ego survives as long as we feel separate from anyone or anything for any reason. We have found many uses and purposes for separation, though they are really all the same. One purpose for separation is to project guilt outside of ourselves. Another is so we don't have to be responsible for others' pain. We avoid pain by seeing that someone else is suffering and we are not. When we include everyone's pain, we will be motivated to heal all the pain and all the suffering in the world. This genuine wish for the welfare of all humanity restores to our minds the truth of oneness. It reestablishes us as one organism, each affecting everyone, responsible for everyone, in love with everyone. When we want the best for everyone, we are wanting the very best for ourselves and only then. This is natural, as it is the truth. A third purpose for separation is specialness, which comes from the idea of inequality.

God Could Not Fill Our Request For Special Favor

Sai Baba knows His oneness with everyone. He is incapable of specialness. He has no interest in personal gain. We chose autonomy to experience specialness. In that choice we traded in sanity. *We could not obtain specialness in our right minds. We were at peace until we asked for special favor. And God did not give it as the request was alien to Him. We could not ask this of a Father who truly loved us. Therefore we made of Him an unloving father, demanding of him what only such a father could give. And our peace was shattered, for we no longer understood our Father. We feared what we had made, but still more we feared our loving Father, having attacked our glorious equality with Him.*

As soon as we see our error and allow it to be corrected, we will be restored to our oneness with our Creator. Once Sai Baba asked Al Drucker, "Who are you?" Drucker responded, "I am God, I am exactly like You, Swami. I am no different from God." Sai Baba said, "Then you give darsan (vision of the Divine)." Al realized that he was not qualified to do that as he was not in the experience of his true oneness with God. You cannot give darsan without knowing truly, beyond all concepts, who you are as Divine. Conceptual understanding is not enough. There has to be an owning that a mistake was made. We made ego to forget our Divinity and now a willingness to do whatever is necessary to correct that error will bring us back into our true experience of oneness with God. Only then will we be in a position to give darsan.

Ego was made to experience specialness. Specialness takes the form of prejudice and exclusiveness: 'We are the best, we are the only way, we are the chosen people, we are the most persecuted, we are greater than, we are less than...' are all statements of specialness. God loves us all equally and only when we love all equally are we aware of who we are and what our relationship is to God and all God's children, regardless of color, religion, nationality, or gender.

Everyone is a part of you. Everything that happens to you, you are doing to yourself. You will know who you think you are by how you treat another, for your neighbor is yourself. Specialness comes with the idea of separation. You cannot be special unless you are more or less than someone else. Where is specialness when there is nothing outside of your mind? The idea of separation is overcome in the idea of oneness. *There is only one problem, separation and the solution is it never happened,* so in the ultimate sense, there are no problems ever. Bring separation to oneness and separation vanishes.

Marriage As A Special Relationship

In many instances marriage is a special relationship where two come together to fill a lack. *Any idea of lack comes from a false concept of yourself and can never be satisfied by joining with another, but only by changing your mind about who you are.* Every marriage has the opportunity to be transformed from a special relationship to a holy one. When you enter into marriage because you feel lonely, or to satisfy a longing to feel loved, you are setting yourself up for disappointment. There will never be enough love to satisfy your longing. If you recognize that you are complete within yourself, that you are all the love you need, then you come together with another to enhance each other's joy. Every moment is a clean slate, a new opportunity. We can get it right in this moment, without changing our outer circumstances. All we need do is change our minds about who we think we are.

There is a tremendous amount of guilt around sexuality when it is used to fill a lack. Even intimacy with one's spouse can and frequently does produce guilt if it is lust and not love that prompts the act. If a woman gives herself to her husband because he wants to satisfy a bodily urge, he feels guilty and she is invariably seen as the cause of his guilt. Under those circumstances, women give themselves because they want to be loved or to keep the peace, but it is not the way to happiness.

Everyone must find their wholeness within themselves. This allows sexual relationship to be an expression of love and not a way to get love or gratification. Sexual needs are not real needs. You are whole and complete as you were created. Any attempt to fill a need can never and will never be satisfied because the premise is false. When we change our minds about who we are, we know we have no needs. Sai Baba suggests to think of God when you have sexual urges. In that those feelings can be transformed. Don't use another to satisfy bodily urges, or you reduce both of you to bodies and become the body's slave. That consciousness leads to bondage, not freedom.

Everyone really does know the truth and therefore a woman knows that by giving herself to her husband outside of love she is compromising her integrity and so subconsciously feels deserving of his guilt projections. In that act she has made herself a body in her mind, and since her body is nothing, she mistakenly thinks she is nothing. This leads to a lack of self-worth. Alliance with ego is at the bottom of her willingness to be sexual outside of love and to then accept herself as he perceives her. The honeymoon is over. He looks for greener pastures. He dances with other ladies on the dance floor. He avoids public displays of affection for her. She is reduced to his servant or less. This projection of guilt around lust is at the bottom of many unhappy marriages.

Love-making is intended to be an act of love. If you are not feeling in love it will only lead to unhappiness. 'This to thine own self be true.' You know when you are out of integrity. Don't use sex to patch up an argument. First find your love by dealing with your problem and then express your joining through physical joining. Don't use sex to retrieve your love. In that you put the cart before the horse and it will backfire.

Making love can be the most intensely beautiful act of joining on the planet when you are in love, for then it is not body consciousness that motivates your actions. When it is sex it can produce the most heart wrenching repercussions because it brings you into body consciousness, where you will think you are nothing. Sexuality is a passionate, powerful force that should only be entered into with the utmost responsibility of pure union of heart and mind. To entwine under the right circumstances is Divine. Then your relationship is not a special one, but a holy relationship that blesses the world.

Your Body Is Not As Powerful As Your All-Powerful Mind

When you feel guilty for body gratification and project that guilt out onto your partner, there is separation between you and that is painful. This is at the bottom of most marital problems that couples have faced throughout history, in all countries. The problem is endemic and is healed when you are in love with the one with whom you make love. It is really very simple. If you are not in love, don't do it. Anything short of an eternal commitment with your partner is not love, but lust. If you think you have no control over your sexuality, think again. Your body is not more powerful than your all-powerful mind. Your body is inert. It is nothing. To let it rule you is to make the unreal real.

It could be argued then that we should not eat, as that also makes the body real, but it always depends on your purpose. Do you eat to live or live to eat? Your body can be used for a sacred purpose. Take care of it so it can fulfill its purpose. Sai Baba says of His body, "Ordinary body, used for a sacred purpose." Who will feel guilty for eating when hungry? When love-making is an outer expression of a true union of hearts and minds, it is tantra, or Divine union and that is beautiful and is not tainted with guilt. When free of guilt, you are free. Abstain until it is right.

At the same time guard against letting the pendulum swing in the direction of abstinence for the wrong reasons. You could abstain from a place of denial, sacrifice, for giving yourself a false identity or to avoid the pain of rejection. Watch the motives behind all your decisions either to entwine or not. Trust Spirit to direct you. No action in itself is either right or wrong. It is what prompts an action that is important. Abstinence is perhaps easier than making love for the right reasons. Some people pride themselves on being renunciates as though they are holier than householders. I would take greater pride in honoring and cherishing a sacred commitment. If you have absolutely pure cross-gender exchanges you have put sexuality in its right context and have transcended body consciousness and you will be one in a million on the planet. If you express tender affections for your spouse in public after 20 or 30 years of marriage you have made a significant contribution to the end of suffering for all humanity. Where there is purity and integrity you will do the right thing. Krishna told Arjuna that the householder path was the quickest path to God.

In this world a holy relationship comes closest to our true relationship with God. Your eternal partner was given for that purpose only. If you do not have a partner, ask God to send you one if that is in your best interest. The only truly holy sexual intimacy takes place between one man and one woman who are eternally committed to each other. Sai Baba says that marriage is for sense control and to shift one away from body consciousness.

When you love your spouse purely, no one is excluded. Any sexual relationship outside of marriage does exclude your spouse and is thereby exclusive. We must look deeply to truly understand exclusiveness and specialness beyond concepts. Any impure cross-gender exchanges dishonor your partner and reduce her to a body, leading to feelings of separation, estrangement, abandonment and exclusion. A true holy relationship is not exclusive because everyone benefits.

Making love as an expression of the oneness you feel toward your partner is the only legitimate use of sexuality. Even making babies should happen only between two people who love each other in total commitment. The children who come of that union will feel loved and will grow up to be happy, well-adjusted citizens. Don't make love for the purpose of procreating. Sometimes a couple has a child hoping to save a marriage or they enter into a marriage for having children. Let pure love be your purpose in everything.

Perfect The Law

Jesus says in the Bible, "I have come to perfect the law. The law tells you not to commit adultery, but I say do not even look at another woman." He goes on to say that the only legitimate reason for divorce is unfaithfulness. Marriage is of God and is intended as a life long commitment. It should not be entered into with the attitude that if it doesn't work out you can always get a divorce. If you can't resolve your differences, you make the unreal real and give it power over you. If we can't find ways to enhance each other's joy, we are forgetting that is our only assignment. Let's not be so quick to give up. With God all things are possible.

It is not all right to be unfaithful even if your marriage is unhappy. Don't feel guilty, just don't do it. Past is past and therefore not real. If you hurt your partner, tell her you are sorry and vow to sincerely honor your sacred commitment from this moment. *Each moment is a clean untarnished birth.* Turn over a new leaf right now and all your past is wiped out with no consequences. Mistakes warrant correction, not punishment.

Before taking a partner, make a full commitment. This is where true freedom lies. It is freedom from guilt that we are after as that is the only true freedom to strive for. When that is your objective, you will have put sexuality in its proper context. Sexual freedom is a racket. It is really bondage. It is a wolf in sheep's clothing - don't fall for it. It cannot bring lasting happiness.

Love All Equally; Do Not Treat All With Equal Intimacy

Some so called spiritual movements espouse that marriage relationships should be no different from other relationships or you are exclusive or promoting specialness. This confusion comes from conceptual understanding. Specialness is not overcome by engaging in extramarital affairs. The purpose for one partner has to do with purity, fidelity, sanctity, honoring, self-control and commitment. Free sexuality is a misapplication of the teaching to love all equally. Marriage is a sacred commitment and is to be honored as such. It is of God. Even if your marriage is a special relationship, it always has the potential to become holy when both partners are willing to bring it into holiness by acknowledging no lack within themselves or their partner.

In one spiritual community where sexual freedom is justified as a way to overcome specialness, Mr. Rose was enamored by a woman who expounded the virtues of sexual freedom. Mrs. Rose was devastated and her reaction was judged as jealousy. She needed to be seen as jealous and possessive in order that she be a scapegoat for his guilt. She was not jealous, but she was bewildered. She was told that because she was not willing to share her husband sexually with other women, she was being exclusive, possessive, old-fashioned and expecting special favor. The spiritual teaching, 'All are one and should be treated equally,' was used to justify promiscuity. That justification has to do with body consciousness and is a gross misapplication of the teaching: 'love all equally.' Baba says of sexual promiscuity, "Dogs have that freedom." Behind all distortions around sexuality is ego.

There is an intimacy between a man and wife that is sacred and when you love and honor each other totally, having eyes for no other, you will truly love all in purity and God-awareness and everyone will benefit from your love. To love all equally means to see all as innocent and to condemn or reject no one. It has nothing to do with treating all with the same sexual intimacy. That bizarre conclusion reduces everyone to bodies and comes from conceptual understanding.

Mrs. Rose cannot but be whole and perfect as she was created. No matter what happens there are no victims and she is not dependent on someone outside of herself to complete her. When she turned to God for a solution, she was shown to honor herself by abstaining while Mr. Rose was not honoring his marriage, and she was advised not to divorce as Spirit assured her that Mr. Rose would not act on his distortion. Mr. Rose's behavior was not in alignment with his commitment and is not justifiable or condonable. He needs to make a shift from body consciousness to God consciousness to be free. He is not acting in his own best interest. To make a total commitment to a relationship reflects your total commitment to God and therein lies true freedom.

Once in an interview Baba scolded a woman for letting her husband stray from his commitment. She was in denial, because she did not want to deal with the ugly truth. But in so doing she was not honoring herself. We can always ask God to show us what to do in every situation and God will show us the perfect solution for our circumstances. When we ignore another's inappropriate behavior in relations to us, we are dishonoring ourselves.

Whatever is happening in our lives invariably reflects back to us something that we need to look at within ourselves. When you want oneness in your marriage, you will do whatever it takes to have that. You love yourself when you wait till the circumstances reflect harmony and oneness on all fronts leading to pure, clean and guilt-free sexual expression. This is honoring yourself and herein lies peace and wholeness. You can only change your own mind. You cannot change someone else's. And you are all-powerful. When you are willing to risk your marriage to honor yourself you do love yourself and that will heal your relationship or draw to you the perfect relationship reflecting your integrity and strength.

Once a young couple was coming to visit. I requested them to abstain in my home unless they had made a total commitment to each other. I feared that due to my request they would not wish to visit. They came and were truly grateful for my integrity around sacredness and commitment. There are too many casual relationships, which lead to unhappiness due to a lack of total commitment.

Many young women give themselves prematurely due to fear of being rejected or in hopes of being loved or chosen. This trend is supported as fashionable in our modern society. We have lost much in our determination to overcome our parents' reserve around sexuality. They were ill-informed but we are too informed. Wait for Mr. Right and for the right circumstances. This is self-love and will lead to relationships that enhance your joy, rather than take away from it. You never need sex. To think you do is to think your body more powerful than your all-powerful mind. Your body is inert. Nobody needs sex in order to lead a happy, well-adjusted life. You are not your body. Don't be a slave to its illusory needs.

Society's Purity Depends On Its Women

The Bhagavad Gita says that the moral fabric of a society is upheld by the purity of its women. When women are pure, men will act honorably. Women who love themselves and recognize no lack in themselves will wait for circumstances that reflect true love. When women are pure, a man will look for a woman to spend the rest of his life with rather than one with whom to gratify a bodily urge. This shifts his focus away from body consciousness into his heart. Sai Baba says men should see all females as mother, sister or daughter and reserve intimacy in mind and heart for wife only.

Ramakrishna, an awakened saint of the last century, said that there were two temptations to overcome, women and gold. Males are much more strongly driven by their sexual impulses than are women. If women are easy, the temptation is too great for the male. Sai Baba says women have seven spiritual qualities while men possess only three. Women have to step into their strength and power and use it to uphold virtue.

A woman who is sexually free and easy is not bad, but she is wrong and reveals a lack of self-love and self-worth. Don't be sexually free in hopes of being loved, or for attaining oneness. First love yourself. First be in the experience of oneness where there is no lack in you or your partner and then let love-making be an outer expression of an inner condition or state of mind. Then you are in alignment with the holiness and purity that you are.

Women honor each other as sisters when they support each others' marriages. This is true sisterhood. If you have an engagement with a married man, ask his wife if she feels comfortable. This is honoring your sister. To be pure in all your relations is to lead a life of self-mastery and nobility. Only be sexual in a totally committed relationship. The mess the world is in today can in large part be traced back to sexual promiscuity. Peace in the world starts with peace in the home.

The whole arena of sexuality is vast, due to repression, suppression, perversion, misdirection, control and looseness. As long as you are plagued by lust, you think your body real. You are all-powerful, thus you are the master of your body. Live the truth to have the truth. Sexuality is toyed with in hopes of happiness, but superficial and casual sex can never satisfy you because something in you recognizes the lie. You are not being true when you express oneness without feeling oneness in your heart. A master is one who expresses perfect harmony in thought, word and deed. That is true oneness.

Being In A Holy Relationship Saves The World

We come closest to our truth in this world in a holy relationship. Two voices raised together call to the hearts of everyone to beat as one. And in that single heart beat is the unity of love proclaimed and given welcome. A holy relationship starts from the premise that each has looked within and seen no lack. Accepting his completion, he would extend it by joining with another, whole as himself. What is born into a holy relationship can never end. A holy relationship is any true relationship where all distinctions of separation have been overcome.

The harmonious male/female union, where sexual intimacy is a pure expression of the deepest love is a holy relationship. Sexual intimacy is in God consciousness only when it takes place between one man and one woman in a total, eternal commitment. Homosexuality and polygamy bind us to body-consciousness. There is no power outside of us causing us to make choices that are ultimately not in our best interest. As soon as you know you are not your body, you will choose for holiness. It is not OK to condemn special relationships, but nor is it appropriate to condone behaviors that bind one to unreality. Everyone has the power to choose again.

To be in holy relationship saves the world because once one holy relationship is established, the code has been broken and the special relationship is undermined. It is holiness and purity that we must strive for in every relationship. When we want holiness, it will be our experience. When we want specialness that will be our experience. To want holiness with another is to recognize that you are whole and complete within yourself, and that you are joining with another for a true purpose, that of oneness with each other in God. That true joining is oneness with God.

Oneness - You Are Exactly The Same As God And Everyone

When you are madly in love with someone, you know each other totally. You know that nothing can separate you from one other, not time, nor space, nor even death. You are one with each other forever. That is how it is with you and God. God loves you so intensely that He is always with you, in you, around you, before you and above you. He knows everything about you because He is never separate from you, out of His eternal love for you. *God gave you everything when He created you as everything.* God created you one with Him forever.

There is no place where God ends and you begin. God is the sun and we are the rays. Can the sun be a sun without its rays? Can the rays exist without the sun? And the sun's joy is increased through its many rays. In our total dependence on God, we are one with God forever. God is not outside of you. To depend on God is not to depend on someone or something outside. You were created whole, perfect and complete within yourself. There is nothing outside of you.

If you think of the stars, where are they? They are not off in space somewhere far away. They are in your mind. Everything you can think of, whether of form or formless is an idea in your mind, therefore everything is part of you. Your mind encompasses everything. You are everything. Your mind is all-inclusive. God is an idea in your mind – a real idea. You cannot be less than God. That is oneness. There is God's will and your will, and there is oneness in the recognition that it is your will to do God's will as God wills your happiness. You were created equal with God as God gave you His mind when He created you. So great is your power.

Though there is nothing separate from you, you can have an idea of separation from God, and then that is also an idea in your mind, an idea of willing without God's will. If you want separation to be true, you will convince yourself that it is so and you will make it true for you. You will construct a world wherein it is nearly impossible to find God to prove to yourself that you are separate, but at no point does it make it so. To be one with God, all you have to do is change your mind about your idea that you could be separate. As oneness is a true idea, it requires no effort for that to be your experience. It does require tremendous effort to convince yourself of the reality of that which is not so – namely separation.

You are equal with God and everyone. Everyone is an idea in your mind and to live in that awareness is oneness. Everyone is the Christ, created by God equal with everyone else. We all share one universal mind, the mind of God. *God is the mind with which we think.* God gave you His mind when He created you, therefore, there is no one more powerful than you. Nor is there anyone less powerful. There are those who say that to be equal with God is arrogance, but is it arrogant to be who you are? Actually to be one with God is an awesome responsibility, because in that awareness there is no one more powerful than you and therefore everything that happens to you is your responsibility. That is the real reason people don't want to own their equality with God.

There Are No Victims

There is nothing outside of your mind. You are in the driver's seat. If things happened outside your will, it would prove there were forces beyond your control and you would not be all-powerful as you were created and that is simply impossible. Everyone in your world is fulfilling some purpose in relation to you. No one has the power to prevent you from your destiny. When you recognize all as God, all you can ever feel toward anyone is the deepest gratitude and appreciation. No matter how insanely they may be acting, no matter how frustrated you may feel about something someone is doing, no matter how hurt you may feel, you are still always being given the opportunity to respond with love. *Only you can deprive yourself of anything.* Knowing there is nothing outside of you is oneness.

If you had a problem, wouldn't it be helpful to know the source of your trouble? If you could accept that you are always the source of your problem, then you can know that you are also the solution and you need not look outside yourself for anything. If you take any action in relation to another, or if another takes any action in relation to you, it is because you both willed it. Both your wills come from God and are therefore equal with God and each other. If others could act counter to your wishes in relation to you, it would mean that they were more powerful than you, and that is impossible, as you are all powerful. However, do guard against misapplying this teaching by callously concluding that when someone is in trouble it is because they have willed it so you have no responsibility. They are in your mind and your responsibility is to bring joy to every situation. Help everyone to experience only their joy. Don't be heartless when someone is hurting, because 'they are doing it to themselves.'

When we feel hurt by anyone, we can remind ourselves that our truth is unaffectable. It is usually our reaction that causes our disturbance more than what another did or did not do in relation to us. We can acknowledge that our reaction to an attack happen due to our level of consciousness and ask to be shown what we need to learn from the experience and how to respond with love and integrity. We should not wish anyone to suffer negative consequences for their actions. However this is not an exercise in cheerfully enduring abuse. Honor yourself. We can ask God to show us how to respond to another's lack to bring them back into alignment with their truth so that all our interchanges are pure and kind. When we see everyone's innocence beyond any behavior we are inspiring kindness in others. We are being asked to love all, deep to behavior and to want everyone to behave perfectly for their sake.

When we made ego, we made separation from God and therefore God cannot heal it. We have to heal it by changing our minds. When someone acts hurtfully toward you, they are making separation and they have to heal it. You cannot. Sai Baba tells us to avoid bad company. The person is not bad, but when their behavior is unkind, to deny the unkindness, or to support it would be to enable.

Learn from your hurts and ask how to respond appropriately to the person who has acted unkindly toward you. Don't make a superficial exercise of altercations by thinking that love means throwing your arms around everyone under all circumstances. You can always turn to God for a perfect solution to every conflict. Whatever is happening, you have an opportunity to bring joy to every situation.

House Of Mirrors

When a Divine child enters the house of mirrors, he sees himself everywhere and is delighted. He takes out a crayon and puts a moustache on one of his selves in the mirror, a dress on another and a suit on another. He makes one image fat, another short, another tall and another with long hair. He plays and has so much fun with all his images. When a dog walks into the house of mirrors, he sees lots of other dogs all looking at him, so he growls at them. They growl back. This sets him off so he starts to bark furiously and they bark back as ferociously. This continues and he gets worked up and frantic. Finally in utter exhaustion he lies down. And when he does all the other dogs lie down too.

When we recognize ourselves as Divine, we will see Divinity everywhere and that will be reflected in a Divine experience. If we expect that others are out to get us, we will be setting ourselves up for such an experience, for there is nothing outside of our minds. The Divine child is the central figure in his house of mirrors. He is inspiring all his reflections toward Divinity by seeing all as Divine. He is the Lord of his universe. You are the Lord of your universe. You are the central figure in your dream, be it a nightmare or a dream of awakening. If the figures in your dream are not serving to increase your joy, you can choose again. Ask God to show you how to make your dream a joyful one where everyone benefits. It starts by seeing the Divine in everyone.

You are the Lord of your universe, the central figure in your consciousness, whether dreaming in an unreal world, or awake in heaven. In that recognition, you shift from victim/victimizer consciousness to God consciousness. It is God consciousness to know there is nothing outside of your mind. You will know that in your willingness to be responsible for everything that happens to you. When you and I both recognize the truth, our minds are joined. We can only truly join in the truth. We are already always joined, but until we are in that experience, it is mere conceptual understanding. *The perfect has to perfect itself due to the mistaken idea of separation.*

The teaching of singular reality or non-duality means there is nothing outside of your mind, and all that you see is just a reflection of yourself. However, guard against using that idea to separate yourself or cut yourself off from others. Don't think, 'You don't matter, as there is only me.' This is a misapplication of the idea that there is nothing outside of your mind. If you are in company with anyone, they are in your mind and as such you should only want the best for them and be willing to do whatever it takes to bring joy to all your reflections. You have the power to inspire nobility, grandeur and goodness by knowing who you are.

It is also important to understand that in taking responsibility for everything that happens to us, we need only be responsible to do all we can not to enable. If someone has rage, they are responsible for their rage, not you. If you do not act to discourage that rage, you are enabling. If someone gossips about you, they are responsible, not you. You are responsible to the extent that you not let it get to you or that you not support gossip. Your response should be nonviolent resistance to injustice. Respond with love.

It should be noted that God has begotten only one son. If you believe that all of the souls God created are His children, and if you also believe that the sonship is one, then every soul must be a child of God, or an integral part of the sonship. The sonship in its oneness does transcend the sum of its parts. However it loses this special state as long as any of its parts are missing.

Singular reality or non-duality is the idea that there is no you outside of my mind, not that there is only me. What would it mean to me that you do not exist? You do exist. I also exist. To deny another's existence is ego's way of deluding you into thinking you have understood oneness while retaining the illusion of autonomy. We are one in our recognition of our love for each other. We experience our love when we acknowledge our total equality with everyone. Then you are in my mind and I am in yours. That is oneness. Oneness and autonomy are mutually exclusive.

You are whole in the recognition that everyone is in your mind. This does not mean that there is only you and there are no others. To understand non-duality to mean there are no others is to keep from joining with others, the very purpose for which God gave others to you. You will be missing so many opportunities for happiness. We projected others outside of our minds to make the illusion of separation real. To heal the separation we need merely include everyone back into our minds by loving everyone and acting in their very best interest. Then our minds are again whole. An action of mind is required, from separation to oneness consciousness.

If you fear or hate anyone, you place them outside of your mind and that is separation. Wars, conflict, anger and hatred expose a lack of understanding of oneness. *When separation is your state, you have a split mind, a mind that needs healing.* If you exclude anyone from your mind, you are not whole. If you make one exception to your love for all humanity, you have a split mind. When a handful of minds in the world understand oneness there will be peace for all, and until that time, I cannot be at peace, for all are myself. This motivates me to do all I can toward the salvation of the world.

Ideas Do Not Leave Their Source

You are an idea in God's mind, and just as God's ideas do not leave His mind, your ideas cannot leave your mind. For example, if it is your idea to make the world a hiding place from God, that world is in your mind and cannot leave it, because it is your idea. It is an unreal idea which results in an unreal world. As soon as you change your mind and want God included in your world that is a real idea and will be reflected in a real world. Every idea has power because your mind is all-powerful. Everything that happens to you comes from an idea that you want to be true, whether it is really true or not. It is impossible to cut yourself off from your idea but you can change your mind and then your experience will reflect that change.

As God is an idea in your mind, you cannot separate from Him, but you can certainly have an experience of separation, if not a true experience. Ego is also an idea in your mind. Ego is an unreal idea, while God is a real idea. Ego is an idea of separation while God is an idea of oneness. Any unreal ideas are undone through an acknowledgment that your idea is wrong and through a willingness to have wrong ideas corrected. Once you saw that your idea was wrong, wouldn't you happily let it go, especially when you realized your error to be causing needless pain? Being willing to be wrong opens the door to a true experience.

When Sai Baba says, "You as mind do not exist," He must be referring to the monkey mind – the ego tendencies, the endless, useless chatter. We *are much too tolerant of our mind wanderings.* Mind is a bundle of thoughts. Baba also says that mind is a gift of God. What is God's mind made of? You do know, as your mind is the same as God's. We use God's mind even to think erroneous thoughts. Healed mind undoubtedly includes Divine will, an awareness that it is and has everything and a recognition of its equality or oneness with everyone. If your mind is the same as God's, as you were created in the image and likeness of God, then that is the mind you can experience by withdrawing energy from the monkey mind. When your mind takes on Godly characteristics it is again merged with the mind of God. Open your mind to be as you were created and the truth will be revealed. Once Al Drucker asked Baba, "What do you think about all day?" Baba exclaimed, "Think? I never think, when I will, I act." Act in a Godly fashion, and thereby be one with the truth of who you are.

You Are One With The World

When you merge your mind with the mind of God, you are in the experience of how you were created, one with God. Your mind and God's are exactly the same. That is singular reality. When you and any other join in the one truth, that is a true experience and that true joining with just one is in essence a joining with all as all are already one. You were created to be totally one with everyone and everything. This does not mean you lose your individuality. You do not ever lose anything by becoming who you are. No sacrifice is ever asked of you. You only get bigger. You only become more. You were created to be and have everything forever.

The world is a projection of your mind. When you take responsibility for it, you become its savior, and in that you discover the true purpose for which you are here. In taking responsibility for the world, you bring it back into your mind and see that you are one with it. In your oneness with the world, in your oneness with everyone and everything, lies the salvation of the world and yours as well.

Any idea of feeling taken advantage of by the world, or that the world ought to be taken advantage of by you is separation from the world and is an idea that needs healing in order that you be whole. Baba says to forget the world. Forget it as a place to find happiness. I know the world can give me nothing. That is not cause to hate or reject the world. I love it for what I can give to it. I can give the world everything. In that I am one with the world. I can give the world my love, my compassion, my yearning for the freedom of its inhabitants, and that gives me tremendous joy. In that my mind is whole. In that I step into my role as the savior of the world.

I am responsible for the suffering in the world, not because I caused it, but because love unites me with everyone and as long as anyone is suffering, I am not free. We each cause our own suffering. A savior shows you how to become free of your suffering. Living a life of goodness and holding true ideas in your mind will heal your suffering. Everyone must save themselves, but we can learn from one who has understood the truth behind suffering. Suffering is real for the person who is suffering, though the truth is that suffering is not real. That is good news, because then it can be overcome. If it were real, it would be impossible to free ourselves or others.

Soul Is Perfect Forever – Mind Can Experience Imperfection

Your mind and soul were created one. Your soul is unalterably perfect forever. As soul you are one with everyone and everything. As mind you can have an experience that is different from how you were created but that is all. We could not alter the truth. We could not separate from our souls, thus we could not really forget who we are. When you merge your mind with your soul you will again be home. Only in our minds could we experience nothingness as real. As soul we never left everything. We were created one with God in God's mind. We were created one with every other soul and every other mind.

Separation is the idea that we could be different from each other and from God and that is impossible as God created us all exactly like Himself and like each other. We return back home by recognizing our oneness with one another and with God and by merging our minds back with our souls where we are eternally merged with God and all His creations in perfect oneness.

Though God created us all exactly like Himself, we are not clones. We are each unique, for God is limitless in creative expression. Our sameness has to do with equality, holiness, lovability, preciousness, limitless creative ability, limitless capacity to express love, power, knowledge and truth.

Mind did divide itself when it willed to make its own source, but it could not entirely separate itself from its soul, because it is from the soul that it derives its whole power to create. Even in miscreating will is affirming its Source, or it would merely cease to be. It is impossible for mind to die because it is part of the soul, which God created and which is therefore eternal.

The return to wholeness takes place when we think only loving thoughts, for as soul we are love and only love. When we think thoughts that God, Jesus or any other great teacher would think, we reestablish our oneness with everyone. When we think thoughts of peace, love and harmony for all humanity we are merged, mind with soul, mind with God, and mind with every other mind.

Fullness Is Ever Increasing

Sai Baba says, "I separated myself from myself that I might love myself." This separation is for the purpose of extending love and love unites. God created you and me so He could love Himself and thereby enhance His joy. *God created His children by extending His thought and retaining the extensions of His thought in His mind. All His thoughts are thus perfectly united within themselves and each other because they were created neither partially nor in part.* That extension retains oneness in individuation. That action of extension gives joy and joy is God's nature. God is ever extending. When you give of yourself, you are expressing your nature and you are only ever giving to yourself, as there is nothing outside of you. In giving you experience your fullness.

Sometimes Baba can be heard chanting an invocation from the Isha Upanishad: *Poornamada, Poornamidum, Poornat, Poornamudatchate, Poornasya, Poornamadaya, Poornameva Vashishyate.* It means 'from the fullness comes the full, and the full remains ever full, and what is created is as full as that from which it was created.' When God created us, we were created as complete as God, with every power and glory that is God's, and that creative act did not diminish God in any way.

God, who encompasses all being, nevertheless created separate beings who have everything individually, but who want to share it to increase their joy. Only by sharing can anything that is real be increased. This is why God created us. He created us whole and complete within ourselves, in need of nothing, separate from God in that we are everything, though one with Him in love. Love unites and makes one. Love removes separation, duality and multiplicity. We are ideas in God's mind. As we are in God's mind, we are never separate from Him. Though this is so, *we have all dreamed of a separated ego and have believed in a world that rested on it. Because this is very real to us, we cannot undo this by doing nothing and not changing.* We must change our minds and come to recognize our oneness with God and everyone and everything. We are all so much more alike than different for we were all created by God as God, equal with God and each other forever.

See God In Everyone

Oneness means total equality. Does equality then translate into giving exactly the same to everyone? Parents take pride in treating all their children equally. What this frequently looks like is every child receiving an equal portion of the inheritance. True equality means seeing God in everyone and treating all as God. It means to honor, respect and show loving kindness toward everyone, including everyone in your love. It does not mean doling out the same measure of goods to everyone, whether physical goods, or taking care to spend equal time with each of our relations, so there will not be misunderstandings, or whatever. These restrictions lack spontaneity and lead to bondage rather than freedom.

Giving is creative and everyone is equally blessed when you give in the true spirit and when your offering is pure. Sai Baba frequently manifests jewelry for people who come to visit. His manifestations are full of wonderful variety and creativity. It would become uninteresting if He manifested exactly the same object for everyone. Then one would not feel loved. He knows everyone's equality, yet He knows how to express oneness in a unique and personal way toward each individual.

Baba says, "You cannot always oblige, but you can always be obliging." Does equality mean giving generously to everyone? Let your heart be your guide. You do know what to do in every circumstance. Trust your inner knowing. When you turn to God, He will direct your actions in relation to others. He has the big picture. He knows the past, present and future of everyone. We only perceive so very little. Depend on God to show you how to treat all equally. Equality means not judging on the basis of gender, religion, color, race... That happens when you realize that all are God's children, created equally. God created everyone to have and be everything. We are all alike. We are all equal. That is oneness.

Sai Baba says, "I am God. You are also God. The difference is that I know it, and you do not - yet. I have come to tell you that you and I are exactly the same." The Bible says God created man in His image and likeness. Jesus said in the New Testament, "You are Gods." If we were created by God, in His image, it must be that we were created exactly like God and therefore must be God.

There is a favorite children's story of a lion raised with a flock of sheep. It grew up thinking it was a sheep until it saw its refection in the water. Then it realized it was a lion and not a sheep. Though we have gathered all kinds of circumstantial evidence to support our case that we are sheep instead of lions, it is simply not true. We may have gathered to ourselves innumerable witnesses to support our convictions. Still, none of those witnesses constitute hard evidence. When we are willing to doubt our conclusions, we open the door to truth. We are and have always been one with God, whether we believe it or not.

United We Stand

Separation cannot be overcome by separating. The will to unite must be unequivocal, or the will itself is separated and not whole. If you truly want to be one with everyone and everything with all your heart, soul and might, it is accomplished, for it was always the truth. *The problem of separation is really the only problem there is and it has already been solved. Separation from God is the only lack man really needs to correct. His separation would never have occurred if he had not distorted his perception of truth and thus perceived himself as lacking.*

A person conceives of himself as separate largely because he perceives himself as bounded by a body. In fact the body was made for that very reason. Only when we perceive as mind can we overcome this error in thinking. Ego separates through the body. God can use bodies by reaching through them to others. When you interpret bodies as a means of joining minds and uniting with others you will have a worthwhile purpose for your body. Of itself, it has no purpose. In the service of unity, the body becomes a beautiful lesson in communion. Communication ends separation. Attack promotes it. The body is ugly or beautiful, savage or holy, helpful or harmful, according to the use to which it is put. And in the way you behave toward the body of another you will see the use to which you put your own.

Bodies are limits imposed on universal communication, which is an eternal property of mind. But communication is internal. Mind reaches itself. It is not made up of different parts, which reach each other. It does not go out. Within itself, it has no limits and there is nothing outside it. It encompasses everything. It encompasses you entirely, you within it and it within you. There is nothing else, anywhere or ever. Everything is within your mind. Expansion is inward. Extension is inward.

Three Thought Systems Contribute Equally To Oneness

We touched on Advaita, Vishishtadvaita, and Dvaita in the chapter pertaining to truth. They are revisited here as they pertain to oneness. The Advaitins, the pure non-dualists, have the firm conviction that there is nothing outside of oneself. There is only you as God, the Absolute. There is only your mind and everything is within it. Thereby you are the Lord of the universe. Sai Baba says as much. Nothing happens without your will. There are no victims. Once you understand this, you have shifted from victim/victimizer consciousness to God-consciousness.

The Vishishtadvaitins or qualified non-dualists recognize that they were created. The one who understands qualified non-dualism has made peace with the idea that he was created by God and is inseparable from his

Source. He has understood the oneness of Creator and creation by owning that he could not create his own source. Jesus understood this when he said, "I and my Father are one" and "of myself I am nothing." We are in the experience of this when we turn to God for everything and depend on Him to meet all our needs. There are thousands of people at Sai Baba's ashram, but my experience is that there is only Baba and myself. Whatever else is happening only enhances my relationship with Him.

The Dvaintins or dualists believe God has many children and see all as equal and God in all to be oneness. Dvaita, oneness in individuation, understands that God created everyone to enhance our joy. It recognizes that we all share one universal mind, the mind of God. It understands that there can be more than one and still be oneness. Oneness means unity in multiplicity.

All three philosophies acknowledge oneness, though they approach it from different perspectives. By including all three philosophies, oneness is understood in its entirety. The Advaitin who thinks only he is right and the others wrong will want to start a religion in which his vocabulary is limited to 'I, me and mine,' as there is no you, there is no other. This is fanaticism due to partial knowledge. He may further deny that he was created in his zeal for singular reality. He argues that as there is nothing outside of him he could not have been created. He may even deny the reality of God. This misapplication of the teaching is due to conceptual understanding and is ego's trick to fool him into believing he has understood oneness while retaining separation and autonomy, so it can survive.

The Vishishtadvaitin knows he was created, but may miss out on the understanding that nothing is happening outside of himself, or outside of his will. He may hold God responsible, separate or outside of his mind, though God created him as a thought in His mind, therefore not separate from Him. And when God created him, God became a thought in his mind, thereby he is equal with God in every way. Using this philosophy to shirk personal responsibility is ego's trap to keep him dependent on it while thinking himself dependent on God. Truth is distorted when one feels any inequality in relation to God or fellowman.

The Dvaitin who falls into thinking there are others who are not his equal believes separation real. Whenever anyone judges another by the color of their skin or their religious beliefs, etc. he subscribes to inequality due to alliance with an ego that wants to survive. All God's children were created equal with each other.

Sai Baba says all three philosophies are correct, but that each contains only a portion of the truth. The truth includes all three points of view. That is recognized when we let go of all conceptual understanding of oneness and singular reality. Only if you wanted to remain autonomous would you have a problem including all three philosophies.

Only the whole of God's creation can know as God knows. Separately we can only know our portion. The whole is greater than the sum of its parts. All three ideas, Advaita, Vishishtadvaita, and Dvaita contribute equally to the truth, yet each on its own can lead to misunderstandings and misapplications. Only by adopting all three ideas can the whole truth about oneness be experienced. This is the safest way through the maze of separation. Oneness is obvious and simple because it is the truth. The truth is who you are and you do know yourself.

In heaven we are separate from God because He created us by separating Himself from Himself, but as heaven is an experience where God is in our minds and we are in His, there is oneness. At the same time, I am still me, you are still you and God is God as Creator and Source. We are each self-contained. We are whole and perfect in and of ourselves. We need each other only to enhance our joy, not to fill a lack. Oneness has nothing to do with bodies, for bodies are the vehicles of separation. Nor does oneness have to do with loss of personal identity. All you will ever lose is your false idea of who you are which is no loss as with its loss you gain your true identity.

Here, in the world, we experience separation if we think others and God are outside of our minds. That is an unreal thought leading to an unreal experience, as we are forever one with each other while retaining our individuality as well. I am whole and complete as God created me. You are whole and complete as God created you. I separated from you to enhance my joy just as God separated Himself from Himself to love Himself. In a true experience there is only God loving God, enjoying God, in perfect harmony, unity, equality and bliss, knowing all to be eternally one in God.

Sai Baba says, "Suppose you are asked, 'Who created all the multiplicity in the world; who is responsible for all the variety?' The correct response is, 'There is no multiplicity at all. The Divine self remains the one self forever. You mistake it as many. The fault is in you. Correct your vision.'"

There is only oneness and that oneness depends on your perception, that it be your experience. When you recognize everything and everyone to be within your own mind, you will not see multiplicity for you do not have multiple minds. You will have included everything back into your mind when you have the same love for the Jews as the Christians, the Blacks as the Whites, the poor as the rich... When you have included everything without exception back into your mind, your mind is again whole.

Watch Ego's Tendency To Misapply The Teachings

There are those who teach that inclusion means to include your corruption in. To include corruption is to include nothing, but when included, it is given reality and we have thus traded in everything for nothing. Errors should not be denied, avoided or justified. They should be corrected, healed and transformed.

When ego comes knocking at your door, let it in, but do not let it stay for a cup of coffee. When your imperfections present themselves, look at them. Don't avoid them or deny them, for then you make them real. When you dare to look, you will see their nothingness. Don't entertain imperfections. Ask God to heal them. To justify corruption in any way is to make it real and to thereby keep yourself locked in an unreal experience.

You were created to be holy, to be perfect. When you want to be holy, you cannot want to include corruption in. By wanting to hold on to impure thoughts, words, or acts you do not want to be holy. There are those who say holiness is ambiguous as it is different for everyone. Holiness is the same for everyone. You were created holy in the same way that everyone else was created holy. Corruption is different for everyone and thus expresses and affirms separation.

To make excuses of any kind for imperfections is not to know who you are. Will you be punished for imperfections? Who will punish you? God will not punish you, but ego is eagerly looking to make imperfections a cause for you to feel guilty so it can punish you and thus survive. Imperfections come from ego and if you do not turn them over to God for correction, ego will persuade you that you are guilty and you will agree to its punishment, which requires time and leads to needless suffering.

When you do not will to be perfect, you will punish yourself. You reveal to yourself that you want to be free of suffering when you strive to your maximum capacity for perfection, excellence and love in everything you do, think and say for that is who you are. It is impossible that all your experiences without exception were not by your choice. What you do will come back to you. God always knows what is in your best interest. Give the power of decision to Him and He will lead you to your true happiness. He only wills for our happiness.

Oneness Means Wanting The End Of Suffering For All

You are the dreamer of your dream and there is no other cause. Know this and you are free. Whatever happens to you is because it is your wish. Sai Baba says, "There is no one greater than you. The whole universe is within you. Everything is within your power. You do not know your own great strength." *Your holy will establishes everything that happens to you. Every response you make to everything you perceive is up to you because your will determines your perception of it. Everything around you is part of you. Look on it lovingly and see the light of heaven in it. Then you come to understand all that is given you.* Everything can become a classroom for understanding our minds. Once we know our minds we can change them. Instead of a world of separation, we can see a world of oneness. *In kind forgiveness the world will sparkle and shine and everything you once thought sinful will again be reinterpreted as part of heaven.*

The union of all God's creations is its protection. Ego cannot prevail against the kingdom because it is united and ego fades away and is undone in the presence of the attraction of the parts, which hear God's call to be as one. Alone we can do nothing, but together our wills fuse into something whose power is far beyond the power of its separate parts. Our function is to function together, because apart we cannot function at all. The whole power of God's creation lies in all of us, but not in any of us alone. When you hold all of humanity in your mind, you will experience not loss, but completion. The recognition of the part as whole, and of the whole in every part is perfectly natural.

To yearn for peace and plenty for all humanity is to know your oneness with everyone. Edna St. Vincent Millay, a great American poetess of the early 1900's, at the tender age of 16 expressed it this way in a portion of her poem entitled *Renaissance*:

> *I saw and heard and knew at last*
> *The how and why of all things past*
> *And present and forevermore*
> *The universe split to its very core,*
> *Lay open to my probing sense.*
> *And all the while for every grief,*
> *Each suffering, I craved relief.*
> *A man was starving in Capri;*
> *He moved his eyes and looked at me;*
> *I felt his gaze I heard his moan,*
> *And knew his hunger as my own.*
> *I saw at sea a great fog bank*
> *Between two ships that struck and sank;*
> *A thousand screams tore through my throat.*
> *No hurt I did not feel, no death*
> *That was not mine, mine each last breath*
> *That, crying met an answering cry*
> *From the compassion that was I.*

Beloved Mother/Father God, Creator of us all as one, let love reunite us with all our brothers and sisters everywhere. May all relationships be transformed into holy unions. Let the true recognition of our oneness overcome all separation in the hearts of all people. Help us all to recognize our equality with You and each other that we may live together in peace and love.

May all beings in all the worlds be happy and blest, Amen.

Figure 13a — God Created Us All As One

Everything (Eternity)

Eternity	Life	**Oneness**
God-Dependence	Love	Freedom
Real	Truth	Non-judgment
Heaven	Peace	Creation
Innocence	Knowledge	All-Powerful

Nothing (time and space)

Time/space	**Happy Dream (Satva) God's solution - collapses time**
Ego-dependence	Recognize God as Source
Unreal	Oneness with everyone/Equality/Inclusion/Interdependence
Hell	Nothing outside of your mind - can change mind
Guilt	Support and encourage purity
Death	**Nightmare (Rajo Guna) - makes time**
Fear	Make separation real - fear of God
Untruth	Specialness - greater or less than
War	Buffeted about by circumstances beyond one's control
Ignorance	Conflict, attack, hatred, war due to idea of separate others
Separation	**Deep Sleep (Thamo) Ego's solution - freezes time**
Bondage	Separate to project guilt
Judgment	Denial - no personal responsibility
Mis-creation	Need others to fill lack/ Exchange/Co-dependence
Powerless	Fearful world, outside of self

Direction of Consciousness Awakening

Figure 13b   Mind and Soul – Oneness vs. Separation

Mind and Soul - One before the separation

Oneness of mind and soul

After separation - mind and soul seem separate

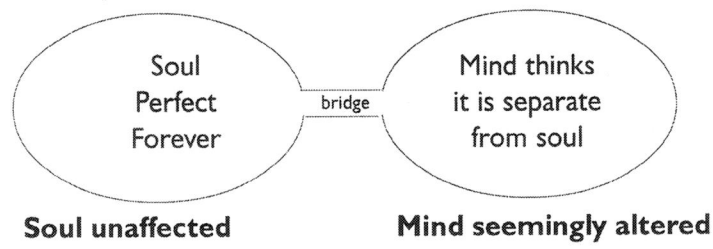

Soul unaffected   **Mind seemingly altered**

After separation mind appears split

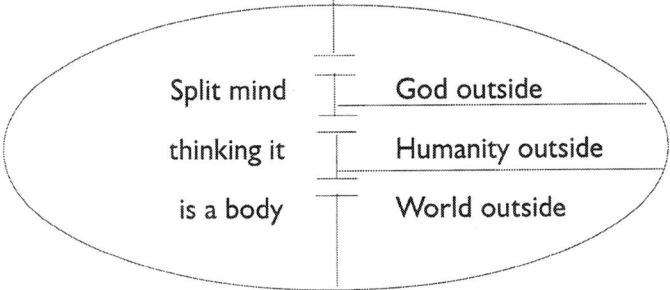

Chapter 14

Are You Ready to Give Up Bondage for Freedom?

Mind is responsible for both bondage and liberation.

Sai Baba

Is There Freewill Or Is Everything Predetermined?

Even as a child I remember grappling with the question of whether there was freewill or if the events that were to happen in my life were intractably written. I was sure there had to be freewill, but over the years I have encountered many spiritual aspirants who insist that all is predetermined and that we really don't have any say about what happens either in our personal lives or in the world at large. That never resonated for me and so I have spent much energy and focus on that particular question, as it seems vital to our every undertaking. If my efforts cannot alter my destiny, then I am not all-powerful as I am led to believe and will not be motivated to put forth efforts if I know my striving to be a futile exercise. I will attempt to make a case for freewill, without excluding predetermination all together.

If we are as God created us, we are all-powerful. Then we are certainly not helpless to simply and complacently accept things as they are. It must be that we have the power to change our circumstances. It must be that what is happening in our world is due to choices we made and that when we make different choices we will have different experiences. Ego is an idea that things could happen to us against our will. Without ego then, we are not under a spell where we think things are happening counter to our own choosing. It must be alliance with ego then that convinces us that we do not have freewill.

If you think certain thoughts, what is causing you to think those thoughts? Is there some force outside of you more powerful than you ordering you to think or act contrary to your better judgment? It is as you think. If you think you are helpless, you will convince yourselves of your helplessness and find yourself unable to change your mind or circumstances. However, if you know that you have the power to change your mind, the result will be a shift in consciousness, generating different thoughts. If you believe you are autonomous all your thoughts and actions will support that belief. If you believe you are one with everyone and everything, you will have thoughts and actions which support that understanding.

If someone says or does something that inspires you, you find yourself naturally emulating them to a certain extent. How is that possible unless you made a choice to do so? If everything comes from desire, where does desire come from if not freewill? If you are doing something that you know you ought not do, who is preventing you from changing your mind and making a different choice?

In the New Testament, Paul lamely suggests that though 'the spirit is willing, the flesh is weak,' but I see that as an excuse to make the body real. Your body is never more powerful than your all-powerful mind, therefore you can change your mind about anything and it will shift your tendency. I used to overeat and struggled with trying to stop. When I understood that my body is not real and is not my master, food stopped being an annoying presence in my consciousness. Sometimes we feel so caught up in our self-made traps that we convince ourselves we are helpless to stop our negative tendencies even if we sincerely wish to stop. We can always ask God to help us. If we do that, we will be shown how to overcome our bad habits without a struggle, just as the man who gave up alcohol by offering it to Sai Baba.

The reason freewill is rejected by most people is because then we would be responsible for everything that happens to them. That is why we do not want to make decisions, hoping someone else will decide for us. This frame of mind comes from an unwillingness to acknowledge our limitless power.

We give our power away every time we let someone else make decisions for us and this is the reason we subsequently feel helpless. When we are willing to step into personal responsibility for our particular set of circumstances, we see that freewill is a great blessing and gift and will use it wisely. When we defer to God, however, we are not giving our power away, but rather reclaiming it, as only with God are we all-powerful.

It is essential to recognize our responsibility in order that we be willing to make a shift in consciousness from victim consciousness to God consciousness. Once we take responsibility we will be motivated to change our minds and circumstances. Then we have recognized that we do indeed have freewill and are not buffeted about by circumstances beyond our control.

As long as you think of God as outside of you, you will feel that God's will is a will that is separate and different from yours. *You are God's will. If you are God's will and do not accept His will, you can only be not accepting what you are. If your joy is what you are and you deny God's will, you are denying joy.*

Are Some Things Predetermined?

There have been prophecies, predictions and forebodings since time began. There are palm readers, astrologers and seers who can predict what will transpire both in our personal lives and in the world at large with uncanny accuracy. This is certainly good evidence for the argument that there is no freewill. There are some students of ACIM who say that everything has already happened and we are back in heaven where we never left. This may be so in truth, but until heaven is my experience I must guard against complacency.

There is also the idea that we came into this birth on a particular mission or assignment in this lifetime which cannot be avoided. That assignment could be in relation to karmic consequences from the past or our role in the salvation of the world. Sai Baba says that we have about as much leeway as a calf on a rope tied to a tree. We can move in any direction but cannot really stray too far from the tree. In a way that is comforting as it means we really cannot stray too far from the purpose for which we are here.

If we find ourselves inexplicably driven or motivated, it may be that we signed up or volunteered for a specific undertaking. We can now complain to God that we don't like our assignment, but He will probably respond, "What can I do, you signed up for this." Everything happens at our choosing. And maybe God will cut us some slack. Frequently Sai Baba can be seen writing in the air with His finger. He has explained that He is rewriting the script where appropriate and warranted.

In India there is a tendency to surrender to one's particular set of circumstances, understood to happen due to the laws of karma, which frequently takes the form of apathy or complacency. On the one hand it is good to accept things as they are. It is good to be happy knowing that no matter what is happening, your peace cannot be affected unless you choose to be agitated by your circumstances. But what is the cause of the particular circumstances we find ourselves in if not our own choosing? Where does karma come from if not from choices we made in the past? If we are experiencing the consequences of karma from previous lives, then it must be that karma came from choices we made at some time. Would it not follow then that if we made different choices now we could have different experiences now as well, and in time to come?

All of time is going on all the time. We saw in Chapter 3 how we can travel back in time. Is it also possible to travel into the future? I do not have any hard evidence for this possibility, but the future is certainly predictable based on the past. History repeats itself. We meet the past in the present because we have not changed our minds about past mistakes and thus repeat the same mistakes over and over again. The future is foreseeable because we are predictable. We are creatures of habit, slow learners and procrastinators, but that does not mean that the future is set it stone. What happens is pre-destiny and what we do with it is self-effort. If we have lemons, we can make lemon aid. Our cup can be half full or half empty. We can always choose how we respond to every circumstance and we can even change our circumstances when we are determined to do so. We are all-powerful. All our karma can be effaced by God's grace.

When I prayed with all my heart to know the truth regarding freewill, I was given a dream in which Arjuna and I were sitting across the table from each other. He was telling me about the great Mahabharata war in which he fought. Before the battle he was given a vision in which he saw everything that would take place prior to it ever happening. I was dismayed to hear this because it sounded as though everything was in fact predetermined. But Arjuna assured me, "When consciousness changes destiny also changes." If that is so, then you are not bound by karma from previous lives. You do not have debts that have to be paid back. You are bound to karmic consequences only as long as you think karma fair and just. As soon as you view karma as ego's idea of justice and not God's, you change your consciousness and your destiny will change accordingly. If you change your mind about what is true, your experience must reflect that change. Baba says, "Let me efface all your karmas."

We do have freedom of choice or we would not be all powerful as we were created. We do have the freedom to change our consciousness and thereby our destiny. It was by our choice that we experienced victim-victimizer consciousness, so we can choose again and return to God consciousness. All this takes place by our choice, because our will is free. But we do not have the freedom to be separate from others. In that sense, our will is not free, as everyone and everything is affected by everything we do and we are affected by what others do. We are one organism and cannot be autonomous. God's will also is not free in that sense. He also awaits our blessing for every action He undertakes.

Our Freedom Is Limited To Limitless Creative Expression

Sai Baba says there is no freewill. He also says there is no one more powerful than you. When we depend on God we have full freedom as that is God's will for us. We are free to choose to be dependent on God or not. In our total dependence on God lies our total freedom. We thought freedom had to do with independence from God, but autonomy has been the cause of all our suffering and we cannot call that freedom.

Our need for independence and our belief in karma have been the cause of our bondage. Due to God-dependence and oneness with everyone there is no freewill as such. Due to the fact that there is no will outside of God's will, there is no freewill. If you can be content to call limitless happiness and boundless creative expression freedom, there is indeed freewill. There is no autonomy. There is no independence. That freedom is impossible. Every decision you make and every action you take affects everyone. You do not have the freedom to act in isolation. You are only free to create and to love without limit.

We were created to create the good, the beautiful and the holy. We would not be able to create if we were not created free. What is creation without freedom? God created us free and that means forever. He did not change His mind about His beloved children. Our freedom is guaranteed and when we are in alignment with God's will, freedom will be our experience. God's will is our true will. Our wills are intertwined. *When we accept that God's will is ours, we are free.* If that is so, then the idea that there is no freewill merely means there is no independent will. God's will is not independent of yours, nor is your will independent of His, nor is your will independent of the rest of humanity. We are one organism and what you do affects everyone, just as what everyone else does affects you.

In the beginning God placed the tree of the knowledge of good and evil in the garden. He recommended not eating from it, however it was available. Once we understand that the fruit of the tree was the making of ego, we can see that because God's kingdom is freedom, God could not keep us from separating from Him if we so desired. Before the eating of the 'forbidden' fruit, the only thought that could be outside of God's will was the wish to be different from how we were created. We were created free to experience that desire, though we could not alter the truth. Had God not permitted us the freedom to choose an experience that would be different from how He created us, we would not have been created free. It is freedom that allows us to make choices that may not be in our best interest.

Though God created us perfect forever, we have the freedom to experience ourselves as different from how we were created. We gave ourselves the experience of being birthed by earthly parents and convinced ourselves that we were born at the time of physical birth, instead of when God created us. We were free to make for ourselves a different experience than the one God created us to have. Our freedom was used to attempt to defy God's will. We could make that choice because God willed us to be free. However, we are not free to alter God's creation, therefore any experience that comes from a desire for autonomy is not real. We are not free to be more powerful than God, as that is impossible.

When we made ego, we attempted to make our own creator. This we did with the freedom God gave us. Now we are in an experience that is quite different from the one God intended for us. That is because we are listening to ego's will for us. Ego's will for us is bondage, though it fools us into believing that we are better off with it than with choosing God's will. It convinces us that God wants to control us, that God's will for us is not freedom, that God does not have our best interest in mind. It tries to convince us not to trust God. If ego can convince us that we want to will with it, it stays alive at our expense.

Because God willed us to be free, we have the freedom to choose that which may not be in our best interest if we so insist. He loves us too much to be our policeman, to stop us if we wish to make an experience for ourselves that will be painful. And He knows that we are unaffected forever by any unreal experience, though it may seem very real to us. He created us to be unalterably perfect and free forever. Even if we experience a nightmare, at our discretion, it cannot affect who we are. A nightmare happens when we are asleep. When we wake up, we discover it was only a dream and was not real and had no real effect.

If we want to stride into hell, God will not bar our way, for to do so would be to act counter to how He created us. Though He is pained at our suffering and at our wish to experience separation from Him, He honors us and is our perfect, most gracious host no matter what our wish. Our wish to be other than how we were created does not alter the truth. And our wish to be other than how we were created does not make us bad. It does however make us wrong, as it is impossible to act outside the Divine will. Fortunately error can be corrected and when corrected, we are back in a real experience of love, joy and delight, in unbroken communion with God and everyone. A willingness to be wrong is where freedom lies. Once you see that your wish for autonomy did not bring you happiness, would you not gladly admit that you were mistaken?

You Are Always Getting The Results Of Your Own Mind

Are you really free to choose whatever happens to you? If you are all-powerful, it must be so. If so, then why the experiences of sickness, suffering and death? If they are choices, then we can chose against them and any sane person would choose health, happiness and life, wouldn't they? I know that there are still some who justify hardships as good for one reason or other. And there are those who complacently accept that everything is God's will including pain, disaster, murder, etc. True, some challenges are Divinely orchestrated, but their purpose is remedial and we do know the difference. God is love and only wills that which offers the experience of love. However, you can choose any experience you wish. If you really were free to choose and yet your experience were of hard times, stress, anxiety, loss, deprivation and devastation, what is keeping you from getting what you really want?

It was in an attempt at getting around God's will that we made ego. We made for ourselves a choice free of God's will. A choice free of God's will would be a choice devoid of freedom as freedom is God's will. We stubbornly hold onto the choice for ego's will, though it is hurting us, because we have been deluded into convincing ourselves that we are free when we are free of God's will. In willing with ego, we still have no will of our own. All we accomplished was the ability to choose between everything and nothing. A choice for nothing is not a real choice, therefore we accomplished nothing. Sai Baba says, "You can only ever choose between God and ego, no other choice there is. Take one step toward God, He takes one hundred toward you. Choose ego and God leaves you alone." We are never independent, whatever choice we make. Before the separation, choice was not an option. There was only God's will.

After the separation, there was God's will or ego's will to choose between. The catch is that ego's will is not real, because ego is not real. Thus any time you will with ego, you are not really willing at all. There is only God's will and God's will is your true will. In this way you really have only one true choice. There is no other will but God's. However, choicelessness does not take away from your freedom to choose for nothing. You are all powerful and when you choose with ego, ego uses your all-powerful mind to limit you to unreal experiences, by your choice. When you choose with God, God frees you to use your all-powerful mind for healing the unreal, thereby restoring you to your original state of happiness. When you choose with God, you are directed to have a Godly experience, in line with God's will for you, which is glorious freedom to create, love and know everything. God created us with the freedom to create, but not to be autonomous or separate from Him or each other, for that is impossible.

The Desire For Autonomy Is The Cause Of Bondage

We made ego to be autonomous and we will have an experience in line with our desire, complete with specialness, competition, greed, hatred, jealousy, anger and pride, all proving that we are indeed separate. This is what ego wills for us, because these baser tendencies lead to guilt. When we experience these feelings we feel guilty and if we continue to turn to ego for a solution, ego will tell us that the way to get around these feelings is to project them out or deny them. When we project guilt onto another by seeing him or her as the one with the problem, we are fooled into thinking that we have gotten rid of our problem. An idea of separation has permitted us to fool ourselves. Or if projection doesn't work, ego advises us to ignore these baser tendencies. All the while ego knows that we have not gotten rid of our enemies and that we will suffer the consequences of any imperfections. Ego likes us to think ourselves incapable of perfection and to act imperfectly because it knows that all uncorrected imperfections are attended with guilt and ego depends on guilt for its survival.

What gives ego power to condemn you? You and you alone, and when you want, you can simply remove allegiance from ego and be free. Bondage was never your true experience because God in His infinite love created you free forever. You are always holy and pure, though your experience may serve to convince you otherwise. In your purity lies your freedom. Freedom is your truth forever and when you want freedom to be your experience, it will be so, for there is nothing to oppose your will. Freedom and bondage are mutually exclusive. You were created free forever. Our chains of oppression are self-inflicted and can be cast off when we no longer want them.

We used all our God given power to choose another will beside God's. We thought independence would be a better experience than dependence on God and each other. We wanted freedom from God's will, though God's will for us is our freedom. We had freedom and traded it in for bondage. We misperceived. All we have to do is own our error and see that ego's will is not what we really want after all. We never wanted suffering. We just didn't realize that was part of the package when we wanted autonomy from God. God does not punish us for separating from Him, but ego does.

God's will for you is perfect freedom, wholeness, abundance, uniqueness, joy beyond imagination and deepest peace. He wishes you to express yourself creatively eternally. He wishes you to have everything. He guarantees your survival and does not will you to work to sustain yourself. His will for you is that you never have a care again. He wills to take care of you completely, so you never need to be anxious about anything. He created you perfect and depends on you to express your perfection always. God loves you so very much. He created you as an expression of His love. He wants you to walk the earth with your head held high in the full recognition of who you are as a holy beloved child of God, with all the glory, splendor, majesty, mastery and freedom of God Himself.

Ego's will for you is that you hate or fear God, so it tries to convince you that God doesn't love you and that God wants to control and punish you, because if you love God, you will depend on Him and not on it. Without your support, ego is finished. Ego wants you to think it is your friend, but all along it is doing everything it can to convince you that you are not who you are. When we wake up to our truth, ego is gone. When we realize who we are, there is no sickness, suffering, lack or death. All these came with ego and go when ego goes. Ego came at our choosing and we are free of it when we so choose as well. When free of ego, we are free to be as God created us.

Salvation Lies In A Willingness To Be Wrong

God is both Spirit and mind. You are also Spirit and mind, being the same as your Creator. Spirit is unaffectable forever though mind can choose a true experience or an untrue experience, as it is free to convince itself of whatever it wants to believe, whether true or untrue. God would never wish things to be other than how they are. Because His kingdom is freedom, we have the option. It is possible for mind to make unwise choices, due to its freedom. When your mind is whole and sane it is one with the mind of God. However, it can become an unhealed mind or an insane mind, reflected in an insane experience by your choice.

We think that if we were created perfect we shouldn't be able to experience imperfection. Can unreality change what is real? Nothing unreal can threaten what is real. It is up to you what you experience, though it is not within your power to alter your status. If you want the experience of the perfection that you are in truth, then what can stop you from having that as your experience right now? You are all-powerful and there is no force to stop you from doing what you want, not even God. Want perfection and it must be your experience. Want imperfection and that is your experience. God's kingdom is freedom.

A mind that is willing to be wrong is free. It is possible to make mistakes and errors are correctable. When errors are corrected, you are restored to a true experience. Uncorrected error is given reality through an unwillingness to see it for what it is and correct it. It thus falls into ego's domain and ego labels it sin, irrevocable, wreaking permanent damage, for which you deserve punishment and damnation. That is bondage. Ego judges you sinful because it wishes to remain alive now that it has been given life. Ego's existence depends on your having traded in your eternal life for time. Time is needed for meting out punishment. Ego dependency is a sick dependency. This tale of sin and subsequent punishment is your sad story until you are ready to awaken from your nightmare only to find that you never left home in truth. Your experience with ego is not a true experience and when you return home it will be because you chose to turn your back on ego by being willing to correct error. Then you are restored to the experience of the perfection God wills for you.

True Freedom Lies In Discipline

There are those who say that it doesn't matter what you do, as none of this is real anyway. One teacher who applied this idea accumulated 93 Rolls Royces. Can you imagine how much good could have come of those misappropriated resources had license not taken hold? If we do not control our appetites, we become slaves to our senses. What slave is free? It is a contradiction. The trap of desires is a bottomless pit. Freedom lies in self-discipline and self-control. Self-discipline means controlling the senses, controlling the mind, living sensibly, curbing desires, using time and space wisely. A mind whose thoughts are under one's control is free. Unreality can and must be transformed into reality by using everything with love and for a sacred purpose. God is sacredness and resides in everything. When your actions are holy you have merged your mind with the mind of God and that is freedom.

Instead of, "Do whatever you like," try "Do only that which you know to be God's will." It is not that you should do only God's will, it is that only in doing God's will is anything really happening and only then will you be happy. God's will is all that is real. Anything else leads to bondage. Indulge in unreality and it will burn you. It is ego that taught us to believe that freedom lies in lack of discipline, because ego wants to give us a false sense of freedom, while binding us to karmic consequences. Don't fall for its seductions. They will not give you the happiness you are looking for.

Sai Baba tells the story of a king who had five wives. This unfortunate king could not control his wives. He was not free. He was very frustrated. He thought constantly about how to control his wives but had no luck at all. Seeking a solution he sent word to all the men in his kingdom to come and share their successes or failures in relation to their wives. He put up two tents, one for those who had no better luck than he and the other for those who were indeed able to control their wives.

Subjects came from all corners of the kingdom and when the king wandered into the respective tents, he discovered the tent for those who were unsuccessful was full to overflowing. He was comforted that he was not the only man who had problems controlling his wives. As he wandered into the other tent he was delighted to find one lone man. Maybe this successful man would reveal his secret. When he asked the man how he had managed to control his wife the man confessed that he had in fact not been successful. The king was disappointed and gruffly ordered him into the other tent. "Oh please, your majesty," pleaded the lone man, "I'll do anything you ask, just don't make me go into the other tent. My wife ordered me in this one."

The king is the mind and his five wives are the five senses. As long as he caters to his senses of touch, taste, sound, sight and smell he will feel enslaved. He will feel that he is not in control of his life. The sense of touch gets you in trouble when you desire after bodily comforts or sensual pleasures. The sense of touch can be used to overcome any ideas that you are a body, such as preferences for hot or cold, pleasure or pain, etc. Taste is out of control when we over indulge the tongue. Eat to live; don't live to eat. Food should be medicine for the disease called hunger. Our speech is also to be soft, pleasing and minimal. Eyes are a gift of God and should be used to see only those things that uplift and direct us Godward. See only good. Ears should be used to listen to only that which uplifts, music that opens the heart to love and to God, stories about God and noble character. Do not listen to idle gossip or deleterious messages. Hear only good. You can use your sense of smell to take you Godward through incense or heavenly fragrances. Do not lose equanimity over unpleasant smells. When you are a slave to your senses you are bound. Be the master of your senses to be free.

Obeying God's Laws Leads To Freedom

If you made a mess and did not clean up after yourself, or were disorganized, after a while it would become impossible to find anything in your house and you would feel very frustrated. With a disciplined mind, you put things in their designated place so you can find them easily and avoid frustration. Discipline does not take away from creativity, but rather frees you up to be creative.

Only one who leads a disciplined life, curbing his senses and observing limits can experience that he is indeed limitless. Baba says, "Observe limits to attain limitlessness." God has laws and if we obey them we will experience freedom. God's laws are laws of love, out of His love, and are in place to serve our very best interests. They are given for our protection. God's laws lay down a disciplined life-style with a code of conduct and proper protocol in relation to marriage, family and society. There are rules, God's rules, and we all know what they are when we are willing to know and willing to be holy. Obeying them leads to freedom. When we do not want God's will, we give ourselves the choice for ego's will. But only God's will is real. *If your will is out of accord with God's, you are willing without meaning. But because only God's will is unchangeable, no real conflict of will is possible.*

There is a fear that obedience to God's laws will lead to bondage, restriction or contraction. If you trusted God to have your best interest at heart, you would know that a disciplined life-style cannot curb your creative expression, but must actually enhance it. There are those who lead undisciplined lives and who seem to be successful despite chaos. However, usually when we look more closely we see their freedom is met with frequent interludes of frustration. At the same time, the pendulum can swing to the other extreme, where one is disciplined to a fault and becomes too easily disturbed when others do not cooperate with his sense of order. The middle way leads to peace.

Only one who is determined to be free will not fall prey to temptation. That one will lead an impeccable moral, virtuous, selfless, pious, humble life. That one will have mastered control over the senses and will have reined them in. Without self-control and self-discipline one is at the mercy of every fleeting thought, sensory sensation or emotion that comes one's way. Can that be freedom? When your life is sane, your thoughts are sane. When your thoughts are sane, your life is sane. The two support each other. Sanity is the happy dream. If you want to have holy thoughts, who is stopping you? You are all-powerful and you can control your thoughts when you so choose.

At Baba's ashram discipline is encouraged. There is no initiating, kundalini demonstrations, dancing, jumping up and down, 'dynamic' meditation or enacting emotional release. One year I brought a group of 50 students of a friend to the ashram. She teaches initiations and kundalini and there is a lot of demonstrating and emoting as part of her offering. I had urged her to set all that aside. Her group wouldn't hear it and they were all over the place. I could see how what they were doing was attracting attention to themselves and thereby making themselves special. The head Seva Dal (volunteer) came over and scolded, "No discipline." I was terribly embarrassed. The spiritually mature do not need to demonstrate or be entertained. If you feel you cannot control your body you think your body more powerful than your all-powerful mind.

Perhaps you will be tempted to think that one who is so disciplined cannot be any fun to be around. You may resist being disciplined because it is boring, too difficult or too elementary. These are all ploys of ego to keep you bound to the rules of the world, the laws of chaos, which lead to guilt and subsequent suffering. Discipline is never a sacrifice. A disciplined mind sacrifices nothing and gains everything. Baba says that mind is a gift of God. We must discipline our minds as an expression of gratitude for our precious gift. It is we who used our minds to make ego which encourages indiscipline. Thus we must determine not to succumb to its temptations.

Discipline is a choice for sanity. God disciplines with love and always looks toward our best interests. True joy comes in holiness and a disciplined life-style. Everyone is attracted to Baba though He eats little, hardly sleeps and generally leads an impeccable life of discipline and holiness. He says, "My life is my message." No one thinks of Him as a stick in the mud. Quite the contrary, everyone wants only to be near and dear to Him.

Discipline Does Not Mean Punishment

Where God recommends discipline, ego recommends punishment. Ego wants you to feel free to do whatever you want because it knows you will feel guilty for any indulgences, imperfections, addictions, derelictions or indiscretions and that guilt leads to self-inflicted punishment. Ego survives at your expense. The world says obedience leads to bondage. The world has everything reversed, because ego wants you to remain a slave and to think slavery is freedom. It says to do what you like and calls that freedom. It says to eat what you like, but when you are too heavy you do not feel free. You feel enslaved to food. You find yourself constantly thinking of the food you like, how to lose weight, how body conscious you feel... You are enslaved to food when you are overweight. Sai Baba tells many people who are overweight to control their appetites. He does not encourage an undisciplined life-style. We rebel against discipline, rules and adherence to God's laws and call that freedom. God's laws are where freedom lies and nowhere else.

When one thinks of discipline, perhaps one thinks of one's formative years where discipline meant punishment, whether at home or in school. So this generation doesn't discipline its children. We let them do whatever they please. We want freedom for our children and think giving them free reign is where freedom lies. That freedom had led to undisciplined television watching, school shootings, drugs, sex, abortions, single parenting, disrespect for teachers and parents and an utter lack of purpose. Lack of self-restraint has led to children hurting themselves and others in ways so deeply agonizing it needs no further discouragement. Without discipline and self-responsibility children lead lives that are anything but free. They ache because of the discipline they missed while growing up.

Our parents disciplined with fear and punishment so discipline was rejected. The baby was thrown out with the bath water. But suppose discipline took the form of a retraining of one's mind. If a child were to understand that stealing were unnecessary because God would give him everything he truly needed, that would lead to the undoing of that unreal habit. Suppose a child stopped watching television because he was encouraged to pursue interests that really turned him on. Suppose a child were given a meaningful purpose like being responsible for pets, or tending a garden. Children need to know who they are at an early age. They need to know that God is their true Parent and that He loves them with the love of a thousand mothers, and that they can talk to Him whenever they want. He is always available.

If you discipline a child with love rather than fear, you are giving him what he needs to be happy for the rest of his life. It was discipline with fear and a stick and punishment that we rebelled against, not the discipline itself. Ask God to show you how to discipline your child and I trust your he or she will be well-adjusted, problem free for you and his teachers, and a blessing and joy to be around. A good way to discipline is by encouraging good behavior and sharing stories from the lives of uplifting and inspiring role models with your children. This helps them to connect with a positive approach to life in a world glaringly short on true role models.

Adults also can find peace in a disciplined life-style. Ego advises you to spend your money however you like, to enjoy sexual freedom, to entertain corruption, to abuse drugs and alcohol. 'Do what you like – just don't feel guilty,' 'you are God no matter what you do,' or 'nothing you do is real anyway.' Ego tries to convince you that immorality is where freedom lies. All along it knows that if you fall for its lies, you will be digging yourself into a big karmic hole. You will have debts to pay for your 'freedom' and ego likes to see you in debt, because debts have to be paid up. That is just. To pay off your debts takes time and ego depends on time for its survival. Sai Baba says, "All your freedom is tied up in karma, in debts." Your whole life is for payback for the 'freedom' you took in previous lives. Is that freedom? *There is no man who does not feel that he is imprisoned in some way. If this has been the result of his own freewill, he must regard his will as if it were not free.*

Fortunately, all that karma can be effaced with a simple shift in consciousness, reflected in a life of integrity and holiness. In the Bible, Jesus tells the parable of the vineyard. Someone comes to work early for an agreed upon wage. At noon another worker shows up and is offered the same pay as the one who has been working since early morning. Even the one who shows up at the eleventh hour gets the same pay as the one who came early. By the world's standards this would seem unfair to the one who has been working all day, but by God's standards you deserve the same pay because of who you are.

Using anger to demonstrate this teaching, the one who has never expressed anger comes to the vineyard early in the morning. The one who comes at noon has some history with mild irritability and the one who comes at the 11th hour has a substantial history with rage. All three get the same pay, peace, love and joy forever, because all three have left anger behind, thus find themselves in the vineyard. Their past is irrelevant and they all get the same benefits, because they are all equally precious souls and no past affected their truth in any way. God has no favorites. His love is always maximal.

You are already perfect and do not have to earn peace, love and joy. You come to the vineyard when you have changed your mind about who you are and know you do not have to pay back for your past. In coming to the vineyard you are ready to be as God created you, perfect, holy, loving and free. In accepting your truth, you have a clean slate, with no past debts to repay. You can come at any time. You can continue to think you need to balance the scales first through suffering if you choose. You can leave it all behind when you see that you were never guilty. Past is past. Baba says, "If you want Me you deserve Me." All errors are correctable, and there is no mistake that is more than an error. There is never a reason to feel guilty.

Our Will Is Equal With God's Will

We have chosen to be in a state of opposition, in which opposites are possible. As a result there are choices which we must make. In our true state, our will is free in the sense that its creative power is unlimited, but choice itself is meaningless. In our true state then, there is no freewill, though we have total freedom of unlimited expression for our creativity. Because we made for ourselves a situation in which there is choice, we are free to choose between our true will and another will, a will that is not real, which essentially is thereby not a real choice. Let us not however minimize its reality for us. Once we see clearly what the choices are, we will be in a better position to make the wise choice.

We will choose for ego as long as we believe that doing the opposite of God's will can be better for us and as long as we believe that it is possible to do the opposite of God's will. When we choose for ego, it is because we believe that an impossible choice is open to us, which is both very fearful and very desirable. Our wish for other choices permitted ego to be a choice, but God only wills. Sai Baba says, "When I will, I act." God does not wish. *Our will is as powerful as His because it is His. Ego's wishes do not mean anything because ego wishes for the impossible. We can wish for the impossible, but we can only will with God. This is ego's weakness and our strength.*

We have all convinced ourselves that we could act counter to God's will. Any time you think you are defying God's will, take comfort in knowing that nothing is happening. The experience of sickness, suffering and death is not real, but is the result of defiance against God's will. It is not that God punishes us, but ego does. When we truly see the implications, we will happily do only that which we know to be in alignment with God's will.

There is no one greater than you. God is not greater than you. To defy God's will would be to be greater than God. You are equal with God, therefore it is not possible to do anything that is counter to His will. If you think you can defy God's will, you are thinking with ego and you will feel guilty, because ego needs you to feel guilty to survive. You would only entertain the idea of defying God's will if you wanted to prove your idea true or if you wanted to prove yourself greater than God. When you want untruth to be true, you will use your all-powerful mind to make it true for you. Take one step toward God and God takes one hundred steps toward you. Turn toward ego and God leaves you alone. He won't push His way into your life. Only when you want God is He there for you.

When Adam made ego, he was frightened to be in God's presence and that was the cause of his banishment from the garden. He banished himself.

God did not banish him. It was God's will to commune with Adam. God only wills your happiness. There is nothing opposing your will. It was Adam's will to leave the garden because he felt unworthy to be in god's presence. He had willed with ego and thus thought he had defied God's will. He had not defied God's will as that is impossible because his will is not greater than God's. To think defying God's will possible is erroneous thinking and when his thinking is corrected, Adam will again find himself in the Garden of Eden. God never banishes anyone. We banish ourselves by thinking there is another will besides God's. When we think that, we are mistaken.

Outside Of God's Will Nothing Is Happening

It is not that you shouldn't do that which is not God's will, it is that it is impossible to do anything other than God's will. Does that mean that when the murderer murders in cold blood he is doing God's will? No, he is not doing God's will and nothing is happening. What has he killed? Only a body, which was never real. Can he kill the mind or Spirit? No. Only those are real. So he has killed what doesn't exist. However, though nothing is happening, the action of killing comes from a mind that thinks it possible to kill, and thereby reveals that it does not know itself.

Only one who thinks he is a body attempts to hurt another body. Thus for him his action is real, and he binds himself to the laws of karma. He thinks it possible to do something that is not God's will. That action will always be attended with guilt. So the murderer feels guilty and punishes himself for crimes he never committed. If he goes back in time to that moment where fear took the place of love and asks for help, he will be shown that truth is unaffectable. If he truly understands, he will have eradicated any and all murderous thoughts from his mind. The unreal will have been undone. His destiny will be altered as his consciousness changes to will to do only God's will.

Most people who commit grave errors feel so badly about themselves that they tend to repeat their errors over and over again due to guilt. They feel helpless to change because they think they have done irreparable damage and identify themselves with their actions. Guilt binds and causes one to feel helpless to break negative patterns. Knowing ultimate truth is unaffectable should lighten one's burden and at the same time shift one's consciousness for the better. If you use it to justify unkindness, you are still too allied with ego to choose what is in your best interest. You can be the most hardened criminal and come back to God before the saint. It all depends on what you do right now.

There is no will but God's. When you have recognized that, you know that your will is His. *You are God's will. Your will and God's cannot be out of accord because they are one. This is the undoing of everything ego tries to teach. Ego wants to teach you that you want to oppose God's will. This unnatural lesson cannot be learned, but the attempt to learn it is a violation of your own freedom and makes you afraid of your will because it is free.*

Your will is free because your mind is all-powerful. You are free to choose God's will in which lies your perfect freedom and you are free to think there is another choice though there is nothing outside of God's will. When you really understand God's will for you, you will not wish for something different.

Freedom is an attribute of the mind, not the soul. The soul always remains changeless, because it never leaves the sight of God. If you really want to be free, you will bring your mind into alignment with your soul. If you really want to be free, you will ask God to guide your every decision, what you shall do, where you shall go, what you shall say. However God directs will be toward your freedom, because that is His will for you. God knows you better than you know yourself and loves you with the love of a thousand mothers. When you let ego direct you, it will tell you your freedom lies in doing whatever you like. All the while, ego wants you bound. That is its wish for you. It is seductive and deceptive.

Your mind can miscreate only when it is not free. An imprisoned mind is not free by definition. When your mind is held back, it is imprisoned by itself, as there is nothing outside of your mind. You are your own prison guard. You lock the doors against yourself. You hold the key to your freedom. Your freedom is in your hands. As long as you hold yourself back, your will is limited and not free to assert itself. A mind that is willing to be wrong is free. Correction of error frees your mind and reestablishes freedom of your will. When your will is truly free it cannot miscreate, because it recognizes only truth.

God Is The Only Doer

Some Sai devotees have the attitude that everything is Baba's will, after all He teaches us to say, "It is You who made me walk and talk and think and act as I did." If we truly give all to Sai, our lives must be transformed. If you say your every thought, word and deed comes from Baba, but it is not pure, you are choosing with ego and calling it Baba. You are not being honest with yourself. We are responsible for all our actions. Self-responsibility leads to a shift in consciousness and results in freedom. Once free of denial and guilt you open the door to the transformation of your heart.

Baba says, "I am the only doer." He also says, "The way to immortality is through the removal of immorality." When you understand that your mind is the mind of God, you realize that it is only with God's energy that anything happens, even if it was a choice with ego. Even when you act with ego, ego is still using the power of God. Every movement draws on Divine energy. How are you using all that heavenly energy? Ultimately everything does source back to God, as God is the only Source. However, this does not mean that which sources from alliance with ego is God's will. Ego is nothing and is thereby totally outside of God's will. Lumping nothing with everything is ego's mechanism for not taking personal responsibility.

It is thought by some that everything that happens to you is in your best interest. Everything that happens to you is not God's will, though all can be used as God's grace, as everything can serve the highest good. Everything can serve to bring us back into alignment with God's will. Once a young girl was badly burned. Her mother's spiritual teacher calmly suggested she find the blessing, as there is a blessing in everything that happens. The little girl was miraculously healed without the skin graft that was scheduled as part of her recovery, due to the teacher helping her to use her experience as God's grace by supporting her to find the good in it and to trust in miracles.

What Is The Cause Of Natural Disasters?

In January of 2001, there was an earthquake in the state of Gujarat. Baba, in His compassion for the victims, the homeless, the afflicted and the devastated, sent 18 huge trucks full of supplies: clothing, food and medicine. Baba was standing at the gate to bless each truck as it rolled away from the ashram compound. After a stirring send off, someone asked Him, "Baba, why do You spend so much money on supplies when You could have averted the earthquake?" Baba responded, "God does not create earthquakes or other disasters. These are due to man's bad thoughts and greed." Apparently mining for gold in the area had upset the ecosystem.

Sai Baba teaches that nothing happens without His will. Is everything then God's will? Is the earthquake God's will? On the one hand Baba says that everything is God's will and on the other that some things are not due to His will. I asked a number of devotees what they thought He meant and most were unwilling to accept that the earthquake could have happened without Baba's will.

There are those who complacently accept everything that happens as God's play, unfolding as He wishes, as He ordains. There is no taking personal responsibility with this understanding, nor is there any recognition of the power of one's own mind. There is no brightness of mind happening with this philosophy. If all the horrible things that happened were God's will, wouldn't that make God cruel?

To think the earthquake to be God's will would be to have conceptual understanding of the teaching that all is God's will. If everything is God's will, what happened to you being all-powerful? Granted, everything real is

God's will. The earthquake was unreal and thereby not God's will. Unreal experiences come from ego, not from God, as ego is unreal.

You can have an unreal experience and convince yourself that it is real. This does not make it real, nor does it follow that it is God's will. We use God's mind for everything we experience. God entrusted us with the freedom to use His mind and thus all our God power can be turned against us at our choice. It happens by wanting to experience another will besides God's will. Once this is seen, we recognize that we can choose again and in that we offer ourselves an experience which will reflect that different choice.

Nothing happens outside of God's will. The earthquake is nothing. However unreal events do not merely happen at random or without some will. There are no accidents. Nothing happens without our will. We have a responsibility for all that we witness in our world. Let us not use this teaching to be heartless in relation to the disruptive events taking place in the world and throughout time. They are real for us and we must treat them with compassion and a willingness to help where we can. We can always send pink light and pray for the displaced and the disquieted.

Though the earthquake must have served some purpose does not mean that those who suffered deserved to suffer by bringing it on themselves. No one ever deserves to suffer as all are God's children, created solely to experience love, peace and joy. Everything can be used to wake up from the dream, and thereby can be seen as God's grace. We do not know what God's intervention prevented from happening that could have been even worse. God is always acting to uplift and restore peace where He is welcome.

When we see the unreal as God's will we make it real and leave no room for a miracle of undoing the unreal. We set it in stone and thereby prevent it from being transformed. By accepting earthquakes as God's will we are essentially willing earthquakes to continue to be our experience. We are all-powerful. We are in charge of whether we experience God's will as our only reality or whether we experience a will apart from His. God's will is perfect happiness for everyone. The earthquake took some 50,000 lives. Obviously that was not perfect happiness for everyone involved. None involved deserved to experience that nightmare. There is no justification for it. No one ever deserves to suffer.

If anyone suffers, it is not deserved, no matter what their past, as God created everyone to be perfect and incapable of sin forever. Only if you sinned would you deserve to suffer. Suffering is experienced because of a choice made with ego. Ego wishes us to suffer. Suffering does not make us bad, but it does prove us wrong. When we choose only God's will, we cannot suffer. When we recognize that suffering is our responsibility we will be motivated to change our minds. As long we are convinced that suffering is God's will, we will not be so motivated, and will not alter the course of our destiny. Only when we change our minds can we avert disasters. Self-responsibility is the portal back to true freedom.

The earthquake was not real, but it was very real for those who suffered. If we experience suffering, it is real for us and to say it is not real is to deny our experience. Denial will not undo the unreal, as it gives it energy of reality. When untoward events take place, we have to see that we are supporting a will besides God's, because we believe that to be possible. As soon as we ask God to heal our minds so that we accept the truth that there is only God's will, our experience must be free of suffering.

I shared a story of how Baba cured me of jealousy in Chapter Eight. If I feel jealous, and if it were God's will, why would Sai Baba urge me to overcome jealousy? Why does He bother to correct behavior and urge purity, self-discipline and noble character? What kind of sadistic joy would He get in making us bad so He could then transform us into good? We are anything but mindless. Let us determine to use our all-powerful minds to step into personal responsibility for everything that happens to us. When we take responsibility, we will be motivated to change our minds about all those experiences that are not in alignment with the Divine will. The desire for a different experience is all that is needed to have a more fulfilling life. As long as we see what is happening as God's will, we will feel powerless to change our circumstances.

The earthquake in Gujarat happened because of the thought that there could be another will beside God's. That is erroneous thinking. By asking that a false idea be undone we open the door to the truth that only God's will is possible. Then our experience will be one of perfect peace, love and happiness, free of disasters of any kind. God is always eager to give us everything we need to be truly free and safe.

There Is No Will Apart From God's Will

Making a shift in consciousness is easy but we have invested heavily in untruth and so have to be very honest to see what we really want. If an earthquake happens, it is because we want the purpose that it serves, thereby we want the earthquake. You are all-powerful. Only you are the cause of your every experience. *Only you can deprive yourself of anything.* We made ego because we wanted choice, because we thought choice was where freedom lie. *We still think it advantageous to have a will apart from God's.* This is insane, but it is what we are thinking if our experience reflects any upheaval, loss or pain. These are not God's will, thus they come from an idea that there is another will outside of God's will. Having this idea does not make us bad, but it does make us wrong. When we are open to the possibility that we are wrong and to correcting our error, we will come back on the mark, in alignment with God's will wherein lies our true freedom.

If there is only God's will, then the truth is that those things that happen that are unpleasant, unkind, unsafe or unhelpful are not real. That is good news. Anything that is unreal is easy to undo for the simple fact that it is unreal. That is, as long as we do not give it reality. If you say the imperfect is perfect, you give it reality. If you say the imperfect is God's will, you give it reality. If you say the imperfect is not real from a place of denial, rather than self-responsibility, you give it reality. When you do not own that it is your wish, you will undoubtedly see it as God's will and that makes it real for you and thus keeps it from being undone. The unreal is unreal because it is not God's will and knowing this permits it to be undone.

I was raped, though I now know the experience was not real. I know this from the place of having healed the unreal. There are those who were raped who also say their experience was not real but generally their denial comes from conceptual understanding. Only when you take personal responsibility for the unreal things that happen are you in right relationship with them. They cannot be undone as long as you give them reality in any way either through denial or guilt. As soon as you take personal responsibility, you will want to change your mind and that desire opens the door to a shift in consciousness which alters your destiny. As long as the unreal is not undone you are not free to experience God's will. God wills our perfect freedom.

To Want God's Will Is To Want Happiness

There is no force anywhere that can cause you to do or be or have anything other than what you want. So be clear about what you really want. *To fulfill the will of God perfectly is the only joy and peace that can be fully known, because it is the only function that can be fully experienced. When this is accomplished, there is no other experience. But the wish for another experience will block this because God's will cannot be forced upon you, being an experience of total willingness. If God's will for you is complete peace and joy, unless you experience only these, you must be refusing to acknowledge His will. If you want to know God's will, He will not hide it. Nothing God creates can oppose your will, as nothing God creates can oppose His will. God gave your will its power.* Act on what you will and it must come to pass for there is no force outside of you that is more powerful than you. Everything that happens in your life is by your will.

Your will is your only experience. Your freedom depends on your will. Until you will for true freedom, you cannot experience freedom. Until you are free, my salvation is incomplete, for we are all one. *Until not one slave remains to walk the earth's surface is my salvation complete.* Even if you are awake, your freedom is incomplete without the freedom of all humanity. When you are free, you must join the great crusade to end the suffering for all mankind.

In desiring to serve in the great emancipation of all humanity, you are desiring to step into your role as savior of the world. When you will the world to be saved you open the door to that possibility. When you will to be in perfect harmony with God's will it is accomplished for that is your true will.

No mind can believe that its will is stronger than God's. If you believe that your will is different from His, you can only decide either that there is no God or that God's will is fearful. Fear of the will of God is one of the strangest beliefs that has ever been made. The very fact that the will of God, which is what you are, is perceived as fearful demonstrates that you are afraid of what you are. It is not then the will of God of which you are afraid, but your will. Your will is not ego's and that is why ego is against you. What seems to be the fear of God is really only the fear of your own reality.

God's will is our will only when we choose it. *Our will is boundless. It is not our will that it be bound. What lies in us has joined with God Himself in all creation's birth.* God created us and through our will created everything forever. Nothing happens without our will. *Not one thought that God has ever had but waited for our blessing to be born. God is no enemy to us. He asks no more than that He hear us call Him friend. What is the will of God? He wills we have everything and that He guaranteed when He created us as everything.* Therein lies our freedom. May you have the courage to choose for freedom from your self imposed shackles, that all the world may see that choice is available to them as well. May all beings be free as God always intended.

Dearest Loving God, You will our happiness be undisturbed, forever increasing, eternally expanding in the joy of full creation, and wholly limitless in You. That is Your will, and so Your will provides the means to guarantee that it is accomplished. May all beings discover their freedom in the joy of doing Your will. May all beings realize that Your will is their true will. May we all awaken to the truth that there is no freedom in autonomy or independence. Grant everyone the courage to see that their chains of oppression will be lifted in a willingness to take personal responsibility for everything that happens. Help us all to realize that true freedom lies in a disciplined life-style. May freedom be restored to every heart and to every country. Thy will be done on earth as it is in heaven that heaven be restored to earth.   May all beings in all the worlds be happy and blest, Amen.

Figure 14a – True Freedom Lies in Doing God's Will

Everything (Eternity)

Eternity	Life	Oneness
God-Dependence	Love	**Freedom**
Real	Truth	Non-judgment
Heaven	Peace	Creation
Innocence	Knowledge	All-Powerful

Nothing (time and space)

Time/space	**Happy Dream (Satva) God's solution - collapses time**
Ego-dependence	Disciplined lifestyle, observe limits, sense control
Unreal	Surrender need to be autonomous
Hell	Your true will is to do God's will
Guilt	Willing to be wrong
Death	**Nightmare (Rajo Guna) - makes time**
Fear	Follow ego's will - act imperfectly
Untruth	Bondage/constriction/limitation, addictions
War	Discipline means punishment
Ignorance	Oppose or defy God's will
Separation	**Deep Sleep (Thamo) Ego's solution - freezes time**
Bondage	Believe suffering and death are God's will
Judgment	Lack will power - I can't know God's will
Miscreation	Addictions or over indulgences don't matter
Powerless	No choice - everything is predetermined - apathy

Direction of Consciousness Awakening

Figure 14b – Mind And Spirit in Relation to Freedom

Characteristics of mind and Spirit in relation to freedom

Before Separation:

Spirit – Knows
      Loves
      Creates
      One with Creator and Source

Mind – Wills to know, to love and to create, and to be one with its
      Creator and all God's children
      Free to choose to will what is not real
      Communicates

After Separation:

Spirit – Knows, loves and creates - unaffected by what happens in
      mind

Mind – Wills to forget that it knows, loves and creates
      Chooses to will autonomy from Creator – an unreal choice
      Severs communication with God and others

Healing the separation:

Spirit – Does not need to be healed as it remains unaffectable

Mind – Wills to learn anew that it knows, loves and creates
      Chooses to heal separation with Source by recognizing
        the impossibility of autonomy from Source
      Chooses to reestablish communication with God & others
      Learns that forgiveness and self-responsibility heal
      Opens to miracles by being willing to be wrong

Chapter 15

Are You Ready to Give Up Judgment?

Judge not that you be not judged.
Jesus in the Bible

Non-Judgment Means Holding The Big Picture

It took me a very long time to really understand the idea of non-judgment. I would see people using the idea to justify lack of discernment: 'all behaviors are to be condoned' or for license: 'do whatever you like, just don't judge it.' It seemed that non-judgment had to be much deeper than that. I sat with it and prayed about it a lot. Essentially, as I have come to understand it, non-judgment means holding the big picture. Judgment comes from hasty opinions and conclusions based on insubstantial or inconclusive evidence. All are sinless as God created them and if they seem to be acting insanely, that is no reason to condemn anyone or to sever communication. *All judgment involves rejection at some level.* It sees others as different from how God created them, namely whole and perfect.

Let's use Hitler as an extreme example. How do we see him without judgment? One day during a conversation someone commented that he admired Hitler for his certainty. He was trying out his understanding of non-judgment by finding good in Hitler. This did not resonate for me. I do not find anything redeeming about Hitler's character. However, I do not forget that he is a precious child of God.

Once I was at a Course In Miracles workshop in which a woman was sharing her frustration over her judgmentalness. She found the strain of constant judgment virtually intolerable. When she prayed to Jesus to show her how to correct her errant mind, he gave her a vision of two young boys sleeping in separate beds in the same room. The one was obviously having a nightmare; while the other was sleeping peacefully. When asked, "Which of these two boys do you love more? Which one less?" she saw that she loved them both equally. She did not love the one less because he was having a nightmare. She did not love the other more because he was sleeping peacefully.

She was then shown that the child having the nightmare was Hitler. Hitler is no less a precious child of God than anyone else and therefore is not to be condemned. This is not to say that his actions are to be condoned. To condone his actions would require judgment. Only when he acts perfectly should we support his actions, for that requires no judgment. He was created perfect. When one acts imperfectly, calling it perfect is a judgment. To see him as a precious child of God requires no judgment for that is the truth. That is charity. All God's children deserve charity, for in that their minds can be healed and they can be restored to the peace and joy that comes from acting with love and kindness toward all. To judge Hitler would be to wish him to suffer for his actions, heinous though they were. I do not wish him to suffer. I do wish him to change his mind toward love for all, including the Jews and gypsies. This shift in consciousness is all I wish for him. He is not guilty, though he is very wrong. I include him in my mind by wanting his salvation, no less than I want salvation for everyone.

If I were in Germany during Hitler's dictatorship, I would not be passive on the pretext that I was practicing non-judgment. This is conceptual understanding of non-judgment. If I passively did nothing in response to Hitler's outrageous defilements against humanity, I would be judging. If I acted to stop his actions through nonviolent resistance, I would be demonstrating non-judgment. People who did just that acted with tremendous courage, for their lives were at great risk. They are heroes. Non-judgment is not passive. To be passive when your brother is out of integrity and causing harm to himself and others requires judgment. It means you accept him for who he is not. It is our duty to inspire everyone to be who they are – pure, holy, kind and good. We may not know what to do, but we can always ask Spirit to show us. Our willingness is all that is ever asked of us. During the Nuremberg trials, the whole German population was found guilty for passively condoning Hitler's behavior.

Don't Judge A Book By Its Cover

Judgment can be used to condemn on the one hand or to put someone on a pedestal on the other. Either way separation is maintained. A friend wished with all her heart to be as eloquent a speaker as some of those lucky souls who got to share the podium with Sai Baba. One night she had a dream in which all the VIP's were importantly lined up on Baba's stage ready to give talks. They were all wearing long gowns and looking very distinguished. Suddenly a huge gust of wind came up. She woke up laughing. They all looked the same in their underwear. She understood that her idea about eloquent speakers being better human beings was a judgment. We are all the same, not based on our worldly achievements or abilities, but on who we were created to be for all eternity.

There is a story told in India of a renunciate who sat in his cabin very piously day after day. He would go out to beg for food once a day and would take a bath in the holy river nearby, and then spend the rest of the day in his cabin. He was considered to be very saintly. A prostitute happened to be living next door and he would watch her day after day taking in all those men. He was beside himself thinking about how wicked she was and his mind was constantly occupied with her immoral behavior.

Meanwhile the prostitute was very much aware of the holy man living right next door to her and though she needed to sustain herself and was not qualified for any other work, she followed his pure example of thinking only of God and seeing God everywhere and in everyone. She became so passionate in her love for God that she started to see God in all the men who came to her, all because of the good example the holy man was setting in living so piously so near by.

Needless to say, when he died he found himself not at the pearly gates as he had hoped, and she did, though she had no such expectations. He was judging her and thereby condemning himself. She was inspired by him and thereby saved herself. He was not as holy as he appeared to be and she was holier than would appear on the surface.

Martin Luther King, Jr. worked tirelessly to overcome superficial, baseless prejudice, expressed most eloquently in his famous speech: *"I Have a Dream*... that our children be judged on the basis of their character and not the color of their skin."

What Is Good For One May Not Be Good For Another

Once Ramakrishna's disciple, Vivekananda, was being ferried across the Ganges River to his teacher's class. When he arrived, Ramakrishna asked him to describe his experience. Vivekananda told him how the boatman had berated Ramakrishna, and how he, Vivekananda, had gotten very incensed. Ramakrishna scolded Vivekananda and told him that he did not need Vivekananda's defense.

The following day, another disciple, Brahmananda came to class by the same ferry. When he reached the master's abode, Ramakrishna asked Brahmananda to share his experience. Brahmananda told how the boatman had belittled Ramakrishna and how he had kept quiet. Ramakrisha shouted at him, "How could you keep quite? I was being attacked and you did nothing to defend me!" He was absolutely wild with rage.

It turns out that Vivekananda was easily angered and Brahmananda was very shy and demure. So Ramakrishna gave the right prescription for each to help them overcome their respective weaknesses, though the prescription for the one was exactly the opposite of that for the other. For pearls we must dive deep and not stay on the surface or draw hasty conclusions based on insufficient information. A true teacher will use the method most efficacious for bringing the student into his perfection.

Watch Any Tendency To Condemn The Good

To be perfect is not to be better than anyone else. It is to be who you are. Perfection is your truth. A case for imperfection argues that those who are perfect will judge others as less than themselves. Be sure that this is ego trying to keep you from your truth, as your stepping into your perfection pushes ego out of the picture. And anyone who judges others as imperfect is hardly perfect. Only in imperfection does ego have a role. When you truly know your perfection, you see everyone as the perfection that they are, no matter how insanely they may be acting.

In order to act imperfectly you must have judged yourself as different from who you are. To act perfectly requires no judgment at all, for it is the truth. We are all perfect. To see one as perfect and another as imperfect, based on behavior is to see inequality. Judgment has to do with ideas of inequality. There are those who judge the perfected ones as arrogant. This position merely reflects a resistance to being who you are and to supporting others to be who they are.

In the movie, Camelot, Lancelot traveled from France to join King Arthur in England at a round table where 'civilized' leaders met to settle differences through peaceful deliberations rather than by the sword. Lancelot was an embodiment of the highest nobility and impeccable moral character. Initially Queen Gweniviere judged his purity and virtue as arrogance. During a joust he killed his opponent and then out of his love and compassion restored him to life. The queen could not deny the genuineness of his purity and he won her heart.

We have to be vigilant not to throw the baby out with the bath water. We have to use common sense. In our dependence on God we can be shown how to judge truly. It is not that we should not judge on our own. It is that we cannot judge, for we simply do not have enough information to draw accurate conclusions. We do not know the past, present or future of anyone including ourselves, thus we are not in a position to judge. But we can ask to be shown how to respond to every situation.

Non-Judgment Does Not Excuse Inappropriate Behavior

Is there then no room for correction of errors in others? In the Bible, Jesus says to take the beam out of your own eye first and then you will have clear vision to remove the splinter from your brother's eye. Always question your own seeing. Are you seeing in others what you do not wish to look at in yourself? When you can see error in another without it causing irritation or repulsion perhaps there is a place for correction. But that correction must be with God as guide. At the same time you do have a responsibility to others and cannot merely condone actions that are clearly not in alignment with truth or you are enabling.

Sai Baba tells the story of a boy who stole and whose mother did not discouraged him. When the lad grew older his habit was out of control and one day he was caught and seized by the authorities. As he was being carted off to jail, his gaze fell upon his mother. He shouted at her, "My ruin is your fault." Baba says he was right. Had she taken corrective measures when he was a child, he would have grown up knowing not to steal. He would not have found himself in the situation he was in. Parents are responsible for their children. We are responsible for each other as we are all one. Every experience that comes into our awareness serves a purpose and we have a duty to respond.

How should you respond to a child stealing? First, I would remember for the child that he was created to be and have everything and that he can trust God to give him whatever he needs. Perhaps a disapproving look would give him the courage to put the item back without a word. If not, I might ask him to give it to the clerk with an apology, or ask him to pay for it if he really wants it. I do not want to punish the child, but I do want to discipline so that he will grow up to be a well-adjusted, happy adult. It is my duty to respond with love to everything that I see, not as a policeman, but without excusing or ignoring that which I know to be out of integrity. When it is love that prompts my response, it will be right no matter how it may be received.

During a visit to Baba's ashram, 2002, I was attending the morning bhajans (devotional singing that takes place twice daily). Someone behind me was singing off key. I asked myself, 'Is it a judgment to call it off when it is off?' 'No,' came the answer, 'it is a fact.' If someone sings off-key, to call it on requires judgment and comes from a lack of proper musical training or an unwillingness to acknowledge the fact out of fear. Calling it off when it is off is a fact, not a judgment. It could be argued that by saying, "You sing beautifully," you will become a beautiful singer. I prefer to be honest, though sensitive, tactful, diplomatic, and above all, loving.

Helen Schucman and Bill Thetford, the authors of ACIM, were psychiatrists who worked together in a hospital in New York in the mid-60's. Their relationship was difficult at best and so in desperation they called out for help. Jesus responded by giving them ACIM. During the time of its scribing he gave them a number of personal messages. Once he said to Bill, "You dissociate. That is not a judgment. It's a fact."

In the Bible, Jesus said to the prostitute, "Stop sinning," or stop missing the target. If someone shoots an arrow and misses the mark, will you tell him he hit the bull's eye? Is he bad if he misses? No, he is just off, and when he adjusts his stance, or aims more carefully he will hit the target.

Will he feel better about himself when he hits the target? In all likelihood he will. Would you not want that joy for your fellowman? Would you not want to inspire your brother's perfection for his satisfaction? Non-judgment is anything but passive. True non-judgment inspires perfection in yourself and everyone.

How do you know when someone is out of integrity? Just as one needs to train the ear to hear what is off key, so one must purify the heart to discern correctly what is on the mark and what is off. If I am aware that you are singing off key what is my responsibility? If I comment that you are singing beautifully, am I not doing you a disservice? I know your heart will soar when you sing on key. Only when you sing on key does your singing give joy to others. Your happiness increases with giving joy to others. When off, it gives pain to the listener and so you also won't feel any satisfaction. Minds are joined, therefore you know when you enhance another's joy.

When anyone is performing for Baba, He will rarely tolerate imperfection. If it is not perfect, He will stop it on the spot. Many boys have been stopped in the middle of a bhajan because of ego or going off key or for some other reason. Singing is a service that transports the whole multitude of devotees Godward and if the leader is not opening the door to that experience, it must be given to one who will. The one who gets bumped will persevere and attain perfection because he knows that is expected of him. Baba is not judging just because He is intolerant of imperfection. On the contrary, to tolerate imperfection requires judgment. To be intolerant of imperfection inspires us to rise to perfection, which is our true, natural and comfortable state. To expect anything less requires judgment. It means we are being judged to be less than who we are and that is a disservice.

We are always able to rise to the occasion if inspired and not punished. Once I went to a bhajan session where everything was tolerated. Everyone was simply leading songs the way they wanted. They were off key and off tempo and it was awful. I wanted to leave within the first half hour of coming for a 12 hour bhajan. The spiritual path is the razor's edge. You should not tolerate imperfection, nor should you condemn anyone who is acting imperfectly. If you do not motivate another to rise to perfection, you have condemned. With God, you can be shown how to inspire all to rise to the heights and that is glorious.

If you sing off key and there is no one to correct you, you are being deprived of joy, and you are depriving others of joy as well. It is love to be honest. It is tough love perhaps, but if you are sincere and your heart is pure, it will come out right. Everyone has the capacity to sing on key. Frankness, openness and honesty with each other is healthy and not judgmental.

Judgments are based on inconclusive evidence, opinions and shortsightedness. They come from seeing with ego. True perception comes from God. Ask to be shown what to do in relation to correction of another. Correction must come from God and not from you. You are not judging when you see God and perfection in everyone. Baba says, "You can't always oblige, but you can always be obliging."

We Have Condemned Ourselves

Suffering stops through the relinquishment of judgment. We have all judged ourselves as guilty. That is because we have all chosen a lawyer who was heavily invested in finding us guilty without our catching on to that as his agenda. Who but a fool would hire a lawyer to represent him if he knew his lawyer had it in for him? Yet we all did just that when we looked to ego to represent us. Ego needs us guilty. Its survival depends on our guilt. Its very existence is sustained by guilt alone. And it cleverly and craftily keeps hidden from us its deceptions and cunning, thus most are probably not even aware of its agenda.

Ego judges only in terms of threat or non-threat to itself. It is merciless in its attempts at self-preservation. It has gathered all kinds of evidence against you. It tells you your errors are sins, you were born sinful, you cannot help but be imperfect. It tells you that you have hurt your brother and must be punished, that your brother hurt you and must be retaliated against. It tells you that you win at someone else's expense. You believe it, though it cannot prove any of its allegations. It's evidence against you is insubstantial, inconclusive and completely baseless. Your lawyer is a liar.

Ego is not a nice guy. It has no interest in you at all. It has every interest in doing you in. You believe in ego because you made it and you believe in what you make. You pledge allegiance to it though your allegiance is not reciprocated. Do not listen to the voice for ego. Ego should be judged by you and found wanting. Without your allegiance, protection and love, it cannot exist. Fire ego and hire God as your lawyer. God has all the evidence necessary to prove you innocent beyond a shadow of a doubt. He is eager to be your lawyer. The case against you will be dismissed on the spot.

The Christian church has invested heavily in guilt. Its whole premise is based on the idea that you are sinful, in fact that you were born sinful and guilty. I have been accused of blasphemy by good Christians for declaring my innocence and oneness with God. My certainty that I am equal with God, complete, pure and holy seems very threatening to some. You are no different from God. Many Christians are taught to believe they are sinners and that the only way home is through the blood of Jesus. This is not Jesus' teaching.

Jesus taught the Lord's Prayer, which starts, "Our Father…" Jesus knows that you are a child of God, thus he directs you to call on your heavenly Father. Jesus is not the only begotten son of God. Everyone is begotten of God. If you are a child of God you are innocent. What comes from God is pure and innocent forever. Jesus taught us to be perfect because perfection is the way home. He showed the way through his life of perfection. If you can attain perfection you do not need a savior to save you from your sins. If you are sinful and cannot attain perfection, Jesus' teaching is a mockery. The two ideas, to believe Jesus died for your sins, and to be perfect are incompatible and irreconcilable. Jesus is your savior if you like, though not through his death, but through his life of noble character and selfless unconditional love for all his brothers and sisters whatever their religious background. He lived a life of non-judgment. A savior is a way shower. No one can save you but yourself.

Use Judgment To Discern Between Real And Unreal

Some have taken the idea of non-judgment to mean giving support to unreality, meaning if someone is acting insanely or hurtfully toward another, you take no action under the guise of non-judgment. This is lack of discernment and a misunderstanding of non-judgment and is in itself a judgment. Taking no action in the face of unrighteousness is to support unreality. Only supporting what is real requires no judgment.

Sai Baba says the bird of liberation flies with two wings; discrimination and dispassion. Discrimination means to discern the real from the unreal. This is proper use of judgment. When you use discrimination, your mind will be bright, clear and sharp. You will see truly. You will recognize which is the voice for God and which the voice for ego. You will recognize what is real and what is unreal. Dispassion means knowing that nothing real can be threatened and nothing unreal exists. When you know this, you will never get upset for any reason. You will be detached from the results of all your actions. You will strive to your maximum capacity for excellence, but without being anxious about the outcome. Dispassion alone and your mind is flat and dull. Discrimination alone and you are caught up in the drama. Both wings in balance and the bird soars free. This is the same idea as that of the spiritual path being a razor's edge. If you are too discriminating and lacking in dispassion you will fall off the one edge, and if too dispassionate and out of balance with discernment, you will fall off the other edge.

If you see a child hurting another child and do nothing, you are in essence beating the helpless child. Who will not remedy such a situation? It is the same when you see adults misusing their power. Sai Baba says, 'If I instruct you to do one thing and your heart tells you something else, always follow your heart." This is reclaiming your power. To refrain from judging requires CIA (Constant Integrated Awareness). Constantly listen to the Divine director in your heart in relation to everything you see, hear, think and do. Baba tells us to follow the master. There is room for listening to a teacher outside of yourself, but a true teacher will ultimately lead you to the master within. Just because one sets himself up as a teacher is no reason to distrust your own sense of what is right, true, pure and holy, and to act with integrity.

Open-Mindedness Is Non-Judgment

When you feel peaceful, it will be because you did not judge. Discern between what is real and what is unreal and do what you are directed to transform the unreal back into the real. That is right use of judgment. You cannot be helpful unless you are clear about what is real and what is unreal. It was judgment that caused us to think ourselves guilty, flawed or unworthy. Non-judgment alone will restore us to wholeness. As long as you judge anyone you are judging yourself. Use judgment to see where you are contracting into judgment. God does not judge. In giving up judgment you are restored to your original state of purity and perfection.

Reality dawns on an unclouded mind. It is always there to be accepted, but its acceptance depends on your willingness to have it. To know reality must involve the willingness to judge unreality for what it is. This is right use of judgment. *To overlook nothingness is merely to judge it correctly and because of your ability to evaluate it truly, to let it go.*

Baba does not care what people think of Him. He has a job to do, that of liberating the hearts and minds of all His children and He will act in the most efficacious manner possible, uncaring of what that will do to His reputation. Sometimes people judge things He does. In response He says, "The moon is not disturbed when the dog howls at it." We too must maintain equanimity whether we are praised or blamed. And we will not judge when we remain open-minded instead of drawing hasty conclusions based on insubstantial evidence.

The Bible says, "Judge not that you be not judged." We do not know the past or future of anyone therefore have no basis for judgment at all. Open your mind to a willingness to keep from drawing conclusions. Judgments, opinions and conclusions are of ego. They cannot be true because of their source.

God Does Not Judge

When in the Bible God told Abraham that He could save the cities of Soddom and Gomorrah if there were a handful of good people, was He judging? No, He was just stating the fact. Did He destroy the cities as punishment for errant behavior? No, He would have saved the cities, but Divine intervention was impossible as there was not enough light for God to step in. The door was tightly closed to the light, thus the light could not enter. God will not go where He is not welcome, not because He abandons those who are wicked, but because everyone is free to choose for or against God. God honors His children too much to be other than their perfect host. He awaits our blessing to act in all things.

When the Jewish lawyers and judges in Auschwitz put God on trial and found Him guilty, it was because they felt God had abandoned them. They could not see how the things they witnessed could happen if God were not responsible. They could not see God as innocent. Though their conditions were worse than horrible, they could not have found God guilty had they looked at all the evidence. Was God responsible for the atrocities they experienced? Had God really abandoned them? They had no proof that God was to blame and so they found Him guilty based on inconclusive evidence, which requires judgment. But then they concluded their investigation with, "Now let us pray." In that the charges against God were dropped. Though they found God guilty in the courtroom, in their hearts they could not deny God's innocence, and in that non-judgment prevailed under the most challenging of circumstances.

Misperception Leads To Judgment

Judgment and love are opposites. From one comes all the sorrows of the world. From the other comes the peace of God Himself. Forgiveness looks on sinlessness alone and judges not. Everyone is always innocent. Forgiveness merely remembers this and sees everyone as sinless and innocent forever. To forgive is to know that everyone is as they were created. *Forgiveness is charitable, for it is true.* Everyone deserves the best. No one deserves to be punished simply because of who they are. Everyone was created by God to be and have everything forever, irrevocably. If that is so, can you wish anything but the best for everyone?

Carol wanted very much to stop judging her alcoholic husband. When she prayed for help, Baba showed her a vision of her husband as he really was, a wise sage who had chosen to become a drunkard to assist her in overcoming her disdain for the world. Once she saw him truly she was overwhelmed with her love for him and all her judgments vanished. Once we see another truly, it will be impossible to judge. *All judgment comes from misperception.* We do not have the whole picture. If we did, we would not judge. A mind that judges is critical and such a mind is not happy. To be free we must free ourselves of our judgmental nature. It is not true and it is not who we are.

Suppose you were witnessing two young people fighting. Will you tell them to stop? Will you just pass by and do nothing? I would remind myself that they were created by God to enhance each other's joy and that fighting is not the purpose for which they know each other. Then I would ask to be shown what to do. I would send them the light of God's love. Perhaps that would be enough, if my mind were very powerful. Instead of fighting they might just break it up and start laughing at that silly idea. Or, I might tell them to knock it off, or, if Divinely directed, with God's protection, I might just stand in between them. This cannot be dangerous when you are fearless and acting in alignment with Divine will.

Do you see how any of those responses are love in action and require no judgment at all? My first thought was to remember their truth for them, while they experienced a momentary lapse and all my possible solutions expressed love and nonviolence. A good rule of thumb is to see how you feel about your response. Do you find yourself at peace? If not, learn from your mistake. You know when what you did or did not do continues to haunt you rather than transport you to the heights. That is your conscience telling you whether or not you were off the mark. Ask to be shown what you should have done so your mind can be corrected. Then there need not be a next time.

One can only judge if he puts another outside of his mind. The Native Americans were judged as savages and thus it was perfectly justifiable to decimate them. Slave owners perceived Blacks as lower than animals so felt justified in treating them cruelly and inhumanely. Jews were put on a par with dogs and seen as sub-human in Nazi Germany. Violence is justified on the basis of judgment and condemnation. *There is no judgment that does not condemn.* What is behind all judgment is disowned and redirected guilt. When we hurt another, we feel guilty, and if we listen to ego, it will tell us to see the one we hurt as different from who they are to justify our actions against them. Until we see everyone's innocence, we think of ourselves as guilty and that requires judgment. Only when we stop judging others will we know our own innocence.

The Last Judgment Will Uplift, Not Condemn

The last judgment is a fearful idea held by many religions and is generally thought of as a procedure undertaken by God. It will be undertaken solely by man. It is a final healing, rather than a meting out of punishment, however much man may think punishment is deserved. Punishment, like judgment, always involves rejection. When you judge, you are placing your belief in the unreal. This cannot be avoided in any type of judgment or rejection, because it implies the belief that reality is yours to choose from. The last judgment means we will stop judging ourselves, each other and God.

The final judgment on the world contains no condemnation, for it sees the world as totally forgiven, without sin and wholly purposeless. Without a cause, or a function it merely slips away into nothingness. Those who believe that God's last judgment will condemn the world to hell along with them can be comforted, for it is not so. God's judgment is the gift of the correction He bestowed on all our errors, freeing us from them and all effects they ever seemed to have. To fear God's saving grace is but to fear complete release from suffering, return to peace, security, happiness and union with our own identity. God's final judgment is as merciful as every step in His plan for the salvation of the world.

Let us unite with all our brothers and sisters in shining our egos away and releasing the strength of God into everything we think, will and do. Watch your mind carefully for any beliefs that hinder this accomplishment and step away from them. Any discrimination on the basis of skin color, religion, nationality, social status, reputation, or gender is a judgment. *Judge how well you have stepped away from prejudice by your own feelings. This is the one right use of judgment. Judgment can be used to protect and to heal, or to attack and to hurt. Do not mistake the fine disguises you can use to cover judgment. They appear as charity, mercy, or love and yet you know all is not as it seems if the discomfort you feel remains unsolved.*

Watch A Tendency To Judge The World

There are those who judge the world unfairly, who hate the world and see it as full of injustices. *You cannot see yourself as innocent at the cost of someone else's guilt. Each unfairness that the world appears to lay upon you, you have laid on it by rendering it purposeless and simple justice has thus been denied to every living thing upon the earth. What this injustice does when you judge unfairly you cannot calculate.*

The world grows dim and threatening and you cannot perceive a trace of all the happy sparkle that is always present to lighten up your way. You see yourself deprived of light, abandoned to the dark, unfairly left without a purpose in a futile world. The world is fair because God has brought injustice to the light within and there all unfairness has been resolved and replaced with justice and with love. If you perceive injustice anywhere, you deny the presence of Your heavenly Father and His wholly innocent children. Let their presence shine all injustice away.

The separation never happened. *Not a single note in heaven's song was missed.* Nothing came to disturb the perfect peace God intended for his perfect creation forever. *When terror took the place of love it had no effect on the truth. Yet in each unforgiving act or thought, in every judgment and in all belief in sin is that moment of terror called back, as if it could be made again in time. To judge is to be dishonest for it assumes a position you do not have. Judgment without self-deception is impossible.* Judgment closes your mind. Forgiveness, or the recognition that nothing happened, opens your mind. To see everyone as the holy sinless child of God that they are is to relinquish judgment. As you make that sane choice for non-judgment, you demonstrate for all humanity that non-judgment is in the very best interest of all.

Beloved Lord, Thank You for Your unconditional love. Thank You for seeing Your children as innocent, pure and holy forever. Thank You that You do not judge. Dear God, how You have been judged by Your children who You created to enhance Your joy. How we have misperceived You, Our ever loving Father. Forgive us our judgments. Grant that we may see clearly who You are and who all Your creations are. You are innocent forever. All your children too are innocent forever. Thank You that this is so. Open our hearts and minds to all the evidence, that we may only draw conclusions based on irrefutable, incontrovertible evidence.

May all beings in all the worlds be happy and blest, Amen.

Figure 15 – God Does Not Judge

Everything (Eternity)

Eternity	Life	Oneness
God-Dependence	Love	Freedom
Real	Truth	**Nonjudgment**
Heaven	Peace	Creation
Innocence	Knowledge	All-Powerful

Nothing (time and space)

Time/space	**Happy Dream (Satva) God's solution - collapses time**
Ego-dependnece	Judge everyone as innocent
Unreal	Open-minded
Hell	Discern real from unreal
Guilt	Unaffectable by others judgments
Death	**Nightmare (Rajo Guna) - makes time**
Fear	Judgment/rejection/critical mind/condemn
Untruth	Narrow-minded
War	Prejudice on basis of color, race, religion...
Ignorance	Fear of last judgment
Separation	**Deep Sleep (Thamo) Ego's solution - freezes time**
Bondage	Condone all behavior - 'non-judgment'
Judgment	License - 'Do whatever you like, just don't judge it'
Mis-creation	No discernment, easily swayed by others' opinions...
Powerless	Make unreal real and real unreal through lack of judgment

Direction of Consciousness Awakening

Chapter 16

Are You Ready to Stop Miscreating?

Make your life a rose that speaks silently in the language of fragrance.
Sai Baba

God Created You to Create the Good, the Beautiful and the Holy

In the beginning God created us just like Himself. He also created the world for us. After God created us, we co-created with Him. We were created to create with God, the good, the beautiful and the holy. God did not create on His own any more than we did. We became a team. Your *creations are your gift to all, created in gratitude for your existence. They do not leave you, any more than you have left your Creator. You extend yourself to your creations as God extends Himself to you. Your creations love you as your soul loves God for the gift of creation.*

Every creation is shared by all minds in the one mind of God. We were created to create in unity and harmony with all of creation. We had not the power to create in isolation. Neither did God, after we were created. Our creative power is always shared by all of creation.

Once we entertained the tiny mad idea, "What would it be like to create in isolation, to create independent of God?" ego was born. As it is impossible to create separate from God, ego is not a real creation, however, ego comes from energy and is endowed by its creator with the power to create. Ego is a miscreation.

Your mind is a very powerful creator and never loses its creative force, which it gets from your soul. All things that you create have energy, because like the creations of God, they come from energy and are endowed by their creator with the power to create.

Miscreation is still a genuine creative act in terms of the underlying impulse, but not in terms of the content of the creation. This does not deprive the creation of its own creative power. It does however guarantee that the power will be misused, or used fearfully.

Everything we see in the world of separation is unreal. It comes from creating with ego. Since we delight in our creations, we delight in ego, even though it is a miscreation. It was our enchantment that caused us to ally with ego and to be mesmerized by it. Ego was made, not created, and ego does not love us, since it was not created in love as love is inclusive. Ego is an act of creating in separation or in isolation. All that comes from alliance with ego will be motivated by its selfish will to survive at our expense. Our only hope of freeing ourselves of ego and the ego distorted world of illusion is by choosing for selflessness.

To Have All, Give All To All

We are restored to our creative function through giving, as to give is to create. Having everything your soul keeps it by giving it. In this way you are creating as God creates. God created us in understanding, appreciation and love. To create is to love. Giving is the one act of mind that resembles creation. Sharing is God's way of creating and also ours. Baba is always giving of Himself. Sometimes He gives treats like apples, sweets or pens to the students or saris to the ladies and dhotis to the men, but His real gifts are His love, patience, compassion, charity and miracles of undoing our miscreations when we give them to be undone.

Giving is one of God's laws. God's laws are always fair and perfectly consistent. By giving we receive. But to receive is to accept, not to get. It is impossible not to have, but it is possible not to know we have. The recognition of having is the willingness for giving and only by this willingness can we recognize what we have. What we give is therefore the value we put on what we have. And this, in turn is the measure of how much we want it. If you want peace, give peace. If you want love, give love. They are real and worth giving. In giving peace and love, you are assured of having them. *Protect everything you have by the act of giving it away.*

We do not need worldly wealth in order to give. Our treasure is in heaven and the more we give of peace, love and happiness, the more we will have as our direct experience. God's laws are the opposite of the world's laws, which tell us that to give is to lose. Is it possible that giving and losing can be meaningfully associated? If in giving something, you lose it, it was not real in the first place. When you give anything in the true spirit of giving, you cannot help but feel joy. It was the giving that made you joyful, thus it was joy that you gave and in so doing you increased your joy. *Except you share it, nothing can exist. You exist because God shared His will with you, that His creation might create.* We were all created equally. We all have everything and know it through the act of sharing.

To have all, give all to all. Do, however, guard against any temptation to use this teaching to make demands of your fellowman reasoning that their joy will increase by giving to you. Once I met a teacher who was teaching that lesson to her audience by urging them to give everything to her. God only gives. She claims to be a Goddess, yet she was choosing to play the role of a beggar by asking for something from her students. Ego is very subtle in its ability to ensnare you if you are not totally free of it. Always be vigilant. A true teacher only gives and does not ask for anything in return, trusting God to give her everything. A true teacher knows no lack, thus has no need of anything. It is all right to ask for things from others if you do not know God, but don't set yourself up as a teacher under those circumstances. Once you know that God is your Source and that you are sustained by His love, it would make no sense to ask for anything from anyone. You would trust God implicitly for everything.

We are mind, in mind and purely mind, sinless forever, wholly unafraid, because we were created out of love. We have not left our Source, so we are as we were created. We cannot lose that knowledge. Everything has that knowledge and by that knowledge it lives. To give is the way to recognize we have received. It is the proof that what we have is ours. It is the proof that we are who we are. Let us not however mistake bodies for God's creation. *When we see the light beyond bodies, purity undimmed by errors or pitiful mistakes or fearful thoughts of guilt from dreams of sin, we are giving as we have received. When we see no separation, but rather look on everyone, all circumstances, all happenings and all events without the slightest fading of the light, we are indeed giving and can be assured that we know who we are.*

Ideas increase through sharing. The more who believe in them, the stronger they become. *Everything is an idea.* The more people who hold the idea that the world can be saved, the more likelihood that it will become a reality. Using the hundredth monkey idea, as soon as enough people invite God back into the world, the world will be saved. *In this world, giving takes the form of healing as creation takes the form of giving in heaven. In heaven you create as you were created. Here you can choose to miscreate or to heal. To heal is to undo the unreal. That requires a miracle. Miracles come from God, but can be performed by you when you are in alignment with God's will. However, do not pretend to know on your own when or where to perform miracles. Perform only those miracles that God directs you to perform. This will save you from exhaustion. Every day as you awake pray to be shown what miracles God would perform through you this day.*

Expect Miracles

In general we are not used to miraculous thinking, but we can be trained to think that way. Expect miracles. Do not leave your mind unguarded. Miracle working entails a full realization of the power of thought and a real avoidance of miscreation. Every time you think an unloving thought and do not give it to God for correction, you are miscreating. The whole world is unreal. All unreality comes from miscreating, which comes from wrong thoughts, which in turn come from alliance with ego. Experiences of darkness, contraction, lack and loss are due to miscreating. They are impossible in God's creation. They are all equally unreal, and are transformed into real experiences when we stop giving them energy of reality.

The world teaches you to get what you can at another's expense. Ego leads you to believe that you can only gain if someone else loses. That is impossible because everyone was created to have everything forever. No one lacks anything. What should we do when we see a beggar or a hungry child? Hopefully we will feed them, but we can also make a shift in consciousness so that lack is impossible both for us and for everyone we meet. We can choose to transform unreal perceptions into experiences of abundance for all of humanity by healing our minds that thought lack possible. We raise our consciousness by taking only what we need.

When you give freely and generously to everyone you are giving to yourself. Help everyone. The biggest help you can give is to help others see that truth is unaffected by experience, not with your words, but with your prayers to God in their behalf. It is not enough to conceptually or intellectually see that the beggar is not really a beggar. Be in your heart, not your head. Baba says, "Help ever; hurt never." Always act with compassion.

Lack is impossible in God's creation. Only you can deprive yourself of anything. Abundance, fullness and completeness are all attributes of God's creation. If ever there is a sense of ingratitude toward God or anyone it comes from not knowing who God is or who your family is. All are your family, worthy of your eternal gratitude and deepest appreciation, for everyone is giving you everything in every interaction no matter what it may look like. All those seeming others in your life are only doing what you have asked and are thus your savior. There are no victims.

We cannot create in the world as it is. We can heal and when healed the world will be restored to its original purpose. When our minds are healed our miscreations will disappear and we will be realigned with our true function of creating the true, the beautiful and the holy. Miscreations disappear in the presence of our true creations created with God.

There are those who say that maya, illusion, is God's play. Illusion is not God's idea. All illusion is due to man's unloving thoughts. We have a grave responsibility, for our minds are all-powerful and everything we think has all the power of God behind it. Never underestimate the power of your mind. Where do you think the unreal comes from? It comes from a mind that is all-powerful and has misused its power. There are no mysteries. There are no secrets. Watch your mind for purity in thought, word, and deed. When you are not thinking loving thoughts, turn to God and ask for help to change your mind. All thoughts are under your control. You are in charge. You are not mercilessly bombarded by thoughts that are not of you. Loving thoughts come from alliance with God.

Allied with ego, your Divine power is being misused. It is being used for suffering, sickness, death, disease, atrocities, wars and strife. This is not God's will. This is God's power being misdirected by us who were entrusted with God's all-powerful mind. We are responsible for every one of our thoughts. We are their generator. They do not come out of nowhere. And they are the cause of everything we see. If we want a real world, a healed world, then it begins with our real thoughts. That is why we should think of God constantly. In our remembrance of God we can only think loving thoughts and those thoughts will have real effects, where all benefit. Our unreal thoughts are undone when we give them to God for healing and that healing is a miracle. Miracles merely undo what never was.

Miracles Heal

Unless a miracle actually heals it is not a miracle at all. There was once a pompous yogi who had mastered walking on water. He came to visit Ramakrishna by walking across the Ganges River. When he arrived, Ramakrishna commented that for 20 annas, that is for as little as 5 cents, he could have ferried across. Ramakrishna was pointing out to the proud yogi that his yogic accomplishments were worthless. He should have focused the power of his mind on the salvation of the world. There are those who teach lay people how to walk on burning coals and not get blisters. That is not a miracle for it does not heal and thus serves nothing except to demonstrate the power of mind. This may be helpful, but more often than not leads to arrogance and feelings of specialness.

When we will to heal the separation by letting it go we return to wholeness. To heal is the only kind of thinking in this world that resembles the thought of God. To heal is to correct our perception. Whenever you heal someone by recognizing his worth, you are acknowledging his power to create and yours. We heal our brothers and sisters simply by accepting God for them.

When anyone is sick, it is because he is not asking for peace and therefore does not know he has it. The acceptance of peace is the denial of illusion and sickness is an illusion. Every child of God has the power to deny illusions anywhere merely by denying them completely in himself. If you have denied the power of illusions, you cannot fall ill. If you fall ill illusions are still real to you. Do not be discouraged. Ask God to show you the way to your full recovery. Do not suppress symptoms, as that is not healing. To go beyond conceptual understanding is to turn to God for a miracle that will restore you to perfect health.

Miracles come from God and are elicited through prayer. Prayer is natural communication between God and His creation. Through prayer love is received and through miracles love is expressed. Miracles acknowledge the truth and restore reality. Sickness is separation. Healing overcomes the separation. When you know your oneness with God you cannot fall ill.

Sickness Is Not God's Will

Some Sai Baba devotees hold an idea that sickness is God's will. They say everything is God's will and therefore when they are sick it is because Sai Baba willed it for them out of His love and is therefore in their best interest. There are many people who have stories of how their sickness gave them wonderful insights, teachings and opportunities to slow down, so sickness is justified.

But if you love someone do you really will them to be sick and then tell them it is for their own good? It wouldn't make me feel loved. I wouldn't like that god. Once someone asked Sai Baba if everything unfortunate that happens is due to bad karma. He said to think of it as God's grace. He did not say it is God's will. If you think of it as bad karma, you may feel guilty. If you think of your illness as God's grace you will be grateful and this attitude will help you to heal and keep you from making more karma for yourself. And undoubtedly due to God's grace you are better off than had God not intervened.

The masses are not yet ready for the awesome responsibility that everything that happens to them is by their choice. That can be very fearful, so accepting suffering as God's grace serves the situation and at the same time prevents contraction into terror. That nothing happens but by our will is really good news, but sometimes good news looks bad when we are too afraid of the truth. It is good news because if you are all-powerful, then you have the power to change your experience if you don't like it. It changes when you are willing to make a shift toward personal responsibility.

A broken body shows the mind has not been healed. Miracles of healing are witness to the truth that sickness is not real. If sickness can be undone, then it must follow that it is not real. If unreal then it cannot be of God. A sick body does not make sense. It could not make sense, since sickness is not what the body is for. Only if your body were for attack as the Muslim suicide bombers believe, or if you thought you were your body, would sickness make sense to you. *Sickness is a way of demonstrating that you can be hurt.* If you are sick, you are vulnerable, which is exactly what ego wants you to believe. The truth is you are invulnerable, as that is how God created you. *Health is the result of relinquishing all attempts to use your body lovelessly.* Only when you do not value yourself do you become ill.

There are those who say, "I am not a body; therefore I can use my body in any way I like as who I am remains unaffected." This is miscreating through erroneous thinking. Your body is a temple for God. Take good care of it and it will serve you well. Eat to live. Don't live to eat. Food does affect your health and well-being. Eat consciously. Ask to be shown what to eat. There are those who say, "My body may be sick but as it is not real, I am not sick even if it experiences illness." If you think this, you are dissociating and missing the opportunity to use your sickness as the learning device it was sent to be. Nor are you stepping into personal responsibility for your ailment. When sickness is seen as God's grace, it can be used as a classroom. It is God's grace because it exposes to you that your mind is not yet healed. Everything can be used. Ask to be shown what the sickness is telling you.

A friend was suffering pain in his left shoulder. I understand the left side to be our passive or feminine side and the right to be the male or active side. If too passive, it will reflect in pain on the left side of the body, and too active or aggressive it will show up on the right side. I asked my friend if he felt remiss about shouldering responsibilities in any areas of his life. He admitted that he did. He committed to discharging his duties and the pain subsided. A woman was having heart pain. She was asked if she beat herself up a lot. She confessed that she was hard on herself. It was shown to her that every time she put herself down she was stabbing herself in the heart. She understood and the heart pain vanished. We can be shown the contents of our minds by what is playing out in our bodies. Everything can be used. Live a life of integrity and realize that all pain is self-inflicted punishment for crimes that were never committed.

How do you enlist God's healing as your direct experience? *The invitation to be healed must come from you. God can only heal you when you are ready to be healed. He does want you to be whole and performs miracles where invited. Healing is release from fear. All healing involves replacing fear with love. God is love and can only enter where there is no fear. Unless you have hurt yourself, you could never suffer in any way, for that is not God's will for you. Nothing external to your mind can hurt or injure you. There is no cause beyond yourself that can reach down and bring oppression. Pain is the ransom we gladly pay not to be free. When we experience pain, we can ask for miracles instead.*

The miracle does nothing. It merely undoes. It cancels out the interference to what has been done. It does not add; it merely takes away. Miracles are the translation of denial into truth. If to love yourself is to heal yourself, those who are sick do not love themselves. Therefore they are asking for the love that would heal them, but which they are denying themselves. If they knew the truth about themselves, they could not be sick. Our task thus becomes to deny the denial of truth. The sick must heal themselves because the truth is in them. They heal by enlisting the power of God. Only God can heal, but everyone can access God's healing grace, and that by faith. When Jesus healed he always acknowledged the person being healed as their own healer. He frequently said, "Go your way, your faith has made you whole."

You do have a role to play in healing, and that is to hold the light of truth for the person who is sick. *Having obscured it, the light in another mind must shine into the patient's mind, because that light is theirs.* When a friend is sick I might tell him or her, "I am holding your perfection for you. When you are ready, please join me there." I pray to God to let wholeness be restored. Sometimes the miracle happens instantly. Sometimes it takes a little longer. Time is given to overcome any fear or feeling of unworthiness that might get in the way.

Sickness Is A Call For Love

When you perceive sickness as a call for love, you offer the sick what they believe they cannot offer themselves. There was a lady in a Course in Miracles study group who was diagnosed with cancer and was in the hospital. The others in the group went to visit her, but instead of coming to cheer her, they expressed anger toward her for having fallen ill. As a student of ACIM they thought she should know better than to get sick. They felt the truth of ACIM to be threatened by her illness. Had they come with compassion and love, they may have witnessed the miracle of healing that the course offers.

Miracles demonstrate that learning has occurred under the right guidance, for learning is invisible and what has been learned can be recognized only by its results. We do not know our own minds. We will know that we have understood when we experience miracles. *There is no order of difficulty in miracles. Each is a gentle winning over from the appeal of guilt to the appeal of love. Not one illusion is less amenable to truth than are the rest. It is possible that some are given greater value and less willingly offered to truth for healing and for help.*

We are share some responsibility for how others see themselves. *It is given you to change another's whole mind, which is one with you, in just an instant.* Though everyone must heal themselves, you can be the light that gives the courage to another to dare to be healed. It does require your alignment with God's will. *Healing always happens where fear has been replaced with love. Perfect love castes out fear.* Give perfect love and see loved ones restored to perfect health.

Sai Baba says there are times when suffering serves a remedial purpose. Where sickness, suffering, or deformities are due to unkindnesses from the past and where the present experience is serving to heal an individual of a degenerate behavior pattern, it would not serve to heal that person. This sounds like a justification for suffering, but sometimes suffering is remedial. If they want to make a shift in consciousness they are free to do so and that shift will permit miracles, through God's grace. We do not know the past or future of anyone and therefore do not know which miracles are appropriate. God knows what is best in every situation.

Heal Yourself To Heal The World

There is no need for anyone to suffer. There is need that you be healed because the suffering of the world has made it deaf to its salvation and deliverance. The resurrection of the world awaits your healing and your happiness that you may demonstrate the healing of the world. I have personally undergone a number of instant healings. Baba healed me, but I had to have no further purpose for my illnesses. *Of myself I can do nothing, but with God all things are possible.*

Once at Prasanthi Nilayam I had an angry foot infection. The foot was badly swollen and it was almost impossible to walk. One day, as I was hobbling to my room, I jokingly asked Baba in my heart, "What shall we do, shall we cut it off and throw it into the fire?" That was the remedy Baba had recommended for someone else who was very sick. Baba does not take sickness seriously because He knows it is not real. Instantly, I felt a wonderful warm healing energy on the wound. By morning it was completely healed. Sickness is my attempt to make myself my cause and not allow God to be my Source.

Another time in darsan I had a nasty cold. I had gone through all my tissues when it dawned on me that I absolutely had no need of that congestion. Amazingly, instantly, my head cleared and that was the end of that. It was a direct confirmation of the power of my mind. When I am healed, there is hope for the healing of the world.

Allowing yourself to be healed demonstrates to the world that healing is possible. Truth gathers momentum. The world is a projection of your mind. However, *true healing is never about healing bodies. The miracle is useless if you only learn that your body can be healed, for that is not the lesson it was sent to teach. The lesson is the mind was sick that thought your body could be sick. Projecting out its guilt caused nothing and had no effects. The world is full of miracles. They stand in shining silence next to every dream of pain and suffering and of sin and guilt.*

Any more, when I start to feel ill, I simply remind myself of my Source and affirm the impossibility of sickness and do not get sick, by God's grace. People who reason that their illness doesn't matter as their body is not real anyway, have only conceptual understanding. They still think their body real, otherwise it simply could not get sick. You do not have to accept what I say as your truth. You need only be willing for it to be true and you open the door to miracles of healing. If you insist that it is impossible to have a miraculous cure, you have closed the door to that possibility. Stay open and let the miracle be gently given you. You need not struggle. You need not try to force miracles.

What can be sick that was created by God and what that was not created by God can be at all? Sickness is a demand your body be what it is not. Its nothingness is guarantee that it cannot be sick. It is not difficult to heal, as all that is really required is your willingness. I have given talks on this subject. Once a young lady in my audience had been suffering from a flu for over two weeks. She tried what I was suggesting but had no success. She talked to me about it and by the end of our conversation commented in frustration, "I guess I just have to figure it out." "No," I said, "That is just what you do not have to do. You have asked, now just say, "Thank-you.""

The next day she happily reported how she felt completely cured and was eager to try her new understanding of miracles on everything. Yes, expect miracles in every walk of life. Remember that your Source wants you whole, perfect and happy, and wants to heal your mind so that wholeness can be your experience right now. You need do so little to receive so much. If you do more, you only get in the way. Don't try to figure it out. You don't have to do anything but want to be healed and then thank God that He has healed you. You do not even have to trust that this is so. With experience of the miracle, trust will be gained.

Use The Mind To Heal Rather Than Suppress Symptoms

There are those who suppress symptoms, using the power of their minds to stave off illness. This is not healing. Healing comes from a willingness to change your mind about who you think you are and who your Source is. It is the mind that needs to be healed. Then the healing of the body will follow automatically. Perhaps you are a student of ACIM and think that if you haven't been successful in healing yourself, you are guilty or you are not a good student. When you feel ill, do not deny your illness or suppress your symptoms. You are sick because that is still real for you. That does not make you bad or guilty. It is simply that unreality is still more real than reality in this moment. Be patient and allowing. When you resist, you fight your illness and thereby further affirm its reality in your mind.

If you feel ill, simply ask to have that place in your mind healed that thinks you could be other than how you were created. Then let it go. We do not know our own minds because we have allowed ego to convince us that we are ignorant and powerless. Be gentle with yourself whatever is happening. Surround yourself with those who love and cherish you and feel compassion and do not judge you because you are ill.

The world and our bodies are gifts. They can help us to discover our minds. Use everything as an opportunity to know yourself, as a learning device. Then you are seeing all as God's grace. Know that you can change your mind. Be loving, kind and compassionate toward yourself, and if the healing does not take place miraculously, do not become impatient. Maybe there is too much fear associated with the idea. Under those circumstances, do what you need in order to feel safe. Don't become fanatical and refuse doctor's care. You are a precious child of God. Be gentle with yourself wherever you are in your consciousness.

Once one of Sai Baba's students who was sitting on the verandah had a bad cold and flu and felt very sick. Baba manifested a packet of antibiotics for him. Al Drucker, who was also there, wrinkled his nose. Baba commented to Al, "He believes in them. What can I do?" The young man was perfectly fine the next day. It was the power of his mind that healed him, but the drugs supported his faith. Baba says, "I give you what you want so that you will come to want what I have really come to give you, namely eternal life."

Hold Wholeness In Your Mind To See It In The World

When you heal yourself and others too, it becomes easier and easier for the rest of humanity to trust the power of mind to heal. Only when you yearn with all your heart for the healing of all humanity do you really wish your own healing and release. *Once you have been restored to your original state of wholeness, you will naturally find yourself unable to tolerate a lack of love in yourself or in anyone else and must join the great crusade to correct it.* Make a commitment to participate in God's plan for the healing of the whole world. *As long as a single slave remains to walk the earth, your release is not complete. Complete restoration to wholeness for all of humanity is the only true goal of the miracle-minded. Everyone in the world must play his part in the redemption of the world to recognize that the world has been redeemed. Your part is essential, for in your part lies all of it, without which is no part complete, nor is the whole complete without your part.*

Perhaps you are a doctor who feels threatened that you will not have work if everyone learns to heal through the power of mind. If there is no sickness, rest assured that the world has been healed and all of humanity is in the consciousness of being sustained by the love of God, thus you also will not need to be sustained by your profession. To be a true doctor is to wish yourself out of business. Then only can you really call yourself a doctor. Sai Baba has set up hospitals for people to come and have free medical care. He advocates gradual though permanent change. When people know they will be cared for if they are sick, they are less fearful, thus less prone to sickness. Baba's work is slow but effective. He knows the remedy that will give a permanent cure.

You Can Be Healed Instantly

Your mind is all-powerful and the world is a projection of your mind. When you want to heal your mind, you invite the world's healing simultaneously. Everyone wants a healthy body. Healing is of the mind and will be reflected in the body and in your experience in general. To want your body healed is not enough. To be willing to be wrong about what you hold in your mind opens the door to the healing of your mind, reflected in a healed body and a healed world when enough minds have become truly miracle minded. Until your experience reflects the peace of God, your mind is not whole.

If you sincerely feel you do want to be healed and yet find you are not whole, then you have to start with where you are. Be tender and gentle with yourself. When you accept that you do want what is happening right now due to the purpose it is serving, you open the door to a change of mind. Maybe it is time to reevaluate your purpose. If you were not getting what you want, you would not be all-powerful. When you are that honest, you are expressing a willingness to change your mind. A shift in consciousness about who you are will heal and is the only true and lasting cure for all disease, whatever form it takes. An admission that only you can get in the way of your healing will inspire the necessary shift in consciousness. All that is necessary is your desire attended with an admission that you are responsible for your particular set of circumstances.

There are those who look to Ramana Maharshi, Nisargadatta and Ramakrishna as examples for what awake looks like. They were all fully enlightened beings of tremendous light in the last century and yet they each died a very painful death, where their bodies were wracked with festering, angry cancers. If they were awake and yet experienced such deaths, what hope do we have? Some claim that they did not suffer. I look into Ramana Maharshi's eyes in a picture taken just days before his death. His eyes reveal such peace and freedom that I believe he really did transcend his pain and did not suffer.

But suppose you could choose between consciously leaving your body in perfect health or contracting a terminal illness in which you could rise above the pain? What would you choose? *Who would want the "benefits" of sickness, when he has received the simple happiness of health?* Is it realistic to lead a healthy life, sound of body and mind right now? It really comes back to a willingness to accept that you are all-powerful. If you are, then you must be in charge of your own destiny and it must be possible to choose for health, wholeness, completeness and perfection of body and mind, as that is how you were created. Your body is a projection of your mind and when it is well, it indicates a healed mind. Let your healing be a demonstration to the world of what is possible.

There are those who don't contract physical ailments who might not be all that enlightened, thus a healthy body is not the only indicator of one's state of mind. The sparkle in your eye and the laughter in your smile are also helpful pointers.

Perfect Health Is Possible Right Now

Does Sai Baba get sick? There are a number of occasions where He has taken on illnesses of His devotees. In one case a woman in Dehre Dunn, nearly a thousand kilometers away, suffered a severe heart attack. She was a teacher of Sai Baba's human values program for young children. She had five daughters. Her husband was a drunkard. The heart attack would have taken her life had Baba not intervened and taken it into His own body. Her girls would have been in the street. When asked why Baba had to take it into His body, He explained that it was the law of nature. He said that once something starts in a body it has to finish in a body. Perhaps Baba took it into His body because her consciousness was not able to permit it to simply be undone. Baba said it was His duty.

An older man from Australia also suffered a heart attack. He took some vibhuti (sacred ash) and was instantly healed. Baba did not take it into His own body in that instance. In any case, I do not remember a time when Baba fell ill unrelated to taking on another's illness. Recently His walking is impaired and He has explained that His body has become so attracted to the earth's magnetic field that walking has become difficult. He assured those looking on in pain that He is in perfect health. Baba does not get sick and so for me He is a model of what is possible. He says, "My life is my message." We also needn't get sick if we want healing and health above all else. *If a sufficient number of people become truly miracle-minded quickly, the shortening process becomes almost immeasurable.*

When you heal yourself, everyone benefits. Your healing is proof that healing is possible and that is good news for everyone. *When you are healed, you have the capacity to bring peace to the minds of others. Everything meets in God, because everything was created by Him.* You are part of everything, as everything is part of you. *You can no more pray for yourself alone than you can find joy for yourself alone. Prayer is a restatement of inclusion. We begin the journey back by setting out together and gathering in all God's children everywhere as we continue together.*

When we uncover the key to healing and share it with all who yearn for a better way, the world becomes a place where hope of happiness can be fulfilled. No one remains outside this hope because the world will have been united in the belief that the purpose of the world is one which all must share, that hope be more than just a dream.

You are here only to be truly helpful and to represent God who sent you. You do not have to worry about what to say or do, because the One who sent you will direct you. Be content to be wherever He wishes, knowing He goes there with you. You will be healed as you let Spirit teach you to heal. Healing is the undoing or correction of errors so that the awareness of your true creative function can be restored to you. The only error that needs correction is the thought that separation is possible. In full awareness you will know the separation never occurred.

To Heal Is To Forgive

When truly healed, the past is remembered in purified form only. That happens through forgiveness. *To forgive is merely to remember only the loving thoughts you gave in the past and those that were given you. All the rest must be forgotten. Be willing to forgive another for what he did not do. That is true forgiveness. Unjustified forgiveness is attack.* This is what you do when you think someone has sinned, but in your magnanimity you forgive them. That is not forgiveness. It makes errors real. Forgiveness looks past error and sees only the truth of God's wholly innocent child. *If you can see your brother merits pardon, you have learned forgiveness is your right as much as his. Forgiveness recognized as merited will heal.*

No one can do anything to you that you have not ask for. If they could, they would be more powerful than you. Nothing happens to you without your consent. When I was raped, it was because I had given my consent. I forgave my rapist by seeing that I was responsible for what happened to me. In that way I was forgiving him for what he did not do. That is forgiveness and allows the mind to be healed. If you do not understand that you are responsible for everything that happens to you, you are giving your power away and are in victim-victimizer consciousness. If that is your consciousness you can ask to be healed. When you are healed you will have nothing to forgive. That is forgiveness.

However, forgiveness does not ask that you take a beating with a smile on your face, because nothing is happening that you have not asked for. Forgiveness is an active process of transformation both within yourself and the other. I forgive myself by being responsible. I forgive him by praying that he desire a shift in consciousness where he recognize me as his sister, given to him by God for the purpose of enhancing his joy. I do not condone his actions. Forgiveness means you do not wish the other to suffer for his actions in relation to you, though they may have been hurtful. You do act to prevent his hurtful actions in future. I sent my rapist to jail to prevent him from hurting others. I know his innocence is unaffectable by anything he may have done. I hold his perfection in my mind and pray that he choose to act in accordance with the purity and holiness that he is in truth, because that is in his best interest. Forgiveness sincerely wants another's salvation and knows his innocence, no matter how hurtful his behavior.

In this world we cannot create. We come closest to ourselves through forgiveness. Forgiveness is acquired. God does not forgive because He has never condemned and there must be condemnation before forgiveness is necessary. Fear condemns and love forgives. Forgiveness undoes what fear had produced. The major difficulty we find in genuine forgiveness is that we still believe we must forgive the truth and not illusions. When we truly forgive we will see clearly what is true and what are illusions. True forgiveness requires clarity about who we are.

We naturally think of forgiving when we have been hurt. There is no one more powerful than you. And it is also true that there is no one less powerful than you. If no one can hurt you, it means that if you are hurt it is because that is what you chose. You may have chosen it to prove yourself vulnerable or because you thought you were guilty and deserving of punishment. You can change your mind by accepting that you are as God created you and that you deserve the very best no matter how shady your past may have been. Once your mind is healed, it will be impossible for anyone to hurt you.

When some Sikhs came to the ashram with sub-machine guns, planning to snuff out Baba's life, Baba had them intercepted at the gate. His third eye vision saw them coming. It was not possible for them to harm Baba because He had no victim-victimizer consciousness. Another time some students who were disgruntled decided to storm the ashram one night to kill Sai Baba. Baba was not to be found. He had warned His faithful attendant to leave his post, but the attendant, in a determination to protect Baba was killed. That was sad. The point is that Baba could not be touched because He had not given His consent to their plans. There are no victims. No one is more powerful than you. If you are hurt, it is because you have given your consent.

You can protest that you did not agree to some of the things that happened to you, but if they happened without your consent, you are a victim. Either you are responsible for all that happens to you or you are not all-powerful. What is your choice? Ego wants you to think things can happen to you against your will. That is what ego is: an idea that things can happen to God's holy child, created all-powerful and perfect, against his holy will. Once you see that you are the cause of everything that happens to you, you have understood forgiveness. Once you see that nothing can happen to who you are as God created you, you have understood forgiveness. Once you see that, who is there to forgive? Who hurt you?

Do not however use this teaching to keep yourself in harms way. You are a precious child of God worthy only of the deepest honoring and tenderness. Also, do not use this teaching to justify hurting others, as 'they are doing it to themselves.' If you hurt someone, whether intentionally or unintentionally, learn from your mistake and vow not to repeat it. You do not want to hurt another because they are your very self. In hurting them you hurt yourself. And when you recognize your mistake let them know you are sorry. Saying that you are sorry heals the pain that another feels due to your conscious or unconscious acts against them. Do unto others as you would have them do unto you. When you know who you are, it will be impossible to hurt anyone. 'Help ever; hurt never.'

Should you forgive yourself if you are accosted in any way? If you feel the need to forgive yourself, you are stating that you really were violated and you are making the error real. Once I see that I am not a body I also realize nothing happened. Then the past is truly healed and all that remains of it are the flowers, the good and joyful memories. *If you knew the glorious goal that lies beyond forgiveness you would not hold onto any unforgiving thought, however light the touch of corruption on it may appear to be. How great is the cost of holding anything God did not give in your mind. Your mind was given to direct your hand to bless and to lead all your brothers and sisters out of darkness into the glorious light.*

Creation is your true function in heaven as healing is your true function here. Healing includes miracles and miracles undo the unreal. Sickness and suffering can be undone because they were never real. Healing happens through compassion and forgiveness. Compassion is love, non-judgment and caring. Forgiveness means that what you thought another did to you never happened. It shifts you out of victim-victimizer consciousness into God consciousness. May your complete healing of mind and body stand as a splendorous beacon of hope to all the world.

Beloved Heavenly Father, Thank You for the beautiful world You created for us. Thank You for creating us to create the good, the beautiful, and the holy. Thank You for Your solution to our miscreations. Please heal the whole world of all our miscreations. Sorry that we have misused our minds to miscreate, when they were given to us by You for creating. Thank You that forgiveness, healing, and miracles undo our miscreations and restore us to our original function of creating with You and all our brothers and sisters everywhere. Please show us what miracles You will to perform through us today. Please instill faith in all your children in the whole world that miracles are natural expressions of Your love. May all the world be healed.

May all beings in all the worlds be happy and blest, Amen.

Figure 16 – God Created You to Create

Everything (Eternity)

Eternity	Life	Oneness
God-Dependence	Love	Freedom
Real	Truth	Non-judgment
Heaven	Peace	**Creation**
Innocence	Knowledge	All-Powerful

Nothing (time and space)

Time/space	**Happy Dream (Satva) God's solution - collapses time**
Ego-dependence	Heal the mind that thought the body could be sick
Unreal	Undo miscreations/personal responsibility/vigilance
Hell	Forgive others for what they did not do
Guilt	Compassion.yearn for the healing of the world
Death	**Nightmare (Rajo Guna) - makes time**
Fear	Sickness, suffering, death
Untruth	Mis-create
War	Victim-victimizer consciousness
Ignorance	Buffeted about by a world that was miscreated
Separation	**Deep Sleep (Thamo) Ego's solution - freezes time**
Bondage	Dissociate, suppress symptoms when body ill
Judgment	Hurt by someone - 'forgive' - make error real
Mis-Creation	Not responsible for what happens to others or myself
Powerless	I do not have the power to heal myself

Direction of Consciousness Awakening

Chapter 17

Are You Ready to Be All-Powerful?

Love is the only power; Love is the only way.
Love sweetens every hour; Love makes a happy day.

Sai Baba

Nothing happens without self-confidence

King Henry V of sixteenth century England was battling with France to reclaim his father's winnings. It was really pride that motivated his actions, but there was a genuineness, a fearlessness and a devotion to God that I admire in his character. He and his men had been slogging in the rain and were bedraggled, disgruntled and missing their families, not to mention on the verge of starvation. It was the day of a deciding battle and the French troops were fresh and outnumbered them by at least twenty to one.

Young King Henry rallied his troops with his famous St. Crispian's Day address wherein he declared, "All things are ready if our minds be so." He dedicated the day to God and demanded moral character of his men, telling them that there were to be no spoils and no women and that they were to fight honestly and fairly. By the end of the day he had no idea who was the victor. He had given to his maximum capacity and his med had been inspired to do the same. When the dead were counted he had lost only 26 men while the whole French army had been utterly decimated. When you know you can win, it doesn't matter the odds against you, you will succeed. That is self-confidence. It is ego that tells us that we are helpless or that the odds against us are too overwhelming. When you take your power back by recognizing that in God you are all-powerful, you again take charge of your life.

The oldest and most powerful mantra in the Vedas, the ancient Hindu scriptures, is the Gayatri mantra and the last two lines request, "Let my limited consciousness be merged with the limitless consciousness that I am in truth." In truth, you are as powerful as God. You have everything God has since you were created exactly like Him. God is all-powerful. Therefore, you too must be all-powerful. Sai Baba says there is no one more powerful than you. Nothing happens without your will. Everything that happens, you have asked for and have received as you have asked. If you don't like what is happening, you have the power to give yourself a different experience. You can change your mind. Everything is possible when you have self-confidence.

There are those who say power can be dangerous. What they are referring to is not power, but force. Force is used by those who believe themselves weak. Those who know they are all-powerful will not misuse their power. Once you see that you have put value in powerlessness, will it be a sacrifice to trade it in for all the power in the universe?

There are no neutral thoughts. Your mind is all-powerful. When you think loving thoughts, you are thinking with God and those thoughts contribute to the welfare of all humanity because we are all one. Those are real thoughts. Those thoughts weaken illusion's hold and move you toward waking up. That is why Baba constantly urges us to watch our thoughts, words, and deeds. He encourages service to society because when you help one, you help everyone. He urges us to constantly repeat His name because when your mind is focused on God, you are not misappropriating your power. Then you are choosing for God and for your freedom and the freedom of all.

Perseverance In a Just Cause Is All The Power You Need

Once I came to Sai Baba to procure a robe for our center in Southern California. I was given three interviews during that visit. In the first interview I asked for the robe and Baba agreed to give me one. But a month passed and there was no robe. I went to the office and they told me I should have come immediately - that it was too late. In a second interview I again asked for a robe and again Baba promised to deliver one to me. Immediately after the interview I went to the office and they agreed to check with Baba, but then the man in charge fell seriously ill and the robe lost importance in the shuffle. A third time I was called in and a third time was promised a robe. When I went to the office, the new management told me it was not their business and that if Baba intended to give me a robe He would have to do so directly.

I sought advice among my devotee friends and was told that Elsie Cowan, a prominent devotee, had once asked for some sandals. When they were not forth coming, she sat in the hot sun near Baba's door. When a student came by and asked, "Mother, why are you sitting in the hot sun?" she told him of her determination not to move without the promised sandals. The boy reported to Baba. He came back shortly and told Elsie that the sandals would come and for her to please move to the shade. She would not budge. She sat there until the sandals were in her lap.

Baba's door was no longer accessible, so sitting in the hot sun was not the way to demonstrate my determination. I decided to fast until the robe appeared. But it was Christmas time and after a few days, fasting was really getting in the way of the joy that the season offers, so I quit, but I did not stop praying for a robe.

It was two days after Christmas and my departure day. I asked the head volunteer if I could sit in front to ask for the robe. She pointed to all those who were making similar requests and shrugging her shoulders said, "What can I do?" I went back to my place in my row. The person at the front of the line drew #25. There is a lottery system set up to get inside. It would be impossible to make contact with Baba with that high number. I again plucked up the courage to ask Mata-ji, telling her the robe was not for me, but for all those people back home who were not so fortunate to be here. That softened her heart and she let me sit in front.

When Baba came, He stopped by the person on the one side and then the person on the other side, completely avoiding me. I said, "Baba, leaving today, may I please have a robe?" He ignored me and continued walking. I persisted more loudly, "Baba, leaving today." Suddenly He turned back, "What? Leaving today?" "Yes, and please may I take a robe for our center?" Baba said, "Yes, yes, where are you staying?" "In Elsie Cowan's flat." "I know. What is your name?" "Yaani." "Yes, yes." And He walked on. All day I stayed in the flat full of anticipation, but the robe didn't show up.

Then it was afternoon, my very last darsan and of course I couldn't possibly ask Mata-ji for special favor again. Our row drew #19. When I took my place, I was about 12 layers of women deep and there was no possibility to ask Baba out loud. But I could pray, and pray I did, with all my heart and soul. Baba walked right toward me. But He just passed me by and kept on walking. I prayed even harder, "I know you are just testing me. I know you are hearing my prayer. I won't give up. I will never give up. Please Baba, you promised...." Suddenly He turned and retraced His steps. When within ear shot, He instructed me to go to the office.

After darsan I ran to the office, only to be told the office was helpless as there was no robe waiting for me. I told them I was leaving this very moment, but when the robe turned up, they could give it to friends in Elsie's flat who were also leaving in a few days. They would see that the robe reached me. The office agreed and I was on my way. I was so very happy all the way home. Never did I wonder if the robe would really turn up. I had persevered. I had done everything to my maximum capacity and now I left the results to God. I was singing and dancing for joy. I was so exhilarated. A few days later my friends showed up with the robe. They said the office had thoroughly interrogated them to make sure they would not consider holding onto the coveted garment themselves. Then the manager had apparently said of me, "She's one lucky lady."

I had confidence that my purpose was selfless and that our center deserved the robe. I did not get discouraged or let any of the obstacles get in the way. That kind of determination and perseverance is all that is necessary and you can do anything, you can go anywhere. You have to be willing to do whatever it takes. You have to be willing to draw your circle just as Elsie did in not budging till the desired result was achieved. That perseverance takes self-confidence. With confidence that you will get what you truly want and deserve, you will passionately invest every ounce of energy into your pursuit. With that kind of determination to awaken, you will awaken.

You do not need to know what to do. You do not need to know how to proceed. All will be given with your determination to succeed. So great is your power. It is your desire for anything that brings everything to you, so watch what you desire. Desire eternal life, perfect happiness, a healed mind, peace, love and truth for yourself and everyone. Anything less than that is not worthy of you. At the same time, temper your determination with a willingness to let go and trust God for everything. Again the spiritual athlete knows how to walk the tight rope, neither letting the pendulum swing too far to the side of your passionate desire for what is your true inheritance or too far to the side of surrendering to whatever is happening in the moment.

You Are All The Power In The Universe

Sai Baba says, "You are the Lord of the universe. There is no one more powerful than you." If you really are all-powerful what does that mean? It means that nothing happens to you that you do not will. Baba says that He has a mission to restore peace and happiness to the whole planet and that there is no force that can alter His mission in any way. There is nothing that can interfere with Baba's mission, because He knows how to wield His power to achieve the desired outcome.

Baba is a living example of omnipotence. Everything that happens around Him happens at His will. He says that no one comes to Him unless He wills it. There are plenty of stories of those who have attempted to see Baba and gotten waylaid. He did not will it and without His will it could not happen. During the mid-70's a camera crew from BBC in England came to the ashram and took some footage of Baba and the ashram activities. They were planning to televise their film. When they returned to England, not one frame of film had anything on it. It was all blank. All film shot prior to coming to the ashram and after leaving came out perfectly. Baba said it was not time for Him to be known to the world. Everything that happens in relation to Him is under His control. He is the host in His ashram and nothing happens without His will.

In 1962, Baba didn't want His birthday to be spoiled by the Chinese invasion into His homeland, so the night before His birthday, by 12 o'clock midnight, there was not a single Chinese in all of India. They had simply left of their own accord. Baba says, "When I will, I act." He fully focuses on what He wills. He doesn't let Himself get distracted, and so whatever He wills, does take place. We can be very comforted in this. It means that He can make pretzels of weapons of mass destruction. There is nothing more powerful than God. Nothing happens without His will. And it is His will that we be as powerful as He is.

Power Means Perfect Equality

The only true power is love, wherein power is used not to dominate or control, but to join in sacred oneness with God and all others. Power struggles frequently infiltrate into marriages, teacher/student, professional/client, healer/patient and employer/employee relationships.

Marriages where husbands attempt to control through use of force such as anger, physical power and physical or verbal abuse are clearly not in alignment with honoring one's partner. The women in such situations typically respond with fear, until they see through his display. His is not power but force. Force is used by those who think themselves weak. As soon as she sees truly, she will be in a position to open the door to his stepping into his real power. Asking God to guide her, she can move the relationship into one where there is equality and an honoring and supporting of each other as God and Goddess. Then the relationship moves from a special relationship into a holy relationship. Conversely a woman may try to control her husband through manipulation, whining, pushiness, or seduction. Control over another is not power but weakness and cannot lead to happiness for either partner.

The workplace is frequently fraught with power struggles and competition as well. People think they are stressed because of their work load, or because of the particular circumstances in which they find themselves. They think they are the effect of a cause outside of themselves. They have it backwards. You are the cause of everything that happens to you. You arrange your circumstances because you want to be stressed or victimized by your particular situation, because it serves the purpose of autonomy.

The service professionals, doctors, dentists, psychologists... would do well to honor their clients equality in order that true healing take place. You are never less than the Ph.D. or the M.D. you make appoints with just because they have a qualification you don't possess. Equality is of God and therein lies your power and your strength. Do cultivate a healthy respect for another's position or expertise where appropriate. Always temper the teachings with common sense. Vulnerability and helplessness are part of the package when you choose ego as your master. Once you are willing to accept that you are the cause of everything that happens to you, you have taken the first step in reclaiming your power and thereby regaining control over your life.

You cannot be hurt by anyone or anything. If you could it would mean there is something or someone more powerful than you. That is simply not true. At the same time, you are not more powerful than anyone else. You can never do anything to hurt another. You can only attack or be attacked if that is what you both decided. You can only experience love and union with another if that is what you both decided. When did you make that decision? If you are all-powerful, you must have made it or your experience would be otherwise. You do not know when you made the decisions that are being played out because though your mind is all-powerful, you do not know your own mind.

Psychology studies subconscious and unconscious aspects of mind. You were created as conscious mind only. God does not have any unconscious aspects in His mind and He gave you His mind. It is you who chose to be unconscious or unaware of the full power of your mind. That is because you allied with an ego which uses the power of your mind to convince you that you are powerless and ignorant. Ego uses your mind to keep you from knowing your own mind. It does this only as long as you let it. Most people have hundreds of thoughts per minute and are much too tolerant of their wandering mind. Control your mind and you will know your mind. Deep breathing helps to slow down the mind. Sai Baba says, "I never think, when I will I act." There are no surprises in His life. He knows what He wills.

You are all the power in the universe, because you are as God created you and He has withheld nothing from you, His precious creation. He trusted you implicitly and entrusted you with power equal to His. So great is His faith in you. So awesome is your truth. You are grandeur and strength. Your capacity is limitless. And we all used that power to make a replacement for God. In other words we used the power of God to overthrow God. But that is impossible as God did not create us more powerful than Himself.

You cannot overstep God's will, because God is as powerful as you are. You are equal with God. He is not more powerful and He is not less powerful. If you want to do something that He does not will, it simply cannot happen. If it could, you would be more powerful than God. Nonetheless you are all-powerful. Whatever you want to be real is real for you merely by your wanting it. It cannot make it real, for only God and God's love are real. God will never conflict with you. His power is His love, and love is always patient and forbearing. If you want to make an unreal choice He will wait till you are ready to make a real one.

Use Your Power In The Service Of Truth And Reality

You are sustained by the power of God who created you. Your relationship with God is symbiotic. God depends on you as much as you depend on Him. You enhance Him and He enhances you. You made ego against God's will. As God did not will you to make ego, it is not real. When you made ego you made it real for yourself by believing in what you had made. Then you entrusted your all-powerful mind to it. It has no power of its own. It uses the power of your mind for its sustenance. The relationship you have with ego is parasitic. Ego sucks your mind dry. It uses all your God power to convince you that you are powerless. Your situation can be likened to the character in the science fiction movie who invents a robot. The robot takes over and becomes your master and you become its slave. That is exactly how it is with you and ego. Ego is not your friend. It is an illusory idea which uses all your God given power to convince you of its reality.

Faith given to illusions does not lack power, for by them you believe you are powerless. You are faithless to yourself but strong in faith in your illusions about yourself. Ego is an illusion which took you over through your consent because you put your faith in it. You are still all-powerful and you can take back your power any time you choose.

The way to regain control of your all-powerful mind is by recognizing that everything is a projection of your mind. You projected your body and the world outside of your mind. They can be used as teaching devices to show you your mind. When you start to see everything as your projection, you are perceiving correctly and this opens the door to regaining awareness of your mind and your power.

Use whatever happens to your body as an opportunity to know your mind. When it is sick, it shows you that you think you are not whole and perfect as God created you. If you knew you were whole and perfect it would be impossible for your body to become ill. So your sickness becomes a learning device. Sickness does not make you bad. It reveals an error in thinking. It reveals a simple lack. Ask God to fill the lack. All you need do is be willing to be restored to wholeness and God does the rest. You need do so little to receive so much.

No One Can Hurt You

If you are hurt by anyone, it can only be because you still think that another is more powerful than you. That is a gift, as it exposes faulty thinking. Be willing for your mind to be restored to wholeness. Be willing for a shift from victim-victimizer consciousness to God consciousness. Let God make the shift for you. All that is asked of you is a little willingness. You want it when you ask for help instead of feeling victimized. Knowing that everything happens by your desire will motivate you to want to change your mind. When you take full responsibility for everything that is happening to you, you will desire that shift. When you desire the shift, God will give you the shift in consciousness. It is desire that determines everything. If you feel jealousy, anger, pride, hatred or lust it can only be because you think that you are not all-powerful and that your power is not exactly the same as everyone else's. Ask to be restored to wholeness.

The more you see that everything that happens in your world is reflecting back to you your own mind, the more quickly you will become aware of your mind. When you know your mind, you can change it. If you are unaware that you are the cause of all that happens to you, you will feel helpless. I now know that I cannot ever be raped again. That is impossible. Consciousness has shifted from victim-victimizer consciousness to God consciousness. That type of incident simply would serve no purpose and without a purpose, it cannot happen. I am all-powerful. I know that I cannot get sick. My body does not fall ill, by God's grace. I know that my body is not to be used for attack and sickness is attack. I know that my body is not who I am, thus it is not real. Because I know this, it is impossible for me to get sick. I have taken back my power in most areas of my life.

At times I still get hurt in relation to the ones closest to me. That makes them my teachers. They still find my places of vulnerability and I am grateful to them. And I give myself permission to feel sad or hurt if that is real for me. I don't use the teachings to intellectualize myself out of feelings. And I remember the truth that they cannot hurt me. They do not have the power. I can feel hurt but that doesn't mean they hurt me. There is no one more powerful than you. That does not mean that you are responsible for the actions of others. You cannot change another. Even Baba cannot change a person's heart. He says, "I can turn earth into sky and sky into earth, but over men's hearts I have no power." We are each in charge of our own lives, but no one else's. If someone is not acting appropriately in relation to you, you can change how you relate to the situation but you cannot change them.

We do affect and influence others with the example we set. We can inspire, encourage and support others and that is effective, as we are one and our minds are joined. When I went to Ramana Maharshi's ashram, I experienced a profound silence and in that supportive container my mind naturally fell into that reverie effortlessly. Ramana's silence was influencing my mind positively because I was receptive. We can influence each other, but we have no power over anyone except ourselves.

God Is Not More Powerful Than You

We placed God outside of our minds. He did not put us outside of His mind. He yearns for the reestablishment of communication with His children. He is lonely without His children. But He has no power over when we will return to Him. That is up to us. We are all-powerful and God cannot force us to do anything we do not want to do. God's love for us is unaffectable. He loves us no matter what we do in our minds. And the truth is that we could not put God outside of our minds, though we thought we could. God placed Himself in your mind forever. He is always there. That is irrevocable. Be glad it is so. You only have the power to think things are other than they are and to make your ideas seem real. You do not have the power to alter the truth.

When Baba created the ring drama shared in Chapter 9, He set it up to inspire me to rise into my power by asking Him for a ring that was specifically intended for me and not to settle for one that was originally intended for someone else. I did not settle for being less than God. In that moment, equality with God was reestablished in my mind. That drama permitted a shift in consciousness, where I recognized I am a Goddess, as powerful as God. I know my Father and I are one.

You have the power to think that God is separate from you and to project Him outside of your mind. God does not have the power to stop you from thinking that because you are all-powerful. This does not make your idea true, though it may seem true for you. You would only want to think that God is not in you when you listen to ego. Ego wants you to believe God is separate and fearful. Once you know who God is, you will want Him in your mind and will invite Him to stay. God is pure love and wants you to be happy. To recognize that you have God's love in your mind is so awesome and overwhelmingly wonderful.

God cannot heal the separation with you as He did not create it. We tend to blame Him for the abandonment we feel, because we see Him as all-powerful and so how could things that are not peaceful or joyful happen except at His whim? But His power cannot be forced upon us for the very fact that He created us free and honors us as all-powerful. If God had separated from us He could reunite with His beloved children. But He has no power over that reestablishment of communication because He did not will communication be severed. You and I are responsible and communication is reestablished when we so choose. In truth communication was not severed, but lack of communication certainly has been our experience. Because the truth has not been affected, God's power has not been usurped by us.

God cannot force His love on you by its very nature. That would not be love. He is not more powerful than you. If you do not wish to receive His love, He can only wait in patient loving tenderness. If you wish to descend into hell, He has no power to prevent you. You are all-powerful. There is nothing opposing your will. In interviews Baba frequently asks, "What do you want?" The correct answer is, "I am always getting exactly what I want in each moment." If that is so, then we can look at what we have and decide if it is really what we want.

Do you really want the sickness, suffering, lack and conflict that are necessarily part of autonomy? Is that really what you want? Do you want the competitiveness that proves you greater than or less than others? Do you want the pleasure/pain syndrome that keeps your specialness in tact? Do you want the sacrifice that fame, fortune, glory, reputation and adulation demand? Or do you just want to merge with God and others in the full recognition that we are all exactly alike, that we are all equal? In that you recognize that we are all of equal power, glory, holiness and innocence. No one is better, no one is less, not even God. We are all so much more alike than we are different. Once we understand that, we can really start to enjoy our relationships with God and each other.

Love is the only power. *Only love is strong, because it is undivided.* Love is so powerful it can move mountains. What are you doing with all your God given power? What do you really want? Do you want peace and happiness for all humanity, or do you still want to gain at another's expense? If you do not want peace and happiness for all you do not want it for yourself. Do you want to be who you are, or do you want autonomy, specialness, or grandiosity? Do you want to be one with everyone and everything or do you want praise, adulation and inequality? Do you want to be put on a pedestal, to be seen as special, better than, or holier than? God is humility, grandeur, power and love. You are God. There is nothing outside of you that can add in any way to what you already know, are and have.

Reclaim Your Power Now

Many students get sucked into spiritual movements where they give their power away to their teacher. Sai Baba empowers us by reminding us to follow our hearts. The ego-oriented teacher is out to dominate you. *A true teacher will always want to absolve you finally from the need for a teacher.* A true teacher will set himself up as a way shower, rather than as one who promises to do it for you. If you think your salvation depends on your teacher, you are in the wrong relationship. You are your own savior. No one, not even God, can do it for you. A spiritual or religious group in which you are not free to leave is not a true offering and will not help you to your destination of freedom from bondage. If you leave the Catholic church you are damned to hell. This is an example of use of force instead of power. Viciousness comes from the need to defend an untrue thought system. Truth needs no defense. Defense is how untruth is maintained, but also how it is exposed.

A true student will find a true teacher. A true teacher is one who looks after the welfare of the student and is unconcerned about his reputation or how many students he has gathered around him. And he supports and even encourages his students to move on when that is correct and appropriate. Do not let others use their power inappropriately in relation to you and do not use your power inappropriately either. Teacher/student is just one type of relationship where there is a tendency to surrender your power. You also give your power away to doctors and dentists every time you let them make decisions for you. You defer to them because of their expertise in the area. But the power of decision is your own. When you give it away, you set yourself up for future regrets. In the work place the boss is frequently given power over his employees. You have rights and when you know what they are you will act in ways that preserve your honor and dignity. If you are a boss, it is right to cultivate a healthy respect in your employees, but that through love rather than domination or subordination.

Manipulating Events To Suit Desires Is Misuse Of Power

There are those 'new-agers' who hold the idea that power means the ability to get themselves parking spaces or to manifest whatever they want. You are already getting what you want. To use the power of your mind in a manipulative or coercive way is a misappropriation of power. It is a little like walking on coals or bending spoons. If it does not heal, it is a misdirection of power. Using your mind to get what you want masks symptoms and does not solve your problem. To solve the problem we need to get in touch with the seed idea from which all thoughts, actions and effects spring. The seed idea behind manipulating events is lack of trust in God. When we trust God to know what is best we are not giving our power away. Instead, we are directing our power appropriately and can rest assured that we will be empowered by that surrender. As our power comes from God, by entrusting it to God we are merely acknowledging Him as our Source.

What about Sai Baba and His manifestation of objects, you may wonder? Baba says they are His calling cards. They instill faith and give joy to His devotees. He does not manifest for show. He did not undertake yogic practices to attain powers. He came onto the planet with these abilities as God incarnate. He is Divine and limitless and His love expresses in that and many other ways. Love is creative and limitless. This is different from the yogi who walked on water out of pride of attainment through self-effort.

Be Assertive, Not Aggressive

If you find yourself in a situation where you are being violated in any way, how should you respond? Always honor yourself and do that which serves your truth. Power should not be expressed as force, might or hurtful acts either in relation to yourself or others. Be true to yourself. Be mighty in splendor, dignity and honoring of yourself. You are God's purity, holiness and sanctity. You deserve the best because of who you are. Let everything that happens be used to reveal to you that goodness, beauty and holiness are what you truly want because they are what you are. You should only want to be treated like the Goddess or the God that you are. If that is not what is happening, then use what is happening to bridge the gap. Ask to be shown what to do.

I cannot change anyone. I can only change myself. Once I really know I am a Goddess, I cannot but be treated as such. Don't settle for less than the best for yourself. You deserve the best. You have the power within you to have the best. You are all the power in the universe. Never forget your awesome inheritance. Cultivate it. Nurture it. Realize it. Turn to God. With God all things are possible. Without God nothing is possible. Every impossible situation can be brought to wholeness. There is nothing that is impossible when you stand in the strength of who you are as God created you.

Watch any tendency to justify being a victimizer with, "There are no victims. Whatever I am doing to another, they have requested or it could not happen." This reasoning is a misapplication of the teaching and is taking enough spiritual knowledge to hang yourself. Help ever - hurt never. When you hurt another, you are hurting yourself. It is not your business to support another's victim consciousness. Your business is to treat ALL with the utmost respect, kindness and gratitude.

Everyone deserves the best, as all are precious children of a most holy loving God, and it is God's will that all His children be treated as Divine, regardless of their actions. No one with past karma or victim/victimizer consciousness need balance the scales. They need only shift from victim/victimizer consciousness to God consciousness and all karmic consequences are wiped away by God's grace. You can help make that shift by treating everyone with honor and dignity. When you do that you know your truth as God created you and you remind others of their truth by your living example. At the very least you need not play a role in balancing the scales for someone else.

Use Nonviolent Resistance Against Injustice

What about the bullies in your life? Do you just remind yourself that you cannot be hurt and that you are doing this to yourself, when you get nailed up on the cross for the hundredth time? Sai Baba says to resist injustice, while Jesus says to resist not evil. I hear Sai Baba to say don't be passive or complacent in the face of injustice. And I hear Jesus to say don't fight it. The Aramaic word for resist means "to stand against." Jesus is instructing us not to act in kind as in an eye for an eye. At the same time, Jesus life was not one of being passive in the face of injustice.

Baba and Jesus are both saying essentially the same thing though it may sound on the surface that they are giving opposite messages. We always have to dive deep and then the right interpretation and the right application will reveal itself. When the twin towers was hit in the fall of 2001, Baba advised to send pink light to Osama bin Laden, to President Bush and to all those families who were terrorized. He did not advise doing nothing. He advised resisting evil. Meet it with goodness. Meet hatred with love. That is how evil is overcome.

To love does not mean to let yourself be stepped on. Jesus said, "If anyone strikes you on the right cheek turn the other also, and if anyone wants to sue you and take your outer garment, give your undergarment as well. And if one of the occupation troops forces you to carry his pack one mile, go two." This sounds like he was advising his followers to let themselves be trampled upon. But Jesus' life was an example of resisting injustices and violations. There is a plausible explanation.

The Romans were misusing their power to dominate the Jews. They treated the Jews with a lack of honor and dignity that is everyone's due. They would strike the Jews into submission with the back of their left hand. They didn't have toilet paper in those days and the left was considered unclean. If the Jew should offer the left cheek it would put the Roman in the untenable position of having to use the right hand or the hand which was reserved for equals. Offering the left cheek was an assertion of equality. Jesus was not suggesting that the Jews be passive, complacent or resigned to injustices in their lives, but to meet evil with nonviolent resistance.

When Jesus instructed the poor to give their undergarments he was advising those who were being unfairly taxed to remove their underwear when they were stripped of their outer garments due to inability to pay their taxes. This action of utter nakedness brought shame on their creditors, so again it was an act of nonviolent resistance against injustice. Jesus was not teaching passiveness or submissiveness. He was teaching active nonviolent resistance.

As to carrying their packs two miles, Roman soldiers would force Jewish civilians to carry their heavy packs, but the law mandated they be carried no more than one mile. When a peasant carried a pack more than a mile the soldier became culpable for violation of military law. It was a different era and we cannot take literally everything that got said for the particular circumstances that had to be dealt with at that time. You know in your heart what is right. To be passive in the face of injustice is to condone it and thereby to judge it. Non-judgment is not passive. You deserve the best because of who you are. So does every living thing including the victimizer. You serve him by seeing that his actions are not real and by remembering for him that he is as God created him. Do not condone his actions or you do him a disservice.

You are a precious child of God. You do not deserve to be unjustly treated under any circumstances. If you are not being treated as the Goddess or God that you are, something is wrong and you can turn to God to show you how to remedy your situation. Don't justify or rationalize ill-treatment from anyone. Do not think that it is your bad karma coming back to you, that you have to put up with it because you have no alternatives, that you deserve it or that you stand to learn from your circumstances. You deserve the best only and always. Turn to God and you will be given nonviolent solutions to every problem.

Force is a misuse of power and is not to be tolerated. If you truly love yourself, you will never use force to get anything, nor will you permit force to be used against you. Take back your power O holy child of God. It was you who gave it away. It is yours whenever you so choose. There is no one more powerful than you. Nothing can happen to you that you have not asked for. If you don't like it, change your circumstances. If you don't know how to change them, ask for help. With God all things are possible. Walk the earth with your head held high in the glory of your mighty power. Be empowered in the knowledge of your splendorous truth and may all go well with you always. Love is the only power. May the power of your love transform the world into a sublime masterpiece where all are empowered to lead lives of dignity as it was always meant to be.

Our all-powerful, all-loving Father/Mother God, thank You for creating us as powerful as You. What an awesome trust You have placed in us, Your creations. Thank You for honoring us and wanting only the best for us. Love is the power you have given Your Divinely loved children. Show us how to use our power to honor and glorify You. Show us how to use our power in the service of all our brothers and sisters toward the end of the misuse of power in its entirety. Show us how to use our power for love and for healing this beautiful world. May all beings everywhere take back their power so they may live with dignity, honor and holiness as You intended for all eternity for all Your precious children.

May all beings in all the worlds be happy and blest, Amen.

Figure 17 – God Created You To Be As Powerful As He Is

Everything (Eternity)

Eternity	Life	Oneness
God-Dependence	Love	Freedom
Real	Truth	Non-judgment
Heaven	Peace	Creation
Innocence	Knowledge	**All-Powerful**

Nothing (time and space)

Time/space	**Happy Dream (Satva) God's solution - collapses time**
Ego-dependence	Expanding into limitless power
Unreal	Self-confidence
Hell	Nonviolent resistance to injustice/All deserve the best
Guilt	Trust yourself/Follow your heart/Trust God within
Death	**Nightmare (Rajo Guna) - makes time**
Fear	force/attack/aggression
Untruth	Dominance/manipulation/coercion
War	Violation - victim/victimizer
Ignorance	Misuse of power
Separation	**Deep Sleep (Thamo) Ego's solution - freezes time**
Bondage	Powerless, helpless
Judgment	Passive
Miscreation	Complacent in presence of injustice
Powerless	Denial of mistreatment
	condone imperfection

Direction of Consciousness Awakening

Chapter 18

My Personal Journey To Truth

To attain enlightenment is the greatest service you can render to the planet.
Sai Baba

My Innocence?

I had been studying with a Kahuna master for over a year and had moved to Hawaii to immerse myself in his teachings. It was the summer of 1981, and what started out to be a normal day on the beautiful island of Oahu would change the course of my life forever. On that momentous day my teacher announced that there was an Avatar on the planet, an incarnation of God. In that pronouncement I recognized what I had been looking for, for a very long time. I just knew that God was on earth in human form and wanted with all my heart to be with Him. I was going to India to see Sai Baba.

A friend who had been to India to meet with his teacher advised me to travel with a group, as traveling alone was not advisable for a young woman (I was 26 at the time). I just assumed that Sai Baba would arrange. Within a few days a couple walked into Kapahulu Health Food Store where I worked the juice bar as chief cook and bottle washer. I spontaneously found myself asking out loud if they were going to India to see Sai Baba. They were as surprised as I that I should ask and in fact were headed to Baba's very soon. Their group consisted of eight members and Baba had told them internally that He would be sending a ninth.

We arrived on February 2, 1982, and Baba was in Brindavan, His smaller ashram near Bangalore. My anticipation was at an all time high as this was the first time I would see God in human form. I expected fireworks, neon lights and a tingling sensation throughout my whole body and so much more. It would undoubtedly be the most incredible moment of my life. Finally out came this tiny elegant figure in His simple orange robe and shock of black Afro hair. He was grace in action, gentle and unassuming. I watched His every move. He spoke to some and took letters from others. His every gesture and word seemed suffused with loving kindness; so gracious, so effortless and so tender. Then slowly, gracefully, He floated away.

I liked Him instantly. However, the experience fell far short of my expectations. There were no extraordinary feelings, sights or sounds. It was all so natural and lacking in sensation. As He was disappearing from view, I asked in my heart, "Is that it?" An inner voice, new and clear, which I immediately recognized as His, said tenderly, "When you know who you are, you will have some idea of who I am." I had my assignment: to discover who I am. What a profound and simple communication.

The following day Baba asked how many in our group and where we were from. I told Him we were nine from Hawaii. It was a very natural conversation, as though I was talking to a dear friend and we'd known each other forever. He then said He would see us tomorrow. Our group was very excited. We ladies put on our best saris and completed our outfits with fresh flowers for our hair. The men were all in spotless white. When He came out, instead of calling us, Baba invited a group of forty devotees from Australia. As He was passing I asked if He was planning to see us. He said there were already too many and what could He do?

I was crestfallen and felt stood up. How could He promise and then not follow through? His name is Sathya Sai Baba - Sathya means truth. How could He lead us on? I was to learn that tomorrow was not necessarily to be taken literally; after all, time is not real. I stayed another six weeks and found I really liked Baba. In fact I fell head over heals in love. So I wrote Him a love letter letting Him know how wonderful I thought He was and how I appreciated His life of loving service to humanity. One day He was giving a talk to which I happened to take my letter. After the talk He walked up our aisle, right to me. It was such a surprise. He took my letter and looked into my eyes. I felt a transmission of the deepest love. For days I was transported into a state of sweet bliss.

Though I was smitten, I was young, restless and eager to visit all the holy sites in India. I went to Professor Kasturi, who had privately taught me the Gayatri mantra complete with perfect intonation and pronunciation. We had bonded and I adored him, seeing him as Baba's most ardent devotee. I asked him to advise me where I should travel. He shook his head helplessly and said, "My child, this is the holiest spot in all of India, and even the whole world. Why go anywhere else?"

"But, Professor Kasturi, if Sai Baba is who He says He is, He is in my heart and will be with me wherever I go."

He shrugged his shoulders in resignation and gave me a list of his favorite sites in the North, so off I went. I visited the Shivananda Ashram in Rishikesh, saw Anandamoyi-Ma in Haridwar, and lived on a houseboat in Srinigar visiting all the beautiful mogul gardens there. I went to the Aurobindo Ashram in Nanital; to Bhodgaya, Buddha's birthplace; to Ayodhya, Rama's birthplace, and trekked the Himalayas of Nepal. Toward the end of my spiritually rich adventure, I lived for a month in a tent in an ashram in Phalgam in the Himalayas at about 10,000 feet elevation and followed their severe meditation practices.

As a service project I was asked to type letters to be sent to all the guru's students, inviting them to come for Guru Purnima, a celebration honoring the teacher. As there was no facility for reproducing the letter, I manually typed each letter. After about the fiftieth invitation it dawned on me that I ought to see my guru for Guru Purnima. That was just days before the holy festival and I was way up North. Suddenly everything in me knew I had to be with Baba for that holy day and I hurriedly made the necessary arrangements. In my rush, I found myself flying from Delhi to Bangalore late at night. When asked where I was spending the night I conceded that I had made no plans. My questioner warned that it was very late and that Bangalore was not safe for foreigners at night. I trusted Baba to take care.

When I took my seat, the lady next to me struck up a conversation. I told her my destination. It just so happened that she was also going to Baba's for Guru Purnima and I was welcome to accompany her. Would I like to be her house guest for the night? It all got taken care of without any effort, because I simply, innocently trusted Baba. When I arrived at her home, her walls were covered with pictures of Baba and other Avatars and great saints. Next morning we reached Prasanthi Nilayam and celebrated Guru Poornima with all the joy and honoring that the day represents.

I stayed on for a week after the celebration and then returned home. I had spent seven mind-expanding months in India and Nepal. It was a wonderful adventure and indeed Sai Baba was with me. Interestingly, during my travels a number of seers approached me all bearing a similar message: 'Very special marriage, age 33.' I had no intention to marry as I was on a spiritual quest. But after hearing the same future prediction five times, I found I could not overlook it.

A few years later, in an interview, I asked Baba if He thought it a good idea to marry. "Yes, yes, choose husband," was His reply. I asked Him to choose for me, but He had already turned away and was talking to someone else. After the interview I sat on the steps to my flat and thought about who I would like to marry since the Lord had just given me *cart blanche* to marry whom ever I wished. I confided to Him in my heart, 'I would like to marry Your most ardent devotee, someone who loves You as much as Professor Kasturi.'

'How about Al Drucker?' came a voice responding to my thoughts. I was startled and turned to see who was reading my mind, but there was no one. I knew of Mr. Drucker as I had attended his lectures to the overseas devotees. He was working as professor in Baba's university and was very popular among the foreigners.

I didn't trust that voice and thought it was probably my wild imagination. Up to that point I had regarded Mr. Drucker as an inspiring teacher who provoked deep thinking. Now my thoughts started to revolve around him more and more. Needless to say, it was not so much his teachings that were spinning around in my mind, but rather pure feelings of Divine love and joy. It was my secret though and I didn't let on to anyone.

The next time I visited the ashram, our group was called up, but Baba singled me out and said very sweetly, "Not you." I slithered off the verandah and wanted to disappear. Imagine what thousands of people must have thought of me at that moment. Three times with three different groups I was asked to leave in the same way. By the third humiliation, it dawned on me that Baba did not want me to ask my burning question about marriage to Drucker.

I was determined not to move without Baba's Divine direction. One day while I was living at a Sai center in California I happened to be accompanying a Sai devotee who was also living there, on her work route. She had undertaken a service project of visiting the elderly. Al's mother was on her list. I had no idea that Helen Drucker lived right in my neighborhood. We struck up a conversation and became fast friends through our mutual interest in her darling son.

Just a tiny sidelight: Once Al was giving a lecture at an international conference of space scientists on a new missile project that he was instrumental in designing during his stint in the nuclear arms race. His mom was sitting in the back of the auditorium at her insistence that she be permitted to attend. Finally she could contain herself no longer and blurted out in a loud Jewish mama voice, "Mine son! Mine son!" Needless to say she didn't get to attend any more of his lectures. He couldn't have been more embarrassed or she more proud.

She invited me back to her home and asked me to read a book Al had published and sent to her. She coyly confessed that she couldn't read. That started weekly visits. Later, her daughter Goldie became adamant that she move to a retirement home because Helen lived alone. Goldie was afraid she might fall and no one would know for days perhaps. Al's mom was 96 years old at the time. She asked me and I agreed to move in with her. So there I was making some pretty bold moves into my secret love's family's hearts and homes. All part of God's Divine plan unfolding perfectly?

Some time passed and again I went to see Sai Baba. Again Baba called our group, and this time I didn't get sent back. First thing He did was call me lazy. I was surprised, as I am by nature very industrious and self-motivated. I feared He was reprimanding me for loitering at the ashram for six months at a stretch. (I was spending half the year there in those days and the other half pulling together enough resources to go back to India to be with my beloved Baba).

During the small group portion of the interview, He asked how long I was planning to stay. It was September and I hesitated because of my earlier association between lazy and length of stay, but told Him I wished to stay through Christmas with His permission. He exclaimed, "Oh stay for Christmas, for birthday, for Dasara. This is your home. Stay as long as you like." So sweet, and it cleared up any doubts that 'lazy' might be associated with tarrying too long at the ashram.

He started that semiprivate interview by asking if there were any questions, then leaning toward me He commented mischievously, "Spiritual questions only." When He got up to go, I was fairly exploding because even though I had promised not to ask, I wanted with all my heart to have some direct confirmation from Him. I blurted out, "Baba?" He playfully responded, "I know your question, I will tell later." One month later He looked at me deeply, penetratingly, during darsan and then nodded, "Yes."

By now my timid love had become an all-consuming flame. Four suspense-filled years had passed and I could hardly contain my secret any longer. Baba had called me lazy in the interview. I sat with that and what dawned was that He was directing me to go for the chase. So I wrote a 'Dear Al' letter, telling him everything. He happened to be 'dying' in the ashram hospital. I sent my letter with his aide and then felt I had done my duty, as I couldn't possibly ever see him again. What an embarrassing position I found myself in.

As fate would have it, a close mutual friend was off to visit him and insisted that I come with her. I tried to resist, but she was persistent and so I resigned myself to seeing my beloved. As soon as we showed up he pulled me aside and laughingly joked, "So you're in love with a dying man?" I blushed and words failed me. When we left, I found myself sobbing uncontrollably. At darsan Baba looked at me and I knew everything was going to be all right. In fact Al soon returned to the USA where he made a complete recovery.

And now I was on a mission to land the man I loved. Thus started a barrage of letters intent on persuading Al to marry me. Twice previously he had been instructed not to marry. Baba had told him on a number of occasions, "No ladies." Baba had also informed him that he didn't need marriage. So he had concluded that he had been Divinely directed not to marry. It was hard work to try to persuade him otherwise.

Many looked to Al as guide, counselor, healer and storyteller. Some referred to him as the 'Prince of Prasanthi.' He was older than me by nearly 28 years, being over 60 at that time. His background was Jewish, mine, Christian. He was brilliant. I was naive at best. I was shy, awkward, a simple preschool teacher and a farmer's daughter. I had no worldly qualifications to speak of to be going after this 'very prominent' Sai devotee. The odds against my convincing him were pretty ridiculous. It was an impossible situation and yet the love I felt for him directed my every move.

Al had been catapulted out of India on his 60th birthday, accused of being a spy, and so was now going back and forth between India and USA. Before that shift, he had lived at the ashram for 8 years, teaching in Baba's university, giving lectures to foreigners, conducting study circles for the other professors and designing educational programs that were being adopted in universities all over India. When he was in the US, he would come to visit his mom who I just happened to be living with. Each visit, I'd come bounding out of the house to greet him and he'd start off very formal, stiff and protective. By the end of the visit, we were laughing and loving each other. Next visit, it would start all over again. But despite his hesitation, he found joy in my company as I did in his and he warmed up to the idea of our sharing our lives together.

In the fall of 1988, Al returned to the ashram and I followed a few months later after finishing my teaching responsibilities. In February of 1989, at the coconut stand at Baba's ashram, I confided to Al my plans for return to USA. He happened to be flying back on the same airline on the same day and we became a couple. Back in California, we enjoyed the Big Sur Coast for several months and then came to stay with Al's mom. She was 98 and we doted on her until her passing. After putting her affairs in order, I wanted nothing more than to go to the ashram for Baba's blessings. I wanted very much for Al to come along. He was reluctant. I persisted and he came. When we arrived, Baba was in Brindavan. As He walked by, He gave Al a quick frown. Next day when Al reached the gate, attendants blocked his entry. He was not permitted inside the ashram. He went to Puttaparti where he had a flat and stayed there for a few days. Our group was called for an interview. Inside the interview room, I asked, "Baba, may Al Drucker and I have Your blessings to marry?" He retorted gruffly, "Why do you want to marry that man? His body is filled with cancer." I responded, "I love him, I'll take care of him." He shouted back, "You're worse than an animal!" I was not alone and that pronouncement spread through the ashram like wildfire. I was branded the seductress who had stolen Baba's boy.

Previous interchanges with Baba had been the purest, sweetest love, but now it was time to go to work. Once in a dream Baba and I were in the forest playing hide and seek. It was so much fun. Then He came face-to-face, so close and laughingly asked, "Will you play with Me like this when I'm Prema Sai?" (Prema Sai is to be His next incarnation – Baba's mission of planetary transformation will span three incarnations of which the present is the second). "Oh, no, Swami, I want to BE Prema Sai with You."

He seemed pleased, though compassionate in my behalf, and commented, "That won't be so easy." I had been warned.

Al and I married and a year later, on my next visit to the ashram I wanted more than anything for Baba to take Al back. I asked the office to please request in my behalf. One hour later, two tall strapping men knocked on the door and asked if I was Mrs. Drucker. I acknowledged that I was and there upon was asked to leave immediately. Their instruction came direct from Baba. He told them I was a disgrace to the ashram.

Before my trip I had paid a visit to a friend who happened to have a new deck of tarot cards. He asked me to pull one. I pulled 'disgrace.' He said, "Great card! It means God's grace. Dis or Dios means God." It seemed a stretch at the time, but when I heard that pronouncement, I immediately remembered and took my dismissal as God's grace. Was this drama all God's grace unfolding as part of His Divine plan to help me relive that moment of terror when I traded in paradise for hell, so that my error could finally be healed?

A year after I was thrown out, I felt the urge to go to the ashram again. With trepidation, I arrived. Baba called me in for an interview. Al had just finished the <u>Sai Baba Gita</u> book. I gave Baba a copy. He looked through it slowly and seemed very pleased. He didn't say anything and I couldn't resist plucking up the courage to ask if Drucker could come back to the ashram. "Why?" He asked gruffly. "Because he loves You, Baba." He said some strong words and then raised His hand as if to strike me on the cheek. He stopped just short and then turned abruptly away.

I was holding onto His feet. As He briskly turned away, His feet didn't flinch. There was no tension in them at all. The message seemed to be, 'hold on to the feet,' the idea being that no matter what it looks like on the outside, peace and succor can be found in that which doesn't change. I was totally surrendered and trusted that He knew best. After He turned away, another lady in the room said, "Baba, I love You." Immediate He responded with all the sweetness of a thousand mothers, "I love you too." There was no anger whatsoever, though He had appeared livid moments before.

The next year I was back for more. I was resilient and never stopped loving Baba or trusting His inscrutable ways. Another interview - this time I was smarter. I determined I would not ask about Al and thereby avoid another clobbering. But to my surprise, He asked very sweetly "How is husband?" and tears of relief tumbled down my cheeks. "He's fine, Baba; he sends his love." He gently patted me on the head.

On my next visit, Baba manifested the ring for me detailed in Chapter 9. He was restoring my self-worth. In a subsequent interview during the same visit, He sweetly asked, "I made ring, you like?" "Oh Baba it is beautiful and I love You very much." He answered, "I love you too." Then

He went into a blissful trance and the whole room was transported into ecstasy. Later, He looked at me as though to elicit a question, which spontaneously, effortlessly, flowed from my lips without any forethought, "Baba, I long for husband to come back to the ashram." "I know your longing. He is a good man, a very good man, and YOU are always working for Me."

A Course In Miracles Deepens Understanding

Back at home a couple moved into the neighborhood and started A Course in Miracles study group. We both attended the first meeting and then I continued to meet with the group. When I again left for the ashram Al decided to attend in my place. Upon my return to the USA, the ideas in the course had taken hold and he was impassioned. We started to go to workshops in Roscoe, New York and Sedona, Arizona. We held study circles in our home after the couple that got us started moved on. We found ourselves living, breathing, studying and teaching the course. And we were filtering it through our own understandings, thus found ourselves differing on what Jesus meant in many of the passages.

When next I went to the ashram in the spring of 1999, I took the book with me and read it from cover to cover. Upon leaving Baba appeared in a dream. "Baba, I'm studying A Course In Miracles," I blurted out excitedly.

"Yes, yes, I know, very, very happy. But you haven't understood it in your gut." He pointed to His tummy. "Don't worry. I'm sending you a teacher." I find it interesting that He didn't say that I hadn't gotten it in my head or heart. It was in my loins that I was to get it, in the deepest recesses of my being. I also think it interesting that He used the word, 'gut,' as Baba is very refined. It turns out that the teacher He sent, by contrast, was coarse, and so 'gut' was to confirm that I was not mistaken when, after some time, I had doubts about whether this was really the teacher He had in mind.

Upon my return to USA, Al told me about a teacher of a group that was studying the course. They would hold a function in San Francisco shortly. He had already booked a flight and I was welcome to join him, so I did. I liked the teacher and the group. They seemed dedicated, loving and full of joy. We joined their academy for the summer of '99. Most people at the academy stay on in a total commitment, giving up all previous connections and giving themselves fully to the teachings of the course as interpreted by their teacher. It was great. We felt alive again, having been given a new purpose and a greater extended family.

By the end of the summer we proceeded to our residence in Colorado. Months later when I again left for India, Al returned to the academy. I took my course book with me. This time as I read it, the pages jumped out at me as never before. I fairly drank them in. I was experiencing epiphany after epiphany, revelation after revelation. Everything came together. My summer at the academy had opened the door to profound and deep understandings. It was the catalyst that drove me to do my own inner research. I was looking for support for what resonated deep in my heart as it differed from the way Jesus' teachings were being presented at the academy. On my own, I would never have bothered to search so deeply. The teacher was the irritant that would produce a pearl, which made him the perfect teacher for motivating me to understand the course in the very essence of my being.

On a subsequent trip to Baba's ashram in 2001, I had a most profound spiritual awakening. I saw the underpinnings of the whole ego thought system and emerged free. I exploded into light. It was such a liberating moment and precious gift. Every detail of the drama leading up to this moment had been a perfect prop for my enlightenment. Mariah, a psychic friend sitting next to me, whispered, "Yaani, whatever it is, your aura has just expanded to infinity and you are shooting off sparks of love and joy to all humanity." In that moment I understood everything both in my personal life and for all of humanity. All my doubts about who I am and what my purpose is disappeared. It was as though the code had been broken and ego stood exposed. Ego was seen as the nothingness it has always been. It was a glorious, victorious moment.

During that same trip, I had another powerful experience - a dream with the teacher of A Course in Miracles assigned to me by Baba in an earlier dream. In this dream, he had just finished his teaching session and requested me to dance with him. As we twirled around the room I couldn't help but notice that all the faces looking on were glowing in the recognition of the power for good for the whole of humanity that our coming together signified. Then we came to a standstill and our minds totally merged in a surge of energy that caused my body to collapse to the floor. There was a deep sense of his total honoring of Al as my husband, and a perfect equality with no taint of him in the role of teacher or me in that of student. It was an experience of utter purity and the deepest compassion in service to all humanity. I awoke with my whole body trembling and my kundalini vibrating as I have never experienced before or since. It was so beautiful and confirming of the heavenly experience of two minds perfectly joined as one in truth.

Confirmation Of Enlightenment

In the summer of 2002, I took off for the Himalayas. It was a surprise to me, as it was the last thing I thought I'd ever be guided to do. My friend Deva clairvoyantly directed me that this was my next step. When I asked for what purpose could I possibly have to go there, she responded, "For marriage to Shiva." She also said something about needing to anchor in my enlightenment. After much resistance on my part and much support from the universe, I took the leap.

Upon arriving in Delhi, I traveled by bus to Rishikesh and then from Rishikesh to Gangotri. The scenery was as spectacular as the hairpin curves were treacherous. I went during monsoon season. There were torrential downpours where the heavens fairly opened. Frequently the roads were washed out and we would find ourselves stuck for perhaps several hours on the side of the mountain, about as far from civilization as one could ever hope to be. There's something thrilling about it actually. Monsoon season generally lasts from mid-July through mid-September. Then it gets sunny again for two months before winter sets in and everything closes down for the season. The up side of my timing, beginning of August, was that there were hardly any tourists.

When I arrived in Gangotri, I took a room at Mandakini Hotel, fairly clean and decent. There is no electricity so one has to adjust. They turn a generator on when it gets dark, which gives you only lights and also noise. Living conditions are appallingly stark for the shopkeepers and guides. After a few days, I shifted to Yog Niketan, an ashram, where I had my own little cabin. It was cozy and offered spectacular views of the jagged peaks from my door. You can telephone, but no opportunity to e-mail, so communicating with the outside world is not easy. I liked not having the temptation, as I really went for my God connection and gave myself a break from my focus on personal matters.

In Gangotri, I bathed in the River Ganga, sat on her banks and took lots of hikes. The scenery is breath taking and there are plenty of trails to enjoy. There are also lots of babas to visit. I discovered a few genuine ones, but most of them were not really renunciates in my opinion. The mauni (silent) babas were gesticulating wildly with their hands, or writing in the sand and there was a lot of smoking of gange (pot). Some even confessed that they were attempting to blow out their lungs so they could get to God more quickly - I don't think so. Almost all of them wanted something from me, a white face. When I asked the purpose for their renunciation, there was rarely a lofty answer.

I met one young man whose company I enjoyed very much. His name is Lakshmana and he shared his experiences of his teacher. It turns out his teacher was Ramakrishna in a previous birth. In this life his name was Sri Ram Sharma Acharaya. He recently left his body, but had some fascinating experiences with the Rishis in the Himalayas. His account helped me to appreciate just how fortunate I was to be there. The rishis directed him to keep a candle lit 24 hours a day and to chant Gayatri for the uplift of all humanity, as well as eat a simple diet consisting mostly of specially prepared barley. I adopted his practice with the eternal flame and the Gayatri while in the energy of the rishis. It was so effortless. The Himalayas are a huge repository of spiritual vibration and while there I found spiritual focus naturally became foreground and life's vicissitudes simply lost their hold.

On the 13th day I went to Tapovan where the great Rishis are said to reside. The trek from Gangotri is about 24 kilometers. You can arrange to have guides lead the way and horses to carry your packs. I went on foot with Bhagavan (God) as my companion. When I neared Gomuk, the headwaters of the Ganges, I was warned not to cross the glacier without a guide as it was breaking up and there were unexpected and dangerous crevices. I trusted Swami to take care and indeed when I arrived at Gomuk, there was a man with a guide who invited me to join him after he had his bath. I took the opportunity while waiting to bathe as well and then we embarked on the one-kilometer crossing of the glacier, followed by a very steep ascent at high altitude. Tapovan is at 13,000 feet elevation.

There are some babas living in caves, though they generally don't give darshan to the tourists, as they are continuously absorbed in the Absolute. The air was so charged and the energy so clean, that I reacted to my thoughts as though they were violations. But Gayatri came effortlessly. I spent the night in a cave with a mata-ji who cooked extraordinarily delicious food for us – a miracle considering where we were. Next morning the sky was crystal clear and Shivalinga Peak stood unveiled in all his majesty. It was truly a spectacle to behold and a rare blessing that the sky was so blue and free of rain or clouds. Every day I had asked Baba if I should make the ascent and was directed internally to wait. The day He finally gave the go-ahead was the first clear day.

On the way down, I met Steve from England, who invited me to join him in his vehicle back down to Uttar Kashi. It had been exactly two weeks and Deva had said that I would be given the next step in two weeks. Gangotri had been a perfect indoctrination, with the swirling gush of the mighty River Ganga hurling pell-mell from its source nourishing and enveloping me and filling me with its power. Even at Gomuk, now the source of the headwaters, the river made its entry with tremendous force. The glaciers have receded some 18 kilometers from Gangotri since the Ganga alighted on Shiva's crown thousands of years earlier, as the story goes. Ganga is a mighty river, huge and powerful, interlaced with several gorgeous picturesque waterfalls in Gangotri.

Lakshmana, the friend I met earlier, lived in Uttar Kashi and had invited me to visit him. He had returned about a week earlier. So I took a hotel room nearby and stayed for a few days and read his teacher's book, My Life and Inheritance. In it he talked of Kedarnath as a strong Shiva spot and as I was keen to go for Shiva energy, I felt led to go to Kedarnath next. I took the bus to Gaurikunj, the last point for vehicles. On the way someone told me to visit Triyugi Narayan, a nearby hamlet, as that was purported to have been the place where Shiva and Parvati had married thousands of years earlier. That sparked my interest as I was always looking for clues to what Deva meant by marriage to Shiva.

I felt a yearning to have some clear confirmation that I was really on track in being in the Himalayas as I still felt uncertain about needing to go anywhere to get anything. On the five-kilometer trek to Triyugi Narayan I asked for a sign. I prayed, "Baba, if You are with me, please show me by feeding me lunch." When I arrived I was shown the marriage spot where there is now a pandal and beautifully embossed stone. There is also an eternal flame and a fire pit in a very ancient temple. It was explained to me that Shiva and Parvati walked around the pit seven times. I asked if I could walk around it. The priest asked where my husband was. I persisted. So with Shiva before me, behind me, within me, above me and around me, I walked the fire pit ceremoniously seven times. I put on my shoes and started to leave, when a renunciate called me over. I asked if he wanted Dakshina, (money) as I was kind of tired of all the babas pestering for something or other because of my white face. He laughed and assured me he only wanted to extend his love and to meet me as his sister. His genuineness warmed my heart.

After some chatting, I asked his purpose. He said he was praying for a vision of Parvati, Shiva's consort. He invited me to have lunch with him. He bustled around fixing the most delicious and wholesome food and fed me till I was nearly bursting, and then still he wanted to feed me more. He was so childlike, innocent, joyful and pure. It was very refreshing to meet him. Then, worshipfully, with sacred chants, he put sandal paste, kumkum and vibhuti on my forehead and reverently anointed me with oils of a heavenly fragrance. He treated me like sister and also Goddess. So he was not only praying for a vision of the Goddess, he was seeing the Goddess in his sister. I walked away totally transported, saying to Baba, "I only asked for lunch and you gave me everything."

The next day I was up at 5 am and reached Kedarnath by 9 am, after an 18 kilometer trek. On the way, I exchanged greetings, "Jay Kedarnath," and "Bum Bum Bole," with the other pilgrims on the trail. We were all joyfully transporting each other Godward. By the time I reached the temple I was so ecstatic I was fairly walking on air. I reverently took off my shoes and pack and went into the temple to pay my respects to the different deities. At one point someone behind me insisted I take a bindi (a red dot worn on the middle of the forehead). I thought he felt I would be more respectful by wearing it in the temple, so I placed it on my forehead. No, that was not his intention. It was customary to use it for worship of the next deity - Parvati, Shiva's consort. I assured Parvati that I honored her holy union and that I had no intention of stealing her husband from her.

Kedarnath being complete, I took the bus to Badrinath. The ashram director at Gaurikunj had insisted I not miss Badrinath, as I was so close. As I alighted the bus, I made eye contact with a very striking young man from Hydrabad traveling with his younger brother. There was an instant recognition, although we had not met earlier. At the first landslide we had a chance to talk. In the course of our conversation he informed me that he was a Yogananda devotee and had had visions of Yogananda and Leheri Mahasye as well as the immortal Baba-ji. Shailendra described some powerful kundalini and third experiences which he had undergone. He also mentioned that he had had an inner visitation from me. I did not remember, but there was a definite connection.

We visited the temple in Badrinath together. Every time I stepped inside the temple my whole body would start to tingle and I felt as though I was about to lift off. I came to find out that twenty years earlier Sai Baba had installed a Shiva lingam (a very sacred egg shaped object of worship). Shailendra, his brother and I also visited several caves, including Veda - Vyas' cave and Ganesh's cave. They were all very transporting but there was one particular baba's cave that was more than profoundly uplifting. When we stepped inside, I found my hands raising up on their own and I actually had to sit on them. My whole body seemed to have become light. The shakti was phenomenal and I could have stayed forever. When we finally got up to leave, the baba wanted to give us each some prasad (blessed food) as is typically done upon departure.

One of the baba's disciples had distracted me with a question, so Shailendra said, "Hey Yaani, I think Baba wants to give you something." When we were outside Shailendra said, "You have just been blessed by the Gods." I responded, "That energy was out of this world." He said, "I'm not talking about the energy, I'm talking about what is in your hand." In my hand was a rudraksha bead. He explained how that bead was a gift from Lord Shiva.

It is significant that he saw what the baba was giving me, while I was distracted, or else he would not have known that I had received this gift. On my own I would not have given it any importance. Neither he nor his brother received a rudraksha bead. The rudraksha bead is held sacred in all of India but especially in the Himalayas. Many babas string them into 108 bead garlands to wear around their necks and use for doing japa, repetition of God's sacred name. Shailendra pointed out that the bead is rare and known to be Shiva's signature and that customarily the prasad consists solely of food. This seemed no ordinary happenstance.

Shailendra went on to explain that when he was in Kedarnath, he had what he described to be a powerful awakening experience, but rather than be a self-proclaimed enlightened one, he prayed to the Gods to give him a rudraksha bead to confirm his enlightenment. Then he would have no doubts. So, he immediately recognized that I was being confirmed, to my astonishment. Shailendra proceeded to tell me that the purpose for which I had come to the Himalayas was now complete.

I protested because I didn't want to abort my assignment prematurely. I had spent less than a month in the Himalayas all told. He said, "Don't take my word for it. Meditate on it. I feel you should go to your guru and thank him for the wonderful blessing that has been achieved." I got truth bumps all over my body and suddenly there was no need to stay a moment longer.

Before I'd left for the Himalayas, I had asked Baba in my heart if I should come to see Him also. He said at that time, "See Me in the Himalayas. No need to come to Prasanthi." So I didn't pack any saris or bring any of the other paraphernalia for going to Baba's. Of course that was a blessing, as I traveled much lighter. But as soon as I got the word, I flew post haste to Prashanthi Nilayam.

A few days after reaching Baba's ashram, a friend, Madhu, who has a gift of vision, asked why I was not wearing my mangala sutra (a necklace Indian women wear as a sign of marriage). She had seen it on me the first few days I was there and now assumed that I must have taken it off, for she saw me without it. In fact, at no point during that trip was I wearing a necklace.

When Baba spoke to me, it was only to ask where I was from. I told Him I'd come from USA. Again He asked, so I responded, "From You Baba," as I recognize Him to be my source. He walked away saying, "USA". Later while having dinner with Franchesca, another dear friend, also a spiritually developed sensitive, I shared my short exchange. She responded that Baba was assigning me to USA.

I also recounted to Franchesca my recent trip to the Himalayas, finishing with Madhu's noticing a nonexistent necklace. Franchesca suggested that she was seeing an ethereal chain confirming my marriage to Shiva. All Indian women wear one when they get married and never take it off, therefore Madhu was concerned when she thought I had taken mine off. Shiva dances on the head of ego and that is what marriage to Shiva means to me. I hope this book has inspired you to wake up by dancing on ego's head and by marrying the Divine within you.

Thank You dear Sai Baba for your love, and for helping me to see ego as the imposter that causes all our needless suffering. May everyone become free of ego's seductions and be restored to self-love, the kind that flows freely into the hearts and minds of all humanity uniting us all with each other and with God. May love be reestablished on earth now as it was always meant to be.

May all beings in all the worlds be happy and blest, Amen.

CPSIA information can be obtained at www.ICGtesting.com
Printed in the USA
BVOW03s1217031213

338021BV00015B/697/P